D0492604

A Dictionary
of
Rock and
Pop Names

The Rock and Pop
Names Encyclopedia
from
Aaliyah to ZZ Top

A Dictionary of Rock and Pop Names

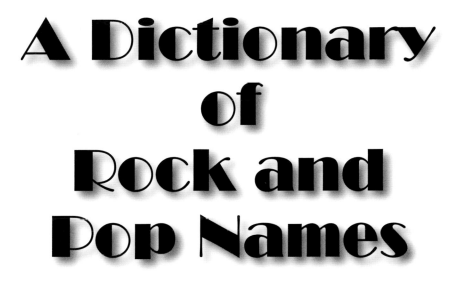

The Rock and Pop Names Encyclopedia from Aaliyah to ZZ Top

Mark Beech

First published in Great Britain in 2009 by
REMEMBER WHEN
An imprint of
Pen & Sword Books Ltd
47 Church Street
Barnsley
South Yorkshire
S70 2AS

ISBN 978 1 84415 807 2

A CIP catalogue record for this book is available from the British
Library

Typeset by Phoenix Typesetting, Auldgirth, Dumfriesshire
Printed and bound by Kyodo Nation Printing Services, Thailand

Pen & Sword Books Ltd incorporates the Imprints of Pen & Sword
Aviation, Pen & Sword Maritime, Pen & Sword Military, Wharncliffe
Local History, Pen & Sword Select, Pen & Sword Military Classics,
Leo Cooper, Remember When, Seaforth Publishing and Frontline
Publishing.

For a complete list of Pen & Sword titles please contact
PEN & SWORD BOOKS LIMITED
47 Church Street, Barnsley, South Yorkshire, S70 2AS, England
E-mail: enquiries@pen-and-sword.co.uk
Website: www.pen-and-sword.co.uk

Contents

The Author

Mark Beech is a journalist, writer, and broadcaster. His articles have appeared in many newspapers worldwide, including most of the British nationals. He has been described by the BBC as "the world's leading expert on music names". He has interviewed thousands of stars and is the author of *The A-Z of Names in Rock* (Robson Books, 1998) which U.K. disc jockey John Peel said was one of the most-needed reference works.

He is pop and rock critic for Bloomberg News and the London editor of MUSE, the cultural section of Bloomberg. He listens to more than 1,000 CDs a year for his column, which is syndicated to more than 400 newspapers, many in the U.S., as well as appearing on Bloomberg's Website and terminals. Mark also writes and edits articles about literature, art, theatre, dance, architecture, restaurants and other cultural issues.

He was in Liverpool as the Fab Four made it big . . . but was far too young to remember any of it. He graduated through The Beatles Fan Club to Bob Dylan, to schools in Shrewsbury and Evesham and St. Catherine's College, Oxford University, where he was a Kitchener Scholar and where his first book was published: *Passionfruit*, edited by the late distinguished poet Howard Sergeant – its title meant it ended up in the cookery section of one bookshop. Mark has an M.A. in Philosophy, Politics and Economics. After graduation, he became a film script writer and one of the founders of *The Daily News* in Birmingham. He has also worked for *The Sunday Times*, ITN and the Press Association among others.

He interviewed many top musicians, as well as their family, friends, managers, concert promoters, roadies, groupies, and anyone else he could think of along the way. This has resulted in articles on Madonna, Bruce Springsteen, Michael Jackson, Sir Paul McCartney, and just about any other star whose name can be casually dropped in conversation at parties. (He has written a book about names, what do you expect?)

Mark's play *Freaks Come Out At Night* was one of the Westminster Prize award-winners in 2005 and was performed in the West End starring Burn Gorman and Robert Mountford. Soho Theatre produced Mark's earlier play, *Happy/Sad*, in 2001.

He divides his time between a house in London and a farm in Herefordshire, where he is usually to be found annoying his tenants by playing his favourite CDs loud for "research purposes". He is an inveterate attendee of concerts varying from rock to classical and an expert on the music of Sir John Tavener. He describes his musical tastes: "Tavener above all. Then Beethoven to *Blonde on Blonde*; Sibelius to The Smiths; Messiaen to Joni Mitchell."

His other interests include painting and photography; travel and collecting everything from books and CDs to antique typewriters and cars. "Sometimes I sleep, but, like Warren Zevon, I won't do much of that until I'm dead."

Epigraph

Where did you get the name of the group? This is the question which plagues every band on the planet.

Whenever you see this question appear in an interview or an article, you know that the journalist has left his/her brain in a matchbox somewhere. It's bad enough that mediocre journalists base whole articles on such secondary matters. Most journalists are worse than mediocre, so they have to actually ask the question first.

– **Andrew Eldritch**, The Sisters of Mercy.

Introduction

This book differs from every other work about rock names.

First, it's up to date.

Second, it's based on research over two decades – and counting – by a professional journalist – well, so I've been kidding people since the 1980s. I started the project shortly after making journalism my misbegotten career.

Third, it's based, where possible, on primary sources and cross-checked facts, not gossip or speculation. I've interviewed thousands of rock stars as diverse as Sting, the Smiths, and Sigue Sigue Sputnik. I've also travelled thousands of miles, scanned countless yellowing newspaper clippings, and contacted many record companies and agents.

Fourth, this is the successor to *The A-Z of Names in Rock*, a work that British disc jockey John Peel thought should become a standard music dictionary. The BBC kindly called me the world's leading expert on rock names. Radio personality Jono Coleman said that it was one of the finest rock reference books, which should grow and be kept in print forever. (Thanks, folks.)

WHO, WHAT, WHERE, WHEN, HOW?

This volume will be of use and entertainment to those interested in names, words and especially popular music. It's an A-Z guide of the stars and groups of today, yesterday, and – in some cases – tomorrow. As its title implies, it provides the answers to one of the great questions in music, from the biggest-selling and best-known down: "Why are they called that?"

- Why were The Beatles called The Beatles?
- Why "The Rolling Stones"?
- How did (insert the name of your choice here) arrive at their name? I can't include everyone within this volume but you'll find an array from The Bee Gees to Elton John, Hear'Say to Nirvana, Badly Drawn Boy to Oasis, Destiny's Child to Linkin Park.
- Why should a band whom everyone knew decide to stick to the name The Who?* What was wrong with their previous choice, The High Numbers?
- Why did she become Madonna?** What about Eminem? Moby? Pink?
- Who or what really inspired Bob Zimmerman to become Bob Dylan?*** Reginald Dwight to (Sir) Elton Hercules John? Dave Jones to David Bowie? Harry Webb to (Sir) Cliff Richard? Brian Warner to become Marilyn Manson?

A Dictionary of Rock and Pop Names

- What of the teen idols: Backstreet Boys, Take That, Wham!, Duran Duran, Boyzone? The Spice Girls or the Sugababes?
- How did Paul Hewson become Bono? And his group become U2?
- Who, or what, are Arctic Monkeys? Eurythmics? A Sex Pistol? A Led Zeppelin? What is a Stone Rose? An Aztec Camera? A Prefab Sprout? A Strawberry Alarm Clock? A Manic Street Preacher? Or a Quiet Riot?
- Why should anyone wish to embarrass their fans who had to ask for records in shops by The The? Or embarrass themselves by naming Gay Dad? Or Ol' Dirty Bastard, Puff Daddy/Diddy, Snoop Dogg or Ghostface Killah?

For those readers feeling smug and sure of the answers, look at the questions above once more – full answers come later in the book – and consider:

* = So that's The Who. Then why did a bunch of total unknowns become the Guess Who?

** = Madonna: a trick question. No, she didn't chose her name as a sacrilegious statement. That really **is** her first name.

*** = Bob Dylan. If you said he named in tribute to poet Dylan Thomas, think again. It's not so simple.

Or try these:

- What band could have sprung to fame called Johnny and The Self-Abusers? Mark Skid and the Y-Fronts? The Golliwogs? The Crackers? Tom And Jerry? The Screaming Abdabs? Hitler's Underpantz? Cans Of Piss?

These were names considered or used by early versions of Simple Minds; the Boomtown Rats; Creedence Clearwater Revival; The Band; Simon and Garfunkel; Pink Floyd; O.M.D. and R.E.M.

While the answers aren't as profound as Einstein or as earth-shattering as a solution to global poverty, they have their uses, at least for pub quizzes and providing an education on dinosaurs (T. Rex), Gaelic swear words (the Pogues) torture machines (Iron Maiden), birdwatching (The Nightingales), science fiction (The Human League) and bizarre sexual practices with rodents (allegedly, The Pet Shop Boys).

This is far more than a compendium of information for trainspotters, geeks, nerds, anoraks or fact freaks. It's for the millions who follow these musicians yet may not know how the names came into being.

WHAT'S IN A NAME?

What's in a name? Sometimes, pretty much everything. The replies given are controversial, hilarious – and often revealing.

Groups as varied as The Doors, NWA, The Clash, Blind Faith, The Beginning Of The End, UB40, The Levellers, Devo, Tears For Fears and The Beautiful South are named after their intention, manifesto, interests or philosophy. To have this fully explained can be insightful.

A Dictionary of Rock and Pop Names

This book will annoy those people who like mystery, and don't want every mythology explained, categorised and defined because it can kill magic. Yet in many cases, listeners can't solve the riddle by buying all the band's records and going to every concert. As you discover the answers from the comfort of your armchair, you might wonder what was the motivation, or obsessive idiotry, that led the author to do this musical detective work – donkeywork, if you prefer.

MY GRANNY, PHIL, AND STING.

I blame three people for this book. My granny, a fellow journalist called Phil Hainey . . . and Sting.

My grandmother Mary Beech was a keen philologist, and spent her life collecting names and their origins. She fired my interest.

Phil was a colleague when I started out 25 centuries ago (it seems like). We were both local reporters at Heart of England Newspapers. He noted my fascination with band names and suggested I write it down.

Sting entered the story when I progressed to national newspapers and was writing about the former Police star. A friend of mine suspected that, in keeping with his serious image, Gordon Sumner's stage name signified something profound or pretentious. At least, she suggested, it must be a reference to "sting" as in a bank robbery? Or an insect name, like The Beatles or The Crickets?

I had heard it was something to do with a jumper. Sting confirmed that my version was true: it was merely a silly nickname because of a black and yellow horizontally-striped Breton-type top which was all he could afford in his career's earliest days. He looked like a bee or a wasp.

Here I saw two steps to an easy book. Step one: Outline the various theories, often entertaining in themselves. Step two: Explain which is correct. (This was potentially the only tricky bit, but I had access to answers few other people have.) Perfect. Instant best-seller! It all looked so simple. The project has been with me ever since.

SOURCES AND ACKNOWLEDGEMENTS

INTERVIEWS

The main source of primary material was my own interviews with a who's who of stars.

After Sting, I included the question: "How did you/your band get the name?" I felt I was doing a service to my readers. I had certain "pay-off" questions usually left to the end of the interview and this was one of them. It came after: "Unless you've anything to add . . . " and ranked alongside some form of: "How much are you worth?" and: "Do you mind if I ask how old you are?" (where I didn't know the answer or it was unclear). I knew it could produce irritation and was best kept until the main interview was in the can.

Most of the stars were very polite, especially if I was writing a long profile for a serious paper. Some gave generously of their time. While this book comes with thanks to everyone who spoke to me, it comes with the biggest appreciation to those with no ulterior motive (I mean no new CD to sell, or tour to hype) who just turned out to be likeable and helpful.

The information so gathered from the stars usually has precedence, although it's important to say that not all gave the true stories. Next on the pecking order, I referred to stars' friends, managers or families.

RECORD COMPANIES

I found much in material which originated from the acts themselves or sanctioned by them: lyrics, record sleeves, press releases, official websites, posters, autobiographies or authorised/official biographies. Thanks to those press officers who provided vintage biographies and statements.

ARTICLES

The secondary source list includes interviews with other journalists which had undisputable quotes – TV/radio tapes or downloads with transcripts. Next came interviews from reliable news sources.

There are yawning gaps in information available. Many other reporters have patently failed to address the sort of questions I posed at the outset, despite many fans' clear interest. They don't bother to ask about names – even in initial articles about new acts, despite it being an obvious starting point.

Some bands become reluctant to reply. The answer might be silly, let slip their influences or spoil the mystique. Others fabricate stories out of boredom at the question – for, yes, it does get asked sometimes. Peter Hook of New Order says he's been asked "hundreds of times" and calls it "a dumb question".

However, some publications were more useful than others. Those I use most are *Q, NME, Rolling Stone* and *Mojo,* and newspapers such as the *New York Times* and *The Guardian.*

INTERNET

When I started research, the Internet was in its infancy. Finding names required much reading and checking. Far from killing the need for this book, the Web has made it more relevant. With the deluge of disinformation online, you can often spend hours trying to find the true story.

In the absence of information on official sites, the vacuum is filled by fan chatrooms, blogs, bulletin boards and sites such as AmIright.com (the name says it all) which allow any school kid to post whatever piece of speculation they want. In some cases this third-hand, half-heard urban myth gets recycled as gospel. Watch for the tell tale phrases "I think I read that . . . " "a friend of a friend told me . . . "

Some acts have forum pages, sometimes with "ask the group" sections, where the question comes up with alarming regularity as fans fail to spot previous instances of the query – forum search functions are often poor. Usually the band gives an answer in the first few days the forum is running, then insults the poor fans for innocently asking the question again.

PREVIOUS BOOKS

Adrian Room's scholarly *Brewer's Dictionary Of Names* and *Dictionary of Pseudonyms* are outstanding. I have to thank him for all his detailed comments on my 1988 book.

A Dictionary of Rock and Pop Names

There are other name books by Glenn A. Baker, Adam Dolgins and David Wilson though none were of use alongside Colin Larkin's 10-volume *Encyclopedia Of Popular Music* from 2006.

There are at least four other U.S. rock name volumes, written by amateur writers and some vanity published. All seem to have had the same idea I did around 1984, except a few years later. I've pretty much ignored these works because they are so bad. The creators seem unaware that there are other works, usually much better than they ever could produce. This ignorance is both frightening and funny: they have neither the access nor the depth of research that the job needs.

PERSONAL SOURCES AND THANKS

My colleagues from previous jobs at ITN, the Press Association and Europe Online were quizzed on their own knowledge and bored by mine as I assembled information. I have my employer Bloomberg News to thank for allowing this book to go ahead. I repeat my thanks voiced in the 1998 book to my Bloomberg colleague, then as now, Richard Vines. In addition to all on the MUSE team worldwide as well as to Maria José Vera and Victoria Cochrane in Bloomberg TV.

Also while I'm in "without whom . . . " mode, I must express thanks to Kazuyo Enomoto, as in my last book, for a decade living with a Mark Beech who is addicted to work, Red Bull and CDs.

Pen & Sword's editor Fiona Shoop and production team did an exceptional job in seeing this to print. I must also thank freelance picture researcher Kate Duffy, who took my often difficult requests and within three months found and negotiated rights for the illustrations.

Thanks to my literary agent Andrew Lownie, who has done an outstanding job since taking over my account. Also to Michael Pead and Jay Dong for Web site advice on www.markbeech.net and elsewhere; and to staff at the British Library and the National Sound Archive.

ABOUT THIS BOOK

This encyclopaedia deals with mainstream rock and pop for the most part; many artists from other genres, punk, soul, reggae, rap, jazz, folk, country, blues, indie, heavy metal, grunge, rock 'n' roll, new age and R&B are included where they are well known or where there is a good story.

While the lengths are not meant to reflect the importance of each artist, major stars generally get a fuller treatment.

EXTRAS

There are many things that this volume includes which most other music encyclopaedias do not:
  (1)   detailed nicknames (for example, see James 'Star Time' Brown or Bruce 'The Boss' Springsteen),
  (2)   anagrams (Madonna Louise Ciccone = Occasional Nude Income),
  (3)   "unflattering derivatives" (Bryan Ferry = Bryon Ferrari),
  (4)   stars' children's names (Moon Unit Zappa),

(5)   details of informal or contracted versions (The Rolling Stones to The Stones),

(6)   CDs/ songs punning on names (Pavlov's Dog's *At The Sound Of The Bell*),

(7)   pronunciation guides (Sade, Björk),

(8)   names of fan clubs (Gary Numan's Numanoids),

(9)   tribute bands (The Bootleg Beatles, Fabba, Lez Zeppelin),

(10)   spinoff groups (R.E.M. and Hindu Love Gods),

(11)   the author's prize ratings for good/bad designations or individual band members;

(12)   origins of some other music-related names – disc jockeys, managers, record labels.

INTERNATIONAL VIEW, SPELLING, GRAMMAR

This book is designed to be worldwide in appeal. Some of the explanations will be obvious to some readers, not to others. British, American, Canadian and Australian references are explained. When I started in 1984 I elected to keep language in informal British English and treat groups as plurals ("The Beatles were," "Radiohead are..")

CROSS REFERENCES

Many entries give cross-references, shown by a ⇨, to encourage browsing. Cf ⇨ means "compare to this similar name" and doesn't necessarily mean a related act.

ALPHABETICAL ORDER

Generally individuals are under surnames, groups under first names. Numbers are listed as if they are spelled in English. The order disregards English definite and indefinite articles before names. Where locations are unclear, a page number is added to cross references to speed navigation.

OFFENSIVE WORDS

Some band soubriquets offend certain people. The controversy may be political (Dead Kennedys), racial (Big Black), sexual (Lovin' Spoonful) or all of these (4 Skins). There's no point in being mealy-mouthed, or excluding offensive words, if this obscures the account.

SOURCING/ CITATIONS/ RIVAL ACCOUNTS

Some of the entries are drawn from perhaps 15 sources. For this concise edition, the attributions are usually used only where there is a dispute over the information presented.

ACCURACY

Wherever possible, multiple crosschecks of spellings and stories have been used. Readers are invited to write in with any corrections, suggestions and documentary proof where possible to mark@markbeech.net, or care of Andrew Lownie, 36 Great Smith Street, London, SW1P 3BU. All the further information used will be acknowledged in future editions.

A Dictionary of Rock and Pop Names

LESS IS MORE

This book is the executive summary of my database which runs to four times its published size. It includes every major entry and trims the background that for example inflates the full Led Zeppelin and Bob Dylan entries to 4,000 words. This is a handier potted version which aims to concisely give all the headlines and more. It's not weighed down, more quick-reference and just as definitive. Less is more. (As I was told when given my first script to write at ITN.)

My database also has much on the history of music names, lists, trivia, quizzes and essays on further adventures I had in finding the names. That's for the next book maybe.

Mark Beech

First edition: Oxfordshire ca 1984-Abbey Road, St John's Wood 1998

This book: Evesham 1998-Westminster 2008

Aaliyah

This Detroit R&B star, who sold 12 million records in a career that ended with a 2001 plane crash, was born Aaliyah Dana Haughton.

ABBA

Swedish singer/songwriters Benny Andersson and Björn Ulvaeus started with The Hootenanny Singers. They teamed with Anni-Frid Lyngstad and Agnetha Fältskog in 1970 in cabaret act Festfolk ("party people"). A 1972 single, *People Need Love*, was credited to "Björn & Benny, Agnetha & Anni-Frid." This was reduced to their first initials. ABBA was also a Swedish canned fish company, which agreed to lend its name.

Agnetha was known as Anna, and Anni-Frid as Anni (many ABBA releases drop the Swedish characters). ABBA was an acronym, palindrome and – with the first 'B' backwards – a registered trade mark.

This Eurovision-winning act spawned many tribute bands after they broke up in 1982. Some have been touring for more than 20 years. They include Abba Dabba Doo, ABBALANCHE, Abbasolutely, ⇨Björn Again, and ⇨Gabba.

ABC

"Because the first letters of the alphabet are known the world over," explained Martin Fry. He thought the choice would put the British band's records "at the top of the alphabetical section. It's vague enough not to be 'limiting'." ABC said the designation stood for "Always Be Cool", to counter suggestions it was "Awfully Boring Crap".

Abraxas Pool

Members of ⇨Santana who played on the *Abraxas* and *Santana III* albums.

AC/DC

Glasgow couple William and Margaret Young encouraged their children to play music. They moved to Sydney, Australia, in 1963. Their eldest son Alexander Young remained in Britain. Renamed George Alexander, he formed the band ⇨Grapefruit.

Another son, George Young (Junior) had a starring role in ⇨The Easybeats before moving into production. A younger brother, Malcolm, was inspired to try music, joining an act called Velvet Underground (no relation to the ⇨Lou Reed act). Their younger brother Angus formed his own group, Tantrum, and AC/DC in 1973.

There have been dozens of Web sites (a) repeating possible name sources, nearly all with sourcing of the sort "I think I heard this" or "a friend told me that" or (b) speculating on possible satanic connections when the group has repeatedly denied them. Of course most of these Internet items are written by fans who can't directly go to the band, like a journalist can, to get answers (so I did). But most can presumably read – even if they can't spell or write grammatically – so they've only to read books such as this to get the answer. It seems their research never extends beyond the Internet, or even as far as checking out some of AC/DC's old TV interviews which give answers.

The name source: "AC/DC" came from a household appliance. The question is, which: a vacuum cleaner or a sewing machine? There's a dispute over who owned the machine – the Youngs' mother Margaret or sister, also called Margaret? Then there are contradictory reports over who noticed it (Angus and his sister Margaret are the people most often cited) and who came up with the name (Margaret, Angus, Malcolm, another relative?)

AC/DC confirmed to the author comments made for a VH-1 interview. Malcolm says the name came from sister Margaret's sewing machine.

The meaning: There's agreement that the moniker was chosen because of its believed electrical connotations. AC/DC means "Alternating Current/Direct Current" to indicate that an electrical device can use either type of power. The brothers felt it summed up the raw energy and power-driven performances they aimed for.

In some countries, including Australia, AC/DC was and is also known as a slang term for bisexuality. Malcolm said he didn't know this in 1973: "It wasn't widely used." AC/DC made it with singer ⇨Bon Scott's macho image and emphasised the electrical theme through albums such as *Powerage*.

The early AC/DC songs didn't contain any especially evil meanings, and even the later ones – hard rock bands such as AC/DC were accused of interest in the occult and devil worship – can usually be explained easily. (*Highway To Hell*, for instance, from a disastrous tour.) The critics suggest "AC/DC" means "Anti-Christ/Devil's Child(ren)", "Anti-Christ/Devil Christ" or "After Christ/Devil Comes". These look badly-fabricated attempts by religious groups to unfairly besmirch the group.

Tribute bands include BC/DC, from British Columbia, and AC/DShe, an all-female San Francisco version.

The name's said one letter at a time "A-C-D-C", "Ay-cee-dee-cee" for English speakers. In Australia "Acca-dacca" is an often-used alternative.

Ace Of Base

Swedish dance-pop outfit, founded in 1987 by Johnny Linden. The band members were masters – or "aces" of their studio, sited in the basement of a car-repair shop – the "base" or "basement".

A Certain Ratio/ ACR

Originally A Certain Ratio, this 1970s-on Manchester, U.K. group renamed ACR. It came from ⇨Brian Eno's *The True Wheel*, on the CD *Taking Tiger Mountain (By Strategy)*. The phrase comes from the thoughts of Hitler on the proportion of Jewish "blood" to determine if a person was Jewish. ACR denied being aware of this meaning.

A Dictionary of Rock and Pop Names

Adam And The Ants
Adam was born in 1954 in London as Stuart Goddard but soon called himself "Adam", after Adam and Eve. He got an ADAM tattoo on his left arm: "Adam's a very strong name; it's the *first* name – you know – the Garden of Eden."

Adam, and his tattoo, left Hornsey Art College in 1977. He added the Ant surname – a play on "adamant", someone determined and hard, and coincidentally recalling Adam Adamant, hero of a 1960s BBC sci-fi series played by Gerald Harper.

Related: ⇨Bow Wow Wow. Fans called: Ant People.

Cannonball Adderley
U.S. alto saxophonist Julian Adderley's nickname was "cannibal" – referring to the amount he ate! The corruption followed a phone mishearing.

King Sunny Ade
The African singer reworked his real name Sunday Adeniyi. Pronunciation: Ard-ay.

Adeva
American singer Patricia Daniels (1960 +) punned on "a diva".

Adolf And The Casuals
⇨R.E.M. side-project linking dictator Adolf Hitler and 1950s bands such as Kenny And The Kasuals. "Adolf isn't a casual name".

The Adult Net
A spinoff from ⇨The Fall and ⇨The Smiths, named from a line in a Fall song.

Aerosmith
Drummer Joey Kramer recalls in an interview: "My old girlfriend Patty Bourdon keeps telling me that she and I came up with the name while we were sitting in her room listening to Harry ⇨Nilsson's album *Aerial Ballet*, which had *Everybody's Talkin'* on it. We were thinking of cool names and the whole 'Aero-something' got hatched."

Note Kramer's wording of Bourdon's account, "keeps telling me". Elsewhere it was previously suggested he was piecing together words Scrabble-style and chose "aero-space" and "songsmith". The result was meaningless but sounded good. Either way, it was offered to his schoolboy band, Strawberry Ripple, and rejected.

Kramer wasn't that interested in lessons, and would sit doodling the word on his textbooks and ring binder. In 1998, contacted by the author, Kramer also confirmed there was no relation to Henry Sinclair Lewis' 1925 novel *Arrowsmith*, a book "everyone hated in high school". The name produced the same reaction, he said, when he first pitched it to his later group, The Jam Band, until they got the spelling.

Bassist Tom Hamilton recalled: "We had to find a name that somehow matched the power of the band and gave you the same sense of 'lift' that we got when we played together."

Also known as The Boys From Boston, and, in part, as ⇨The Toxic Twins.

A Dictionary of Rock and Pop Names

a-ha
This Norwegian pop phenomenon's name was chosen by leader Mags Furuholmen. An early song, *Nothing To It*, had the word "a-ha" in the lyric. He said it's a way of expressing recognition – common to many languages (cf ⇨ABC), with positive connotations (cf ⇨Yes) and short (cf ⇨U2).

Aiden
The Seattle band formed in 2003, named after Aiden, a boy who can see ghosts, in the 2002 film, *The Ring*. Aiden's 2005 debut *Our Gang's Dark Oath* contains songs about the movie's gothed-out world.

Airhead
British band reacting, in a very 1980s "breadhead" way, against 1960's "airhead" hippies. Hippy parlance: breadhead = capitalist; airhead = idiot. ⇨Jefferson Airhead.

Air Supply
A name chosen because this Australian-based soft rock group's music was a counter-attack – "a breath of fresh air" – to the growing popularity of heavy metal.

The Alarm
Works on several levels: alarm for future, human emotion, alarm clock. They came from Wales, and started as punk band The Toilets. *Alarm Alarm* was one of their songs. It was abbreviated because of fears of comparisons to other double-barrelled names (cf ⇨Duran Duran).

The Albion Band
Albion means "Great Britain". This band was set up by bassist Ashley Hutchings after he quit ⇨Steeleye Span, inspired by traditional folk. A spinoff, The Home Service, was another nostalgia trip, recalling the old name for BBC's domestic Radio 4.

Dennis Alcapone
Another Jamaican star to name after a U.S. outlaw, in this case Al Capone. He was born Dennis Smith in the year of the gangster's death.

Alexisonfire
You say that as "Alexis On Fire". The Canadian band thought it would be cool to write the name as one word. On the Alexisonfire site, they say "What kind of idiot would name a band 'Alex Is On Fire'?" Presumably the sort of idiot who crunches the words together without realising that it will be misunderstood. It was taken from Californian adult film actress Alexis Fire.

Alf
This singer, not the most feminine of figures, was inappropriately born as Genevieve. Alf, based on her punky nature and short hair, was a corruption of her other prenomen, Alison. Later she reverted to Alison Moyet. ⇨Yazoo.

A Dictionary of Rock and Pop Names

Alice In Chains
Originally, Alice N' Chains was the name of a school band led by singer Layne Staley and resurrected for a spoof project, an ⇨(p.79) Alice Cooper-style group. This U.S. ensemble used the Alice In Chains identity full-time when they couldn't agree on anything better for their day-job performances. Staley said it suited the drag and speed metal.

Alien Sex Fiend
U.K. singer Nick Wade created a science-fiction character as his alter ego, called Demon Preacher – the name of his first band. The character later became the sex fiend, with Wade wearing weird make-up to complete the role.

Alisha's Attic
This British pop duo named from a fictional character, Alisha – "a woman like us, who embraces her demons". It's also a reference to the Dagenham loft in which they wrote their first album.

The All-American Rejects
The band formed in 2001. They couldn't decide between the All Americans and the Rejects, so opted for both.

The Allman Brothers Band
Duane and Gregg Allman, from Georgia, went through names The House Rockers, Allman Joys (a pun on the U.S. chocolate candy) and Hour Glass. The Brothers appellation stayed some time after the death of Duane in a 1971 motorcycle accident.

All Saints
British all-girl quartet whose name comes from the All Saints Road near their homes in London's Ladbroke Grove.

Marc Almond
Almond chose his second Christian name for the stage. Somehow, the tattooed torch-singer – all agony, angst and androgyny – would never have seemed as convincing as an unpierced, stable-sounding Peter, his first name. Related: ⇨Immaculate Consumptive, ⇨Soft Cell.

ALO
Or Animal Liberation Orchestra in full. ALO said they "liberate animals each night they step on stage. That is, set free a bunch of dance-crazed funk lovers and turn them into sweat-soaked animals."

Alone Again Or
A band which evolved from ⇨The Shamen. Their psychedelic style is shown by the name, the same as the lead-off track on ⇨Love's album *Forever Changes*, which encapsulated 1967's "summer of love".

Altered Images

Glaswegian Claire Grogan's band name came from a graphics consultancy, Assorted Images. She altered it to avoid any trademark disputes.

Altered States

From the 1980 science fiction film. The band thought it could also relate to the U.S.A.

Amboy Dukes

There have been several groups of this name. Of the best-known, founder Ted Nugent said he appropriated the Dukes name in the 1960s from the earlier Detroit Amboy Dukes. Both were referencing a Brooklyn street gang.

Amen Corner

They came together in 1966 in Wales, moving to London and taking their name from a district of the capital. The alias was a humorous comment on sanctimonious Welshmen! It was also a play by U.S. activist James Baldwin.

America

Formed in the U.K. in 1967, this band contained three sons of U.S. servicemen. They hardly knew America at the time and only went there after chart success.

Tori Amos

This flame-haired American singer-songwriter was born Myra-Ellen Amos. Yet Tori's a diminutive of Victoria. She's produced intriguing music and many "kooky chick" / "ginger nut" headlines. The author approached with care. Tori renamed herself "after a tree" because she has an affinity "with all things natural". Plants are "beautiful, so still".

Anastacia

Another single name: the American singer's full name is Anastacia Lyn Newkirk.

Anberlin

This Florida band formed in 2002 and namechecked the German capital, though they didn't live there. They also echoed the name of ⇨Berlin (too young to remember the first one?) It's not a reference to ⇨David Bowie's Berlin phase or ⇨Lou Reed's *Berlin*. Singer Stephen Christian heard the name in the background of the ⇨Radiohead song *Everything In Its Right Place*, the opening track of 2000 album *Kid A*.

. . . And You Will Know Us by the Trail of Dead

If you laughed at the title of this entry, then this Texas-based art-rock band would say they're doing something right. They suggested it's from an ancient Mayan chant. Mayan rituals did include human sacrifice and fans dutifully went off to try to find it. Founder Conrad Keely later confirmed it was a false lead: "People like to be entertained, they like to hear stories."

A Dictionary of Rock and Pop Names

Horace Andy
Jamaican singer; no relation to Jamaican star Bob Andy but renamed in his honour by ⇨Coxsone Dodd, who thought him Andy's heir. Originally Horace Hinds.

Angelband
Named by Emmylou Harris in memory of ⇨Gram Parsons, and their work together on 1974's *Grievous Angel*.

The Angry Samoans
In the tradition of misleading names such as ⇨Barenaked Ladies, this Los Angeles punk band's members weren't from Samoa. They were paying tribute to the Wild Samoans, a wrestling team.

The Animals
The band formed in Newcastle, U.K., in 1962. Singer Eric Burdon said they needed a name with impact. His choice was in honour of a then-friend of his, "Animal" Hogg, a tough Army veteran, whose squatting-freewheeling lifestyle they wanted to emulate.

Though the moniker didn't come from their stage act, the choice was confirmed by an outraged audience's comments following early frenzied performances: "Like wild animals!"

Burdon later recorded with ⇨War. The Animals featured Chas Chandler (1938-1996, born Bryan James Chandler), who managed ⇨Jimi Hendrix and ⇨Slade.

Anthrax
This band, formed in New York in 1981, is the only heavy metal group to be named after a scourge of cattle and sheep. The infectious disease can spread to humans.

There's a convoluted theory that it's homage to ⇨Curved Air, who named from Terry Riley's album, *A Rainbow In Curved Air*. Riley's fourth album, with John Cale in 1971, was called *Church of Anthrax*. This theory can be discarded: guitarists Scott Ian and Danny Lilker learnt about anthrax at college. They chose it purely for its sound rather than its repulsive meaning involving throat inflammation, malignant pustules, boils and fever.

It's also nothing to do with the 1979 ⇨Gang Of Four track *Anthrax* or a 1980-84 British punk band, which had to become Anthrax U.K; they formed first but the American act was more successful.

The Anthrax Web site got bombarded with requests for information in September 2001 when letters containing anthrax spores were mailed to news offices and two senators, resulting in several deaths. Anthrax joked about renaming as "something more friendly, like 'Basket Full of Puppies.'" A month later, at a 9/11 benefit concert, they wore suits spelling out "WE'RE NOT CHANGING OUR NAME".

Apple
⇨The Beatles named their business arm because of the joke: Apple Corps. = "apple core". They liked its simplicity and echoes of the Adam/Eve and apple "first temptation" story. In addition, Yoko Ono had used apples as an image and the

Japanese had long been amused by the name "Ringo", which sounds like their word for "apple". There was later a name dispute with Apple Computers.

Apple Boutique

This group paid tribute to ⇨The Beatles. The Fab Four's ⇨Apple was intended to cover film, investments, publicity, publishing and retailing. Only the record business proved a success. Two – then trendily-named – fashion "boutiques" failed spectacularly, prompting the comment: "They should stick to what they're good at."

Aqua

This Danish-Norwegian dance-pop group's lead vocalist Lene Grawford Nyström recalled in an interview: "We were doing a concert in Copenhagen [in 1996] and had to think of a name really quickly for the poster. René [Dif, male vocalist] saw a poster for an aquarium [in a dressing room] and thought it would be a great, positive name."

Arcade Fire

Texas-born vocalist Win Butler is leader of one of the most acclaimed bands of 2004-8+, so it might come as a shock that he performed briefly with a joke student act called Willy Wanker and the Chocolate Factories. (⇨Cf (p. 287) Veruca Salt.)

Fans of the serious Canadian band have said surely it cannot be possible that it named after something as literal and mundane as a fire in a shopping mall.

Still, there was a blaze in the arcade and bandstand of Exeter, New Hampshire, where both Butler and fellow band member, his brother William, attended Phillips Exeter Academy preparatory school. The band is fully aware of the symbolism of a commercial building, such as an arcade, going up in flames.

Arcadia

When ⇨Duran Duran members briefly went their separate ways in 1985, two formed ⇨The Power Station. The rest – Simon Le Bon, Nick Rhodes and Roger Taylor – "wanted something that sounded different". "Arcadia" was a rural area of Greece with mythological connections and they thought it sounded "heavenly".

The Arctic Monkeys

The Monkeys' story began in Sheffield, England, when Alex Turner and Jamie Cook got guitars for Christmas aged 16.

In summer 2002, they were practicing with their friends Andy Nicholson (bassist) and Matt Helders, who had reluctantly become the drummer because the others chose guitars. The rehearsals in Alex's garage went under the initial handle Bang Bang, though this only lasted weeks. It was later recycled for the label (Bang Bang Recordings) on the 2005 release *Five Minutes with Arctic*

[1] Spot the little monkey: The Arctic Monkeys put their cards on the table about the new name.

Monkeys. There are Internet suggestions that the Monkeys were reconsidering the name around that time, but were already getting attention.

Lead singer Alex said: "We had the name before we got our guitars. While we were still at school, Jamie was saying he wanted to get a band together and call it the Arctic Monkeys." He was doodling random ideas during lessons.

The most common story was that they named after an earlier band including the uncle, or even the father, of drummer Matt Helders. The Monkeys told *Prefix* magazine: "We made that up 'cause we got so many people asking us that in the U.K."

It used to be the case that when musicians were challenged about such silly band names, they would regularly fall back on the old defence "⇨The Beatles had a silly name and it didn't stop them". It could be in future that musicians will replace this with the Arctic Monkeys.

Noel Gallagher of ⇨Oasis said in a radio interview that the name was so bad it would stop them from winning awards. He was proved wrong. One of the few to instantly approve was another Manchester man, poet John Cooper Clarke. Turner said: "Everyone tells us we've got a shit name but he was like 'That's great! There's no trees in the arctic! How would it survive?' He painted this picture instantly, a real creative mind!"

They are called both the Arctics and the Monkeys for short.
⇨Death Ramps.

Area Code 615
These musicians from Nashville, Tennessee, were regarded highly by some, including ⇨Bob Dylan. They played on his 1969 release *Nashville Skyline* and emphasised their origins by naming after the Nashville telephone code.

The Arizona Cowboy
Nickname for American country singer Rex Allen, who came from an Arizonan cowboy family.

The Armoury Show
This Scottish band misspelled the 1913 Armory Show that introduced post impressionist art to the U.S. It fitted the pretensions of founder Richard Jobson and was more elevated than his previous choice ⇨The Skids.

Army Of Lovers
Taken from the title of a movie about gay rights activist Rosa von Praunheim.

Kokomo Arnold
The U.S. bluesman was born James Arnold and named from his 1934 hit *Old Original Kokomo Blues*, about a type of coffee.

Arrested Development
A reflection of their early rap lyrical concern about police repressing free expression. Individual names: Headliner (born Timothy Barnwell) and Speech (born Todd Thomas), first known on stage as DJ Peech.

Art Of Noise

Luigi Russolo was a leader of the Italian twentieth century art futurist movement. He urged a new view of music in a 1913 pamphlet *L'Arte Dei Rumori* or *The Art Of Noises*.

He said mechanical movement had a new beauty for visual art and "one day . . . every factory will be transformed into an intoxicating orchestra of noises". The name was coined by ⇨ZTT Records boss Paul Morley when the band, consisting of three British producers working with Trevor Horn, formed in 1984.

[2] The Art of Noise and ZTT Records both got their names from artist Luigi Russolo, seen here with his Noise Machine.

The Artwoods

Because they were led by Arthur 'Art' Wood, the brother of ⇨Faces and ⇨Rolling Stones guitarist Ronnie Wood.

Ash

Ash started young, at age 12 in the 1990s as part of "the worst band in Ireland's County Down", ⇨Iron Maiden wannabes Vietnam. They wanted a simple name and picked up a dictionary. According to Ash's Web site, it was a speedy search. They picked the first short word they liked. Job done.

Asia

Contenders for the most Boring Band Name. British 'supergroup' consisting of players from other by-then dinosaurs such as ⇨Yes, ⇨ELP, ⇨King Crimson and ⇨Uriah Heep. The four wanted a short name which would print up well, never mind they'd no links with Asia. They later became U.K. – just as boring, but at least they lived there.

PENGUIN MODERN CLASSICS

William Faulkner
As I Lay Dying

As I Lay Dying

This Californian metal band formed in 2001, namechecking *As I Lay Dying*, William Faulkner's stream of conscious-

[3] As I Lay Dying found this book heavy going but still named after it.

ness 1930 novel. It fitted both the members' death themes (with albums such as the 2001 debut *Beneath The Encasing Of Ashes*) and their Christian commitment.

Singer Tim Lambesis said: "It's kind of depressing but it's not my style of novel. We've been able to adapt and make it work. Just the ring of it sounds cool."

The Associates
They began in Dundee, Scotland. Leader Billy Mackenzie (1957-1997) said the name came from his vision of the group as "a concept". The idea was that anybody who wanted to join could be an associate member, "even someone you met at a bus stop, or your mum who wants to play spoons or something".

Fred Astaire
Anglicisation of Frederick Austerlitz, made by his parents when the future dancer/singer was only two.

Asthmatic Kitty Records
This record label is owned by singer-songwriter Sufjan Stevens and his step-father, Lowell. It's named after Lowell's beloved cat Sara, who suffers acute feline asthma.

Aswad
British reggae band from the 1980s on. "Aswad" means black in Ethiopia's Amharic language. It encapsulates their militant politics.

Atilla/ Attila
The real Attila (circa 406-443), invading King of the Huns from Asia, was a brutal tyrant. He inspired (1) three metal bands, two from the U.S. and one from the Netherlands, who traded as Atilla; (2) Atilla The Hun (ironic stagename of a gentle Trinidad calypso singer) and (3) Briton John Baine, who was on his way to a City career when he turned to performance poetry, as Attila The Stockbroker.

Atomic Kandy
From the book by Phyllis Burke. Cf ⇨Ned's Atomic Dustbin, a nuclear name.

Atomic Rooster
This British prog rock band was formed in 1969 by Vincent Crane and Carl Palmer. They had met members of the U.S. band ⇨Rhinoceros, one of whom said he'd just had a dream about an "atomic rooster". It was a "fundamental" name, like the 1970 ⇨Pink Floyd title *Atom Heart Mother*. Related: ⇨ELP.

Atreyu
The band named after a character played by Noah Hathaway in the 1984 movie *The Neverending Story*.

At The Drive-In
The critics' raves about this post hardcore band (1993-2001) might have been less fulsome had they known that the oh-so-cool name was lifted from glam metal band

Poison, whose single *Talk Dirty To Me* includes the lines "'Cause baby we'll be/ At the drive-in/ In the old man's Ford/ behind the bushes." Related: ⇨The Mars Volta, ⇨Sparta.

The Attractions

⇨Elvis Costello's backers chose the name as a play on sexual characteristics and showbusiness attractions. Cf ⇨Fairground Attraction.

Audioslave

There have been two Audioslaves, the better known being an American rock supergroup (2001-7) made up of former members of ⇨Soundgarden and ⇨Rage Against The Machine. Guitarist Tom Morello said it was the suggestion of Chris Cornell. It "came to him in a vision. We're all on the two-way pagers, and Chris one night said: 'I got it. It's Audioslave.' To paraphrase ⇨Elvis Costello, talking about band names is like dancing about architecture—there's just no point in it because the band name becomes the music and the people."

Augie March

This bunch of Australian rockers named after *The Adventures of Augie March* by Nobel laureate Saul Bellow, joking his poetic language dwarfed the efforts of their own singer-songwriter Glenn Richards.

Au Go-Go Singers

Named after the New York venue at which they played, the Café Au Go Go. Members of this 1960s act went on into bands including ⇨Buffalo Springfield.

The Automatic

Rob Hawkins, the vocalist with this Welsh post-punk band, said: "It's about the way that a lot of our friends have got it programmed into them that they go to college, they go to university, they get a degree, they get a job. The Automatic is the opposite of that." Legal problems meant they had to be called The Automatic Automatic in the U.S. and Canada.

Automatic Pilot

Automatic Pilot was born in 1980 in San Francisco. The name reflected local anger over Dan White's 1979 famous murder trial. Psychiatrists said White's behaviour was partly explained by excessive intake of sugary food; he was "sort-of on automatic pilot".

Frankie Avalon

He was born in Philadelphia as Francis Avallone. This was an Anglicisation to make life easier. Cf ⇨Fabian.

Avenged Sevenfold

These hard rockers from California formed in 1999 and insist they aren't primarily a religious band, although the name is taken from the book of Genesis where Cain is exiled for murder. Anyone who kills him would have "vengeance taken upon him sevenfold". Several of the group's songs tell this story.

Average White Band

This outfit, formed in 1972 by musicians from Scotland, gets its name reported incorrectly all over the place. The usual error is to say the name was suggested by singer Bonnie Bramlett, who was working with the band. But it's wrong: the group confirmed to the author that the phrase was from a friend, Rab Wyper, then working as a British diplomat, who had a catch phrase "too much for the average white man", applied to temperatures, cooking etc.

It worked on another level though, because they were obsessed with black music and their repertoire includes some songs that are about the closest any white group has come to true soul music.

AWBH

Stands for (Jon) Anderson, (Rick) Wakeman, (Bill) Bruford and (Steve) Howe of ⇨Yes. Most boring supergroups have boring appellations. This because (a) there's a need to placate enormous egos; (b) stars mistakenly believe their names alone will attract interest; (c) all members have to be included. This results in designations which sound like a partnership of attorneys; or which are meaningless acronyms/abbreviations.

Charles Aznavour

Anglicisation of his name Shahnour Aznavurjan.

Aztec Camera

Leader Roddy Frame, from East Kilbride, Scotland, formed the group at 15 during an infatuation with psychedelia. Aztec "sounded right"; Camera came from ⇨Teardrop Explodes single *Camera Camera*. Related: ⇨Neutral Blue.

Babe Ruth

This all-British band, from Hatfield, took the all-American name from their liking for baseball player George Herman 'Babe' Ruth (1895-1948).

Babes In Toyland

This 1990s U.S. female rock band punned on "babes" as in children and "sexy young women". "Happy as a babe in toyland" was a phrase taken by Victor Herbert for a musical. ⇨Riot Grrrl.

Babyshambles

Pete Doherty named his band after their first single from 2004. The title scrambles "Babycham" and "shambles", apt given his reputation for indulgence and musical mayhem. Related: ⇨The Libertines, ⇨Dirty Pretty Things. Not related: Jamaican act Baby Cham.

Bachman-Turner Overdrive

They initially considered the name Brave Belt – as worn by American Indians to indicate success as a hunter and fighter. Their record company complained this was obscure and they should play up links with ⇨The Guess Who.

Their surnames were Bachman (Randy, ex Guess Who; Robbie; and later Tim) and Turner (bassist C.F. 'Fred' Turner). They spotted Canadian truckers' magazine *Overdrive* which suited their top-gear rock and carried the concept through with a logo of a gearwheel. The name was often abbreviated to BTO.

The Back Door Band

Mike Mills and Bill Berry named this band after *Back Door Man*, the Dixon-Burnett song covered by ⇨The Doors among others. ⇨R.E.M.

Backstreet Boys

This U.S. pop act formed in 1993 and has gone on to sell more than 100 million albums worldwide – the best-selling boy band of all time. Producer Lou Pearlman advertised in a Florida newspaper, seeking male singers for a ⇨New Kids On The Block style group. He wanted a local name and used Orlando's Backstreet Flea Market.

[4] Babyshambles star Pete Doherty: in no way a shambles. Or fond of intoxicating substances.

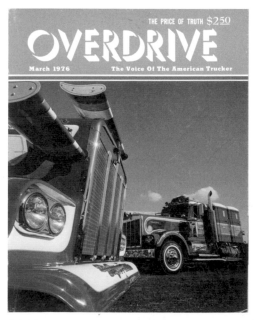

[5] The magazine that got Bachman-Turner Overdrive into gear.

A Dictionary of Rock and Pop Names

Back Street Crawler

Paul Kossoff, one of the driving forces behind ⇨Free, made a 1973 solo LP called *Back Street Crawler,* and decided to recycle it in 1975 for his band.

Bad Brains

The group led the Washington punk movement of the 1980s and named after a ⇨Ramones song on 1978's *Road To Ruin*. They helped inspire ⇨The Beastie Boys.

Bad Company

This U.K. band named from a 1972 Stanley R. Jaffe and Robert Benton western about youths who become outlaws in the U.S. Civil War. The film was released before they started their musical life of crime. They called it a protest at faceless corporations.

Singer Paul Rodgers said: "I had to fight to get the management and the record company to accept the name. They thought it was terrible." He told Peter Grant, who was also managing ⇨Led Zeppelin, "I had been through this before with ⇨Free, as Island wanted to call us Heavy Metal Kids." The belligerent Grant backed him and the name was approved.

Bad English

The name was decided during a pool game when band member John Waite played a poor shot, eliciting the comment that his "English" was bad, meaning the spin applied to the ball. This is as opposed to the once-common explanation that it was a comment on his previous band's misspelled moniker, The Babys.

Badfinger

They started as ⇨The Iveys, in Swansea, Wales. By the late 1960s they were a corollary to the then-successful ⇨Hollies. They later turned against the Iveys: it sounded dated and there were a few other bands with similar choices. In 1968 they signed with ⇨Apple, ⇨The Beatles' record company, and realised it was "now or never" to change their name before releasing ⇨Paul McCartney's song *Come And Get It*: the Macca connection made it a guaranteed hit, and after that a change would be out of the question.

On John Lennon's suggestion, they considered The Prix and Glass Onion, after his song of this name (cf ⇨Glass Onion). In the end though, they passed on the suggestions of a genius to go with Apple boss Neil Aspinal. He suggested a reference to *Bad Finger Boogie*, an early working title of *With A Little Help From My Friends*. Lennon had played a demo version of this song with his middle finger, after hurting a forefinger. This makes more sense than earlier reports that it was an obscure blues record Aspinal had heard – nobody involved in that version seemed to have any idea who recorded it anyway. Either way, Badfinger initially struck the group as ridiculous but they couldn't think of anything better . . . and the record was about to be pressed. They'd been given a name and a Top Five song: few artists are as lucky.

The luck didn't last: after a split in 1981, for two years the rival factions both ran bands called Badfinger. The story ended with a second suicide among the musicians.

[6+7] Badly Drawn Boy and the cartoon that made him laugh.

Badly Drawn Boy

This badly-bobble-hatted U.K. tunesmith is nowhere near as slapdash and lazy as his name and woolly image suggest. From his debut at a Manchester nightclub, he's been making crafted music, aware that his birthname Damon Gough isn't especially memorable. Taking the same sort of cue as ⇨Fatboy Slim, he's gone for humour.

He adopted his name in 1997. A long-time admirer of the *Viz* adult comic, he loved May 1983's one-off *Badly Drawn Man,* with all the jokes stemming from the dashed-off delineation.

Viz responded by parodying a pop singer who failed to sell records and ends up begging and busking – called, naturally, *Badly Overdrawn Boy.*

The source is sometimes wrongly given as the simply-drawn hero of a TV show, *Sam And His Magic Ball.*

Bad Manners

The name was suggested by the manic antics of the vocalist with this U.K. ska revival band, Fatty Buster Bloodvessel. He was born Douglas Trendle, in 1958. This bald-headed, 17-stone, extrovert, bovver-boot-wearing hunk's habits included dressing up as a ballet dancer and diving into vats of baked beans. The Bloodvessel name was used by the bus conductor played by Ivor Cutler in the 1967 ⇨Beatles film *Magical Mystery Tour.*

The Bad Seeds

Nick Cave-led band named after a book called *The Bad Seed.* Related: ⇨The Birthday Party.

Badu

Or Erykah Badu in full. She was born with the surname Wright. Badu comes from scat ad-lib.

A Dictionary of Rock and Pop Names

Long John Baldry

This singer from London was named from his 6'7" height. His bands included ⇨The Hoochie-Coochie Men, and Bluesology, both christened from musical terms. Baldry's first name was adopted by ⇨Elton John.

Afrika Bambaataa

New Yorker Kevin Donovan. The name was adopted to tie in with his musical cohorts The Zulu Nation. The Jungle Brothers, another act, dubbed themselves as Baby Afrika Bambaataa in his honour.

Bambinos

This Italian female band had a rough time with their name. They started as The Barbies. Fears of legal action followed from the doll makers. They became the Bambies – until they were told this could upset Walt Disney. Finally they renamed Bambinos, the Italian word for "babies", because they were "babes".

Bananarama

The U.K. female band's Caribbean dance song *Aie A Mwana* led to the idea for the name The Bananas, and jokes about ⇨Roxy Music's *Pyjamarama*. They hoped their fame would lead to plenty of ⇨Bryan Ferry-like types armed with bananas in pyjamas. Their publishing company was called In A Bunch Music.

The Band

This Canadian ensemble started as ⇨The Hawks, the backing band of rockabilly Ronnie Hawkins. All of his frequently-changing groups used this name. They later deserted Hawkins to become Levon And The Hawks – Levon being drummer/vocalist Levon Helm–, The Crackers, The Honkies (considered) and The Squires in 1965. The Crackers was a derogatory name, for poor white southern trash, which went over the record company's heads. The Hawks name was warlike and meaningless when they moved out from under Ronnie's wing.

They were simply and colloquially called "the band" not long after they started on their own, probably because no other appellation seemed right. Robbie Robertson recalled that everybody called them "the band" when they started to back ⇨Bob Dylan: Dylan himself, their friends and neighbours. "That's all we were known as."

They kept the title because it was so simple and had attitude: THE Band, as if no other mattered. It was also justified because they were a unit able to switch instruments, without inflated egos hampering team work.

It also didn't limit their scope in the way contemporaries found with aliases such as ⇨Strawberry Alarm Clock. The Band were never psychedelic, never hippy: their timeless music was reminiscent of 1868 not 1968.

Cf ⇨The Pop Group.

Band Aid

⇨Bob Geldof's name for his "supergroup" which cut the three million plus-sales 1984 single *Do They Know It's Christmas* to aid the starving in Ethiopia.

The appellation was preserved for the Band Aid Charity which organised the July

1985 Live Aid concerts. The title produced some concern about Band-Aid plasters – which many saw as petty, given the charity purpose (the plasters were written with a hyphen, the band without). Geldof was keen to stress that the designation did not mean they were simply trying to patch over the starvation problem.

Arthur Lee of ⇨Love recorded a 1972 solo album which used musicians collectively known as Band Aid, so-called "because the band helped me out".

Band Of Susans
This New York band started in 1986 with three Susans: Lyall, Stenger and Tallman: two later left and three guys joined.

Ed Banger And The Nosebleeds
Links heavy metal "headbanging" in time with deafening music in the front row of rock concerts, with the nosebleeds sometimes produced as a result. Without Ed Banger, the Nosebleeds searched around for a new vocalist, at one point adding ⇨Morrissey.

Bangles
Supersonic Bangs!, screamed the headline above a U.S. magazine fashion article on retro hairdos. It was 1980. This Los Angeles female group loved it: the pun referred not to jet booms but bangs, as in long tresses of hair. Bang also had meanings linked with pleasure, drugs and sex.

The Bangs they might have stayed. Then they discovered another band on the other side of America called The Bangs; there were fears the New Jersey rivals would sue. They went for a close alternative. The new name recalled "L.A." and the "les" of ⇨The Beatles. (Any link with *Bangles* by ⇨The Electric Prunes seems coincidental.)

Barbecue Bob
U.S. singer Robert Hicks got his name because he used to work at a barbecue in Georgia.

Barclay James Harvest
This band from Oldham, U.K., signed to EMI in 1968. When the recording company launched its progressive rock label in 1969 it had such high hopes for them it named it ⇨Harvest. By 1990 they were simply B.J.H.

In 1993 founder Les Holroyd said he could not remember the origin. "It was probably because they needed the name for posters or something and we gave them the first thing that came into our heads."

Barenaked Ladies
This 1990s pop band from Toronto, Canada, has a very misleading name. It certainly attracts attention – and away from the five chunky guys called Steven, Ed, Jim, Andy and Tyler who make the grungy music. Far from being naked, they favour thick clothes of several layers.

The band said: "It's a term we all used when we were kids of six or seven years old. You looked at someone with no clothes on, or at the picture of a nude woman, and say they were barenaked."

The founders Ed (Robertson) and Steve (Page) met again in 1988, long after they had been at school together. They recalled the name – with its innocent sexuality – while making up stories about bands at a ⇨Bob Dylan concert, bored with the music. Robertson had been in a covers band which had broken up. When he had a call a week later to remind him that his group was entered into a talent concert, he impulsively said it had renamed as "Barenaked Ladies" and called Page to ask for help.

Tribute band: Fully Clothed Gents.

Basher
Nickname for ⇨Nick Lowe, way before his ⇨Rockpile days, from his studio slogan of "bashing it down and tarting it up later".

Basia
Polish vocalist Basia Trzetrzelewska, a one-time member of ⇨(p.189) Matt Bianco, wisely dropped her surname.

Count Basie
U.S. bandleader Bill Basie got his name during a radio broadcast from Kansas City, where a radio announcer called him "the Count." Soon, deejays and others were comparing him to jazz aristocrats 'King' Benny Goodman, Duke Ellington and Earl Hines. Basie said he would have preferred "Buck or even Fats".

Dame Shirley Bassey
Her real name. Her real unflattering-derivative nickname: Burly Chassis. She insisted "Dame" be added to her stagename after being given the British honour.

Bastard
German heavy rock band who picked up on an abortive choice by ⇨Lemmy for ⇨Motörhead.

Bat For Lashes
The words "bat" and "lashes" came into Natasha Khan's mind as she was working out the visual and audio concepts for her 2006 debut *Fur and Gold*. "It just sounds like the music," she said in an interview. The words were "chosen simply because they sounded unusual together". Gothic bats or sporting bats? Eye lashes or whip lashes? Either way, the term has been applied both to Khan and to her all-female backing band.

Bauhaus

Bauhaus was a reversal of the German word "hausbau". This turns "building of house" into "house of building". It was the name coined by Walter Gropius for his German school of radical design, founded in 1919 and lasting until 1933.

The Northamptonshire, U.K., group at first called themselves Bauhaus 1919. This was in 1978. They became simply Bauhaus the following year. They thought the name sounded cool and liked its "stylistic implications and associations", said bassist David J.

Bauhaus has reformed after splits that produced ⇨Dali's Car and ⇨Love And Rockets. There was a 1970s Italian band called Bauhaus (no relation of course).

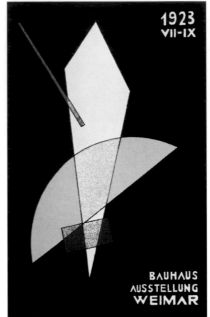

[8] The Bauhaus Weimar Manifesto from 1923 created a new Bauhaus in Northampton 1978.

Bay City Rollers

By the mid 1970s they were simply called The Rollers by their fans, teen-boppers if not weeny-boppers. But this Edinburgh, Scotland, band began in 1967 as The Saxons. Their manager Tam Paton wanted an American handle.

He blindly stuck a pin in a map of the U.S. and came up with Bay City. There's confusion as to whether his pin found the Bay City, Oregon, Texas or Rochester, Michigan – but most suspect the latter, the birthplace of ⇨Madonna. It recalled both surf music and ⇨The Rolling Stones.

The Beach Boys

This is an everyday story of the evolution of a long-lasting California band that started singing simple Four Freshmen style harmonies and using garbage cans as drums. The name changed, the production matured, the ever-youthful music stayed. The beards grew, the drum kit got better, hair greyed and receded.

The Wilson family-dominated act began as The Wilson Brothers, then became Carl And The Passions. This was suggested by Dennis Wilson in 1961, and an identity adopted for retro-sounding 1972 LP *Carl & The Passions: So Tough*. They metamorphosed into the similar-sounding Kenny And The Cadets. Songwriter Brian Wilson, the leader for their early career, was the first-billed Kenny.

A growing interest in surfing – both among the band and Californian youth – led to their third alias, The Pendletones. This was taken from the name of heavy Pendleton-trademarked plaid top worn by surfers and beach nuts. The group wore similar matching shirts on stage, an easy and cheap image. Plus, the name was a pun on "tone" recalling the success of Dick Dale's Del-Tones and other "tone" acts.

Their first record, 1961 release *Surfin'*, was trial-pressed on Robert and Richard Dix's local X Records label. Herb Newman of Era Records wanted to issue it on the

A Dictionary of Rock and Pop Names

[9] The Beach Boys try to live up to their name. Yet only one of them liked surfing.

new State-wide Candix label, which had already had a surfing hit, the now long-forgotten *Underwater* by The Frogmen. But Newman hated the Pendletones appellation, which he thought was too obscure. In a round of phone calls which the Wilsons knew nothing about, Candix A&R man Joe Saraceno played the freshly-cut demo to a record distributor. Saraceno said that he thought the group was called The Surfers. It turned out this pseudonym had been taken by another close-harmony act and Saraceno telephoned back to remark that he preferred something like, oh, say, The Beach Boys. Russ Regan of the local Buckeye Record Distributors took this as a cue. The moniker would also suit the image of the sporty song, put them together with Jan And Dean and was an echo of their West Coast origins, similar to ⇨The Coasters, briefly known as The Surf Boys.

The record was processed before the boys were told. They were scandalised and their father/ self-appointed manager, the outspoken Murray Wilson, had a therapeutic shout down the telephone – only to be told it was too late. Not only would it be expensive to reprint labels but also they had already been sent out to dozens of shops. The youngsters shrugged it off because they were pleased to have a record out; their father worked to make it a local hit.

Hindsight suggests "The Beach Boys" was a better handle than the obscure Pendletones, which would have quickly sounded dated. Similar choices by other acts such as The Silvertones and The Quailtones were soon confined to the dustbin of musical history.

On the down side, critics claim the choice has subsequently suited only song subjects such as *Endless Summers*, hot rods, girls, sex, sea, surf, and sun sun sun. It did them little favours as they moved onto "deeper" subjects such as the environment on the *Surf's Up* album, aging, having children or world politics.

Only drummer Dennis had a long-running interest in surfing – and he died in a swimming accident in 1983. The name also dated as the group aged well beyond boyhood. Britain has seen ⇨Boy George and ⇨The Pet Shop Boys face similar problems. What about The Beach Men? The Beach Granddads?

Inspired: ⇨The City Surfers. Related: ⇨Wilson Phillips.

Beastie Boys

Well, they really were nice middle class kids from New York. But, in the early days, they always acted as repulsively as possible, as if to live up to the Beastly name.

They formed in 1979 as a punk act, The Young Aborigines. Two years later, they switched to the Beastie Boys at the suggestion of guitarist John Berry: this was 1981, as Adam Yauch joined. BB really had no other significance, with other interpretations coming later, according to members Michael Diamond (better known as Mike D) and Yauch (pronounced Yowk, also known as MCA: that's not "Master of Ceremonies Adam" but "Mic Controller Adam", according to the 1989 song *Year And A Day*).

King Ad-Rock, (AKA Adam Horovitz) joined the band slightly later but said in an interview that they could have been called The Beastly Boys.

They all rubbish the suggestion, often slavishly repeated on the Internet, that Berry initially intended "Beastie" to mean "Boys Entering Anarchistic States Towards Internal Excellence". He may very well have come up with this LATER, true.

The Boys were soon winning support slots for Washington punk band ⇨Bad Brains. It's also suggested their initials BB were intended to mimic the main act. The song, *Beastie Boys*, from 1982, was later included in a 1999 compilation, where Ad-Rock says the Bad Brains were their "heroes".

Their antisocial behaviour was celebrated on the B side of a 1983 single with a rant called *Beastie Revolution*.

As the Beasties became one of the longest-lived hip-hop acts, nominated for induction into the Rock and Roll Hall of Fame more than 20 years after their debut, the "Boys" became more than faintly ridiculous. The Beastie Men (Beastly Men?) somehow doesn't work, any more than The Beach Men. Inspired ⇨The Sneaker Pimps.

The Beat

This American group cut their first album in 1979 before ⇨The (English) Beat came onto the scene. The U.S. outfit claimed the legal right to the name and won. They were handicapped, though, because The (English) Beat became better-known. They later tried renaming Paul Collins's Beat, with a 1983 LP called *To Beat Or Not To Beat*.

The Beat (known in the U.S.A. as) The English Beat

Singer David Wakeling was browsing the "music" synonyms and antonyms in *Roget's Thesaurus*, divided into "discord" and "harmony". The latter yielded ⇨Clash. The other started with "Beat". As a name, its drawback was that it was too like ⇨The Beatles. Wakeling liked the harmony aspect: the band had black and white members.

Related: ⇨Fine Young Cannibals.

Beatallica

This band combined both the music and names of ⇨The Beatles (see below) and ⇨Metallica.

A Dictionary of Rock and Pop Names

The Beatles

This British 1960s greatest awesome foursome changed music forever.

The first version of the band, formed by ⇨John Lennon in 1957 in Liverpool, U.K., was a skiffle outfit called The Quarrymen, after the local Quarry Bank High School which he attended. ⇨Paul McCartney and ⇨George Harrison joined later. By the time they briefly disbanded in 1959, the Quarrymen designation had become irrelevant – John had left the school for art college the year before and the others were at The Liverpool Institute.

Later, the reformed trio went through a series of monikers, for example christening themselves The Rainbows one night because they turned up in different coloured shirts.

The drummerless band also entered one talent competition, selecting, on the spur of the moment, the handle Johnny And The Moondogs. This was a reference to the origins of rock with the singer ⇨Moondog and Alan Freed's 1951 radio show *Moondog's Rock 'n' Roll Party*. It also reflected the fact that most acts in those days, such as ⇨Cliff Richard And The Shadows, had a leader – and John was acknowledged the prime mover.

It was he who suggested their final name. He wanted to emulate ⇨Buddy Holly, idolised for his songwriting and guitar-playing. Holly died in 1959, but his music lives on to this day via musicals and much else. John liked the double-meaning of Holly's backing band ⇨The Crickets – referring both to "cricket" = insect and also "cricket" = game. He was annoyed someone had beaten him to it, perhaps especially with cricket being English. John's love of Goonish word play, which later emerged in humorous slim volumes such as the endlessly-punning *In His Own Write* and *A Spaniard In The Works*, caused him to search around for a similar insect designator. He soon misspelled "Beetle" as "Beatle" to make the pun on beat music more obvious. (Lennon's punning later led to his naming another band ⇨Cyrkle).

The term "The Beat Generation", coined by writer Jack Kerouac, was reaching its apogee. In time, Kerouac influenced many bands such as ⇨The Dharma Bums and ⇨Elmerhassell. It would be fascinating to establish an earlier link between Kerouac and arguably the greatest of all bands. There's no evidence to confirm this however.

Still, there's another possible origin here: John may not have read 1957's *On The Road* by Kerouac but he certainly knew of *The Wild One*, the 1953 film which propelled Marlon Brando to greater stardom – wearing the leather jacket look much favoured by the early Beatles. Brando's character led a motorcycle gang against Lee Marvin's rival faction who were called The Beetles: their black jackets made them look like beetles. (Cf ⇨Black Rebel Motorcycle Club, who named from Brando's gang.)

Lennon jokingly referred to "the Bootles" in several interviews, so he knew of a connection with the Liverpool district of Bootle. Still, there's no strong evidence that this was an initial motivation for the choice of the moniker.

Liverpool friend Casy Jones, of Cass and The Casanovas, said the Beatles appellation was too short. Following the fifties trend for "showbizzy" long designations, Jones suggested Long John And The Silver Beetles. The ⇨Baldry-style 'Long John' alias was another reference to the outgoing Lennon, still seen as the leader, possibly by everyone apart from McCartney.

They shortened/ changed it to The Silver Beatles, the billing they used for an audition in 1959, until 1960. Even then, they preferred its further-abbreviated form without the meaningless "Silver" tag. It was as The Beatles they evolved with Stuart Sutcliffe (left in 1961, died in 1962), Pete Best (sacked in 1962) and ⇨Ringo Starr (replaced Best in 1962).

However, they made one demo record in 1961, backing pop singer Tony Sheridan as 'The Beat Boys' because 'Beatles' was thought too confusing.

Clearly, there was some resistance to the handle, revolutionary in its time – the band discovered during their Hamburg days that Germans often said the byword as "Peedles", slang for cock or John (Lennon) Thomas. Top English promoter Arthur Howes, on first hearing of the band, merely thought "another group with a silly name!"

The Beatles often shrouded the choice in secrecy, producing various "entertaining" yarns such as that the name was given to them by a man on a magic carpet. As John put it: "It came in a vision – a man appeared on a flaming pie and said unto us 'From this day on you are Beatles with an A'. Thank you, Mister Man, we said, thanking him." (In May 1997 McCartney released an album entitled *Flaming Pie* and ⇨Oasis referenced it in *Magic Pie*.)

There's more on all four individual Beatles' other pseudonyms in their separate entries. (Paul Ramon, cf ⇨The Ramones; Carl Harrison.) In contrast to the rebellious Lennon, who returned his M.B.E. long before his untimely death, McCartney went on to be knighted, joining a group of pop "Sirs" including ⇨Bob Geldof, ⇨Elton John and ⇨Cliff Richard. His band ⇨Wings named, in part, from his 1968 Beatles song, *Blackbird*.

All four Beatles became household names as their band's identifier passed into popular consciousness and into language: Beatlemania, Beatlesque. They became known as The Fab Four or The Fabs (sometimes made into a joke: The Prefab Four).

Inspired/ related: ⇨Apple, ⇨Apple Boutique, ⇨Badfinger, ⇨Bonzo Dog Doo-Dah Band, ⇨Glass Onion, ⇨The Glove, ⇨The Nerk/ Nurk Twins, ⇨Ricky And The Red Streaks, ⇨The Rutles, ⇨Sgt. Pepper's Lonely Hearts Club Band, ⇨The Smoking Mojo Filters and ⇨Yeah Yeah Yeah.

Among many tribute bands: The Bootleg Beatles and Sgt. Pepper's Magical Mystery Trip.

The Beatnigs
Three black men from San Francisco chose this name, bringing together "beatniks" and "beatings", to remind everyone that racial inequality still exists. Their intentions were frequently misunderstood, not helping radio play.

To quote the liner notes of their 1988 debut album, the word "nig" is "a positive acronym . . . it has taken on a universal meaning in describing all oppressed people". Cf ⇨N.W.A.

The Beau Brummels
This 1960s band from San Francisco misspelled the notorious British dandy George 'Beau' Brummell (1778-1840). Like the related harmony outfit ⇨Harpers Bizarre, plus

⇨The Buckinghams and ⇨Sir Douglas Quintet, the moniker was chosen to sound British, during the "British Invasion".

The Beautiful South

"The beautiful south" is a slogan for several U.S. states. Still, this reference is strictly British.

The band evolved from ⇨The Housemartins, whose patriotism for Northern England led to titles such as the LP *Hull 4, London 0*.

Leader Paul Heaton felt the new band should scrap the previous image, which had meant The Housemartins were not taken seriously, like a ⇨Madness of the north.

This was hammered home by a debut album, *Welcome To The Beautiful South*. Far from portraying the south as a beautiful eldorado, it featured a picture of a woman about to kill herself with a gun in her mouth.

Beck

Band and solo star, named from Beck Hansen. No relation to Jeff Beck of ⇨The Yardbirds.

Captain Beefheart

Another fairy story, of how once upon a time 1940s child TV star Don Van Vliet, from California, dreamed of stardom, became international avant-garde rock star Captain Beefheart and later spent his days eccentrically painting pictures in the Mojave Desert.

It started, for young Van Vliet, with a fantasy called *Captain Beefheart Meets The Grunt People*. He went to school in Lancaster, California, where he became buddies with ⇨Frank Zappa, later moving to Cucamonga to make Beefheart into a film and further aid and abet Zappa. The two worked on the movie scenario, formed a band called The Blackouts and planned another group called The Soots.

Some aficionados maintain Van Vliet first thought of the script, while other fans claim that it was Zappa who came up with the title. Both sides are wrong in one respect: a similar Captain Beefheart had existed as a storybook familiar for a century. Yet both are fundamentally correct: Van Vliet reinvented the character, while there is no doubt that Zappa was soon applying it to him. He said Van Vliet had a "beef in his heart" against convention and the world.

The name was outrageous for a rock artist in the early 1960s, and the critics loved him, perhaps as much as Zappa himself. Beefheart was backed by ever-changing Magic Band members whom he rapidly rechristened such ridiculous things as Zoot Horn Rollo, The Winged Eel Fingerling, Antennae Johnny, The Mascara Snake, Rockette Morton and Orejon: "it means 'Big Ear'," he explained enigmatically of the last.

Inspired: ⇨Dali's Car, ⇨the Zutons.

The Bee Gees

The name variously has been explained as coming from any or all of the following:
1. From "The Brothers Gibb" – Barry, Maurice and Robin – who were born in the U.K. but partly brought up in Australia. They were billed as The Bee Gees (Brothers Gibb) Comedy Trio in Brisbane in 1962.

2.   From Barry's initials. He's several years older than the others and was the early band leader.

3.   From speedway driver and promoter Bill Gates, who spotted the trio singing at a race track.

4.   From local Aussie deejay Bill Goode, who also championed their music.

5.   From the musical notes used in their early close-harmony style in Brisbane.

The correct answer's that they were always The Bee Gees (Brothers Gibb): it was good fortune that Gates and Goode had the same initials so there was no renaming required. It's preferable to two alternative choices – Rattlesnakes and Wee Johnny Hays and the Blue Cats.

B.E.F.

Abbreviation for British Electric Foundation, the production organisation behind U.K. electronics band ⇨Heaven 17. The 1980s was a time when many music stars saw themselves as businessmen or women (cf ⇨Public Image Ltd.)   The aim was to sound like a public corporation with a mission statement: "The new partnership – that's opening doors all over the world." Plus a ludicrous international slogan: "Sheffield-Edinburgh-London."

Beginning Of The End

This U.S. band was protesting at funk creeping into Nassau music. Their concern was spelled out with the 1974 minor hit *Funky Nassau*. The "beginning of the end" phrase's most famous use was by British premier Winston Churchill. Cf ⇨Blood, Sweat And Tears.

Belle & Sebastian

This Scottish rock band formed in 1996 as a duo, neither called by these names. They had written a song based around *Belle et Sébastien*, the tale by French writer Cécile Aubry that had also been made into a TV series.

The Belle Stars

1980s U.K. female pop band with a penchant for western gear and stetsons. Their name and image came from the west's most notorious female outlaw Belle Star.

Belly

Short-lived 1990s band, offshoot of ⇨Throwing Muses, with a name which resembles ⇨Echobelly. Tanya Donelly said in an interview that belly suggests "different things to different people. Some people think of babies, some of beer; others think of dead fish or of sex. I think of the one black hair on my body that grows from my belly and it gets to be very long sometimes." Related: ⇨The Breeders.

Pat Benatar

This New York singer was born as Pat Andrzejewski. Her first husband was Dennis Benatar. Pat kept the name after her 1982 remarriage to guitarist-producer Neil Geraldo, by which time she was an established artist.

A Dictionary of Rock and Pop Names

The Benders

This jazz band explain their name: "It's a word which means nothing in our home, Australia, and that's what we wanted." If it meant the same Down Under as it does in the U.K., they wouldn't have stood a chance.

Ben Folds Five

Not a sentence, as in Ben folding up five somethings. Group led by Ben Folds. A trio, they thought this sounded better, with alliterative prospects for growth.

Cliff Bennett And The Rebel Rousers

In the early 1960s, British bands were trying to sound American. By the mid 1960s, with the success of ⇨The Beatles, this had changed. This U.K. group belongs to the earlier phase, named after Duane Eddy's 1958 *Rebel Rouser*.

Tony Bennett

The U.S. singer was born Anthony Benedetto, and started performing as Joe Bari, after his family's hometown in Italy. In 1949, comedian Bob Hope offered to put him on his touring show on condition he changed his name to something classier. Hope proposed the new name, based on Bari's real name.

Benny Profane

These U.K. rockers loved the name of an eccentric figure in U.S. writer Thomas Pynchon's 1963 debut, *V*.

Bent Fabric

This Danish pianist anglicised his name Bent Fabricus Bjerre. More fabric names: ⇨Felt etc.

Berlin

Like ⇨Anberlin, ⇨Spandau Ballet and ⇨The Berlin Blondes, a group under the spell of the capital of Prussia/ Germany, with its aura of mystery. Like the other three, this lot don't come from there. In this case, from Los Angeles. The nerve of these people *takes your breath away* . . .

They named from ⇨Lou Reed's 1973 LP *Berlin*, which also inspired ⇨The Waterboys.

Berlin Blondes

Another case which violates trades descriptions laws. They may have been blonde but they were from Glasgow, Scotland. Not ⇨Berlin either. Cf ⇨Texas.

Irving Berlin

The pronunciation of famous U.S. songwriter Israel Baline's real name led to a printer crediting an early piece to Irving Berlin. It stuck.

Chuck Berry

There's confusion over his birthplace and birthdate, not his birthname – Charles Berry, called Chuck from an early age. Inspired: ⇨(p.160) Jo Jo Gunne.

Bettie Serveert

In Dutch, the name means "Bettie serves," as in tennis. This long-running band fronted by Carol van Dyk was inspired by the Netherlands women's player Bettie Stöve who made it to three of the Wimbledon Finals in 1977. She was a heroine at home, making a TV show called *Bettie Serveert*.

Beyoncé

The American R&B singer's full birthname is Beyoncé Giselle Knowles. The unusual Christian name is from her mother's maiden French-Creole name Beyincé. She started in ⇨Destiny's Child and is another single-name star. Pronounced bion-say or bee-yawn-say (to rhyme with fiancée) NOT buy-once.

[10] Bettie Serveert means "Betty Serves". So here's the band's inspiration, Betty Stöve, serving.

B-52's

The American Air Force B-52 bomber, delivered between 1955 and 1963, was in regular use 30 years later. The plane, with a wingspan the size of a football pitch, played a role in the Vietnam and Gulf Wars.

A beehive hairstyle popular in the 1950s/ 1960s was so large it acquired the Southern nickname B-52.

Singers Kate Pierson and Cindy Wilson used to go to nightclubs in Athens, Georgia, in the early 1970s. Because they couldn't afford anything else, they went to a second-hand store and bought old sixties clothes. Cindy carried the image through with a pink bouffant so high she looked in danger of falling over and Kate sported a blue version a foot high. Their early music plundered the 1950s and 1960s. Tribute: ⇨The Rock Lobsters. Cf ⇨Voice Of The Beehive.

The B.H. Surfers

Name given by some of the U.S. media – especially in the Bible Belt – to ⇨The Butthole Surfers.

[11] From Destiny's Child to solo star, Beyoncé proves one name's enough.

[12] The B-52s show off the high hairstyles that gave them the name.

Bhundu Boys

These Zimbabweans named from the bush fighters who ended Ian Smith's white regime in what was Rhodesia.

The Bible

Like ⇨The Christians, they had to fend off religious references. This band simply wanted to sell as many CDs/records as the world's best-selling book. Perhaps someone should have told them it's the least-read per number of copies printed.

Big Audio Dynamite

The abbreviation B.A.D was chosen by ex- ⇨Clash guitarist Mick Jones. "Bad" also carries the connotation of meaning "very good" (check out rap, or songs by Isaac Hayes and ⇨Michael Jackson). Jones then had to consider what it might stand for. "Beyond Alien Destruction" was one possibility. His second choice, in 1982, was ⇨Real Westway.

Big Black

If you want to stir up controversy, do it big. This is what U.S. musician Steve Albini managed to do with this, and his subsequent band ⇨Rapeman. He denied allegations of racism (here) and sexism (there). This name's supposedly not phallic and portrays the evils of society through a dark devil figure.

Big Bopper

Born Jape Richardson, in Texas, he adopted the name J.P. Richardson, based on a mispronunciation of his name, when he became a local disc jockey on KTRM Radio, Texas. Because of his size and enthusiasm for the 1950s heel-and-toe 'Bop' dance, he became Big Bopper.

Big Brother And The Holding Company

These San Francisco musicians got their name in 1965, before they started backing Janis Joplin. Manager Chet Helms took "Big Brother" from George Orwell's 1949 novel of the "near future" *Nineteen Eighty-Four*. Helms, as promoter, financier and *éminence grise* saw it as an amusing comment on his role.

The band added The Holding Company to rival ⇨The Great Society's name. Joplin said it was an apposite comment on faceless capitalist institutions, which were becoming Orwellian monoliths. Cf ⇨Public Image.

Gurley added in an interview: "It had a double meaning because of common slang at the time. 'Holding' meant 'possessing' [drugs] – it just was safer to say. It was a long name but it worked well."

Related: ⇨Dinosaurs.

Big Country

Seen by some as applying to Stuart Adamson's original Scottish home. Surprisingly, the rest of the band were non-Scottish, born in England and Canada. The twin-guitars still sounded like bagpipes on 1983's *In A Big Country*.

In an interview with the author, Adamson said the name was meant to imply "vastness, open spaces, ambition and new discovery – in whatever country, in whatever field". Their music was "panoramic" and "wide screen". Any specific geographic reference became blurred when Adamson moved to the U.S.

Related: ⇨The Skids.

Big In Japan

This Liverpool, U.K., band named after one of the music businesses' greatest jokes about bands being "big in Japan" if not at home. A late 1970s *New Musical Express* issue said: "⇨Led Zeppelin big in Japan" (Led Zep was big in many other places of course). Big In Japan said the advent of punk showed it was time for a fresh start. Unrelated: ⇨Japan.

Big Star

This 1970s Tennessee band needed a name, and a rest, after a hard day's night working in a recording studio. As they emerged, sure that they were going to be big stars, their eyes alighted on a display across the street: "Big Star Foodmarket". "It must be a sign," they said.

Big Thing

This U.S. Midwest band's singer-songwriter Robert Lamm said the name was chosen in the optimistic hope that their jazz-rooted rock would become the Next Big Thing. It was also Mafia slang for murder – and saucily suggestive. This may have explained why they spent some years only getting bookings in small clubs. Their mentor Jim Guercio suggested they become ⇨Chicago, when they indeed became the Next Big Thing.

Acker Bilk

Born Bernard Bilk, but known as "acker" from old Southern English slang for "friend".

The Billion Dollar Babies

⇨Alice Cooper was initially the name of the band; later it came to refer to the singer alone. The original line-up without him took a cue from the 1973 LP *Billion Dollar Babies* which showed them wallowing in Greenbacks.

Biloxi Blues

This blues band ripped off the title of a musical about a man called up for service in the dying days of World War II, filmed in 1988.

Bird

Charlie Parker rapidly became Charlie "Bird" Parker. Within years the nickname had become bigger than the name. Within hours of his death in 1955, "Bird Lives" was daubed on the walls of the New York subway.

Arranger and composer Gil Evans insisted the name came when Parker was a teenager in Kansas City. "He would joke: 'Well, I'm going home to catch one of the yardbirds and cook it' – that's what he called chicken".

Cf ⇨The Yardbirds, ⇨Birdland. The nickname was also applied to jazz arranger Bert Johnson.

Birdland

Occasionally it's been said this U.K. Midlands band of the 1990s named after ⇨Charlie 'Bird' Parker's nightclub. Not true. They liked *Birdland*, an arty track on Patti Smith's 1975 album *Horses*.

Birds

This 1960s English band started as The Thunderbirds, after the car; found another band already had the name; renamed The Birds, then found themselves overtaken in popularity by ⇨The Byrds and sued the Americans for loss of income. The Brits lost and had to become Bird's Birds.

Most lucky of these early Birds: Ron Wood of ⇨The Faces, ⇨The Rolling Stones.

The Birthday Party

This Australian band started as The Boys Next Door in 1980. They used both names for a time, conscious that both names sounded thoroughly ordinary and unthreatening. The name was inspired by *The Birthday Party*, a doomy 1957 play by British

[13] *The Birthday Party* by Harold Pinter inspired Nick Cave's first band.

A Dictionary of Rock and Pop Names

Nobel laureate Harold Pinter, in which an ordinary event becomes desperate and dangerous. Related: ⇨The Bad Seeds.

Bitch
The name fitted the sado-masochistic image and lyrical content favoured by this American heavy metal band fronted by Betsy Weiss. They later changed their music – and name to Betsy – in an attempt to be taken seriously.

Bix
Jazzman Leon Bismarck Beiderbeck was generally called Bix; a corruption of his Germanic real name.

Björk
Björk's name is common in Iceland and means "birch tree". The Old English equivalent is "beorc".

U.S. and U.K. fans have had enough problems saying her name. Pronounce it "Be-urk" (rhymes with "work") not "Bee-ork" (rhymes with "York"). Björk has jokingly pointed out it also rhymes with "jerk".

According to Icelandic naming conversion, one name is enough. In full she is Björk Guðmundsdóttir, with the second name variously spelled in other countries. However rendered, strictly speaking this only means "Guðmundur's daughter" and is a description rather than a full family patronym. However this is academic when Icelanders use a second name for ID.

She became the latest in a growing line of one-name stars – cf ⇨Sting, ⇨Madonna etc – as a member of ⇨The Sugarcubes. The second name is said as "Gvuth-munds-doh-tear".

Bjorn Again/Björn Again
There have been about six tribute bands of these names, with lookalikes playing cover versions of ⇨ABBA songs. All use the name of original member Björn Ulvaeus to pun that ABBA and Sweden are "born again".

The most-successful Björn Again, from Australia, has names punning on the real members: Agnetha Falstart (from Agnetha Fältskog), Benny Anderwear (Benny Andersson), Frida Longstokin (Anni-Frid Lyngstad) and of course Björn Volvo-us (Björn Ulvaeus). The band is supported by Rutger Sonofagunn (from session bassist Rutger Gunnarsson) and Ola Drumkitt (session drummer Ola Brunkert).

Black
Black were always white, although they were a trio which became just one. That one was Liverpool singer Colin Vearncombe, whose wonderful lifestyle included a penchant for black clothes. He accepted he would never become famous in the charmingly-named punk band Epileptic Tits.

Blackbyrds
This loose aggregation wasn't named after ⇨The Byrds. Their leader was Donald Byrd, who had a hit with *Black Byrd*.

Black Caesar

Sample of plethora of nicknames for ⇨James Brown, this one was from his score for the 1973 ghetto gangster film of the same name. The name, like ⇨Little Caesar, recalls Julius Caesar, West Indian escaped slave John Caesar, and the "Godfather of Harlem" in the movie.

Cilla Black

The star best known for British TV shows such as *Blind Date* was born in Liverpool as Priscilla Marie Veronica White, and began her singing career as Swinging Cilla in the swinging sixties. She was called Cilla in school. Deciding Cilla White still did not sound right, so she hit back called Cilla Black. She said that a local paper, *Mersey Beat*, made a mistake. The reporter knew her name was a colour and guessed wrong. "My [and ⇨Beatles] manager Brian Epstein quite liked it, though, and put it in the contract."

The Black Crowes

Chris and Rich Robinson, from Atlanta, Georgia, were Mr Crow's Garden after the fairy tale, then developed a logo featuring crows with long black hair cut in ⇨Keith Richards style not unlike their own. They are informally known as The Crowes in the same way as ⇨The Rolling Stones, who they emulated, are often called the Stones.

Black Eyed Peas

This Californian hip hop trio started in 1988 as Atban Klann and renamed Black Eyed Peas in 1995.

Peas co-founder William Adams (better known as will.i.am) got in an ethnic reference when he chose a food name, partly because he wanted something similar to ⇨the Red Hot Chili Peppers, whom he admired. Adams has explained in interviews that black eyed peas are "food for the soul".

Black Flag

Named after the U.S. insect-killer aerosol. This Californian hardcore punk band formed in 1976 under the name Panic. They found another band of that name and went for Black Flag. The band had a neo-anarchist outlook and a black flag was also the symbol of piracy, anarchy and danger/quarantine areas. More importantly, they liked its nihilistic sound: the bug spray "destroys all pests". When ⇨Adam Ant played in the U.S., they gave out badges that said "Black Flag Kills Ants."

Above all, the name reminded them of ⇨Black Sabbath, a band they liked – something that might surprise some of their even more hardcore followers, said guitarist Greg Ginn. Spin-off: ⇨The Circle Jerks.

[14] "Black Flag Kills Ants". So watch out Adam Ant, said a Californian punk band.

Blackfoot

Blackfoot was a U.S. band and Blackfoot Sue a British act, named after American Indian tribes Blackfoot and Sioux.

Black 47

This 1990s U.S. band chose to commemorate Ireland in 1847, the height of the Irish Famine. Some of their ancestors had emigrated from Ireland with a profound bitterness for the English.

The Blackhearts

Named by Joan Jett of ⇨The Runaways. She was a part-time graffiti artist with a predilection for little hearts which became her calling card on walls across America.

Black Moses

Nickname for Isaac Hayes in his mid period, after his biblical robes and mumbled philosophical introductions to songs. James Brown fans hit back by calling their idol ⇨The Real Black Moses.

Black Mountain

This band from Vancouver, Canada, includes members who worked with charities for people with drug and financial problems. Leader Stephen McBean avoids answers to questions about reports that the name is a reference to a pile of hashish, while noting that he has a sideline act Pink Mountaintops for more experimental work.

Black Oak Arkansas

This southern band retreated to Arkansas in 1971. All members lived around vocalist ⇨Jim Dandy's home Black Oak.

Black Rebel Motorcycle Club

The San Francisco band took its name in 1998, from Marlon Brando's 1953 movie *The Wild One*. Brando plays Johnny Strabler, who leads a motorcycle gang called "Black Rebels Motorcycle Club". The film is famous for the exchange: "What are you rebelling against?" "What have you got?"

Violence breaks out when a rival gang, The Beetles, ride into town. (Its leader is played by Lee Marvin). The film is cited as one of the reasons for the name ⇨The Beatles, so it's good to have someone claiming the other site. The Beatles' early leather-jacketed image also led to ⇨The Ramones.

Often abbreviated as BRMC.

[15] Marlon Brando in 1953's *The Wild One* kickstarted Black Rebel Motorcycle Club.

[16] Black Sabbath the band mixed metal, Wheatley, Karloff and black magic.

Black Sabbath

Started in 1967 in Birmingham, U.K., by ⇨Ozzy Osbourne, whose first band went through hippy-inspired names Polka Tulk, Mythology, Whole Earth and Earth. There was another band called Earth, better known and playing soft rock; audiences might turn up expecting that style – and get blown away by Ozzy and his mates at full volume.

A change was in order, and they took the title of one of their early songs to become Black Sabbath, frequently abbreviated "Black Sab". The song came from bass player Geezer (Tony) Butler's interest in black magic, as discussed in a non-fiction book *The Devil And All His Works* by author Dennis Wheatley. There was also a 1963 film of the same name, featuring three horror stories by Anton Chekhov, Leo Tolstoy and Howard Snyder – all introduced by Boris Karloff.

The same interest and image was also followed by many other heavy metal stars, not least Jimmy Page of ⇨Led Zeppelin. Spin-off: ⇨Dio. Partly inspired: ⇨Black Flag, ⇨Masters Of Reality.

Black Snake Moan

There have been at least three professional bands of this name. All named after a track by Blind Lemon Jefferson.

The first, a British 1960s outfit, briefly had Robert Plant as vocalist. He went on into the similar-sounding ⇨The Crawling King Snakes, also paying tribute to his fondness for U.S. blues, and then became famous with ⇨Led Zeppelin. Plant returned to the blues theme years later with ⇨The Honeydrippers. A 1970s U.S. jazz act and an industrial rock band of the 2000s also used the name, long before the Samuel Jackson film with this title.

Black Uhuru

They formed in Jamaica as Uhuru, Swahili for "liberty". Their reggae songs had a strong black political element.

Blind Faith

There are two accounts of the origin. The band contained Steve Winwood, ex ⇨Traffic; Ric Grech, ex ⇨Family; and ⇨Eric Clapton/ Ginger Baker, ex supergroup ⇨Cream.

"My ambition . . . was to recreate ⇨The Band in England, an idea I knew was a huge gamble, which is probably why I named the band Blind Faith," Clapton said in 2007.

Still, in 1994 photographer Bob Seidemann said the name came from the title of his famous photograph which graced the LP.

Seidemann had moved to England and was living in Chelsea after lodging with Clapton. In a 1999 advert to advertise his artwork, the photographer added that in 1967 an assistant of Robert Stigwood, Clapton's manager, called him to ask if he "would make a cover for the new unnamed group." Clapton didn't want to be the cover star. Seidemann wanted a spaceship to symbolise "human creativity" and "the ideal bearer, a young girl, a girl as young as Shakespeare's Juliet." She had to be naked.

He spotted a likely subject for his planned shot on an underground train – 12 year old Sula Goschen, dressed in school uniform. He gave her a card and her parents, Mayfair residents of Bohemian sympathies, gave their consent to the scheme, although it was finally Sula's sister Mariora who posed. Mariora was told by her family she would get "a young horse" as payment but instead got £40 from Stigwood, Clapton's management organisation.

Seidemann had previously kept secret details of the story and his model's identity. Mariora, aged 50, said in a 2007 interview that at the time of the shoot she was

[17] The *Blind Faith* look: the controversial cover that summed up Clapton's band name.

unaware she had any breasts. At least the money "paid for some hay and the travelling expenses".

The final image became one of the most enduring and controversial images of its time. The record company initially refused it until Clapton insisted.

The artist was told she had a trustingly naïve "blind faith" expression, which was exactly what he wanted to create. "It was created out of hope and a wish for a new beginning. Innocence propelled by BLIND FAITH . . . I called the image 'Blind Faith' and Clapton made that the name of the band."

Clapton's version differs. "I immediately loved it [the image] because I thought it captured the definition of the name of our band really well – the juxtaposition of innocence and experience."

It also perfectly fitted Clapton's desire for anonymity after all the "Clapton is God" histrionics but self-doubt led to them self-destructing after just one LP.

Clapton further hid from this acclaim as ⇨Derek And The Dominos.

blink-182

The U.S. punk perpetrators started off just as "blink". The name was chosen for its vague sound – as they said, "just the sound of the word brings a smile to your face." They then ran into claims of copyright infringement, apparently by a techno band from Ireland and added the 182.

The author asked the group about the significance of the number: there have been reports it's a reference to the number of times humans blink. Their reply, alas, is unprintable, suffice to say it could be the number of times band members have indulged in sexual self-satisfaction – "or it could just be that we think the numbers go together well." Go figure. In a subsequent TV interview, founder Tom DeLonge confirmed the numbers were chosen at random. The most common report had been that it was the number of "fucks" uttered by Al Pacino in the movie *Scarface*.

The Blockheads

This London outfit, known for their backing of ⇨Ian Dury, named after a comment at rehearsals about the problems of learning tunes: "Y'er'll block'eads!!" Formed from ⇨Kilburn And The High Roads.

Bloc Party

This English band simply puns on "block party". Bassist Gordon Moakes said it had "a twist that made it sound like something to do with the Eastern Bloc rather than New York. That ambiguity suited us so we stuck with it." While it was both about the merging of eastern blocs and western parties, it wasn't a political choice.

Blodwyn Pig

Spin-off from ⇨Jethro Tull, a name also with an agricultural origin, after a champion breeding hog, depicted on the cover of their debut. They later became Blodwyn, Welsh for 'white flower'. Cf ⇨Henry Cow, ⇨(p. 144) Pearls Before Swine.

Blonde On Blonde

A tribute to ⇨Bob Dylan's 1966 double album of the same name.

Blondie

Naturally-brunette singer Debbie Harry started as a member of folk-rock band ⇨Wind In The Willows. The bottled-blonde look came in a three-girl-singer band The Stilettos, all with fair hair. Harry's ⇨Marilyn Monroe style caused her to be addressed as "blondie".

"Yeah, it was a good choice," she said in an interview. "It was a great visual image and proved that blondes can have more fun."

Harry later used her full name Deborah. Terrible punning album title: *Once More Into The Bleach*.

Blood, Sweat And Tears

This New York band formed in 1968 and used an old phrase for human emotions after toiling in a dark, sweaty rehearsal room on their first songs. Al Kooper said he cut his finger but felt nothing, and certainly didn't cry: the name just jumped out at him when he saw the red puddle on the floor as the lights came up after the session.

The phrase is best known from the 1940 quote by British Premier Winston Churchill: "I have nothing to offer but blood, toil, tears and sweat". Cf ⇨Beginning Of The End.

The Blow Monkeys

Taken from a less-than-complimentary Australian term for aboriginal didgeridoo musicians, heard by singer ⇨(p. 100) Dr Robert during time spent in the country.

Blue

This popular name for a group has been used many times, with the best-known being a 2001-2005 U.K. boy band and another being BLUE, a short-lived 1998 "supergroup" meaning Bruford Levin Upper Extremities (including drummer Bill Bruford and bassist Tony Levin, ex-⇨Yes and ⇨King Crimson).

Blue Angel

This New-York quintet including Cyndi Lauper liked the 1930 Marlene Dietrich film.

The Bluebells

Formed by Glaswegian Robert Hodgens 1979, who renamed himself Bobby Bluebell. The Bluebell Girls of Paris started legal action over the name. The Scotsmen won. The court ruled Scottish bluebells were well known – and there was no way the acts could be confused.

Blue Cheer

A blue cheer is a rude wolf-whistle – and a strain of the hallucinatory drug LSD. This West Coast band, formed in the long-off hippy hazy Boston daze of 1967, was, not surprisingly, named after the drug.

The Blue Flames

A name used by countless outfits, including those led by Junior Parker, Jimmy James – AKA ⇨Jimi Hendrix – and Georgie Fame. Parker's band named after their blues repertoire; Hendrix named his band after Parker's.

Blue Jays

The name has been used several times by successful recording groups. The longer-lasting was formed in Venice, California, in 1958, regrouping in 1989. In the interim a duo appeared with plenty of Blue Jays on their record sleeves – that's Jays from their first names, Justin (Hayward) and John (Lodge); blue in reference to their 'main' band, ⇨The Moody Blues.

The Blue Nile

Not from Africa or even Egypt but Scotland, this acclaimed group, producers of the *Walk Across The Rooftops* and *Hats* albums, were looking through an atlas when they found the Blue Nile river and liked the picturesque name.

Blue Öyster Cult

This Long Island heavy metal band initially tried for size the radically-different names of The Stalk Forrest Group, Oaxoa, The Cows and Soft White Underbelly, mostly suggested by leading light Sandy Pearlman.

Underbelly got well reviewed in U.S. magazine *Crawdaddy* but Clive Davis, president of CBS records, rejected their demo tape. They re-recorded it and decided to resubmit it to him under a new name.

Pearlman had moved from rock journalist to manager and was casting around for ideas while outside a New York seafood restaurant selling Blue Point Variety oysters. He went on to write a song called *Blue Oyster Cult*. The name applied to the band "just because it sounded cool" and the umlaut was put over the O to add mystery.

Pearlman denied suggestions that Blue Öyster Cult, or B.O.C. for short, came about from the link between PEARLman and OYSTER.

The tape under the new name was accepted by Davis at CBS and the musicians took a year to tell him the full story.

B.O.C. inspired other heavy metal bands to garnish their names with cod-Germanic symbols for no reason. Those who succumbed to this umlaut/diereses diarrhoea include: ⇨Mötley Crüe, ⇨Motörhead, ⇨Queensrÿche and Rëktum (⇨Gaye Bykers On Acid spoof).

The Blue Ridge Rangers

Not so much a band, more a smokescreen by former ⇨Creedence Clearwater Revival's John Fogerty to hide his identity and avoid the limelight. He disguised his 1973 solo album as one apparently made by a new band, with this appropriately-rural name. He returned to the style of its silhouette cover for the 2007 solo CD *Revival*.

Blue Rondo A La Turk

This short-lived 1980s U.K. band came complete with a ready-made ⇨Kid Creole-style image with wide-lapel tropical jackets. They wanted to provide the soundtrack for something like an updated *Casablanca* or . . . well, an appropriately swinging tune by Dave Brubeck Quintet, a jazz standard – which they took as their name. Spin-off: ⇨Matt Bianco.

Bluesbreakers

At one stage John Mayall's Bluesbreakers. Mayall, inspired by Alexis Korner's Blues Incorporated, formed The Blues Syndicate first and wanted to break up old blues with new, jazzy ideas. ⇨Cream, ⇨Eric Clapton, ⇨Mark-Almond.

Blues Traveler

The Princeton blues band, formed 1987, named from Gozer the Traveler, demon in the *Ghostbuster* movie.

The Blue Turtles

⇨Sting had a dream one night about a number of cyan turtles digging up his garden. He found the bizarre vision interesting. It led to his 1985 LP *The Dream Of The Blue Turtles* and calling his jazz-tinged band of the time The Blue Turtles.

Blue Whale

⇨Fleetwood Mac founder Mick Fleetwood in blues mode in the 1990s. The hobby-band backed environmental concerns set out in Heathcote Williams's book of the time, *Whale Nation*. It was also the name of Fleetwood's studio.

James Blunt

The British singer-songwriter (1974-) slightly revised his real name James Hillier Blount. He has become part of the Cockney rhyming slang lexicon ("a right James Blunt" etc) and told *Q* magazine in January 2008 that the same rhyming insult had been used on him between the ages of five and seven, and it only came up again as he became a musician, "which says a lot about the music industry and the media world, doesn't it?"

Blur

Britain's pop hopefuls started out under the fairly bland name ⇨Seymour, named in part from one of singer Damon Albarn's characters. One of their concerts was reviewed under the misspelled name "Feymour" in *Music Week*.

Seymour sent a tape to Andy Ross, the former *Sounds* journalist who was head of Food Records, an off-shoot of EMI. Ross and his partner Dave Balfe, ex- ⇨Teardrop Explodes, signed them for a £3,000 advance on condition they change their name. Bassist Alex James, in his 2007 autobiography, says both the record company and the group came up with a list of ten suggestions. "Blur was on both lists, so we changed our name to Blur." It was already known that the proposed lists of alternative names considered in a West End pizza restaurant also included The Shining Path, Sub, Sensitise and Whirlpool.

Blur was chosen for its multi-meanings which could refer to the effect of alcohol, drugs or the passage of time; it could relate to vision, memory or psychedelia.

Albarn has gone under the anagramic pseudonym Dan Abnormal, and wrote a song of the same name. He said it was given to him by his former girlfriend Justine Frischmann from ⇨Elastica: "I thought it was brilliant. It represents a lot of my less savoury habits." He appears as Abnormal on Elastica's 1995 album.

BOB

BOB – note capital letters – formed in London in 1986. In one interview, they had implied that they named after ⇨Bob Dylan. Worried about being pigeonholed like ⇨The Dylans, they back-pedalled, saying they didn't own one Dylan record between them and BOB was meaningless. Songwriter Simon Armstrong said: "When you think about it, the whole concept of picking a name for a band is ridiculous."

The Bodines

Like ⇨The Boo Radleys, another band to name affectionately after an idiot. In this case, from Jethro Bodine in *The Beverly Hillbillies*, a U.S. sitcom about a family of Ozark farmers who strike oil on their ranch and are baffled by the money that results. The series inspired ⇨The Muswell Hillbillies and ⇨The Notting Hillbillies.

Marc Bolan

Born London, U.K., 1947 as Mark Feld, he flirted with the stagename Toby Tyler (title character of a 1881 boy's novel by James Otis) and Mark Riggs (after actor Riggs O'Hara) before forming ⇨T Rex. Bolan came from ⇨ BOb dyLAN.

Bolan's record company ⇨DECCA briefly credited him as Bowland as a result of a mishearing.

His son was called Rolan(d) Bolan – cf ⇨David Bowie's Zowie Bowie. Nickname: Electric Warrior (from a 1971 album).

Bomb Everything

These U.S. hipsters started shakin' the house under the blunt name Bomb Disneyland, reasoning there was no better way of establishing anarchist credentials. A slight switch avoided the wrath of Disney, though the new name was criticised during the first Gulf War. Cf ⇨Massive Attack.

Beki Bondage

It seemed an ideal name for a punk when bondage gear was fashionable. The lead singer of ⇨Vice Squad was born Rebecca Louise Bond.

Gary 'U.S.' Bonds

Florida-born Gary Anderson was renamed U.S. Bonds in 1960 as part of a promotional 'con'; producer Frank Guida sent out the *New Orleans* single in a plain sleeve which ripped off the slogan "Buy U.S. Bonds". He hoped announcers would think it a federal announcement and play it. An angry Anderson only learnt of this later but accepted it as the record charted. Bond authority protests led to the record company calling him Gary 'U.S.' Bonds, with U.S. meaning Ulysses Samuel.

Boney M

This West Indian band wanted to be "M" because three of the members had names starting with this letter. Producer Frank Farian wanted to call them Boney, after a TV show popular in Europe in 1976. They compromised with Boney M.

Bonham

Jason Bonham, son of ⇨the late "Bonzo" Bonham of ⇨Led Zeppelin fame.

Bon Jovi

The singer, a former studio tea boy from New Jersey, was born John Francis Bongiovi Jnr. His name is Italian, his ancestors Sicilian.

Bonnie 'Prince' Billy

This Kentucky-born singer-songwriter was a Will from the start (Will Oldham) and renamed in 1998. He said: "Bonnie Prince Charlie has such a beautiful ring to it, and I was conscious of appropriating that mellifluous sound. I was also thinking about the name ⇨Nat King Cole."

Bono

The hearing aid shop was called BONAVOX. It was spelled out in big red letters. Close to the Gresham Hotel in O'Connell Street. Young Dubliner Paul David Hewson (born May 10 1960) often passed it with his teenage friends.

They were intrigued and amused by the shop. Paul was nicknamed "Bono Vox of O'Connell Street" by his friend Gavin Friday. Paul sang loudly, as if for the deaf. Soon he was called Bono.

The shop's now at 9 Earl Street, around the corner, and has a different frontage, more tasteful than the tatty 1960s plastic. Its gold letters are highly suitable for tourist cameras.

At first Bono hated it: most of his friends used nicknames to make fun of the others.

[18] Bono named from Bonavox. The hearing-aid shop and superstar have both moved on since 1976.

But he went along with it when he heard "Bono Vox" meant something like "good voice", which is fine for a singer, and "Bono" meant just "good" (which is apt for a man seen by some as saint, if by others a pretentious do-gooder).

Later, he told the fledging band to call him Bono. At first, and to their credit he says, they said "Sure, Paul" and carried on. Gradually, after 1976, he became Bono and like ⇨The Edge, everyone now calls him that including his wife, family and close friends. The name was in place before ⇨U2 was chosen as the group's moniker.

Notes: Pronounce "Bah-/no/Bon-oh/ Bonno" as opposed to "Bown-oh/ Boh-no". For the 1995 Passengers project Bono became Pi Hoo Sunn, misspelling his birthname. Other nicknames and *alter egos* include Alton Dalton, The Mother Teresa of Abandoned Songs, The Sonic Leprechaun, The Fly, Mirrorball Man, and Mister MacPhisto. ⇨The Edge, ⇨Feedback, ⇨The Hype.

He was given an honorary British knighthood in 2006 (which technically makes him Mr Paul Hewson KBE rather than Sir Paul or Sir Bono).

Unflattering derivatives: Bozo, Bonio (after the bone-shape dog biscuit).

Compare Bono ("Good") to Simon Le Bon ("Simon The Good") of ⇨Duran Duran, Bono Vox with ⇨Ultravox.

Sonny Bono
Anglicisation of Salvatore Bono. ⇨Cher. Pronunciation guide: Say "Boh-no" not "Bonno".

Bonzo
⇨Led Zeppelin's drummer (1948-1980) had a nickname that referenced (1) his surname, (2) his goofy friendliness like Bonzo, the old English cartoon daffy dog. Cf ⇨The Bonzo Dog Doo-Dah Band. Related: ⇨Bonham.

Bonzo Dog Doo-Dah Band
Captain Bruce S. Ingram, editor of the British newspaper *The Sketch*, created a lovable puppy dog called Bonzo. He was drawn by British artist George E. Studdy in the 1920s.

In the 1960s, a group of London art students wanted a whimsical band name with a 1920s variety flavour and adopted The Bonzo Dog Dada Band, namechecking the Dada art movement of the twenties. (Cf ⇨Dada).

The name got mispronounced so much that the group bowed to popular opinion and became Doo-Dah not Dada. All with a little help from their friend, ⇨Paul McCartney. Inspired: ⇨Death Cab For Cutie.

Bonzo Goes To Washington
U.S. President Ronald Reagan had the nickname "Bonzo", relating to his mental ability – or lack of it – and recalling his 1951 film *Bedtime For Bonzo*. This 1984 band led by ⇨Talking Head Jerry Harrison recorded a protest piece under this name that also recalled ⇨Frankie Goes To Hollywood.

Booker T And The MGs

A shortened version of their full name, Booker T. Jones and the Memphis Group. All were musicians at Stax's Memphis studio. They backed Otis Redding, among others, and also recorded as the Mar-Keys. Jones had an English MG car. However, the car only came after the band was named and successful.

The Boomtown Rats

In 1975 they began rehearsals as Mark Skid and The Y Fronts. (Cf ⇨The Skids.) Leader ⇨Bob Geldof thought the name juvenile and offensive. He explained that he wanted something which was "dark and brooding . . . People have to respond to everything, including the name. It must be exciting."

He rejected Traction (too heavy metal); Darker Days (like a ⇨The Doors out-take) and Nightlife Thugs. This last was liked because it could be shortened to just 'The Thugs', in the same way ⇨The Rolling Stones were often called 'The Stones'.

Then Geldof read folk singer ⇨Woody Guthrie's autobiographical 1943 book *Bound For Glory*.

On page 114, the character Colonel refers to a gang he disapproves of : "yore pack of mangy curs! Boom town rats!" The rats were youths who arrived in Oklahoma after oilfields were found.

The phrase came into the singer's mind in the interval of the first gig. They played the rest after the promoter announced – to everyone's amusement – the sudden name change to The Boomtown Rats.

The Rats then tried many individual names – Max Volume, Max Headroom, the Van Rentl Brothers Hertz and Avis, Cup O'Tea, Ray Di Ator among them. Only two

[19] The Boomtown Rats were fired by Woody Guthrie. His guitar inspired This Machine Kills.

names stuck. Johnnie Moylet became Johnny Fingers: it was obvious for a keyboardist. Bassist Pat Cusack became Pete Briquette. They thought his name was very Irish so made it more so: a pun on Irish fuel cakes made from peat.

Their records include a greatest-hits compilation cunningly/punningly/atrociously entitled *Ratrospective*.

The Boo Radleys

The British alt rock band (1988-1999) took their handle from a mysterious character in *To Kill A Mockingbird*, Harper Lee's 1960 best selling Pulitzer novel about justice – or, rather, the lack of it – in the U.S., Deep South earlier in the Twentieth Century. It was filmed in 1962 with Robert Duvall making his big screen debut as Boo. It was a self-disparaging name which suggested humour rather than pomposity. See entry on ⇨Simple Minds for similar names.

[20] The Boo Radleys named from Robert Duvall's 1962 role, seen here with Mary Badham.

Nothing to do with ⇨Boo Yah T.R.I.B.E.! Lee also inspired ⇨Harper Lee.

After a run of poor sales, they acquired the unflattering derivative: The Do Badlys.

"Boots"

Nickname for Nancy Sinatra, ⇨Frank Sinatra's daughter, from the bossy, assertive persona on her hit, *These Boots Are Made For Walkin'*. Inspired: ⇨Prefab Sprout.

The Boo-Yaa T.R.I.B.E.

Veterans of Los Angeles ghetto gang wars, they decided to turn their energy to creative force and rapped it up by calling themselves The Boo Yaa Gang/Tribe/Family. Boo Yaa is slang for the sound of a shot, especially from an uzi.

⇨A Tribe Called Quest.

The Boss

Nickname for concert supremo ⇨Bruce Springsteen, acquired at the time of his four-hour shows.

David Bowie

Born David Robert Jones, London, 1947, he cut early records as Davie Jones with The Buzz and The King Bees. The names were tributes to ⇨Muddy Waters, sometimes called King Bee – after his *Honey Bee* song. Jones was also in ⇨The Mannish Boys, named after another Waters number, and The Lower Third – modestly billed as "south-east Kent's best rhythm-and-blues group".

[21] Iggy meets Ziggy. Or should that be Bowie goes Pop?

The Christian name change from David linked 'Davie' with the old maritime saying about dead sailors going to "Davy Jones's locker". His first manager Ken Pitt suggested a change in 1966 after hearing a singer called Davy Jones who had been found for U.S. TV creation ⇨ *The Monkees*.

Jones chose the name Bowie from the Bowie hunting knife, in turn named after Col. Bowie, its inventor, who died in 1836. It was an American word he simply liked (some Internet sites report the myth he always carried a "beloved" Bowie knife from childhood).

Bowie's early bands include The Hype – a name favoured by the early ⇨U2. His son was Zowie Bowie, though more generally known as Jowie Bowie, or now Duncan Haywood Jones. *Wowie Zowie* was a track on ⇨Frank Zappa's 1966 ⇨Mothers debut *Freak Out*.

One 1971 single was credited to a fictitious group called Arnold Corns. This name, "the unsexiest one I could think of", was in tribute to Bowie's favourite ⇨Pink Floyd track *Arnold Layne* about a transvestite. Publicity shots showed his dress designer Freddi Buretti in new guise as the singer.

Bowie's *alter egos* include Major Tom, the subject of *Space Oddity*, ⇨The Thin White Duke – *Aladdin Sane* – 1973 album punning on "a lad insane", possibly his half-brother Terry Burns – ⇨Ziggy Stardust. Also The Dame and The Alien.

Bowie's backing bands include The Spiders, from the Ziggy Stardust tale, and The Glass Spiders.

Also ⇨Tin Machine. Bowie inspired the names of ⇨Kooks, ⇨Simple Minds, an early appellation of ⇨Joy Division, Warsaw, and ⇨Slaughter And The Dogs.

Pronunciation guide: Bowie (Boe-ee) rhymes with Snowy, it's not bOW-ee to rhyme with Wow-ee.

Bowling For Soup

This Texas-based band blends comedy, pop and punk. The name, from 1994, is "a takeoff of Steve Martin's 'bowling for shit'" routine on his album *A Wild and Crazy Guy*.

A Dictionary of Rock and Pop Names

Bow Wow Wow
⇨Sex Pistols manager and rock entrepreneur ⇨Malcolm McLaren took it from the dog, Nipper, one of EMI's trade marks. (⇨HMV). ⇨Sex Gang Children was also considered. Related: ⇨Adam And The Ants, ⇨Lieutenant Lush.

Boxcar Willie
Like so many other boys, Lecil Travis Martin wanted to be an engine driver: his father was a part-time railway hand and he became fascinated by trains at an early age. After learning guitar, he wrote a song called *Boxcar Willie* – tramps would climb onto freight trains for free rides across country. AKA Boxie.

Boy George
Londoner George Alan O'Dowd had given "G.O.D." as his initials for years. The "Boy" was partly to indicate what sex the gender-bender night-clubber really was: cf ⇨(Boy) Marilyn. "I also liked the idea of playing with sexual ambiguity."

He was later sometimes billed simply as "George". ⇨Culture Club, ⇨Sex Gang Children, ⇨Lieutenant Lush.

Unflattering derivative: Boy Gorge. This was bestowed on the Boy by his friends in his St. John's Wood days – the author was a neighbour: George would go out for a walk, dodging the fans, and return home with bags of cakes, crisps and chocolate.

Boyzone
A pop teen sensation of the 1990s designed to appeal to all girls whose fantasy was a zone filled with boys. The name came from the British comic *Boy's Own*. Related: ⇨B*Witched.

Boyz II Men
The Philadelphia R&B group named from a song by ⇨New Edition, who they loved. They formed in 1988. Since then they have literally grown up in public. Cf ⇨Soul II Soul.

Bread
Oklahoma, pop band, formed 1969. David Gates and his friends were trying to think of a name when they got stuck in a traffic jam caused by a bread van. They realised the name was staring them in the face: bread meant not just the most basic food but money. Punning LP title: *Manna*.

Breaking Benjamin
This American rock band got its name in 1998 when leader Ben Burnley was singing a ⇨Nirvana song during a karaoke night at a Pennsylvania club. He dropped the microphone and broke it.

Breeders
From gay slang for heterosexuals. Guitarist Kim Deal was alluding to a woman's reproductive powers. Cf ⇨Belly. Related: ⇨Throwing Muses, ⇨Pixies.

Brides Of Funkenstein

Funk star ⇨George Clinton came up with dozens of persona down the years but one of his favourites was Dr Funkenstein, punning on Frankenstein. The name was inspired by the 1935 film *The Bride Of Frankenstein*, a sequel to the best-known Boris Karloff movie.

Brilliant

Spinoff from ⇨Killing Joke, whose bassist Youth, born Martin Glover Youth, teamed up with ex- ⇨Hitmen vocalist Ben Watkins. "We not just CALLED Brilliant: We ARE," Youth told the author. Modesty!

Brilliant Corners

U.K. band named after *Brilliant Corners*, a 1957 jazz album by pianist ⇨Thelonious Monk and tenor saxophonist Sonny Rollins.

Bromley Contingent

An informal grouping, named from their home area of London: ⇨Steve Severin, ⇨Sid Vicious, ⇨Siouxsie And the Banshees, ⇨Adam And The Ants, ⇨Billy Idol.

Bronski Beat

U.K. pop group founded in London 1984. The original line-up included Steve Bronski (Steve Forrest), whose adopted surname christened this unit. Related: ⇨Communards.

Brooce

⇨Bruce Springsteen knew that he had arrived amid the upper strata of stars as his name became abbreviated to just "Bruce". This led to the nickname "Brooooce" – add as many "ooos" as you feel fit – yelled by girls at his gigs.

Elkie Brooks

She was born in Manchester, U.K., as Elaine Bookbinder. Elkie is the Yiddish name for Elaine and she abbreviated Bookbinder. In 1988 she reasserted her own name with *Bookbinder's Kid*. Nickname: Elk.

Tina Brooks

. . . was a man called Harold. The sax player became 'Teeny' Brooks because of his youthful appearance and this became Tina after someone misheard the nickname one day.

Bros

London's Matt and Luke Goss considered the joint name Gloss. This could be confusing given their real names and they played up their brotherly relationship as Bros. Fans were called Brosettes.

Brown Dirt Cowboy

Nickname for ⇨Elton John's lyricist, Bernie Taupin. From his fascination with westerns, as displayed in albums such as *Captain Fantastic And The Brown Dirt Cowboy.*

Georgia Brown

English singer Lillian Knot (1933-1992) named from *Sweet Georgia Brown*, a 1925 Maceo Pinkard song she covered.

James Brown

He made up for the ordinary name with an extraordinary career crowned by plenty of nicknames.

They include: ⇨Black Caesar; ⇨Butane; Mr Dynamite; The Forefather of Hip-Hop; Funky President (after his 1971 meeting with President Nixon); ⇨The Godfather of Soul; The Hardest-Working Man In Showbusiness (from his 400-shows-a-year schedule); The King Of Soul (also applied to Otis Redding); The Minister Of The New Super Heavy Funk; The Original Disco Man; ⇨The Real Black Moses and Soul Brother Number One. He was originally Mr Star Time, after his spot in every show as captured on *Live At The Apollo Volumes One and Two* (1963 and 1968.).

[22] Ladies and Gentlemen, Mr Star Time Himself, The Hardest-Working Man in Showbiz, James Brown!

BT Express

Like ⇨Guns N' Roses, a combination name from previous groups they had worked in: Madison Express and Brooklyn Brothers Trucking. The American disco-funk specialists came together in 1974.

Buckinghams

From Chicago, Illinois, they named themselves after the city's famous fountain, after an agony of indecision. Their manager wanted a British name at the time of the British beat boom. (Cf ⇨Beau Brummels etc.) Fans from Chicago saw it as local reference, others thought it English.

Lord Buckley

Another star with an assumed aristocratic name (cf ⇨Lord Sutch etc), the comedian claimed to have won his 'title' in a card game with a blue-blooded opponent. Inspired: ⇨The Nazz.

A Dictionary of Rock and Pop Names

Bucks Fizz
This Eurovision-winning band named from Buck's Fizz, a cocktail of champagne or sparkling wine mixed with orange juice, first created by a barman at Buck's Club, London. It was less commonly used in the U.S.

Buckwheat Zydeco
Band best known for their support to ⇨Eric Clapton. They were formed by Stanley 'Buckwheat' Dural. Buckwheat is the Creole name for French haricot beans, commemorated in traditional songs. Zydeco is a type of U.S. cajun and blues music.

Budgie
Welsh 1970s rockers with terrible punning LP titles: *Squawk, Impeckable*. Chosen as a budgerigar riposte to ⇨The Byrds and other avian names. No relation to drummer Budgie, of ⇨Siouxsie Of The Bansheess.

Buffalo Springfield
They formed in 1966 and were originally to be called ⇨The Herd – this punning rubric was soon appropriated by a U.K. vocal band. Instead, in January 1967, they named after an old steam-traction roller seen by percussionist Dewey Martin in Los Angeles. He said: "You hear Buffalo Springfield, and think, what does it mean, man?"

B. Bumble And The Stingers
The pun came from "singers". Fitted in with their *Flight of The Bumble Bee* theme, from Nikolai Rimsky-Korsakov.

Burning Spear
The name came from writings by Kenyan Jomo Kenyatta. A reggae band who wore their hearts on their sleeves, they established their black power credentials with *Marcus Garvey*. Cf ⇨Spear Of Destiny, ⇨Spearhead.

Bush
Named from their native Shepherd's Bush in London. This band made it big in the U.S. while still unknown at home. In America, the band's followers took Bush as another short mid-1990s name (cf ⇨Blur) – some might have thought of the Bush political family, though fewer knew what Shepherd's Bush was like. "It must be a pretty groovy place," said one.

Busta Rhymes
Rapper Trevor Tahiem Smith, Jnr. was performing under his own name when he was seen by Chuck D of ⇨Public Enemy, who suggested Busta Rhymes in tribute to former NFL wide receiver George "Buster" Rhymes.

Butane
One of many nicknames for ⇨James Brown, this one from his Famous Flames backing band and dates from 1957.

Butterfield 8

Taken from *Butterfield Eight*, a 1960 film starring Elizabeth Taylor. They were movie soundtrack buffs and liked the flick's advertising slogan: "The most desirable women in town – and the easiest to find!" Related: ⇨Madness.

Butthole Surfers

Usually seen as being pretty rude: the band know it sounds offensive, but maintain it isn't. Asked to explain further, they referred me back to the song *Butthole Surfer* on their first EP. A butthole surfer is apparently a follower of trendy Texas bands, if you can make sense of the lyric, although plenty of people think it a reference to gay sex.

Despite the denials, the name has been censored in some U.S. newspapers, who have self-righteously taken it upon themselves to rename the act ⇨The B.H. Surfers, the BHs, The Surfers etc. (The last recalls early ⇨Beach Boys.)

The Buzzards

These zany punksters took the name from their native Leyton Buzzard, East London.

Buzzcocks

Life was never the same for northern English students Howard Trafford and Peter McNeish after a visit to London in February 1976. They had new names and a moniker for their band, which had been playing ⇨Stooges covers up to then. On arrival, the duo seized listings magazine *Time Out*. Under music, they just found a review of TV show *Rock Follies* headlined "It's The Buzz, Cock!"

This was after news about ⇨The Sex Pistols, who also played a ⇨Stooges song, *No Fun*. The two saw Pistols perform and were blown away. Trafford said they decided to "go back to Manchester and go like them . . . but up North". The initial Pistols inspiration not only influenced their music but their obviously phallic name. Their apt first single was *Orgasm Addict*.

Within hours, McNeish became ⇨Pete Shelley and Trafford was ⇨Howard Devoto.

B*Witched

That this is as bad a pun as ⇨Boyzone is not surprising – given that this all-female group included the twin sisters of a member of the boy band and they shared the same producer. The official story is that they "bewitched" their manager into taking them on in 1998. Believe that yarn or not, the asterisk seemed neat, though it has caused problems with Internet searches. The name also recalls *Bewitched*, the Elizabeth Montgomery sitcom first broadcast in 1964. Not that this would mean much to members of B*Witched, because they weren't born at the time.

The Byrds

In the late 1940s and 1950s – after Sonny Til and The Orioles' *Cryin' In The Chapel* – it was almost *de rigueur* for black vocal bands to name themselves after birds: The Bluebirds, The Flamingos, The Quailtones.

Similar names later became popular among rock bands: for example, The Hawks, precursors of ⇨The Band, ⇨Wings, ⇨The Eagles, ⇨The Nightingales, ⇨The

A Dictionary of Rock and Pop Names

[23] The Byrds up a tree. Acting out their group name, if not their ages.

Housemartins and Rare Bird – to name just a few. The Byrds avoided a possible clash with the U.K.'s ⇨Yardbirds, saying they were unlikely to be confused.

Some of the other "bird" bands were paying homage to the jazzman known simply as ⇨"Bird", Charlie Parker.

James Joseph McGuinn III, the main brains behind this particular ensemble, came to the job after Brill Building work – he co-wrote a song for ⇨The City Surfers. Looking for a catchy name, he latched on to his aeronautics hobby to come up with The Jet Set, while Jac Holzman of Elektra suggested matching the 'British invasion' with The Beefeaters, taken from a gin bottle depicting the Tower of London guards.

The final name came about when the band met for a Thanksgiving Day meal at the home of joint manager Ed Tickner. Gene Clark said the turkey dinner reminded him of Dino Valente song, *Birdsies*, which he really liked.

McGuinn said it met his plan of a name suggesting soaring flight, though "birds" was British slang for girls, which could cause some confusion! This led to the idea of a misspelling such as ⇨The Beatles' pun on beetles. McGuinn's comments on flight led them to aviator Admiral Byrd. The clincher was that it had "the all-important Magic B" of The Beatles and ⇨The Beach Boys, Tickner recalls.

Drummer Michael Clarke was born Michael Dick. He renamed after broadcaster Dick Clark, adding the final "e" to distinguish himself from Gene Clark. (Cf ⇨Fish and ⇨Paul Revere, also born as Dicks!)

⇨Roger McGuinn, ⇨Gram Parsons, ⇨The Flying Burrito Brothers.

Influenced ⇨The Mynah Birds, ⇨Sweethearts Of The Rodeo and ⇨Budgie, although possibly not ⇨The Blackbyrds and ⇨The Long Ryders. Terrible punning LP: *Preflyte*. More name disputes: ⇨Birds, ⇨The Ded Byrds.

C

Cabaret Voltaire

French philosopher and writer Voltaire's name was taken by a 1916 Zurich literary club, focus of the Dada "art/anti-art" movement, later by two bands. One experimental act swiftly renamed ⇨(p. 144) Henry Cow. The better-known Cabaret Voltaire formed in Manchester in the 1970s.

Marti Caine

This English singer (1945-1995) was desperate for a change to her birthname Lynda Crapper. She said in an interview that she opened a gardening book at random on the entry "tomato cane".

J.J. Cale

Disregard stories that he was born John Cale and added a non-existent "J". He was born Jean Jacques Cale in Oklahoma and shortened it, French-style, to produce something like ⇨B.B. King. (Cf ⇨ZZ Top). He kept it as his fame was overtaken by ⇨The Velvet Underground's John Cale.

Randy California

Los Angeles-born Randy Craig Wolfe, renamed by manager Chas Chandler of ⇨The Animals.

The Camden Caner

One of many unflattering nicknames for award-winning singer ⇨Amy Winehouse, this one based on her hard-drinking in north London pubs.

Camille

⇨Prince had a "dark side" which showed itself on *The Black Album* as Spooky Electric. The "good side" was Camille on *Lovesexy*. A Minneapolis magazine said his 1986 *Parade*'s lyrics were as overwrought as the death scene from *Camille*.

Camper Van Beethoven

Californian act surreally named by member Robert McDaniel. Like ⇨Moby Grape, the punchline to a joke: "Who can drive all night, bed six women and write a symphony?"

Can

The German group started in 1968 as The Can, becoming Can in 1970. They noted that the word was short and multi-meaning in English: as in an enabling verb and to do with metal containers, headphones and recording. Cf ⇨Canned Heat. In other languages it has meanings such as "life" (Turkish) or "sixth sense" (Japanese).

They were always an "anarchist community," said keyboardist Irmin Schmidt. Drummer Jaki Liebezeit suggested "Can" should mean "communism, anarchism, nihilism" only later though. Inspired ⇨Ege Bam Yasi.

El Canario
"The Canary" – nickname for José Alberto, referring to his voice.

Candlebox
Taken from a phrase in a song by ⇨Midnight Oil.

Canned Heat
Borrowed from the title of Tommy Johnson's song *Canned Heat Blues*, recorded many times in the 1920s and 1930s, about Sterno, a chemical used in U.S. depression and prohibition as a cheap way of getting "canned". The name could also mean recorded passion, home heating and a Vietnam War-era bullet-holder.

The Johnson single was owned by Bob 'The Bear' Hite (named from his size) who founded Canned Heat in California in 1966. His co-founder was Al 'Blind Owl' Wilson (from his nocturnal studio visits and thick glasses).

Freddy 'Boom Boom' Cannon
Freddy/Freddie Karmin/Karmon (various spellings) thought this name change would make his career go with a bang. It led to LPs such as *The Explosive Freddy Cannon*. Cf ⇨Cannonball Adderley.

Capp-Pierce Juggernaut
An article by Leonard Feather on a U.S. jazz band formed by Frank Capp and Nat Pierce was headed: "A Juggernaut on Basie Street". Feather thought the big band would be impossible to stop once it had momentum.

The Captain And Tennille
Los Angeles keyboardist Daryl Dragon worked with Toni Tennille as "Dragon and Tennille". They toured with ⇨The Beach Boys, and Mike Love gave Dragon the name "Captain Keyboard" from his frequently-worn naval officer's cap.

Captain Fantastic
Nickname for ⇨Elton John. Cf ⇨The Brown Dirt Cowboy.

Captain Sensible
This was a fully-fledged stagename not nickname, so there's more under (p. 244) ⇨Sensible.

Captain Trips
The late ⇨Jerry Garcia, purveyor of all things far out, got this nickname because ⇨The Grateful Dead's music was called "the soundtrack to an acid trip".

A Dictionary of Rock and Pop Names

The Caravelles
This British 1960s female duo liked the then-familiar name of a French airliner. ⇨Lois Lane.

Carcass
The band's members are vegetarians. They cut *Feast On Dismembered Carnage* and *Exhume To Consume*.

Caretaker Race
Taken from science fiction series *Star Trek*. Also a "green" comment on humans as caretakers of the environment for future generations. Cf ⇨T'Pau.

Carlton And His Shoes
Donald Carlton was backed by The SHADES in the 1960s. They renamed after a misprint on their debut record. He wasn't the first star called a "shoegazer" – although early audiences cast curious eyes over his footwear and were disappointed to see nothing unusual.

Carmel
Like ⇨Sade, the name of a band as well as a singer. Her birthname: Carmel McCourt.

Hoagy Carmichael
From his full name Hoagland Howard Carmichael.

Diahann Carroll
U.S. singer Carol Diann Johnson auditioned for TV show Arthur Godfrey's *Talent Scouts* with her friend Elissa Oppenheim, to be told they could not be introduced as "Oppenheim and Johnson". Her friend called her late that night to say she wanted to be Lisa Collins and Johnson would be Diahann Carroll (so spelled). Carroll was half-asleep and mumbled "fine".

The Cars
This Midwest U.S. band's final New Wave name was suggested by David Robinson of The Modern Lovers, because it suggested music that could move you. Similar abbreviations applied to founders Ric Ocasek (Otcasek) and Ben Orr (Benjamin Orzechowski).

Carter USM
This London band's full name: Carter The Unstoppable Sex Machine. Leslie 'Fruitbat' Carter and Jimbob (James Morrison) named in 1988 from a newspaper cutting – about someone else – given to Fruitbat as a joke. Related: ⇨Jamie Wednesday.

Johnny Cash
The singer was born J.R. Cash, in line with the now- rare U.S. habit of giving initial-only names. He only became Johnny when he joined the army.

Cast

⇨The La's closed their 1990 album with *Looking Glass* and its words "everything must pass, the change is cast". Lee Mavers' song was thought apt by soon to be bassist John Power, because the band was splitting. It recalled ⇨George Harrison's *All Things Must Pass*. The change was Cast.

The Cat In The Hat

Nickname for ⇨Jamiroquoi, after his woolly hat. It recalled Dr Seuss's books in *The Cat In The Hat* series.

CCS

British outfit formed by Alexis Korner, who also helped name ⇨Free. Stands for "Collective Consciousness Society".

Cee-Lo

This rapper/vocalist Cee-Lo Green, from Atlanta, was born in 1974 as Thomas DeCarlo Callaway. He adapts the name as Cee-Lo, Cee-Lo Green, Eldorado Lo, HenniCee-Lo and Dracu-Lo.

Related: ⇨Goodie Mob, ⇨(p. 134) Gnarls Barkley.

The Celibate Rifles

Australian rockers named in tribute to ⇨The Sex Pistols.

Chagall Guevara

This Tennessee rock band formed in 1989. They wanted to make revolutionary art and tried attention-grabbing by linking Cuba's revolutionary Che Guevara with painter Marc Chagall.

Champs

Los Angeles record boss Gene Autry named them (an intended compliment) after his pet Champion, "The World's Wonder Horse", who became a film star.

Gene 'Duke Of Earl' Chandler

Chicago singer, born Eugene Dixon, 1937. He wanted a more stagey name so abbreviated Eugene and borrowed the surname from actor Jeff Chandler.

Chantays

Californian band of the 1960s, named by founder Bob Spickard from the French verb chanter (to sing), although they found fame with instrumentals. Cf ⇨The Chantels.

Chantels

Members of this all-girl Bronx group supported the basketball team at their school, St. Anthony Of Padua, which in 1957 played St. Francis de Chantelle college. The rival team's name was their cue. Cf ⇨The Chantays.

The Charging Tyrannosaurus Of Despair

The name, meant as a serious comment on mankind, is a hilarious hippy choice. Later changed to Detroit Edison White Light Company because the drummer refused to be associated with despair.

Charlatans

A name used by bands from the U.K. (from 1989) and U.S. (from 1964). The better-known U.K. outfit felt its definition suited them: "empty pretenders to knowledge or skill they don't possess" as they were still learning music. The ghost of the other group came back to haunt them: they had to rename Charlatans U.K.

Ray Charles

Georgia teenager Ray Charles Robinson, who lost his sight in childhood, was called R.C. Robinson on his debut. He wanted to use his full name, but the following year American boxer Walker Smith billed himself Sugar Ray Robinson. The singer-keyboardist settled on just his first two names. Ironically, fighter Sugar Ray Charles Leonard was named after the singer.

Cheap Trick

After one critic commented that cheap tricks attract big audiences. This Illinois band also played as ⇨The Grim Reaper.

Cherry Ghost

This British indie rock band formed in 2005. The name comes from ⇨Wilco's song *Theologians* on the 2004 album *A Ghost Is Born*. The words go: "A ghost is born/ I'm an ocean/I'm all emotion/I'm a cherry ghost."

Chubby Checker

1958: Young Ernest Evans, an aspiring Philadelphia singer, was said to bear more than a passing similarity to the young ⇨Fats Domino. The wife of TV host Dick Clark suggested the name because Evans "checked with", or resembled, Domino. His first record was promoted as "an imitation of Fats Domino". Related: ⇨The Dreamlovers.

Chelsea

In the U.S., Chelsea means part of New York and the Chelsea Hotel of ⇨Joni Mitchell fame. These British punksters named after their London base, the original Chelsea. ⇨Billy Idol.

The Chemical Brothers

British dance-rave duo Ed Simons and Tom Rowlands had originally formed a disco company.

Simons said: "We thought of London Dust Explosion, then decided it had to have 'brothers' in it."

Hence the Dust Brothers, after the Dust production team in the U.S.

Things changed as the British disc jockeys moved into recording in 1995. The American Dusts saw the choice as a rip-off, not a tribute, and a legal dust-up was threatened before a U.S. tour.

The new name raised drug concerns. Simons said in an interview: "It's just because chemistry bonds things." It came from a 1993 song of his, *Chemical Beat*. His grandmother suggested they renamed The Grit Brothers, an idea they considered and rejected.

Cher

Half American Indian, half Armenian, California-born Cherilyn Sarkesian La Pier sang as Cherilyn before meeting and marrying Salvatore Phillip Bono, known as ⇨(Sonny) Bono.

Their act's name (briefly Caesar and Cleo) became Sonny and Cher – an abbreviation which was both French for "dear" and a reference to her Cherokee origins. Her 1973 album was called *Half Breed*. (Rita Coolidge is also half Cherokee; cf ⇨Redbone).

Name notes: Child, with Sonny Bono: Chastity Bono. Pronunciation guide: Share not Sheer or Chur. Nicknames: The Great American Navel (her outfits have often gone for the bellybutton-on-show approach); ⇨Queen Of Flash.

Cherokees

While ⇨Cher is Cherokee and dozens of U.S. bands tried to sound British after the success of ⇨The Beatles, this Worcestershire group tried to go the other way. They thought it would be exotic.

Neneh Cherry

Neneh Mariann Karlsson is the stepdaughter of late jazz trumpeter Don Cherry.

Chicago

Chicago businessman Jim Guercio chose a new name for his jazz-rock signing The Missing Links (who started as ⇨Big Thing). All but one of the band came from the Windy City and Guercio liked the corporate anonymity of Chicago Transit Authority. The first LP was released in 1969 titled *Chicago Transit Authority* – and the CTA complained. There have been dozens of similar cases, many missing the point that (for example) it's not easy to confuse a band with a bus company. They became Chicago.

Chicken Shack

From the song *Chicken Shack*, recorded by Alex Korner's All-Stars among others. Like Korner, they championed obscure U.S. blues; Christine Perfect went on into ⇨Fleetwood Mac, then doing much the same. Cf ⇨CCS, ⇨Free.

Chi-Lites

They formed as the Chanteurs (cf ⇨The Chantays etc) in Chicago, 1960. They rapidly renamed The Hi-Lites, after a local club. Then another band claimed the name. Their then-leader Marshall Thompson suggested The Chi-Lites, which was just about different enough to stop legal action. The "C" was meant to show they came from Chicago.

A Dictionary of Rock and Pop Names

Chilli Willi And The Red Hot Peppers

Not to be confused with ⇨The Red Hot Chili Peppers, this 1970s U.K. pub rock band named by a friend as a joke. They couldn't think of anything better in time for their first gig.

China Crisis

Gary Daly, one of this U.K. duo, had said they named from a 1982 newspaper headline about Asian politics. Later his musical partner Eddie Lundon said it was really his revenge after years of jibes at his 'Chinese' appearance.

Chinnichap

Abbreviation for songwriters (Nicky) Chinn and (Mike) Chapman.

Chocolate Watch Band

U.S. band formed 1965 with appropriately psychedelic-surreal name (cf ⇨Strawberry Alarm Clock). They started with a band pun, adding chocolate for a Dali-esque tag like The Soft Watches.

The Christians

The Christians are a family of 11 from Liverpool, U.K., and three (Garry, Russell and Roger) decided to form this vocal band. They considered naming the Gems before going with their surnames "because it's honest". They had to endlessly explain they weren't as religious as it might imply.

Chumbawamba

This British band refuse to play the game of explaining names and usually say it's a nonsense word. That hasn't stopped them coming up with a few ideas down the years. Among a few suggested explanations:

- a contraction of "Chimp Eats Banana";
- the mascot of a soccer team;
- the chanting of African street musicians;
- the word produced by a chimp left alone with a typewriter;
- a dream of men's and women's toilets, labelled CHUMBA and WAMBA.

La Cicciolina

The Italian star was born Ilona Staller. Her name means "the dumpling", an Italian lovey-dovey expression.

Ciccone Youth

New York musician Thurston Moore watched ⇨Madonna's career after he formed ⇨Sonic Youth in 1981. The 1986 track *Madonna, Sean And Me* showed his fascination wasn't totally admiring though. Ciccone Youth took "youth" from Moore's other band, "Ciccone" from ⇨Madonna's original surname. Moore commented: "She's good. I was saying it's got a bit out of hand though."

Circle Jerks

Circle Jerk is defined by Robert Chapman's *New Dictionary of American Slang*: "(Especially teenagers) a sex party of mutual masturbation. Any futile occasion." Outside the U.S., the name was meaningless and naïve reporters were referred to the dictionary.

The name ran into as many protests as ⇨The Butthole Surfers. The C.J.s, as they were then known, were a spinoff from ⇨Black Flag and called their first album *Group Sex* (1980). Cf ⇨Limp Bizkit.

The City Surfers

Named to match their ⇨Beach Boys spoof song, *Beach Ball*. The piece, the rainy East Coast answer to the sun, sea, sand and sex of West Coast surfing sounds, was co-written by Jim McGuinn, later of ⇨The Byrds.

Clannad

Folk band, at one time containing ⇨Enya, consisting of the sons and daughter of an Irish band leader. The name comes from Gaelic "clan a Dobhair": family from Dore, or Gweedore, County Donegal.

Eric Clapton

Eric Patrick Clapton grew up with his grandmother, Rose, and her second husband Jack Clapp, believing that they were his parents and that his mother was his older half-sister.

His grandmother was married twice, first to a Clapton and then to a Clapp (the similarity is quite coincidental). Her first marriage produced two children, the second of whom is Clapton's mother, Pat Clapton. She had him aged 16 after an affair with a man thought to be Edward Fryer, a (married) visiting airman from Canada. Fryer's name was omitted from Eric's birth certificate, leaving him with just Clapton. Eric only discovered that Pat was his true mother when he was nine. Much later a journalist confirmed that Fryer had died. (There's been confusion as to whether the star was ever Eric Clapp.)

Clapton's bands include The Roosters (after the blues number *Red Rooster*), ⇨The Yardbirds (more rooster influence), ⇨Bluesbreakers, ⇨Cream, ⇨Blind Faith, and ⇨Derek And The Dominos. Nicknames: ⇨God, ⇨Slowhand.

Clap Your Hands Say Yeah

This New York indie rock group formed in 2005. Bassist Tyler Sergent said they named after Brooklyn graffiti – a story backed up by *The Gothamist*, which carried a picture of a 30-foot slogan on Baltic Street. (Singer Alec Ounsworth has much more off-the-wall – pun intended – explanations, all of which seem unlikely, such as it's something to do with a medical procedure called trepanation.)

The name is often abbreviated to CYHSY. Cf ⇨the Yeah Yeah Yeahs (similar name, New York band).

The Clash

They formed in 1976 from singer/guitarist ⇨Joe Strummer's outfit ⇨The 101'ers and ⇨London SS. The latter had just split, with some joining Strummer and others going into ⇨The Damned. Management hopeful Bernard Rhodes had been trying to get London SS to change their name anyway because it offended his mother, a European refugee.

Strummer told writer Jon Savage: "For about a week we were the Psychotic Negatives, then The Weak Heartdrops, after a Big Youth lyric, then Paul [Simonon] thought of the name The Clash." (Big Youth inspired ⇨Sonic Youth.)

Simonon, on the liner notes to *The Clash On Broadway*, recalls that the discarded possibilities included The Mirrors, while author Marcus Gray adds they rejected The Phones and The Outsiders.

Simonon told MTV in 1991: "It came to my head when I started reading newspapers and a word that kept reoccurring was the word 'clash', so I thought 'the Clash, what about that,' to the others."

It's often incorrectly reported on the Web that it's "thought" (thought by whom?) that the name came from a specific *Evening Standard* headline about "A Clash With Police."

The Internet bloggers suggest too that "it's largely believed" (again, by who?) that the Clash took it from a track by Jamaican band Culture called *Two Sevens Clash*. It's true the Clash liked reggae. Still, the Culture album was only released in 1977 (its release date being 7.7.77, hence the name) – more than a year after the Clash was christened.

Strummer liked the word because it was short. As they became a leading group, they realised the name meant Clash not just as in a mild shock-horror headline. They were fed up with the bloated state of music and U.K. politics, as expressed in the 1980 factional film *Rude Boy*, countless songs and the name ⇨Tory Crimes.

Related: ⇨Real Westway, ⇨Big Audio Dynamite. Inspired ⇨Four Horsemen.

The Clean

This New Zealand 1980s band made ironic reference to their "dirty" live sound. ⇨The Great Unwashed.

Clem Snide

This American alt-country band formed in 1991. Singer-songwriter Eef Barzelay was a fan of "beat" literature and liked the name Clem Snide, a character in ⇨*The Naked Lunch* and other books by William Burroughs.

Jimmy Cliff

Born James Chambers in Jamaica. Bad album title: *Cliff Hanger*.

Climax Blues Band

From their love of Chicago Blues; they considered Chicago Blues Band as a name. The band said: "We should have stayed with the Chicago Blues thing, even if it produced problems with ⇨Chicago. People think our name's kinda rude. It's not what we meant."

Climie Fisher

From their names, Simon Climie and Rob Fisher. Fisher also worked with ⇨Tears For Fears.

Patsy Cline

This Virginian country star was born Virginia Patterson Hensley. She was known as Patti or Patsy from her second name then married Gerald Cline. Nickname: ⇨Country's Leading Cowgirl. Cf: ⇨The Queen Of Country. ⇨The Reclines.

George Clinton

The leader of ⇨The Brides Of Funkenstein, ⇨Funkadelic and ⇨Parliament(s). Fanciful nicknames include: Dr Funkenstein, Interstellar Cosmic Funkfather, Minister of All Funkadelia.

Clouds

A tribute to ⇨Joni Mitchell and her 1969 second album *Clouds*, specifically the track *Both Sides, Now*.

The Coasters

This Californian group's name, and its predecessor, The Surf Boys, reflected their surfing obsession and later influenced ⇨The Beach Boys' name.

Kurt Cobain

⇨Nirvana, ⇨Courtney Love. Pronunciation guide: Co-bane, not C'bane.

Cochise

This band, playing American music, named from Cochise (ca 1812- 1876), who led the Chiricahuas. Cf ⇨Blackfoot.

Joe Cocker

He hails from Sheffield, U.K., but is no relation to Jarvis Cocker of ⇨Pulp. His bands include Mad Dogs, a name also considered by ⇨Led Zeppelin, and The Grease Band. Nickname: Cowboy Joe, derived from his interest in westerns; no relation to ⇨The Brown Dirt Cowboy. Inspired: ⇨Delta Lady.

Cockney Rebel

⇨Steve Harley. ⇨The Sex Pistols, on tour at one point, named themselves Acne Rebel in jokey reference to this band, also punning on Hackney in London.

Cockney Rejects

Londoners who were beaten by ⇨Steve Harley for the name Cockney Rebel. They chose the nearest they could get.

The Cocktail Cowboys

Band formed to back Dave Pegg (⇨Jethro Tull and ⇨Fairport Convention) for the promotional tour of his solo album, *The Cocktail Cowboy Goes It Alone*.

A Dictionary of Rock and Pop Names

The Cocteau Twins

The name came from a line in a song by fellow Scottish musos ⇨Johnny And The Self-Abusers. It's often wrongly stated that the Cocteaus (as they were known) named from France's Jean Cocteau (1891-1963), author of *Les Enfants Terribles*. The vocalist is Elizabeth Fraser; the twins of the book (which inspired ⇨The Rich Kids) are Elizabeth and Paul.

Coldplay

A group of London students, playing under the name Starfish, were led by singer Chris Martin. He lived in the same building as guitarist Tim Rice-Oxley, who had a band called Coldplay, which wasn't having much success. Martin got agreement to use the name as Rice-Oxley's band became ⇨Keane.

Coldplay were, for some time, reticent about the name. Its origin, according to newspapers, was from a book of poems. Fan sites had speculated it's from a ⇨Paul McCartney song or to do with playing "cold" to an audience.

In the face of constant questions from fans (and the author), Coldplay has now put a short note on their official website. It confirms the original Coldplay took it from *Child's Reflections: Cold Play* by American Philip Horky.

Horky's publisher calls it "a stark collection" which "escapes the stylistic and structural conformity to explore the psychological realms". According to fan site coldplaying.com, Rice-Oxley "didn't like the name any more because it was too depressing".

Lloyd Cole And The Commotions

Singer/songwriter Lloyd Cole chose his band's name to match his own, in the manner of 1950s groups, though only early tracks sounded like old rock 'n' roll. ⇨Bloomsday, ⇨The Bob Dylan Band.

Nat King Cole

Nathaniel Coles got his regal name from the rhyme Old King Cole – another of music's "aristocracy", along with scores of "Dukes", "Counts", "Lords" and "Earls". His daughter is also a "Nat": Natalie Cole. Nickname: Mr Velvet Voice.

Collective Soul

The founder of this Georgia rock band Ed Roland lifted "collective soul" from *The Fountainhead* by Ayn Rand in 1992. He said he did not know if he agreed with Rand's views but thought that the name was good for a group.

Colorblind James Experience

Inspired by countless "blind" blues players and ⇨The Jimi Hendrix Experience. Among those being referenced: Blind Lemon Jefferson; 'Blind' Willie McTell and 'Blind' Willie Johnson.

The Comets

Bill Haley might never have been successful if his band had remained The Saddlemen, chosen to fit their cowboy-country music. As Haley drew up plans for what became rock 'n' roll, discoveries were made about his near-namesake Halley's Comet – then at its furthest point from Earth – and this suggested a suitable tag for a group chasing stardom.

Commander Cody And The Lost Planet Airmen

More sci-fi inspiration, recalling the likes of ⇨Captain Beefheart. Cody was George Frayne IV, who named after a 1940s film, *Adventures of Commando Cody, Sky Marshal*; the band after another old movie, *The Lost Planet Airmen*.

The Commitments

Fictional band in Roddy Doyle's first novel, 1988's *The Commitments*. Their manager Jimmy Rabbitte tells them their music (and name) should reflect "sex and politics" and show commitment to their origins. The novel was filmed by Alan Parker in 1991 and the band became real, later renaming The Committed.

The Commodores

When two fledgling groups – The (Mighty) Mystics and The Jays – came together in Tuskegee, Alabama, in 1967, a change of name seemed to be sensible to keep peace among members.

Singer Lionel Richie said in an interview for this book: "We had all kinds of wonderful ideas – 'The Fantastic Soulful Six', 'The Mighty Wonders'. We almost broke up trying to come up with a name.

"We turned to the dictionary and [trumpet player] William King stuck his finger on a page and came up with 'commodore', a naval term describing someone who ranks between captain and admiral. We were lucky because that word was close to 'commode', and we might have ended up as 'The Commodes', wearing suits made out of toilet paper!"

The Communards

Campaigner Jimmy Somerville wanted to sing about social and sexual politics and saluted inhabitants of the Paris Commune in the 1870s. Related: ⇨Bronski Beat. Cf ⇨Consenting Adults.

Perry Como

U.S. singer Pierino Como anglicised his name.

Company Of Wolves

U.K. writer Angela Carter (1940-92) included this novella in her 1979 collection *The Bloody Chamber*. Based on *Little Red Riding Hood*, it became a horror movie five years later and a heavy metal band's name.

Comsat Angels

This post-punk band from Sheffield (1978-1995) named from short story *The Comsat Angels* by J. G. Ballard.

A Dictionary of Rock and Pop Names

Comus
This 1970s progressive rock band named after a 1630s play by John Milton. Cf ⇨Eyeless In Gaza.

Concrete Blonde
⇨R.E.M.'s Michael Stipe gave this to DreamSix because he wasn't convinced by their old name: "Sounds like *Number Nine Dream*. (⇨John Lennon song.) Concrete Blonde is much better." The band, bemused, thought he was right and didn't press for an explanation.

Confederacy Of Dunces
This British band named after Jonathan Swift's line about when a genius appears, "the duncess are all in confederacy against him." It was also the title of *A Confederacy of Dunces*, John Kennedy Toole's posthumous 1980 novel.

Consenting Adults
A 1970s Midlands, U.K., band, named from a phrase in legislation legalising homosexual relations between "consenting adults" of over 21. (⇨Bronski Beat's 1984 first album was later named after the same laws, *The Age of Consent*, and it was also considered by ⇨The Communards.)

Sam Cooke
He began as a gospel star, working with the Soul Stirrers, but when he also tried to enter the pop market he was credited as Dale Cook in a bid not to alienate his specialist audience. The similar name and his distinctive voice soon gave the game away and he reverted. Nickname: Mr Soul. He inspired ⇨The Kane Gang and ⇨The Pretenders.

Coolio
American rapper Artis Leon Ivey Jnr. got the name as a joke reference to Spanish singer Julio Iglesias because of his "Joe Cool" clothes.

Alice Cooper
The band went through suitably-disgusting names such as The Earwigs, The Spiders and Nazz. The last, suggested by drummer Neal Smith, had to be changed because of Todd Rundgren's ⇨The Nazz.

"Alice Cooper" related at first to the band, but after 1975 to the singer, born Vincent Damon Furnier in Detroit. In an interview, he said the name was meant to fit their "Alice in Wonderland" act. He came up with it "on the spur of the moment" and could have as easily said "Carrie Carter," "Suzie Smalls" or "Billy-Jo Melons". The act featured axes, snakes and electric chairs with Alice dressed as a ghoul with "blood" dripping off his face.

These shock tactics, combined with loud feedback guitars and screams, caused entire audiences to walk out of concerts: some expected to see a quiet ⇨Joni Mitchell style act, not an over-the-top hard rock combo. The confusion impressed ⇨Frank Zappa, who signed them to his record label.

The appellation also has the same ring of innocence as axe killer suspect Lizzy Borden, although it's subtler than ⇨(p. 196) Molly Hatchet.

Alice offered bizarre explanations, all of which he has now admitted to be false. He had once suggested the idea was that "people are male and female biologically". He now says he hates ⇨New York Dolls drag and sexual politics. He had also claimed an Ouija board session showed him the incarnation of a 17th-century witch – now admitted to be a publicity stunt.

⇨The Billion Dollar Babies. Cf ⇨Alice In Chains.

Cornershop

This name was chosen as a comment on how British Asians are racially stereotyped as corner-store owners, and how they are being forced out of business as out-of-town supermarkets take over.

Cortinas

Readers other than in the U.K., or younger readers, may need to be told this British punk act wasn't named after an Italian resort. The word was in common usage in the 1970s thanks to the Ford Cortina family car.

Corvettes

Following ⇨The Cortinas, we have another car name. This time from the U.S., after the speedy and sexy Corvette Stingray. The car's name recalled a fish and a warship.

Cosmo

No relation to the magazine *Cosmopolitan*. Rather ⇨Creedence Clearwater Revival's Doug Clifford, for whom everything was "cosmic". Hence the LP *Cosmo's Factory*.

Elvis Costello

The singer-songwriter was born Declan Patrick MacManus in London, son of Joe Loss singer/bandleader Ross MacManus (usually written McManus).

The name's seen by some as a cheeky attempt to combine ⇨Elvis Presley and 1950s American funnymen Abbott And Costello, by virtue of his own early appearance – not that of the typical rock star.

In fact Costello came from his mother's maiden name: he used it when his parents separated and moved with her to Liverpool. He played early gigs as D.P. Costello. The name Costello was also used by his father who charted in some countries in 1970 with a version of

[24] Elvis Costello was worried about pinching Presley's crown, but he got used to it.

A Dictionary of Rock and Pop Names

⇨The Beatles' song *The Long And Winding Road*. Ross said: "MacManus wasn't a very good name for a rock star."

Jake Riviera became Declan's manager and signed him to the independent Stiff Records, on the condition he became Elvis. Costello said the idea initially struck him as insane. His first success coincided with Presley's death, which led to the shock value nearly backfiring. Costello was later seen as a worthy successor to ⇨The King. His 1986 album, *The King Of America*, featured his own name, McManus, which also cropped up on film soundtracks.

He used the pseudonym The Imposter for 1983-84 political protest songs *Pills And Soap* and *Peace In Our Time*. Costello fans know this pseudonym was appropriated from a track he recorded in 1980.

Costello also hid his identity, electing to be credited as Eamonn Singer, for the artwork of the 1986 LP *Blood And Chocolate*. He had once produced a painting, entitled *Napoleon Dynamite*. The album's vocals, apparently referring to the painting or the track *Poor Napoleon*, credit one Napoleon Dynamite – again, Costello in disguise.

He may have inspired ⇨The Tragically Hip. Related: ⇨The Attractions. Cf ⇨Reg Presley.

The Cotton Club
Several acts, most famously ⇨The Crickets, considered this name, from a Harlem nightclub, later immortalised in a 1984 film.

Counting Crows
Post-grunge Californian rockers. The band's singer-songwriter Adam Duritz said the name was inspired by a scene in the film *Signs Of Life*, starring his ex-girlfriend Mary Louise Parker. In the sequence two men stand contemplating their lives as crows fly by. Duritz told the author the scene inspired *A Murder Of One*, the closing song on their debut album, *August And Everything After* (1993).

Country's Leading Cowgirl
Billing name for ⇨Patsy Cline; only seen, sadly, after her death. Cf ⇨The Queen Of Country.

Jayne County
The singer was born a he and christened Wayne. Jayne was "as close as you can get" to her former self.

The Cowboy Junkies
Members of this Canadian quartet said this misleading moniker doesn't really mean anything: "we were just thinking of a name which would make folks think, what the hell . . . " It sums up their stoned-sounding country songs.

The Cramps
U.S. band revived rockabilly with racy lyrics and shockabilly tactics . . . even to the name, which refers to reactions beyond one's control. In the U.K. it refers to muscle

81

spasms after working out; in the U.S. it's menstrual pains and in parts of mainland Europe, it's a male erection.

Members include Erick Purkhiser, who went under the nom de kitsch Lux Interior, 'Poison' Ivy Rorschach (née Kirsty Wallace) and Slim Chance.

Cranberries

Like ⇨Moby Grape, a name from the punchline of a joke. This Irish band was originally known as The Cranberry Saw Us, a pun on Cranberry Sauce; and liked comic songs. They abbreviated as singer Delores O'Riordan joined.

Crash Test Dummies

They wanted an "unusual collective" name, thankfully rejecting The Bad Chemotherapists and The Skin Grafts.

Crass

Prototype anarchistic band whose name was a reaction against crass ordinary pop pap, party politics and glib punk solutions. Individual names: Steve Ignorant, Joy De Vivre. Album name: *Stations Of The Crass*.

Crawling King Snakes

This band's Robert Plant, later of ⇨Led Zeppelin fame, liked the John Lee Hooker song *Crawling King Snake*. Cf ⇨Blind Snake Moan.

Crazy Horse

Before working with ⇨Neil Young, they were The Rockets. He convinced them the "rock it" pun was old-fashioned. Young suggested the name of an American Indian leader to describe the music, "like a bucking bronco". It wasn't a reference to the Parisian nightclub of this name. With Young, they recorded the 1969 track *Requiem For The Rockets*.

Cream

This 1960s British supergroup was named by ⇨Eric Clapton who says in his 2007 autobiography: "I came up with Cream, for the very simple reason that in all our minds we were . . . the elite in our respective domains." He was joined by bassist Jack Bruce (ex ⇨Manfred Mann, John Mayall's ⇨Bluesbreakers) and drummer Peter 'Ginger' Baker.

It also had orgasmic overtones (cf ⇨10CC, ⇨The Lovin' Spoonful) and related to milk, suggesting titles like *Fresh Cream* and *Cream On Top*.

Related: ⇨Blind Faith, ⇨George Harrison (L'Angelo Misterioso while working with Cream).

Creaming Jesus

This book attempts to be as comprehensive as possible. If this entry offends, well this exactly why this name was chosen by this confrontational U.K. 1990s band. It also guaranteed them minimal publicity, which they said was a sad reflection on free expression.

Creation
London-based musician Alan McGee liked a 1960s band called The Creation so much he named his group Biff Bang Pow! after a Creation song, and then record label, Creation.

Creedence Clearwater Revival
This Californian band began as Tommy Fogerty and The Blue Velvets, then traded as The Visions.

Their manager christened them The Golliwogs in a misguided attempt to make them sound British. The band hated both it and their uniforms but promotional posters had been printed. Fortunately their 1965 debut single didn't chart: in a racially-naïve yet divided America, they didn't realise the fury the name might cause. Among many similar U.S. bands who used supposedly "British" names: ⇨(p. 250) Sir Douglas Quintet and ⇨The Byrds (at one stage called The Beefeaters). The new name grew over a few weeks in 1967:

1. "Creedence" came from an acquaintance, Credence Newball. They thought his name had a ring of truth but amended it slightly so as not to offend him.
2. "Clearwater" was from an advert about the benefits of pure drinking water used in Olympia beer. They liked its refreshing sound with environmental overtones.
3. "Revival". There are a lot of errors commonly promulgated about this last name. Myths have mushroomed round it, partly because John Fogerty was for years evasive when asked to elucidate.

Some reference books say the Fantasy Label boss Saul Zaentz ('Zaentz Can't Dance') urged the band to change their name and revive American roots music. In fact, Fogerty told the author that Zaentz urged neither. The name showed their hope for better times at home after a disastrous few months, being forced into an image and name they "despised". "Both the name and the new records seemed to strike gold."

Related: ⇨The Blue Ridge Rangers, ⇨Cosmo. Inspired: ⇨Green River, ⇨Willie And The Poorboys.

Kid Creole And The Coconuts
U.S. producer Darnell Browder was of Haitian origin hence the "Creole". The "Kid" added echoes of the ⇨Elvis Presley film *King Creole*.

The Kid wanted to get away from his native Bronx and dreamed up the idea of a band with a visual image akin to those in the nightclub scene in 1930's film King Kong – zoot suits, panama hats. His musical collaborator Ray 'Sugar Coated' Hernandez chose the similarly fanciful Coati Mundi.

Crew-Cuts
Canadian 1950s-on singers whose clean-cut name fitted their image, if not the ethics of record bosses who used them to make white close-harmony versions of ethnic black radio hits. They didn't have short-back-and-sides cuts for long: their first album was *The Crew-Cuts Go Longhair*. Cf ⇨The Ivy League.

The Crickets

Members of the band best known for backing ⇨Buddy Holly named in the 1950s after consulting encyclopaedias. Founder Niki Sullivan said he found a page about insects. One earlier group had been named The Spiders. Remarkably, they considered Beetles. "Jerry [Allison, drummer] said, 'Aw, that's just a bug you'd want to step on,' so we immediately dropped that." They chose Crickets as a joke "because they make a happy sound . . . they make music with their legs".

Their 1957 album carried through the insect reference, being titled *The 'Chirping' Crickets*. The band members were not very bothered about its double-meaning – it also could refer to the English sport, never very popular in the U.S.

In fact it was this very double meaning which not many years later helped inspire ⇨The Beatles, great admirers of Holly (though the Britons were unaware he could have had their name first!)

The moniker was needed partly because Holly's could not be used for their first recording: ⇨DECCA had an option on him, although the company showed no sign of picking it up. It was needed only to disguise his presence.

They were initially doubtful about the name, even considering The Cotton Club as an alternative. (Cf ⇨The Cotton Club.) During one of their early tours, staying in Corpus Christi in 1957, Holly and his friends were given a hotel room infested with crickets – which they took as a good omen.

There was another omen during the summer of 1957, while they were recording *I'm Gonna Love You Too*. A cricket got into the echo chamber. On the last version, its chirping came only on the fade-out and at the right tempo. The Crickets kept its sound and this reinforced their commitment to the name.

Both the hotel and studio incidents actually happened, although it's wrong to say – as several books have done – that they inspired the moniker, which had already been around for some time.

Tory Crimes

The original drummer with ⇨The Clash was born Terry Chimes. The "Tory Crimes" farewell credit was given to him by his bandmates on the first album after he left, citing the usual "musical differences".

Crispy Ambulance

The band formed in Manchester, England, in 1978, with a silly, surreal name. The novel moniker was suggested by Graham Massey, later of ⇨808 State. Singer Alan Hempsall: "I thought it was such a nondescript name (silly too) that we decided on it. It gave nothing away, but captured the imagination."

The Cro-Mags

Cro-Magnon means "the grotto of Magnio" and the New York thrash metal band chose it in 1982 because "cave men are hardcore".

Bing Crosby

Harry Lillis Crosby, born in Washington, U.S. was renamed in 1910. The six-year-old Harry Lillis found a feature in the *Spokesman-Review*. It was entitled *The*

A Dictionary of Rock and Pop Names

Bingville Bugle, written by humorist Newton Newkirk, and parodied a hillbilly newsletter. A neighbour, 15-year-old Valentine Hobart, noted Crosby's amusement and named him from one character, "Bingo from Bingville." It's not because of any supposed similarity with big-eared Bingo, as is sometimes suggested. Nickname: The Old Groaner.

Christopher Cross
This U.S. singer/songwriter chose the surname in preference to his own, Geppert, which lacked star appeal. Unrelated: Chris Cross of ⇨Ultravox.

Crowded House
Band founded by ⇨Split Enz founder Neil Finn, after his move from New Zealand to Los Angeles. The name is a reference to the hectic life at his crowded house in Hollywood as he was putting together the band and planning their first album in 1985–86. Related: ⇨The Mullanes.

Crucifucks
The result of a Michigan band that set out in search of "the most offensive name ever." Outcome: success, no success; complete commercial crucifixion. Cf ⇨Creaming Jesus.

Cry Of Love
This rock band's guitarist Audley Freed's ⇨Jimi Hendrix fixation was clear in his playing and the name, taken from a 1971 Hendrix LP.

The Crystals
Shortly after forming, the New York all-girl group met musician Leroy Bates, who suggested the name after his daughter Crystal. Bates co-wrote some of their material including *There's No Other Like My Baby*.

CSS
This Brazilian band's name means "Cansei der Ser Sexy" or "tired of being sexy," from a reported comment by ⇨ Beyoncé.

The Cuban Heels
Crawling from the wreckage of seminal punksters ⇨Johnny And The Self-Abusers, were two bands; the lucky ones became millionaires with ⇨Simple Minds: the unlucky ones had a clever name but no money. They were Cuban Heels. The tall built-up shoes were part of their dress code. The band lasted from 1978 to 1982.

The Cult
Band from Bradford, U.K., which started off as a punk band called Violation.

Singer Ian Astbury, who developed a fascination for American Indian culture and clothes, said Southern Death Cult, the new name, was a Mississippi delta tribe. He has offered several accounts on how he found it: from a book in Bradford library, a sticker off the book or a volume found lying on the road. It could also be seen as an attack on prosperous southern England from the recession-hit north (a line pursued later by ⇨The Beautiful South).

Astbury has been the only constant in the band's development as they reformed, regrouped, moved from punk to heavier metal and abbreviated the name to the Death Cult. This didn't last long – "we realised we might not sell many records called that", he told the author. They became simply The Cult.

The Cult's later music, coincidentally, also recalls the driving rock of ⇨Blue Öyster Cult.

Spinoff: ⇨Four Horsemen. More American Indian influence: ⇨Crazy Horse etc.

Culture Club

The central figures in the British band were 'discovered' in 1979-80 by the U.K. media exploring the New Romantic trend and fashions in nightspots such as Heaven, Blitz and Hell across the "Club Culture" capital. ⇨Boy George switched round this headline to get his group's new name: "We all agreed ⇨Sex Gang Children was the wrong name. We toyed with new names, Caravan Club, Can't Wait Club. Jon said: 'Look at us: An Irish transvestite, a Jew, a black man, an Anglo-Saxon.' That's how I came up with the name Culture Club. Night-clubbing, roots and culture."

Related: ⇨The Damned, ⇨Marilyn, ⇨Visage.

The Cure

The British indie band was founded in 1976 by Robert Smith in Crawley. The new group named Easy Cure, after a song by first drummer Lol Tulhurst, who thought love a cure for all ills. Singer Robert Smith thought this bland: he wanted the group to be a more definite article, THE Cure for problems.

Spinoff: ⇨The Glove. Playing small venues, they have adopted ⇨R.E.M.-style "coded" names such as Five Imaginary Boys, referencing their song *Three Imaginary Boys*. Tribute band: The Lovecats.

Curiosity Killed The Cat

Ensemble formed in London in 1983. Singer Ben "The Cat" Volpeliere-Pierrot's surname came from his celebrity photographer father and model mother. His nickname, he claimed, was because he was "a cat . . . a cool dude". Later the band abbreviated to Curiosity. It was killed as their nine commercial lives ran out and people lost curiosity . . .

Curved Air

U.K. art-rock band formed 1970, named from Terry Riley's 1969 *A Rainbow In Curved Air*. Punning LP title: *Air Conditioning*. Related: ⇨The Police.

Cybernetic Serendipity

Far out 1960s band with suitably far out cosmic (comic?) name. They put out a "manifesto" which said that their music aimed to improve brain communication (cybernetics) and maximise fortune (serendipity).

A Dictionary of Rock and Pop Names

Cypress Hill
This Los Angeles-based band named after part of their suburb of Southgate.

Cyrkle
A Pennsylvania singing group, they started as The Rondells. A rondel or rondeau is a musical or poetical form suggestive of a circle or recurrence. They signed with the same management company as ⇨The Beatles. ⇨John Lennon asked: "What's a Rondell?" They said: "Well.. like a circle." He came up with the misspelling.

Dada
Dada's French for "hobby-horse", a word chosen randomly for a new movement in the early 20th century. It inspired three bands: Dada, dada and ⇨The Bonzo Dog Doo-Dah Band.

Puff Daddy
⇨(p. 97) Diddy.

Daddy Stovepipe
U.S. guitarist Johnny Watson named after his trademark top hat. He married the equally wonderfully-named Mississippi Sarah.

DAF
The German name means "Deutsche Amerikanische Freundschaft" (German-American friendship). Nothing to do with DAF, a carmaker: cf ⇨New FADS.

Daft Punk
The masked French synthesizer wizards were first called Darlin', after a ⇨Beach Boys song they recorded. *Melody Maker* reviewed this single as "a bunch of daft punk". The duo said in a press release this was a compliment (they deliberately mangled the original tune).

The Daintees
Leader Martin Stephenson said this British band's name was "a response to the humourlessness and angst of much music of the time". Not all 1980s critics were impressed. Writing in the Birmingham *Daily News,* I said: "The Daintees make catchy pop. How many people will be turned off by the twee name and won't give them a chance to find out?"

Dalek I

This U.K. group named from somebody with a cold saying "Darling, I love you". It was also a joke about the sinister Daleks from BBC sci-fi TV series *Doctor Who*. Related: ⇨O.M.D. Cf ⇨The Mekons.

Dali's Car

Mick Karn (born Tony Michaelides, ex- ⇨Japan) and Pete Murphy (ex- ⇨Bauhaus) named their band after a track on ⇨(p. 39) Captain Beefheart's 1969 *Trout Mask Replica*.

Damien Thorne

Chicago metal band named from the main character Damien Thorn in *The Omen* films.

The Damned

Might have been called ⇨The Sex Pistols according to some reports, both favoured by impresario Malcolm McLaren. This isn't quite correct: McLaren had considered The Damned as a name for The Pistols however. He planned to name the new boys Masters of the Backside – adding Chrissie Hynde, later of ⇨The Pretenders.

[25] Dave Vanian, Captain Sensible, Rat Scabies and Brian James: in no way damned.

⇨(p. 244) Captain Sensible said McLaren and ⇨Johnny Rotten heard them play with Hynde and weren't impressed. Sensible said: "We were damned really: everything that could go wrong did."

The Damned also matched singer David Vanian's Dracula-meets-⇨Alice Cooper costume. He was born David Letts, was briefly David Zero and had been a cemetery labourer. Guitarist Brian James suggested the name from Luchino Visconti's 1969 *The Damned* starring Dirk Bogarde featuring Vanian-style gore make-up.

Drummer called: Rat Scabies (Christopher Miller). Related: ⇨London SS, ⇨Lords Of The New Church, the Doomed (used during a dispute over name rights).

Damned Yankees

Ted Nugent was asked to describe this band in 1989 and – recalling a 1950s musical – said they sounded like "Damn Yankees". Related: ⇨The Amboy Dukes.

The Dakotas

The Coasters, from Manchester, were one of many U.K. bands trying to be American in the early 1960s. They backed ⇨Billy J. Kramer, who renamed for similar reasons. The moniker, suggested by ⇨John Lennon, is now linked with him after he was killed outside the New York Dakota Building.

A Dictionary of Rock and Pop Names

Dana
Belfast-born Rosemary Brown, a Eurovision winner, was nicknamed as a girl 'Dana,' a Gaelic word for mischievous. It rhymes with "Ghana" not "gainer".

Jim Dandy
The ⇨Black Oak Arkansas singer Jim Mangrum was known as Jim Dandy after one of his favourite records, LaVerne Baker's 1956 hit.

Danger Mouse
U.S. disc jockey Brian Burton (1977-) was too shy to perform under his birthname. He started to wear a mouse outfit as disguise when he did sets. This led him to British comic book character DangerMouse, a small but fearsome secret agent. Later, as a producer and member of ⇨Gnarls Barkley, he wore ever more outlandish costumes along with his collaborator ⇨Cee-Lo, reproducing characters from *A Clockwork Orange*, *Star Wars* and *The Wizard of Oz*.

Danny Wilson
Scottish band named after the 1952 film *Meet Danny Wilson*, starring ⇨Frank Sinatra as a crooner who breaks into the big time with criminal help.

Danzig
These U.S. rockers named from leader Glenn Danzig, formally of ⇨The Misfits. Not a reference to the Polish town now known as Gdansk, birthplace of the Solidarity movement.

Dare
This band named after leader Darren Wharton, ex ⇨Thin Lizzy, but shaved a few letters off at the suggestion of ⇨Lemmy.

Bobby Darin
Walden Robert Cassotto, from The Bronx, chose his stagename after hours, with help from the telephone directory.

Dark Star
The best-known Dark Star, a U.K. rock outfit, named from a sci-fi film. A more recent band liked the ⇨Grateful Dead song *Dark Star*, also used as the title of a Dead fanzine.

The Darling Buds
This Welsh act referenced *The Darling Buds Of May*, a 1958 novel by H.E. Bates, made into a U.K. television series. Their LP *Pop Said* is titled from a quote from the novel, betraying their name's origin as Bates rather than Bate's inspiration, which was Shakespeare's *Sonnet 18*: "Rough winds do shake the darling buds of May".

Dave Dee, Dozy, Beaky, Mick and Tich

Harman was known as "Dee" in school, from his prenomen. This U.K. novelty group started as Dave Dee And The Bostons, confessed on BBC television this was "rubbish" and put together their other childhood nicknames.

Skeeter Davis

Kentucky-born Mary Penick became Skeeter as a girl, from slang for a mosquito: her family said she was always buzzing around. She first performed with Betty Davis, as The Davis Sisters. A 1953 car crash killed Betty and injured Skeeter; she changed her surname in honour of her dead friend.

Lady Day

⇨Billie Holiday became known as "Lady" on the 1930s Harlem circuit for her near-regal bearing. This nickname was used as the credit for 1943's *Trav'lin Light*.

Deacon Blue

Leader Ricky Ross named this Scottish group in 1985 from the ⇨Steely Dan 1977 track *Deacon Blues*: he wanted to emulate its sophisticated music and aspirational lyrics about seeking stardom.

The Dead Boys

There's a chicken-and-egg dispute over these Cleveland punks' name. One U.S. book says the moniker inspired an early lyric *Dead Boys*. Actually, the song came first, called *Down In Flames* and including the line "dead boy, running scared".

Dead Fingers Talk

This 1970s band named after a book anthologising work by William S. Burroughs. Cf ⇨Naked Lunch.

Dead Kennedys

The name referred to the assassinations of President John F. Kennedy (1963) and Senator Robert Kennedy (1968). Leaders Jello Biafra and East Bay Ray's calculated offensiveness included records such as *Too Drunk To Fuck*. Cf ⇨Foetus.

Deadly Hume

Australian band named after notorious accident blackspot, The Hume Highway, running into their native Sydney.

Dead Or Alive

This Liverpool band started in 1980 as Nightmares In Wax, "before we got serious", said frontman Pete Burns. This seriousness was marked by ripping off the old wild west slogan from "reward" posters. Related: ⇨The Mystery Girls.

Deaf School

The members came together in 1974 at Liverpool Art College, partly based in a building which was once a deaf school.

Death
Exponents of thrash rock named from Chuck Schuldiner's phrase "death metal". He said: "The name perfectly describes the music, and it's not a joke."

Death By Milkfloat
They topped ⇨Lawnmower Deth by saying the most ironic way to die was to be run over by a milk wagon.

Death Cab for Cutie
This American indie rock band formed in 1997. They admired the satirical madness of Britain's ⇨Bonzo Dog Doo-Dah Band and named after *Death Cab For Cutie*, on 1967's *Gorilla* album. It's one of the best-known Bonzo tracks since it makes an appearance in ⇨The Beatles' 1967 film *Magical Mystery Tour*.

Death In Vegas
This U.K. band's name is misleading because it refers to the death of ⇨Elvis Presley. Founder Richard Fearless said: "A lot of people think Elvis died in Vegas. He didn't, but that's where he did his sell-out gigs to fat, middle-aged American women and that was the death of him creatively." ⇨The King died in Memphis. Dead Elvis, the act's original name, became their first album title.

Death Ramps
Alex Turner of ⇨The Arctic Monkeys told *The Guardian*: "The Death Ramps is my favourite name for a band. When we were kids, there were loads of hills and woods where you'd go and ride your bike. We called them death ramps. They probably weren't that deadly."

In December 2007, The Arctic Monkeys had a single *Teddy Picker*, with two tracks credited to Death Ramps – the Monkeys in thin disguise.

DeBarge
Like ⇨The Cowsills and The Jacksons (to name but two), they were related – in this case a family of 10.

Chris De Burgh
Christopher Davidson chose his stagename to reflect his Irish roots. It was his mother's maiden name.

DECCA
The U.K. record company took its name from an early gramophone, which played a tune on notes D-E-C-C-A.

The Ded Byrds
This British band tried a ⇨Led Zeppelin misspelling for ⇨The Byrds. Legal arguments from the latter left the project as dead as its name.

A Dictionary of Rock and Pop Names

Kiki Dee
Bradford-born singer Pauline Matthews was given her stagename by songwriter Mitch Murray in the 1960s. Later an ⇨Elton John protégée.

Deep Purple
The story began in the U.K. in 1968 when drummer Chris Curtis of ⇨The Searchers contacted keyboardist Jon Lord (then of ⇨The Flowerpot Men) about forming a band he planned to call Roundabout, because he envisaged a circular stage which musicians would jump on and off.

This idea was deservedly ditched, Ritchie Blackmore (ex ⇨Lord Sutch's Savages) recruited, and they shared a house where a card was pinned up for anonymous name suggestions.

One entry said "Deep Purple", which sounded intriguing. In time it had the same colour references as ⇨Black Sabbath and ⇨Pink Floyd and, later, purple fanatic ⇨Prince. It wasn't – as has been suggested – chosen to contrast with ⇨Vanilla Fudge.

Nobody admitted the choice, until they discovered *Deep Purple* was a light song by ⇨Bing Crosby, made into a hit in 1962 by Nina Tempo and April Stevens. Few fans knew their favourite band was named after a slightly embarrassing song which would be out of place in any rock record collection. Blackmore later said the Hoagy Carmichael version was a favourite of his granny's.

The Purps made some lighter music, such as the ballad *Hush*, though the name became better as they got heavier. Spinoffs: Gillan (from leader Ian Gillan), ⇨Rainbow, ⇨Whitesnake. Inspired: ⇨Stormbringer, ⇨Machine Head.

Def Leppard
The Sheffield, U.K., heavy metal band started as Atomic Mass (1977), renaming on suggestion of singer Joe Elliott. He said many HM fans accept deafness as a hazard; plenty of other bands have named themselves after big cats but rarely leopards. He didn't mean specific homage to ⇨Led Zeppelin but the spelling of "Def" recalled the bigger band. Elliott later found it fitted U.S. street slang: "Def," short for "definite/definitive". Often called Def Lep, like Led Zep.

Del Amitri
This Glasgow, Scotland, act named at an embryonic stage, after "in the womb" in Greek.

De La Soul
This band combined hip-hop with soul to produce a hybrid, DAISY Age Soul, standing for "Da Inner Sound Y'All" and abbreviated to French, "relating to soul".

Delfonics
Producer Stan Watson adapted it from the ⇨Del-Vikings, with whom he'd worked.

Del Fuegos
Del Fuego, the furthest south on the American mainland, sounded to this U.S. outfit "like a hot car or a cool band."

The Del-Rons

In honour of similarly-named groups ⇨the Del-Vikings (sometimes "Dell-Vikings") and The Del-Satins.

Delta Lady

Named from ⇨Joe Cocker's 1970 song *Delta Lady*.

The Del-Vikings

The Vikings was the name of a basketball and social club which founder Clarence Quick supported in Brooklyn. The "del" was fashionable although redundant because it means "the". Cf ⇨The Del-Rons.

John Denver

Singer Henry John Deutschendorf Jnr. thought his favourite city was better than his own surname.

Depeche Mode

This British band from Basildon formed from school acts No Romance In China, The Plan, Norman And The Worms (really), The French Look (close to the same origin as Depeche Mode) and Composition of Sound.

A copy of French trade and general interest fashion magazine *Dépêche Mode* found its way to nearby Southend, where vocalist David Gahan was studying fashion. Band member Martin Gore said: "It means hurried fashion or fashion dispatch. I like the sound of that."

It actually means "Fashion Dispatch" or "Fashion Express". It's often translated incorrectly as "hurry up fashion", "fast fashion" and even "by telegraph". These interpretations are a péché (sin)!

Fans are called Modeheads. Vince Clarke left for ⇨Yazoo and ⇨Erasure. Thank heavens they didn't stick with Norman And The Worms.

[26] *Dépêche Mode:* Full of fashion tips and name ideas for Basildon bands.

Derek And The Dominos

This was British guitar hero ⇨Eric Clapton's attempt to hide under a pseudonym and take a back seat. He had been soured by the hysteria over ⇨Cream and ⇨Blind Faith and teamed up with three ex-members of Delaney And Bonnie's backing band, whom he had met on tour. They were slated to debut as Eric Clapton And Friends at a June 1970 charity concert in aid of Dr. Spock's Civil Liberties Legal Defense Fund at the Lyceum in the Strand, London.

Clapton notes in his 2007 autobiography: "In the excitement of just forming the group, one thing had slipped our minds and that was right up to the last minute . . . we had no name for ourselves."

Backstage, opening act Tony Ashton, who used to call Clapton "Dell", offered to introduce the next band as Del And The Dominos. He felt it had a "fifties feel", like Billy Ward's band The Dominoes or ⇨Fats Domino.

Ashton stumbled when he finally made the announcement, narrowly avoiding saying Eric and coming out with Derek And the Dominos. Eric liked it.

Derringer

U.S. star Rick Zehringer simplified his name before his hit with ⇨The McCoys, *Hang On Sloopy*, who were signed to the Bang label, which had the picture of a small pistol in its logo. Derringer became his band name too.

Destiny's Child

This band started with a talent search in Houston, Texas: the 10-year-old girls selected considered Girl's Tyme, Cliché, Something Fresh, Destiny and The Dolls. Then, founder ⇨Beyoncé Knowles said in an interview: "Whenever I'm confused about something I ask God to reveal the answers to my questions, and he does. That's how we found our name — we opened the Bible, and the word 'destiny' was right there."

Beyoncé's mother Tina Knowles, the group stylist, said it was from the Book of Isaiah. Beyoncé's father Matthew, their manager, added Children (soon abbreviated). The R&B act became one of the biggest-selling female groups of all time.

Destroy All Monsters

The U.S. band, ex-members of ⇨The Stooges and ⇨MC5, saw a 1968 Japanese Godzilla film which is meant to be spine-chilling and is just soppy. The group said: "The title still makes us laugh every time we say it."

The Detroit Wheels

⇨Mitch Ryder's backers, originally The Rivieras. The name reflected their origins in the U.S. auto-making capital.

Devadip

Used by ⇨Carlos Santana during his time following Buddhist teachings. Cf ⇨Roger McGuinn, ⇨The Byrds.

Devo

Devo is short for devolution, the opposite of evolution. The U.S. group was formed as The De-Evolution Band in 1974 as the by-product of a Kent State University documentary video project, *The Truth About De-Evolution*.

It was a prize-winner at the Ann Arbor Film Festival and in 1977 they made another film, *In The Beginning Was The End*, to further advance their view that the world was going backwards biologically; fast information processing will overtake human

[27] Devo: Okay guys, look robotic and don't admit the name means "devolution".

mental power and as we need to use our brains less we will regress back to monkeys or robots.

They extended the concept to a stage show designed to show the de-humanising aspects of high-tech life. They pretended to be automatons in "Devo-robot" costumes and called their first album *Q: Are We Not Men? A: We Are Devo!*

Fans called: Devo-tees.

Howard Devoto

Howard Trafford renamed in 1976. Devoto was the name of a bus driver mentioned in a moral story recounted by one of Trafford's teachers. It mysteriously sounded like "devoted". ⇨The Buzzcocks, ⇨Magazine.

Dexys Midnight Runners

This British group started in 1978. Their name refers to amphetamine dexedrine, taken in pills known as Dexys. These drugs were taken by troops in wars; bored housewives (*Mother's Little Helper* of ⇨Rolling Stones fame); and young soul rebels attending all-night northern soul parties. Their early sound resembled 1960s soul (debut album: *Searching For The Young Soul Rebels*).

In an attempt to play down the drugs reference, leader Kevin Rowland encouraged journalists to shoot them in alarmingly literal interpretations, out jogging in darkened streets.

[28] Kevin Rowland always ensured Dexys Midnight Runners lived up to their name.

A Dictionary of Rock and Pop Names

The Dharma Bums

The Dharma Bums (1965), an account of Zen truths written with poet Gary Snyder, is not as important as *On The Road* (1957), yet liked enough by this band to join those naming after Jack Kerouac. Cf ⇨Elmerhassell, ⇨The Subterraneans.

Neil Diamond

Neil Diamond says he was born Neil Diamond, has never toned down his heritage, and many reports and books are wrong that he was Noah Kaminsky. Still, it's true that many stars ditched Jewish-origin names (cf ⇨Bob Dylan). The name Kaminsky/Kominsky was also thrown away by ⇨Danny Kaye and Melvyn Kaminsky, who became film-maker Mel Brooks.

Bo Diddley

He was born in McComb, Mississippi as Otha Ellis Bates and was put out for adoption. He became Elias B. McDaniel after his adoptive mother, Gussie McDaniel. (Both names are variously spelled: Bo's indifferent to which is correct.)

The derivation of his stagename is the subject of debate. There are about a dozen different accounts. Even Diddley said in an interview with the author: "I'd like to know where it came from, do you know?"

The most likely is that it was from Bo Diddley, a comic character that had been around a while, named from a slang phrase meaning "nothing at all", as in "he ain't bo diddley", "he ain't worth diddley squat".

In a separate interview with *Rolling Stone*, Didley seemed surer: "My name came from grammar school in Chicago. Some kids started calling me that, and it stuck." There's evidence he was known as Bo before he turned to music and certainly while training as a Golden Gloves boxer. Bo said this also came from Southern patois and means "a bad boy" ("bad" in the complimentary sense).

His rebirth as singer and rock 'n' roll legend Bo Diddley came after he was signed to Chess Records in 1955. Harmonica player 'Billy Boy' Arnold recalled how one time, walking along the street, bass player Roosevelt [Jackson] said: "Hey Elias, there go Bo Diddley', speaking of a comical-looking, bow-legged, little short guy. To me it was the funniest word I'd ever heard: I just cracked up!" White notes that the name was used for any comical bow-legged man.

Diddley later found another southern singer had been called the same 20 years before, while Chess found a Diddley had been performing in Chicago around 1935. There was even another – in Shanghai, of all places, around 1929. They might have been named after the comic Diddley figure, and one of Diddley's guitarists suggested he might have stolen it from one of the vaudeville troupes. Still, Diddley himself states he wasn't named after them since he didn't know of them.

Diddley dismissed another theory while talking to the author in 1985: "Only the other week, I read there was a folk instrument in the South, in the old days, called a diddley bow. People played in it the fields." So his name was an inversion of this – but only coincidentally – since he had not heard of it until much later, he insisted.

Inspired: ⇨The Pretty Things. Nicknames: Black Gladiator, Big Bad Bo.

A Dictionary of Rock and Pop Names

Diddy

The more famous Diddy is Sean John Combs, a U.S. music mogul and rapper. He was known as Sean "Puffy" Combs and N. Diddy as he started out. In a 2000 CNN report, industry experts speculated on whether the "puffy" referred to the young Combs's hair or face. Journalist Alan Light said: "I think it's probably not terribly flattering."

Combs recorded as Puff Daddy, then P. Diddy, before in October 2006 announcing he wanted to be called just Diddy because "the P was getting in between us."

This led to a fine legal mess as another artist, Richard "Diddy" Dearlove, took issue with this, claiming the switch was arrogant. This means that the rapper is Diddy in some countries and P. Diddy in others. For the Diddy Web Site, hits from British-registered computers, for example, were automatically rerouted to a special page with the P. Diddy name.

British band ⇨Gay Dad denied naming after Puff Daddy.

Dido

The English singer's (1971-) full birthname is Dido Florian Cloud de Bounevialle O'Malley Armstrong, and she gave it the most radical name-trim since ⇨Eno. Dido, a 1960s throwback, was taken from a Carthaginian queen.

Die Kreuzen

This Milwaukee band heard the German word as "cruisin'," assuming it meant "the crucifixes". It's a verb, for "to cross".

Dillinger

Another Jamaican reggae star named after a U.S. mobster. Lester Bullocks remembered John Dillinger.

Dinosaur Jr.

They named after a children's show, denying any ⇨T Rex homage. The "Junior" was added after complaints by ⇨The Dinosaurs.

The Dinosaurs

An ironic name chosen when these aging West Coast rock stars came together for an ad hoc "supergroup". One newspaper said they were a bunch of dinosaurs. Related: ⇨Big Brother And the Holding Company, ⇨The Grateful Dead, ⇨Country Joe And The Fish, ⇨Jefferson Airplane, ⇨Hot Tuna, ⇨Quicksilver Messenger Service.

Dio

Named after singer Ronnie James Dio. Related: ⇨Black Sabbath, ⇨Rainbow.

Dion And The Belmonts

New York-born Dion DiMucci said the name was an affectionate childhood memory of the Belmont area.

Dippermouth

Big-breath trumpeter Louis Armstrong's mouth was so big he could put a water dipper into his cheeks. ⇨Satchmo.

Dire Straits

Reflects the near-insolvent state of 27-year-old Mark Knopfler in 1977, a part-time teacher and musician playing with pub rockers such as Brewer's Droop. Knopfler, sharing a South London home with two others, toyed with the name Café Racers and scraped together £120 for a demo tape. The Straits name was at first too close for comfort and later ironic (cf ⇨Willie And The Poorboys). Brewer's Droop got a knowing reference in the 1982 song *Industrial Disease*. Related: ⇨The Duolian String Pickers, ⇨The Notting Hillbillies.

Dirty Pretty Things

Carl Barat, who formed this band after Pete Doherty left ⇨The Libertines to form ⇨Babyshambles, named them after the night-time music event he hosted at London clubs. The choice caused problems, both with his club shows, which became Bright Young Things to avoid confusion, and with two other acts who had also been playing as Dirty Pretty Things. Agreements were reached and the others renamed, leaving the name to him.

Disposable Heroes Of (The) Hiphoprisy

Founder Michael Franti said the San Francisco band played "news you can use", disposable like newspapers. The name punned on "dis" (showing disrespect to others), "hip-hop" and commented on the hypocrisy of politics. ⇨Spearhead.

Divine

U.S. drag singer Harris Glenn Milstead (1945-1988) made crossdressing first into a movie career, developing the Divine personality with Baltimore friend and director John Waters in the 1970s, then into a rock phenomenon.

The Divine Comedy

Italian poet of about 1320 inspires rockers of 1990. Singer Neil Hannon was an atheist; his father, a Church of Ireland bishop. Alighieri Dante (1265-1321)'s *Divina Commedia* including *The Inferno* also inspired the very different ⇨Styx. From the divine to the ridiculous.

Divinyls

This Sydney band, known for the 1991 hit *I Touch Myself*, was formed by Mark McEntee and Christina Amphlett, who says they liked the vinyl pun. Within a few years, the advent of CDs made it a dated reference.

PENGUIN CLASSICS

DANTE
Inferno

[29] Dante's *Inferno* suggested names for The Divine Comedy – and Styx.

The Dixie Chicks

This Texan act started in 1989 as a bluegrass-style foursome, naming from ⇨Little Feat's 1972 *Dixie Chicken*.

The Dixie Cups

Little Miss And The Muffets wisely renamed, in reference of their origin, after New Orleans cocktails.

DJM

U.K. record label and publishing company with a name standing for Dick James Music. Cf ⇨Elton John.

D-Mob

These Britons had the briefly *de rigueur* soul "D" (cf ⇨D-Train etc). Countless bands have named after mobs (⇨The Amboy Dukes, ⇨Sigue Sigue Sputnik) while this added a "wicked demobilisation" pun.

DMX

Earl Simmons started out beatboxing for other New York rappers. His vocal skills surpassed many drum machines and earned him the name DMX, after the Oberheim DMX, an early electronic percussion device.

DNA

This name means ⇨(Rick) Derringer 'n' Appice (drummer Carmine Appice), i.e. D and A. The name's been used by two other bands, all referencing the chemical that contains genetic information.

Doctor Feelgood

This U.K. band, formed 1971, recalled 1960s music such as the early ⇨Rolling Stones. They named after the 1961 song and album *Doctor Feel-Good*, by ⇨Piano Red. Inspired: ⇨Roxette.

Doctor Hook (And the Medicine Show)

This U.S. group had to explain Ray Sawyer's patch over one eye, like the character in Peter Pan, after an accident. (Another eyepatch = piratical name ⇨Johnny Kidd.) The quack "doctor" name tied in with an act, inspired by shows selling dodgy potions to gullible cowboys.

Doctor John

New Orleans session player Malcolm John 'Mac' Rebennack helped to organise the AFO record label which included Prince Lala, who adopted black magic trappings akin to ⇨Screamin' Jay Hawkins.

'Mac' became interested in voodoo himself. He became Dr. John Creux The Night Tripper (the latter part often said to be an answer to ⇨The Beatles' *Day Tripper*) with witch doctor clothes and massive head-dresses.

Doctor Robert

⇨Blow Monkeys' singer and solo artiste, Bruce Robert Howard, got the description "The Good Doctor" while at school in Norfolk "because I was a sympathetic listener . . . I got lumbered with everyone else's problems".

Coxsone Dodd

An "aristocrat" in the Jamaican reggae world, Clement Dodd became styled "Sir"; the Coxsone came from the then-popular cricketer. He named ⇨Horace Andy and ⇨The (Wailing) Wailers.

Dodgy

When they were called Three Cheers For Tokyo, these British musicians were told that being in a band was a "dodgy" (i.e. shady, unreliable) career option. They backed it with "The Dodgy Club" in a London bar – and "Dodgy press releases", one said to contain "dodgy" cannabis seeds.

Dojo

U.K. label named after founders, Dougie Dudgeon and John Beecher.

Thomas Dolby

This English musician was born Thomas Morgan Robertson in 1958. Dolby (from Dolby Laboratories, maker of the best-known systems of noise reduction – and a registered trade mark) was a nickname he got at school because he was inseparable from his cassette recorder. Dolby Labs moved to sue him for trade mark infringement in 1987. The star argued that the company could not stop anyone called Dolby from using the name. The company got him to agree to only use "Dolby" with "Thomas" attached.

[30] Thomas Dolby, the man who survived a row with Dolby Laboratories.

Dollar

This British pop band wanted a word in wide circulation. Dollars are indeed used in many countries but the name was a liability in the U.S., and seen as an English eccentricity. Cf the American misunderstanding about ⇨The Fall.

Fats Domino

This New Orleans singer, born Antoine Domino, was in Billy Diamond's Band when their leader gave him the 'Fats' nickname because of his 220 lbs frame. Inspired ⇨Chubby Checker, partly ⇨Derek And The Dominos.

Lonnie Donegan

Glaswegian singer Tony Donegan got his name from New Orleans blues player Lonnie Johnson. He was on the same bill at a London concert (that's for certain) and (not confirmed) he was mistakenly introduced as "Lonnie Donegan". The gig went well and young Donegan decided not to confuse the new fans. Nickname: ⇨The King Of Skiffle.

Donovan

Born in Glasgow, Scotland, Donovan Phillips Leitch always used his prenomen only on stage (although his name was used in full to provide the title of a 1970 album).

The Doobie Brothers

The Californians' name was suggested as a joke by acquaintance and housemate Keith 'Dyno' Rosen. The band weren't brothers and claim they didn't know what "doobie" meant and innocently thought it had something to do with "dooby-doo music" and the like. Caught on the hop a few hours later, they gave it as their name rather than "Pud", their previous choice, which was unlikely to lead to success.

They soon found a "doobie" was slang for a cannabis cigarette. It had already found its way into literature via Armistead Maupin and Richard Merkin. After the truth dawned, the Doobies often said it was a family name to avoid radio bans. Cf ⇨Jefferson Airplane.

The Doors

James Douglas Morrisson (as he then was) stumbled on the name for his future band in conversation with fellow U.C.L.A. student Dennis Jakob.

They were discussing Dionysus (as one does) and remembered a line from William Blake, the 18th century English poet and artist: "If the doors of perception were

[31] The Doors reflect on a name laced with Huxley and Blake, Dionysus and drugs.

cleansed, man could see things as they truly are, infinite" (*The Marriage Of Heaven And Hell: A Memorable Fancy*, 1790.)

They knew the quote had been borrowed by British writer Aldous Huxley in 1954 for his *The Doors Of Perception*. This was his long essay about experiments with the drugs mescalin and lysergic acid diethylamide (LSD). This book was studied closely by Jim, who was soon conducting "experiments" himself. (Cf Huxley references ⇨Eyeless In Gaza, ⇨the Feelies.)

Jim and Dennis were planning an imaginary rock duo based on their reading and contemplated the name The Doors: Open and Closed. Dennis was no longer involved by the time The Doors came together from LA bands Rick and the Ravens and the Psychedelic Rangers.

⇨Jim Morrison, ⇨Mr Mojo Riser, ⇨The Lizard King. Tribute band: The Australian Doors.

Lee Dorsey
U.S. singer Irving Lee Dorsey also had a short boxing career as Kid Chocolate. Nickname: Mr T.N.T.

Judge Dread
An entry which appears under "D" rather than "J" because the Judge wasn't a band but solo Alex Hughes, christened after ⇨(p. 224) Prince Buster's ska song. That's "Dread" as in "dreadlocks": no relation to comic book character Judge Dredd.

Dread Zeppelin
Another Californian spoof on ⇨Led Zeppelin. Extent of joke: "Dread", as in dread-locks; "Zeppelin", as the Led Zep catalogue sampled and translated into reggae form. The Zeps had already tried reggae thanks to the offbeat *D'Yer Mak'er*. Singing star: Tortelvis (Greg Tortill, inspired by tortilla-loving ⇨Elvis Presley in overweight Vegas mode).

Dream Academy
U.K. group named after 1964's The Dream Syndicate, an avant-garde New York project by LaMonte Young and John Cale, later of ⇨The Velvet Underground. Cf ⇨The Dream Syndicate.

The Dreamlovers
⇨Chubby Checker's band formed in 1960 but couldn't become The Checkmates: the name had been snapped up by Emile Ford in 1958. They named after a number one hit of the previous year, ⇨Bobby Darin's *Dream Lover*.

Dream Syndicate
The Dream House was an American 1960s experimental ensemble which became The Dream Syndicate. It inspired ⇨Dream Academy, and this American West Coast rock outfit.

A Dictionary of Rock and Pop Names

Drella
Nickname for artist Andy Warhol, nominal producer of ⇨The Velvet Underground's debut album. This combination of Dracula and Cinderella was revisited by ⇨Lou Reed and John Cale for 1990's *Songs For Drella*.

DRI
This Texas band named after a newspaper column that said all young people who listen to rock are "Dirty Rotten Imbeciles".

The Drifters
Formed around lead singer Clyde McPhatter, ex- The Dominoes. (Unrelated: ⇨Derek And the Dominos, ⇨Fats Domino). Named because the founders had moved through many bands. They moved from McPhatter's blues (1953-1957) to Ben E. King's pop (1958-1979). The name was also used by the early ⇨ Shadows.

The Droogs
Los Angeles 1970s garage band making reference to Anthony Burgess's book *A Clockwork Orange*, like ⇨Heaven 17, ⇨Korova Milkbar *et al*. The book's hero Alex is surrounded by a gang of "droogs". The word translates well as "dudes": the characters are hardly friends.

D-Train
Tom Waits wrote of a *Downtown Train* full of Brooklyn girls trying to break out their world. ⇨Bob Dylan had *Visions of Johanna* which included all-night escapades on the D-trains. Then these New Yorkers named after their local line.

Duffy
This Welsh singer was born Aimee Anne Duffy – in 1984, about the time that ⇨Stephen 'Tin Tin' Duffy, also known as Duffy, was having his first run of success. She became just Duffy, presumably unaware of 'Tin Tin', and was promptly branded "the new ⇨Dusty Springfield" (whose success was even more before her time).

Duffy, Stephen 'Tin Tin' Duffy
British musician Steven Duffy was said to look like comic character Tintin, created by Hergé's Georges Rémi, because he had a quiff in the front (though his hair was black not red). In a farcical dispute, Hergé moved to protect its "intellectual property" and "attendant earnings potential"; but how anyone could confuse the kid detective with The Man Who Left Duran Duran Before They Made It Big is beyond comprehension. Duffy always said he was nothing like Tintin. ⇨The Thompson Twins escaped heavy-handed legal threats from Hergé.

Unflattering derivative: Stephen 'Duff Duff' Tinny. In his Duran daze, he was also billed as "Steven Dufait". Later known as (simply) Duffy. Related: ⇨The Lilac Time.

The Duolian String Pickers

Named a twangy instrument made by National Guitars. Included members ⇨Dire Straits – a National's pictured on their 1985 *Brothers In Arms*. Related: ⇨The Notting Hillbillies.

Champion Jack Dupree

Louisiana musician William Dupree started as a boxer and retired an undefeated champion.

Duran Duran

Simon John Charles Le Bon (translating as "Simon The Good") is the singer's real birthname, though his bandmates call him "Charlie" because their first driver was also called Simon. Le Bon said in an interview that the Duran Duran name was chosen "because it meant nothing to most people", so didn't tie the band to a particular image.

It was taken, by bassist John Taylor, from the 1968 Roger Vadim film *Barbarella*, where Milo O'Shea plays a pervy, mad scientist called Durand Durand. Female space-farer Barbarella had been created five years before by Frenchman Jean-Claude Forest. Jane Fonda played the title role in the film, making it a cult classic.

The young band played many early gigs (1978 on) at the Barbarella Club in Birmingham, U.K., and the venue seemed to confirm the name as right. Later (1988) they briefly tried the ploy of dropping one Duran from their name, then (circa 1989) they were billed for a time as duranduran.

One of their bootleg records inspired the name of ⇨the Lostprophets. Related: ⇨Arcadia, ⇨The Power Station, ⇨Stephen 'Tin Tin' Duffy. Fans called: Durannies. They in turn dubbed John Taylor "Mr Beautiful" (cf ⇨Japan's ⇨David Sylvian, "The World's Most Beautiful Man"). Not the only ones with a double name: see ⇨Talk Talk, ⇨The The.

[32] Duran Duran's starting point: Milo O'Shea, Jane Fonda and an Orgasmatron machine.

Durutti Column

Don't be misled by the columns on the Mancunians' record covers: this is a political not an architectural term. The Durutti Column, named after its leader, was an extreme left-wing faction in the Spanish Civil War. The name was also used by a ruthless group of European anarchists, Situationiste Internationale.

Related: ⇨Simply Red.

Ian Dury

After ⇨Kilburn And The High Roads, this London-born singer favoured ironic names: ⇨The Blockheads followed by The Music Students. Dury's 'Lord Upminster' nickname, used as a 1981 album title, comes from his Essex home.

Bob Dylan

The spokesman for a generation – or more – has said much, and very eloquently. Yet Robert Allen Zimmerman has uttered little about his stagename. And when he has spoken, he's given contradictory accounts of what it means (if anything), or where it comes from (if anywhere).

When he left Duluth, Minnesota, he'd wanted to call himself Robert Allen: it sounded like a Scottish king. Then he heard of saxophonist David Allyn. "I had suspected that the musician had changed the spelling of Allen to Allyn . . . it looked exotic." He considered Robert Allyn. Some of this is set out in *Chronicles Volume 1* (2004). It confirms the present author's own research, save to note the headline, Dylan did NOT rename after Welsh poet Dylan Thomas (1914-1953) as was widely reported.

It's quite correct that he saw Thomas's poetry and thought "the letter D came on stronger." Therefore Allyn became Dllyn/ Dylan. It's also true that Dylan's lyrics are poetic and the singer chose to be known as Robert Milkwood Thomas when working with Steve Goodman. But he's several times dissed this theory of a direct connection, saying Thomas's poetry "isn't the same as mine." After Robert Shelton published

[33] Bob Zimmerman didn't name after Dylan Thomas. Now read on...

a 1986 biography, Dylan told him: "Please correct your book. I didn't take the name from Dylan Thomas." Shelton expressed his frustration to the author, saying we needed to find out the true explanation if this was wrong.

We dismissed evidence that "Dylan" came from a cowboy sheriff called Matt Dillon in the fictional Dodge City or that he named after a 1950s folk singer called Dylan Todd. More promising was a 1965 interview in which he said: "I took the name Dylan because I have an uncle named Dillion." He deliberately changed the spelling because it "looked better."

I ran birth record checks on "Dylan Zimmerman", "Dillion Zimmerman" and similar spellings. Yet I found no direct proof of any person related to the Zimmermans of Duluth on either side of the family tree. I'd more luck with Dillion as a surname: there have been many Dillions in Hibbing, where Bob grew up: a James Dillion was the town's first drayman.

Dylan was unknowingly following ⇨Ethel Merman, a major star of the 1930s, who was born Ethel Agnes Zimmermann – two 'n's on the end in her case.

As for the first name, he felt that "Robert Dylan" didn't work: he was often called Bobby but this sounded skittish and there were already many other Bobbys – ⇨Bobby Rydell, ⇨Bobby Darin, ⇨Bobby Vee and so on.

A new name gave Dylan the opportunity to create whatever myths he desired, free from the identifier of being a middle-class Jewish kid. This made sense if he was to emulate his hero, ⇨Woody Guthrie, and sing about paupers: *See That My Grave Is Kept Clean* and so on. "Dylan" sounded like a down-and-out drifter's name.

Another reason for a pseudonym: protect your real identity and shield your family, maybe emphasise the break with them? Dylan concluded his poem *Advice For Geraldine On Her Miscellaneous Birthday* with the thought that when asked for one's real name, one should never give it.

Dylan's other names: His Bobness, to use his *Q* magazine nickname, has played on many other people's songs, often under more assumed names. These include Tedham Porterhouse (with Ramblin' Jack Elliott); ⇨Blind Boy Grunt (with Richard Farina); Roosevelt Cook (backing Tom Rush); Elmer Johnson, Big Joe's Buddy, Egg O'Schmullson and Keef Laundry.

Dylan played as part of the ad-hoc superstar band ⇨The Traveling Wilburys as Lucky (1988) and Boo (1990).

He took the part of Alias in Sam Peckinpah's now-classic 1973 film *Pat Garrett And Billy The Kid*.

Dylan's backing bands have often been nameless, apart from: ⇨The Band and The Hawks, The Billy 4, and The Rolling Thunder Revue, named after 1976 The Rolling Thunder Revue tour. ⇨Area Code 615 formed after backing him.

His work inspired ⇨Marc Bolan, ⇨Dylan's Trashcan, ⇨fiREHOSE, ⇨Blonde On Blonde, ⇨John Wesley Harding, ⇨Mystery Trend, ⇨Starry Eyed And Laughing and ⇨The Weathermen. He did NOT inspire the name ⇨Judas Priest but may have influenced ⇨Yazoo. Not related: ⇨The Bob Dylan Band, ⇨BOB and ⇨The Dylans.

Related: Jacob Dylan, his son, also a musician.

Nicknames: to many people, Bob is simply Bob or simply Dylan. He is also known as The Zim (from his surname), The Great White Wonder (title of legendary bootleg recording) and (less kindly as he gets older) Bob Zimmerframe.

Dylan followers sometimes style themselves as Bobcats.

The Dylans
Vocalist Colin Gregory says: "It had to be The Dylans didn't it?" He suggested the 1990s Sheffield combo is a tribute to, first, the rabbit Dylan in the children's TV series *The Magic Roundabout*, and second, to ⇨Bob Dylan. Closer examination shows the second is the right one: the Dylans admitted loving "Our Bob's Music."

Dylan's Trashcan
British band named after the fascination for ⇨Bob Dylan. One man, A.J. Weberman, made something of a career of going through the superstar's garbage in search of clues, discarded lyrics etc. Cf: ⇨The Trashcan Sinatras.

The Bob Dylan Band
This New York group is nothing to do with ⇨Bob Dylan and formed by ⇨Lloyd Cole because he had learned to play the harmonica and because they covered Dylan's *She Belongs To Me*.

Vince Eager
One of many stars named by entrepreneur ⇨Larry Parnes. Roy Taylor's enthusiasm was the quality which struck Parnes.

Eagles
The U.S. band's precursors included the Soul Survivors, North Serrano Blues Band, Teen King And The Emergencics and The Poor. Some accounts say guitarist-singer Glenn Frey found the name. Many recent articles, though, have credited fellow guitarist and founder Bernie Leadon, who left the band in 1975.

Both wanted a simple, enduring and all-American word. "Eagles" fitted the bill. The bird is

[34] The Eagles prepare to fly high in their private plane, August 1974.

the symbol of the U.S. and its currency. It also has American Indian and astrological tie-ins. "In the Hopi mythology, the eagle is considered most sacred," Leadon said. "It symbolised the highest spirituality and morals. I would hope that the music would soar that high. Frey wanted a name that could have been a Detroit street gang and everybody wanted a name that was just tough . . . . Hey we're the fuckin' Eagles man!"

The "king of birds" follows dozens of other avian names: cf ⇨The Byrds. Related: ⇨James Gang.

Earth, Wind And Fire
Founder Maurice White became fascinated with the three elements in astrology, mythology and Egyptology.

East Of Eden
A Biblical story; Miltonian phrase; 1952 John Steinbeck book, 1955 film, 1970s band. The latter denied paying tribute to ⇨Iron Butterfly's 1968 *In-A-Gadda-Da-Vida*.
More Steinbeck: ⇨The Grapes Of Wrath.

Sheena Easton
Sheena Shirley Orr, from Glasgow, had a short marriage to singer Sandy Easton before stardom.

East 17
Londoners, 1990s teen sensations, named after their home postal district. Higham Hill and Walthamstow weren't considered.

Easybeats
Many American bands pretended to be British after the invasion led by ⇨The Beatles. This Australian band tried the same trick, adding a Liverpool-born member and echoing a BBC reference to "easier beats" after ⇨Merseybeats.

Eater
This London group came together in 1976. They were fans of ⇨T Rex and named from ⇨Marc Bolan's 1970 *Suneye*: "The rider of stars, Tyrannosaurus Rex, The eater of cars". Still, their music was punk – with names to suit: drummer Roger Bullen was Dee Generate, later replaced with Social Demise (Phil Rowlands).

Eazy-E
This American "gangsta" rapper (1963-1995), a star in ⇨N.W.A., had a drug-dealing past. He claimed the name wasn't about drugs and meant "easy entrepreneur".

Echo And The Bunnymen
The name of this Liverpool band, formed in 1978, produced controversy, sparked by the group's evasiveness in interviews. Guitarist Will Sergeant now says a friend called Paul Ellenbach kept suggesting strange soubriquets, such as The Daz Men, Glisserol (Glycerol) And The Fan Extractors and Echo And The Bunnymen.

The outfit formed as a support for ⇨The Teardrop Explodes. There wasn't much time to find a billing for what was planned as a short-lived unit.

Sergeant's always thought the alias too off-the-wall, cutting airplay. Vocalist Ian McCulloch said the appellation meant nothing and would counteract pretentiousness. He denied he was Echo – this was the name the early group gave to a drum kit for record demos.

Ellenbach may have been thinking of the *Liverpool Echo* newspaper.

The "Bunnymen" tag also produces false trails. If it's meaningless we can discount Internet suggestions that it's anything to do with "bunny girls," talkative people who "rabbit" a lot or *White Rabbit* by ⇨Jefferson Airplane. *NME*'s Dave Quantick declared: "The Bunnymen bit is the result of too much dope."

Echobelly

The U.K.-based band formed in 1992. Founder Sonya Aurora Madan said: "I wanted a word quite female and organic and voluptuous. It also had the meaning of being hungry for something."

Cf ⇨Belly.

Eddie And The Hot Rods

The "leader" of this U.K. 1970s band wasn't the vocalist but a dummy he attacked in early shows. "Eddie" was "retired" before all the stuffing and joke value was knocked out of him. The rest of the name was a hot *double entendre*.

The Edge

The name "David Evans" is little known. Born in 1961, he played with (long-gone, commercially unsuccessful) acts ⇨Feedback and ⇨The Hype.

Contrast that with The Edge, world famous as a guitarist with Irish band ⇨U2.

Evans and The Edge are the same man; the stagename came during his teenage years in Dublin.

The Edge and his musical partner ⇨Bono say in 2006 book *U2 by U2* the moniker comes from his angular head. The Edge told U.K.'s Channel 4: "It's the nose." Bono, in 2005 book *Bono: In Conversation with Michka Assayas*, said: "It had something to do with the shape of his head, his jaw."

There are some extra reasons that Bono adds, which have sometimes been taken as the only reason for the name.

First, it's something to do with his reputation as an outsider. Their circle of teenage friends, from Lypton Village, at first called Dave by the nickname 'Inchicore' – the name of small town on the outskirts of Dublin. Dave, with his Welsh origins, was on the edge of the group: quiet, watching and listening on the fringe rather than joining in.

Second, the name is sometimes said to relate to what Bono calls, in the Assayas book, "the insane love he had for walking on the edges of very high walls, bridges, or buildings." This seems to be secondary.

Among other reasons put forward: David's mind was sharp (yes, but so were their other friends) and he was like The Edge, the hero of Western novels by George Gilman (yes, but the band apparently didn't know of the character as teenagers.).

⇨Bono last called him Dave about 1978. The Edge says: "Just about everybody calls me Edge, or The Edge if it's a formal occasion. I'm only David Evans to people who don't know me well, immigration officers and the like."

Unflattering derivative: The Hedge.

Editors

There's an Internet myth that this English indie band named because its singer Tom Smith edited a fetish porn magazine. In fact his previous CV just has him studying at university and working in a call centre (along with bassist Russell Leetch).

Smith said they came up with Editors and its overspaced logo because they "loved how it looked on paper . . . We all like the idea of an editor overseeing the world and telling people how he is seeing it." Note the name is simply "Editors", in 2000s-style of "no definite article", as opposed to THE Editors.

Eek-A-Mouse

The Jamaican reggae star was born Ripton Hylton in 1957, renaming in 1979. On his Web site, the bio says: "Hylton's unusual name was originally that of a racehorse upon which he frequently lost money; when the horse finally won a race, he had, of course, refused to back it."

E-40

U.S. rapper Earl Stevens combined his first initial with his favourite 40 ounce bottles of malt liquor.

Efua

Efua means "Girl born on a Friday" in Ghanaian, although her parents don't come from that country. They just liked the name.

Ege Bam Yasi

Homage to influential band ⇨Can, whose 1972 LP *Ege Bamyasi* is titled in reference to okra vegetables.

18 Wheeler

Singer Sean Jackson said this Scottish combo named after "a gay black truckers porn magazine in the 1970s which featured enormously endowed men and their vehicles".

808 State

Manchester musician Martin Price said he took it from an early Roland beat box, the TR 808. His earlier choice was even better: The Hit Squad.

801

⇨Roxy Music's Phil Manzanera recycled the lyric of ex-colleague ⇨Brian Eno's 1974 song *True Wheel*: "We are the 801, we are the central shaft". The same song inspired ⇨ACR.

A Dictionary of Rock and Pop Names

Einstürzende Neubauten
These Berliners used drills, girders and power tools for a grating beat. The name translates as "collapsing new buildings". Their first album, from 1982, was *Kollaps*.

Eire Apparent
This Irish band considered "hilarious" patriotic puns such as Eire Today or Eire Style. (Possibly worse puns: Plimsouls, The Jive Bombers.)

Elastica
Leader Justine Frischmann chose Elastica in 1993 on suggestion of Jane Oliver, a housemate of guitarist Donna Matthews. It was said to be a "flexible name" which would allow them room for growth. ⇨Blur's Damon Albarn guested on one CD, under the anagramic Dan Abnormal. Related: ⇨Spitfire.

Eldritch
The black-clad prince who founded ⇨The Sisters Of Mercy surprisingly wasn't born wearing shades in a bat-infested Berlin belfry but was Briton Andrew William Harvey Taylor from Cambridgeshire. The stagename means "poetic, weird, uncanny, unearthly". Eldritch said he was nicknamed 'Von' by Tony James, ex-⇨Sigue Sigue Sputnik, "to point out that I was hanging out in Hamburg rather more than Halifax."
   Not to be confused with an Italian metal band Eldritch, or anything remotely gothic.

Electric Prunes
The Seattle surrealists said "electric" came from their instruments and "prune" was a 1960s buzzword, like "strawberry", and wasn't meant in a derogatory sense.

Electronic
This "supergroup" brought together musicians from ⇨The Pet Shop Boys, ⇨The Smiths and ⇨New Order into "A ⇨Blind Faith for the 1990s". Barney Sumner got the idea when someone spiked his drink in a New York nightclub: "Suddenly this electronic music made sense."

Elevation
Like ⇨Marquee Moon and ⇨Friction, named after a track on ⇨Television's debut LP.

Elisa
The singer was born Lisa Barbuscia and started performing as Lisa B. Eclipsed by dozens of other Lisas (Wendy and Lisa, Lisa Marie, Lisa Stansfield etc), she therefore changed, Elisa said in a 1992 interview with the author.

Duke Ellington
Another music "aristocrat," he was born in Washington as Edward Ellington. He acquired the nickname as a child because of his 'upper class' bearing: his father was a White House butler.

Ramblin' Jack Elliott

Elliott Charles Adnopoz knew his family name wasn't stagey. You could hardly sing ⇨Woody Guthrie songs such as *Dust Pneumonia Blues* if it then emerged you're the son of a famous physician. The romantic "ramblin'" referred to his life on tour, though he could afford good hotels and cars.

Elmerhassell

This band named from a minor character in a major beat generation novel, 1957's *On The Road*. Narrator Sal Paradise says Elmer is a "slinking criminal" with "a hip sneer". Cf ⇨The Dharma Bums.

ELO (The Electric Light Orchestra)

This U.K. band was initially the brainchild of Birmingham musical ⇨Wizzard Roy Wood, who wanted to develop orchestral rock with electric instruments. "Light" was the BBC term for non-classical music. The abbreviated ELO continued the trend for reducing orchestras to initials, as in LSO, NYSO etc. LP covers showed light bulbs and titles such as *Light Years Ahead*.

ELP

Keith Emerson, Greg Lake and Carl Palmer felt they were so famous they didn't need a proper name for their "supergroup". Later E and L linked with strategically-named drummer Cozy Powell. Related: ⇨Asia, ⇨(p. 165) King Crimson.

Emanon

This ⇨Manfred Mann jazz offshoot was simply "no name" backwards.

EMF

Founder James Atkins said this wasn't "Electro Motive Force" but "Epsom Mad Funkers". One song had "Ecstasy Mother Fuckers" though – and fans had many other suggestions.

Eminem

Marshall Bruce Mathers III (1972-) reworked the M and M in his real name. He has used Marshall Mathers as a title in its own right. ⇨Slim Shady.

Emmenon

⇨Madonna started as she meant to go on, being provocative. Emmenology means menstruation. They later became Emmy, a name too close for comfort to the U.S. TV awards.

Empress Of The Blues

⇨The Queen Of The Blues is a title claimed by several stars. Supporters of Bessie Smith upgraded her title to fend off the lesser pretenders.

A Dictionary of Rock and Pop Names

Eno
This British producer and "non musician" was born Brian Peter George St. John (le) Baptiste de la Salle Eno. The abbreviation mirrors similar moves by double-barrelled members of ⇨Queen and ⇨The Rolling Stones. He was the mainspring behind ⇨The Warm Jets and ⇨Roxy Music. No relation to ENO (English National Opera). He inspired ⇨ACR and ⇨801 and worked with ⇨David Bowie, ⇨Talking Heads (⇨King's Lead Hat) and ⇨U2, where he used an anagram to become Ben O'Rian in Passengers (He thought of the name for the last; Bono said in 2006, "I still like it.")

John Entwistle
⇨Ox, ⇨Rigor Mortis, ⇨The Who.

Enya
The Irish singer was born Eithne Ni Bhraonain, renamed Brennan as the rest of the family did for showbiz work – the non-Gaelic form of the surname (⇨Clannad) – and became Enya as the closest Anglicisation of her Christian name.

Epileptics
Instead of the punk shock-tactic approach "flirt with Nazism", this lot tried mocking others. When the British Epilepsy Association objected, they became Epi-X and then ⇨Flux Of Pink Indians. The same stunt was tried by punk band Epileptic Tits that included ⇨Black.

EPMD
Erick Semon and Parrish Smith optimistically named for "Erick & Parrish Making Dollars".

Erasure
Vince Clarke is said to have chosen this name because "erasure is more important than recording in the studio". Related: ⇨Depeche Mode.

Esperanto
This 1970s prog-rock band had members from Belgium, Italy and the U.K. Founder Raymond Vincent named after the language created by a Warsaw linguist in 1887 (1) in reference to the international membership and (2) because it roughly translates as "hope". The band communicated in English not Esperanto sadly.

David Essex
Born David Albert Cook in Plaistow, 1947 – then in Essex, made part of London in 1965. Anagram: Sex Advised.

Sleepy John Estes
The Tennessee bluesman (1904-1977) suffered from a medical condition which sapped his energy, hence the nickname.

The E Street Band

⇨Bruce Springsteen's long-time backing band named after the street in Belmar, New Jersey, where keyboardist David Sancious's mother lived and allowed them to rehearse. The group formed informally in 1972, with a shifting membership, though Sancious only later began appearing as a concert regular. The name was effectively in place for the 1973 LP title *The Wild, The Innocent and The E. Street Shuffle,* by which time he'd been on board for a short period.

Eurythmics

British electronic duo Annie Lennox and David Stewart took their name from a regime of bodily movements with a musical accompaniment to teach rhythm, developed in the early 20th century by French Professor Jacques-Dalcroze, originally "Eurhythmics". Related: ⇨The Tourists.

Evanescence

This Arkansas alternative rock band was formed in 1988 by singer Amy Lee. The word means "the process or fact of vanishing away". Lee said in an interview the name is "mysterious and dark, and places a picture in the listener's mind".

Vince Everett

Singer Martin Benefield purloined the name of ⇨Elvis Presley's character in 1959 film *Jailhouse Rock.*

Everything But The Girl

A furniture shop called Turners in Beverley Road, Kingston Upon Hull, Northern England, was the unlikely origin for this band's unusual name. The only noteworthy thing about it was the fascia with its slogan "Everything But The Girl".

The suggestion looked like old-fashioned 1950s male chauvinism: the shop could furnish all needs for cushioned comfort apart from a lover. Musicians Tracey Thorn and Ben Watt, who were attending the city's university, seized on the slogan – which amused some and appalled others.

This name origin is typical of the amount of misinformation on the Internet: the shop is wrongly reported to have been a favourite of students; a Yankee-style seller of second-hand bric-à-brac or clothing; to have everything for sale as it closed down except the staff, and to have a dummy holding a sign saying "For your bedroom F*** needs we sell everything but me."

The choice was obviously potentially misleading for a male-female duo; yet it was also apt, reflecting the soon-inseparable Thorn and Watt's not-for-sale concerns. Related: ⇨The Marine Girls, Grab Grab The Haddock.

[35] "Everything But The Girl" indeed. Turners in 1985.

Exciter

Canadian three-piece, named ⇨Judas Priest's song *Exciter*, best heard on the 1979 album *Unleashed In The East*.

The Ex-Pensive Winos

Unofficial name for the backing group for ⇨Keith Richards's *Talk Is Cheap* tour. It was chosen after he found three of them guzzling a bottle of Lafitte Rothschild behind the drum kit during rehearsals. Rebel Yell tippler Richards told the trio he was spending all his money on winos. They told him it takes one to know one: "We're winos man – but at least we're expensive winos!"

Exploding White Mice

Rodent inspiration makes for silly names: ⇨Eek-A-Mouse, ⇨Danger Mouse, and ⇨Modest Mouse. This group liked ⇨The Ramones and named after the mice that go pop in the 'Mones film *Rock 'N' Roll High School*.

Extreme

This American hard rock band started in 1985. They considered Dream as a name and became Extreme – which can be read as Ex-Dream, or more likely X-Dream, as in an X-rated dream.

Eyeless In Gaza

The British indie band liked the title of Aldous Huxley's 1936 novel. He also inspired ⇨The Doors and ⇨The Feelies.

F

Fabian

Philadelphia-born Fabiano Forte Bonaparte anglicised his name like his friend ⇨Frankie Avalon. After years as a single-name star, he became Fabian Forte in 1970.

The Faces

A "face" was a luminary in the British beat subculture world of the swinging sixties. ⇨The Small Faces were such celebrities. After a shake-up they felt confident to rename.

Factory

The Manchester record label was set up by entrepreneur Anthony H. Wilson (1950-2007). Promoter Alan Wise suggested it as a club name to Wilson after seeing a sign which said: "Factory clearance." Nothing to do with Andy Warhol's factory. Related: ⇨Joy Division, ⇨New Order.

Fad Gadget

The "band" was effectively just Frank Tovey (1956-2002). He said that many people "just repeat themselves and end up going nowhere. That's why I call myself Fad Gadget. It's a stupid name, throwaway, utterly disposable."

Fairport Convention

1967: the tale starts at a home in Fortis Green, North London – a large house that then had a general medical practice on the ground floor with the rest let to lodgers. It was owned by a widow of one of the doctors, who allowed her son Simon's band to rehearse in the attic. The woman was called Mrs Nicol, her son was guitarist Simon, the house was called Fairport, and Simon's group became Fairport Convention. Fairport is still there, a small part of rock history.

1976: The band name was briefly abbreviated to Fairport after years informally being called such.

Related: ⇨The Albion Band, ⇨The Cocktail Cowboys, ⇨Fotheringay, ⇨Matthews Southern Comfort, ⇨Steeleye Span, ⇨Whippersnapper.

Adam Faith

Londoner Terence Nelhams ploughed through books of boys' and girls' prenomens for a stagename.

Inspired: ⇨Sandie Shaw, ⇨Leo Sayer.

[36 + 37 + 38] Fairport Convention, 1969; and their old base Fairport in 2008.

Faithless

From the spirituality underlying this British dance act led by Maxi Jazz (born Maxwell Fraser), a Buddhist rapper.

Faith No More

These San Francisco residents at one stage lied that the name was a greyhound on which they had placed a big winning bet. Bassist Bill Gould now reveals the truth: "At first (1980) we were called Sharp Young Men but we wanted something cryptic. So it came to be called Faith No Man." They were led by singer Mike 'The Man' Morris. When he became too demanding the others left. Gould's friend Will Carpmill suggested the moniker as a joke on Morris, seeing that "The Man" was no more. The band lasted to 1998. One aspiring vocalist was ⇨Courtney Love.

The Fall

Mancunian Mark E. Smith namechecked 1956's *The Fall* by French writer Albert Camus, reflecting the Bible story of the first sin. Spinoff: ⇨The Adult Net. Cf ⇨The Smiths. The name makes no sense to Americans who read it as a reference to one season of the year.

Fall Out Boy

This Chicago-based band had no name for its first gigs in 2001. At the end of the second informal concert, the group asked audience members for a name. One of the "like four" people there suggested "Fallout Boy," a reference to the sidekick of *The Simpsons* cartoon character Radioactive Man.

[39] Albert Camus's 1956 novel *The Fall* energised a Manchester band 20 years later.

Georgie Fame

This was one of the names manufactured by U.K. entrepreneur ⇨Larry Parnes. In this case, Clive Powell had already been fitted up by Parnes with the name ⇨Lance Fortune.

Some days later, Parnes told his assistant: "The next kid that walks through my door, I'm gonna call him Georgie Fame." The next kid was Powell, and Parnes switched his name on the spot, confident that the keyboardist would be famous. Another kid got the Fortune name.

Family

They formed in 1962 as The Farinas, renaming on suggestion of producer Kim Fowley from their close communal life reflected in Jenny Fabian's *Groupie* novel. Related: ⇨Blind Faith, ⇨Streetwalkers, ⇨Traffic. Unrelated: ⇨Prince's The Family.

Fanny

Their record company ditched the handle Wild Honey in favour of this, spelling out the *double entendre* by hailing "the first female rock band". This was in 1969, when sexism was less understood. The name was suggested by no less than ⇨George Harrison.

The Farm

From Walton Farm in the band's native Liverpool. It's known for its links with Robert Tressel (pen name of Robert Noonan), who wrote *The Ragged Trousered Philanthropists*, published in 1914. It was read by guitarist Keith Mullen at 15, while singer Peter Hooton said they wanted to express "the soul of socialism". Their record label was called Produce.

Perry Farrell

New Yorker Perry Bernstein renamed Farrell, after his brother's first name, to pun on "peripheral". Related: ⇨Jane's Addiction, Lollapalooza, ⇨Porno For Pyros.

Faster Pussycat

Former ⇨Guns N' Roses guitarist Tracii Guns decided to name his new band after *Faster Pussycat! Kill! Kill!* The 1965 movie helped erotic film director Russ Meyer to break into the big time thanks to its fetishist and sci-fi overtones. Part of its kitsch appeal is that it has aged terribly.

When Guns decided to reuse his old band name, L.A. Guns, his friend Taime Downe took the name for his 1980s Californian hard act. He particularly loved the big, busty Barbarella-type women figures.

[40] Rockers Faster Pussycat ripped off Russ Meyer's 1965 erotic movie title.

Fastway

Taken from leaders 'Fast' Eddie Clarke (ex ⇨Motörhead) and Pete Way (ex-⇨UFO, soon to join ⇨Ozzy Osbourne). Almost as bad as Way's punning ⇨Waysted.

Fatboy Slim

British musician Quentin Leo Cook dropped his first name in place of Norman as a schoolboy. After working with ⇨ The Housemartins and others, he adopted his stage name in 1996 from blues singer Bumble Bee Slim.

Father Of The Blues

William Handy composed songs such as *Memphis Blues* and bestowed the title on himself.

The Fat Lady Sings

These four Irish folksters were quite thin men. They chose the name because it was misleading in a ⇨Les Negresses Vertes way. It was from the phrase "it isn't over until the fat lady sings": at the end of baseball games a lady used to sing the National Anthem.

Faust

A medieval legend tells of a man who gained skills by handing his soul to Satan. In the 16th century it was linked to a conjuror called Johann Faust who wandered

Germany. Hence masterpieces by Marlowe, Goethe, Spohr, Wagner, Schumann, Liszt and Gounod. And hence this German prog-rock act.

Feedback

⇨The Larry Mullen Band was history within hours of its formation in September 1976. Varying accounts say the name lasted 10 minutes (Larry Mullen Jnr. himself) or perhaps a day (other band members).

The drummer had placed a notice appealing for fellow musicians on a board in his Dublin school. The original six-piece then began rehearsing at Mullen's home. Bassist Adam Clayton was barely competent but the band got its name from the screeching noise that came from his portable amplifier.

"Feedback" was one of the few technical terms they knew, apart from "gig", said ⇨The Edge. In the 2006 book *U2 By U2*, Mullen said they "had a name for the band before we had anything else".

They became ⇨The Hype in March 1977 and then ⇨U2.

The Feelies

Mid-1980s American band who took the name from a children's blindfold "guess the object" contest. It didn't come directly from Aldous Huxley's 1932 *Brave New World*, although they knew the novel, which foresees films with full sensory effects in the future.

Felt

This British 1980s act's ⇨The Velvet Underground experience was a fabric name that was also the past participle of to feel. More puns: ⇨The Herd.

Shane Fenton And The Fentones

Londoner Bernard Jewry became Shane Fenton in the 1960s, seeking a U.S.-sounding name. Unfortunately the "And The" part sounded dated. Retro-chic was getting acceptable in the 1970s and he made it as ⇨Alvin Stardust.

Bryan Ferry

⇨Roxy Music leader, solo star, guru and icon. Unflattering derivative: Byron Ferrari (sneeringly coined by *NME* as "Bry" continued with his tux look while punk revolted into a new style).

Gracie Fields

She shortened her surname Stansfield (thinking it was a little long to put in lights) and made Grace a little less formal and warmer. Ironically, another Lancashire Stansfield, Lisa, used the surname in full decades later.

Fields Of The Nephilim

These British cowboy obsessives told the author the name came from the song, *The Nephilim*, on their first album, 1987's *Dawnrazor*. A lot of this group's early material was a self-mythologizing script with added road-dust talcum powder that recalled the soundtracks to spaghetti westerns, with results ranging from the impressive to the laughable.

The Fifth Dimension

Before this Los Angeles band went *Up, Up And Away*, they were called The Versatiles. Vocalist Ron Townson suggested the new name, not in reference to the five members but to their interests in pop, jazz, classical, gospel and folk.

50 Cent

The rapper Curtis James Jackson III said that in the same way 50 cents is given in change, his stagename is a metaphor for "change". He took it from Kelvin Martin, a 1980s Brooklyn robber known as 50 Cent. He said in an interview: "I'm the same kind of person 50 Cent was. I provide for myself by any means." ⇨Two Five.

[41] Rap attack: 50 Cent (right) vies with LL Cool J for hip-hop name cool.

50 Foot Wave

This American alt rock band's name was the choice of ⇨Throwing Muses's founder Kristin Hersh. It's supposed to relate to the long sound wave of the lowest tone audible to the human ear. Unfortunately, the band launched just as tsunami waves of 50 feet or more hit parts of Asia.

54-40

Band from Vancouver, Canada, whose name was a subtle attack on U.S. colonialism. "Fifty-four forty or fight" was the presidential campaign slogan of James K. Polk who threatened war with Canada unless it accepted his demands.

Fine Young Cannibals

Founded by graduates of ⇨The (English) Beat. Guitarist Andy Cox said he was thinking of 1960 movie *All The Fine Young Cannibals*. Cox said: "It was so weird that nobody would sue us over it." In fact, a garage band called The Cannibals did try to block the trio's first single.

Misguided cannibalism critics made a meal of their 1988 LP, *The Raw And The Cooked*, actually a reference to French anthropologist Claude Lévi-Strauss. Related: ⇨2 Men A Drum Machine And A Trumpet. Included Guinness (nickname for Roland Gift, sporting bleached-blond hair).

The Fire Engines

The aftermath of punk saw this anarchistic Scottish band name in tribute to nihilists of a different kind and time: ⇨The 13th Floor Elevators, who had a song about fire engines.

[42] Look out for a name idea: fIREHOSE found theirs in this Bob Dylan video.

fIREHOSE

⇨Bob Dylan used D.A. Pennebaker's 1967 film *Don't Look Back* to make one of the first true pop videos. As *Subterranean Homesick Blues* plays, he casually discards cards of key words including "LOOK OUT" and "fIREHOSE".

This U.S. band was formed by members of ⇨The Minutemen. They loved Dylan's song and wanted to get a promotional clip with Dylan "advertising" their band 20 years before formation. fIREHOSE's odd capitalisation was carried across to song titles. The same Dylan track inspired ⇨The Weathermen.

The Firm

A Jimmy Page post- ⇨Led Zeppelin band, formed with Paul Rodgers. The name has sexual undertones, means a business and Page added: "The term 'The Firm' in England is when all the boys go out together at night, without the wives or girl-friends. It's the old firm, chaps that are all out together."

The First Lady of Jazz

Usually said to be Ella Fitzgerald, America's First Lady of Song.

The First Tycoon Of Teen

American producer ⇨Phil Spector; nickname from his massive commercial success with a string of hit records in the 1960s. Coined by author Tom Wolfe.

Fish

Singer with ⇨Marillion, later solo, tells the story on *The Funny Farm Interview*, recorded in 1995 for his information club The Company: "At school I was 'Derek William Dick'. I used to get upset with 'Dirty Dick' and stuff like that."

He was working at Fochabers, Grampian, where his landlady, a Mrs Fraser, objected to the number of baths he was taking. In protest he would take beer, radio and books into the bathroom for hours. "One night a friend hung about waiting for me to come out of the bath and he said: 'Are you some sort of fish or something?'

and I said: 'That's it'. I just could not image being introduced on stage as Derek William Dick."

Unrelated: ⇨The Fish. Another famous "Dick" in rock is Paul Dick AKA ⇨Paul Revere.

The Fish

Barry Melton's name came from a Chairman Mao quote about activists moving through streams of society like fish and spreading dissent. ⇨Country Joe McDonald, ⇨The Dinosaurs.

Five Guys Named Moe

This group is a quartet, three guys and a girl, and none is called Moe. They chose it as the most inaccurate name they could think of. The original *Five Guys Named Moe* is an admired track by 1940s jazzman Louis Jordan and a show based on his music. Cf⇨moe.

Five Star

These siblings of the Pearson family from Essex were aspiring five stars – the international term to signify the best hotels, restaurants etc.

Roberta Flack

Her real name, but she self-produced her LP *Feel Like Makin' Love* – and others – under the name Rubina Flake "to avoid the flak".

Flea

Member of ⇨The Red Hot Chili Peppers. The nickname Flea came during a ski trip, according to one report, because he would not sit still and was always jumping about.

Fleetwood Mac

When ⇨Eric Clapton quit John Mayall's ⇨Bluesbreakers, he was replaced with a shy lad from London's East End called Peter Green (born Greenbaum). Like Clapton, he was unhappy with the adulation. Mayall gave him some studio time as a "cheer up" birthday present in 1967.

Green cut an instrumental called *Fleetwood Mac*, named from his two recording colleagues: fellow Bluesbreakers Mick Fleetwood, the drummer and bassist John McVie. Wanting to hide his identity, Green nominated the tune's title as the group name. He was annoyed when it was credited to "Peter Green's Fleetwood Mac". While he got his way on this later, he had quit by 1970.

Fleetwood and Mac have stayed throughout dozens of other personal and style changes. The appellation almost went amid legal action over its ownership in 1974 when their manager put together a "fake" band to play concert bookings.

The Fleetwoods

The Saturns, from Olympia, Washington, added Gary Troxel as lead singer in 1958 to become Two Girls And A Guy.

Liberty Records company promoter Bob Reisdorff telephoned to offer a contract, while urging they choose a catchier name. He glanced down at his telephone and remarked: "Like Fleetwood". This was the local telephone dialling name.

Flesh For Lulu

In the 1960s, ⇨Lulu was a pop star at 15. Twenty years on and her star had faded. Still, she remained a recognisable figure thanks to her television work. This vegetarian band saw her buying a burger in a restaurant. No great Lulu fans, they named as a meat-eating protest.

A Flock Of Seagulls

Britons who named from Richard Bach's best-selling novella *Jonathan Livingston Seagull*. This thin volume was later made into an LP, and a 1973 film. The group said: "We read the book. Saw the seagulls in the sky. Listened to the album an' that was it!" "Nobody liked the name so we thought we'd keep it." "What about ⇨Scritti Politti's name? It's worse than ours."

Flowerpot Men

⇨The Ivy League's clean-cut image matched the style of early 1960s. By 1967 crew cuts were out and dropping out was in. A strategic change of image and name seemed in order.

So, with absurd hippy apparel and repertoire (*Let's All Go To San Francisco*) the Britons renamed . . . after a BBC television children's serial. This starred Bill and Ben – puppets made out of flowerpots – and their friend Little Weed. Rationale: flower, pot and weed got in interesting references for the psychedelic age when "flower power" was everywhere. Related: ⇨Deep Purple.

Flowers Of Romance

Named on the suggestion of ⇨Sid Vicious. Viv Albertine of ⇨The Slits told writer Jon Savage: "It was perfect. You're the flowers and what's romance? Lies. These children are the flowers of romance."

Flux Of Pink Indians

These U.K. punksters reasoned it made sense: they weren't Indians, nor Red (American) Indians but pink. Related: ⇨The Epileptics, ⇨One Little Indian Records.

Flying Burrito Brothers

They weren't called Burrito at birth, they weren't brothers and they couldn't perform Mr. Kite style aerobatic tricks.

The name was first used for a 1960s informal bunch of musicians in Los Angeles – then borrowed by ⇨Gram Parsons for jam sessions before his time in ⇨The Byrds. Davis said it sounded more like a flying circus act or a mob of southern desperadoes: a burrito is a U.S.-Mexican dish, giving a clue to their origin.

When Parsons joined ⇨The Byrds, they nearly took it as an album title (some fans wrongly protested it was a dig at former Byrd, Gene Clark, who left the band because of a reported fear of flying) though in the end he kept it for his next group project. Cf ⇨Sweethearts Of The Rodeo.

Flying Pickets

British *a capella* band who named after flying pickets: activists who travelled distances to help strikers persuade or force others not to work. The sextet acted after Margaret Thatcher's Conservative government restricted flying pickets to six at each site. "We wanted to encapsulate the struggle for a better standard of living, a fairer society", explained singer Brian Hibberd.

Foetus

Bywords for a family of bands chosen by Anglo-Australian, adopted New Yorker, Jim Thirlwell, AKA Jim Foetus, Clint Ruin, Stinkfist, Flesh Volcano, Steroid Maximus and so on: this man likes identity changes and says "shock 'em before you rock 'em". Repulsive names include: Scraping Foetus Off The Wheel, You've Got Foetus On Your Breath, Foetus Interruptus, Foetus Corruptus and Foetus Über (Alles). Related: ⇨Immaculate Consumptive.

Follow 4 Now

Named after a ⇨Public Enemy song *Bring The Noise*, which advises following people power.

Wayne Fontana

He was born Glyn Ellis in Manchester, U.K. His stagename was chosen from ⇨Elvis Presley's 1950s drummer D.J. Fontana. It's coincidental that he later was on Fontana Records. Cf ⇨The Mindbenders.

Foo Fighters

From U.S. military slang for fighter pilots called out to investigate sightings of "foos" or UFOs, i.e. unidentified flying objects. Dave Grohl's band after ⇨Nirvana; their

[43] Dave Grohl's Foo Fighters keep an eye out for flying saucers.

opening song was called *This Is A Call*, with sleeves picturing the Roswell Incident, in which U.S. doctors examine alien-like forms, now said to be dummies. Unrelated: ⇨UFO.

Grohl's repeatedly said the name was picked in haste and he would have thought longer if he had realised he was going to be stuck with it for decades.

Foreigner
Named because they formed in 1976 with two Brits and three Americans. The personnel later changed slightly, making the band 75% foreign for their main, U.S., market.

George Formby
There have been two British singer-comedians of this name, father and son. The first was born James Booth and took Formby from a name seen on a goods train.

Lance Fortune
Chris Morris was renamed by ⇨Larry Parnes with a cast-off name, originally intended for ⇨Georgie Fame.

The 49ers
This Italian house outfit was without a name when auditioning vocalists. Then jazz singer Dawn Mitchell walked in, the 49th person to be auditioned. She knocked them out with her performance. They had a singer and a name.

Fotheringay
British folk-rock band formed by Sandy Denny after her first ⇨Fairport Convention stint and named after her folk composition which opens their 1969 LP *What We Did On Our Holidays*. Fotheringay, Northamptonshire, was the place where Mary Queen of Scots was imprisoned.

Foundations
These 1960 popsters were discovered by a talent scout while playing in a London basement below his office.

Fountains Of Wayne
Bassist Chris Collingwood said they formed in 1996. "We picked this name because we knew we wouldn't have to fight for it. There really is a place in Wayne, New Jersey, called Fountains of Wayne. They sell lawn ornaments and stuff." The garden furniture store is not far from Montclair, New Jersey, the hometown of the band's bassist and cofounder Adam Schlesinger.

Four Horsemen
This spinoff from ⇨The Cult named from a track by ⇨The Clash on 1980's *London Calling* album.

A Dictionary of Rock and Pop Names

400 Blows
Named after a 1959 François Truffaut film, *Les Quatre Cents Coups*, about an unhappy 12-year-old boy on the run.

The Fourmost
Manager Brian Epstein amended this quartet's name from The Four Mosts in 1963 and exploited their connection with another Merseybeat group, who proved to be a foremost fabber four. (⇨The Beatles).

Fourplay
This quartet who thought it better than The Sensational Alex Harvey Band (Without Alex Harvey). If the foreplay was bad, the actual playing was even worse.

The Four Seasons
They had nearly ten years of moderate success as The Variatones and The Village Voices (a reference to the New York city Greenwich Village newspaper).

Given the group's popularity, it's natural that a number of other clubs have claimed to have inspired the final name. The best-known is the restaurant a few doors from their New York record company offices.

Leader Frank Castelluccio became successively Frankie Valley and Frankie Valli. Cf ⇨Wonder Who, ⇨The Sandpipers.

The 4 Skins
A leading *Oi!* hardcore outfit with a skinhead following, their name was seen as anti-Semitic; the band's politics built on the Nazi stance affected by many punks. Cf ⇨Redskins.

The Four Tops
Many 1950s band names were hardly adventurous: that came later. This quartet from Michigan thus started as The Four Aims (1953) and only revised this because of possible confusion with the Ames Brothers. Lead singer Levi Stubbles, often the target of shaving jokes, became Stubbs.

Frabjoy And Runcible
U.K. band, a forerunner of ⇨10CC. The name comes from two nonsense words, the first (frabjous) invented by Lewis *Alice In Wonderland* Carroll and the second (runcible spoon) by Edward *Pobble* Lear.

Connie Francis
Born in 1938 as Concetta Rosa Maria Franconero, she made the change aged 10 based on a suggestion by TV chat show host Arthur Godfrey. He said, before her appearance on his *Talent Scouts* programme, that her name was too long to remember and too difficult to pronounce.

The Frank And Walters

None of this threesome was called Frank or Walters. They were from Cork, Ireland, and named after two vagrants who were well known local characters.

Frankie Goes To Hollywood

The usual explanation is given on the B side of 1983's *Relax*, called *One September Monday*.

"There was a band I was in, I was just learning. We needed a name quickly because we had to get a gig and there was a piece of the *New Yorker* magazine stuck to the wall in the rehearsal room and it said 'Frankie Goes To Hollywood' and showed a picture of Frank Sinatra getting mobbed by teenyboppers."

William Johnson, who gave this account, earlier changed his name to Holly (⇨Holly Johnson), played with ⇨Big In Japan and formed a band punningly called Hollycaust. What he doesn't say is that the headline contained the magic word "Holly" – just as he was reforming the outfit with Paul Rutherford, ex- ⇨Opium Eaters.

Some pop trivia books have said the headline in question related to fellow veteran singer Frankie Laine's film plans or even British comedian Frankie Howerd. This is variously said to have appeared in *Variety* and a Liverpool newspaper. *Variety* is almost certainly correct; it indeed carried a piece on Sinatra moving from Las Vegas.

The band became informally known as "The Frankies" (⇨The Hollies had already been done) and the remnants toyed with the name of The Lads after the departure of the two main front men. Cf ⇨Bonzo Goes To Washington. Spoof band: Paddy Goes To Holyhead.

The Frantic Elevators

Forerunners of ⇨Simply Red. They liked a track by ⇨Television, *Elevation*, on the 1977 album *Marquee Moon*. (Cf ⇨Elevation.) This was ruled too hippy and they switched to The Elevators. Mick Hucknall considered adding a punky adjective such as Rancid or Manic. Then he saw an advert in *New Musical Express* which said: "Are you frantic yet?" Cf ⇨The Thirteenth Floor Elevators.

Franz Ferdinand

This pop/rock band formed in Scotland in 2001. They loved the name "The Archduke", an entry in an equestrian race they saw on the television, rhythm guitarist Nick McCarthy said. This led to them remembering Austria's Franz Ferdinand, added bassist Bob Hardy.

Singer Alex Kapranos pointed to how the Archduke's death was a major factor in starting World War I and changing history. One of their early songs was about the Archduke's assassination. Still, "a name should just sound good . . . like music", said Alex. They hoped that if they got good enough, people would think of them rather than the historical figure.

The name, they agreed, beat those of bands they had played with before in the 1990s, including The Yummy Fur, 10p Invaders and Embryo.

The Fratellis

The Scottish trio formed in 2005 and named from the family of criminals known as the Fratellis – the bad guys in the 1985 movie *The Goonies*, directed by Richard Donner from a story by Steven Spielberg. They liked it because (a) band member Barry Wallace's mother's maiden name is also Fratelli; and (b) "fratelli" is Italian for "brothers". They all adopted it as their last name, becoming Barry, Mince and Jon Fratelli.

Freddie And The Dreamers

Leader Freddie Garrity chose the name for the Mancunian group, originally the Kingfishers, possibly from a 1960 Johnny Burnette song *Dreamin'*. It also fitted a summer residency at Dreamland holiday camps in the U.K.

Fred Zeppelin

Short-lived California band formed by Moon Unit, daughter of ⇨Frank Zappa, parodying ⇨Led Zeppelin's name.

Free

Named by U.K. musician Alexis Korner, after his then-defunct group Free At Last, which featured Ginger Baker who sprang to fame with ⇨Cream. Free called their 1972 LP *Free At Last* – it was too good to waste in the end.

Island Records unsuccessfully implored the band to become Heavy Metal Kids – a misnomer because the musos were always heavy rockers rather than heavy metal exponents. Heavy metal was an integral part of Cream's sound and popularised in its own right through ⇨Iron Butterfly, ⇨Vanilla Fudge and ⇨Led Zeppelin. (⇨Heavy Metal Kids.)

For a while Free had the immortal name of Kossoff, Kirke, Tetsu and Rabbit. Korner also named ⇨CCS. Related: ⇨Back Street Crawler, ⇨Bad Company.

Friction

Named from the third track on ⇨Television's *Marquee Moon* album. The same record inspired ⇨Marquee Moon and ⇨Elevation. Friction was chosen by Peter Laughner, ex ⇨(p.215) Pere Ubu, because of his love for Television.

The Frustrations

U.S. punk band formed by Bill Berry and Ian Copeland – the name expressed their feeling about Georgia, although it could equally apply to the frustrations of life and growing up. ⇨R.E.M.

The Fugees

The 1994-on New Jersey hip-hop outfit started as Tranzlater Crew, then had to rename after threats of legal action by Translator. The chosen replacement is an abbreviation of refugees; the prime movers were originally from Haiti.

The Fugs

U.S. 1960s poets Ed Sanders, Tuli Kupferberg and Ken Weaver shotgun-married works by William Blake to rough-hewn guitar and named from Norman Mailer, who uses "fug" instead of "fuck" to record U.S. service language in *The Naked And The Dead*.

Funeral For A Friend

The common misconception, found all over the Internet, usually as "a friend of a friend told me . . . ", is that this band (often abbreviated to FFAF) named after *Funeral For A Friend/ Love Lies Bleeding*, the 11-minute 1973 segued track by ⇨Elton John.

Wrong. The name came in 2002 from a track called *Funeral For A Friend*, but it's a less familiar piece by the Florida post-hardcore group Planes Mistaken For Stars. FFAF confirmed this in an interview, though in other statements they've not bothered to deny the John explanation.

Funkadelic

U.S. star ⇨George Clinton relaunched ⇨The Parliaments in 1969. The new moniker combined his own funk with psychedelia, then at its height. Related: ⇨The Brides Of Dr Funkenstein. Inspired: ⇨Urge Overkill.

Fun Lovin' Criminals

A New York trio who wear their interests and influences prominently on their well-tailored Mafia suits. Singer and guitarist Huey stole the name from an acquaintance who ran a graffiti crew in Queens. "It represents the duality that goes with living in New York," he told *Q*. "It's hard to always be on the right side of the law."

Billy Fury

U.K. pop entrepreneur ⇨Larry Parnes chose this name because young Ronald Wycherley, from Liverpool, U.K., had obvious vitality and daring. (He had been sacked from jobs for fighting and got a contract by gate-crashing Parnes's room before a gig). The name led to the 1960 LP *The Sound of Fury*.

Fu-Schnickens

The Brooklyn rappers said FU means "for unity". Schnicken is a word they invented to mean "coalition". "Together it means we are together, work together."

Gabba

Tribute band doing ⇨ABBA in ⇨Ramones style. The name combines the Swedish act's name with the Ramones chant "gabba gabba heh". Unconnected with gabba, an electronic music style.

Serge Gainsbourg

The singer (1928-1991) hated his real prenomen Lucien and changed his surname Ginsburg to a French equivalent.

The Game

West Coast rapper Jayceon Terrell Taylor was named by his grandmother because he was "game" for anything.

Gang Of Four

This British quartet showed their political sympathies by naming – not after the politicians who broke from the U.K. Labour Party, but a group engaged in a Chinese power struggle.

The GAP Band

Oklahoma band named from their homes Greenwood Archer and Pine.

Garbage

This rock band was formed by producer ⇨Butch Vig. His Web Site notes: "[Friend] Pauli Ryan heard some of the samples for the ⇨Nine Inch Nails remix that Butch was working on around 1994. He said, 'this shit sounds like garbage to me.' And Butch replied, 'yeah, but at some point I'm going to turn this garbage into a song.'" The remark's often wrongly attributed to Trent Reznor of Nine Inch Nails.

Judy Garland

The U.S. actress-singer (1922-1969) was born Frances Gumm. She renamed from theatre critic Robert Garland and a Hoagy Carmichael song that went: "If she seems a saint, and you find she ain't, that's Judy!"

Jerry Garcia

⇨(p.68) Captain Trips was born Jerome Garcia and is commemorated by Ben & Jerry's Cherry Garcia ice-cream.

Gay Dad

This short-lived British band was seeking attention, not referring to ⇨Puff Daddy. Unflattering derivative: Gay Fad.

Gaye Bykers On Acid

This British band, beset by questions on how the name came about, said Gaye was a fictional character created by artist Ray Lowry. They played up the joke with alter egos Lesbian Dopeheads On Mopeds (supposedly a butch band from down under); and Rëktum (masquerading as German heavy metal freaks).

Crystal Gayle

Brenda Gail Webb was given her stagename by her sister, ⇨Loretta Lynn, and signed with the same record label which already had a Brenda on its books, ⇨Brenda Lee.

Loretta took it from a Krystal hamburger sign: "Crystals are bright and shiny, like you."

Bob Geldof

His pre⇨Boomtown Rats journalism appeared as Rob Geldof; perhaps as well, for his full name was Robert Frederick Zenon Geldof. Daughters: Fifi Trixibelle (from his auntie Fifi and then-wife Paula Yates's desire to be a Southern Belle), Peaches and Pixie. Also: Saint Bob ("beatification" inspired by his tireless campaigns) and "Sir Bob". As an Irish citizen he isn't Sir Robert/Bob Geldof; the knighthood is honorary. He's Bob Geldof K.B.E., though in many people's minds he's "Sir Bob". Geldof doesn't bother to correct those who get it wrong, telling the author he's proud of the honour, that recognises he's helped millions, so the title is irrelevant. "I've got [bigger] things to sort out." Such as poverty, debt and environmental disaster no doubt.

Gene

This British group of the 1990s paid tribute to both 1950s star ⇨Gene Vincent and 1960s sensation Gene Pitney.

General Kane

U.S. band named by Mitch McDowell in tribute to an officer who helped him during his military training.

Generation X

Taken from the title of the 1964 survey book by Jane Deverson and Chris Hamblett owned by ⇨Billy Idol's mother.

Genesis

The name of the first chapter in The Bible was picked by record executive ⇨Jonathan King because these musicians were starting out when he met them, having played in schoolboy combos The Garden Wall and The Anon.

A receptionist asked for the band's name prior to an initial meeting with King, misheard and introduced them as "The Janitors". Their debut was a concept piece called *From Genesis To Revelation*.

Johnny Gentle

Another name cooked up by ⇨Larry Parnes. Ingredients: take a kid who can sing (here, John Askew). Method: saddle him with any name emphasising the sort of music he will perform (in this case, ballads.) Stir well, and you have a 1960s star. (This guy was even supported by ⇨The Beatles; their success swept away names like this.)

Bobbie Gentry

Roberta Streeter, of Chicasaw, Mississippi, named from the 1952 film *Ruby Gentry*, starring Charlton Heston.

A Dictionary of Rock and Pop Names

Georgia Satellites
Came from Georgia – U.S.A., not Russia. A reference to the aerospace industry.

Gerry And The Pacemakers
In 1959, the Pacemakers – as in the leaders who set the pace in a race – sounded a good name. How could Liverpudlian Gerry Marsden foresee the word's common use as an electronic heart stimulator? He also considered The Mars Bars, after the child's favourite, a play on Marsden and naïve attempt to win cash from the confectionery industry.

Stan Getz
The U.S. jazz saxophonist abbreviated his birthname Stanley Gayetzby.

G-Force
This band was formed by Gary Moore, whose pun on the figure representing total gravity is as bad as ⇨Waysted.

Ghostface Killah
Rapper Dennis Coles named in honour of the star of *Ninja Checkmate*. His group the Wu-Tang Clan loved martial arts films. His early appearances wearing a ghostly mask led to reports he was wanted by the police.

Giant Sand
From the *Dune* books (1963-64 and sequels), which were made into a 1984 science fiction film which featured ⇨Sting.

Gigolo Aunts
Named after *Gigolo Aunt* on former ⇨Pink Floyd man Syd Barrett's second album *Barrett* (1970).

Dizzy Gillespie
John Gillespie was named by his friend Fats Palmer because of his onstage clowning – playing inspired trumpet solos while dancing around in circles.

Otis "Elevator" Gilmore
Cincinnati's Danny Adler fabricated the name after record companies refused to release his recordings because he had a "white name" and therefore wasn't an "authentic" bluesman. He took Otis from a make of lift he operated at a Ohio book depository.

The Gin Blossoms
Named from a picture of W.C. Fields's gin-reddened nose, which he likened to "a giant strawberry".

A Dictionary of Rock and Pop Names

Girls At Our Best!
The misleading tag – like ⇨Everything But The Girl, they weren't an all female group – was a line in their first song, *Warm Girls*.

Kenny G
This U.S. saxophonist abbreviated his birthname Kenneth Gorelick, not the best of monikers for anyone other than a horror film star. Bad LP title: *G Force* (no relation to ⇨G-Force).

Glass Onion
Early ⇨Travis. Taken from *Glass Onion* by ⇨The Beatles. Cf ⇨Badfinger, which considered the name, offered to them by the Beatles direct.

Glasvegas
The band, asked about the name in 2007, said: "We think it sounds pretty, sugary and proud. We like that." Glasvegas was the name of a "super casino" which was to be built in their home city, Glasgow. It combines gritty Scotland with Las Vegas glitz.

The Glimmer Twins
Mick Jagger and Keith Richards of ⇨The Rolling Stones. For glam rock, stars don't need to shine, just twinkle. A nickname also used as formal production credit.

Gary Glitter
British singer Paul Gadd had been in showbiz for 12 years in 1971. He had taken his stepfather's surname to become Paul Russell (And His Rebels); then Paul Raven; Paul Monday; Boston International and even Rubber Bucket (for a single about a hippy squat).

He was advised by his record company to "bring more sparkle" into his act, and took this literally. He and manager/co-writer Mike Leander (born Michael Farr) dreamed up a range of flashy sequin jumpsuits and names such as Davey Dazzle, Horace Hydrogen, Stanley Sparkle, Terry Tinsel and Vicki Vomit. (Cf ⇨Larry Lurex, ⇨Alvin Stardust.)

They chose well and glam bam, thank you ma'am, the glitter bandwagon was born. Gary's back-up musicians, The Glitter Band, later became The G Band, while his hunky frame squeezed into silver suits led to the nickname The Bacofoil Bulk.

A legal dispute later broke out round the Glitter Band name. Glitter ran into more serious legal problems over Internet porn and was then jailed for child sexual abuse – which turned him from a star joke to pariah.

The Globs
No relation to ⇨BOB, The Blobs, The Nabob Of Sob or The Nobs! Stands for Global Village Tracking Company.

The Glove

This 1983 band related to ⇨The Cure and ⇨Siouxsie And The Banshees, made psychedelic music and named after a character in ⇨The Beatles' 1968 *Yellow Submarine*.

Gnarls Barkley

This duo formed in 2003. Producer ⇨(p.89) Danger Mouse said the name came about when friends were gnarling celebrities in a punning game. The choices included Prince Gnarls (Prince Charles), Bob Gnarley (⇨Bob Marley) and Gnarls Barkley (American basketball player Charles Barkley, 1963-). The duo's other half, rapper ⇨(p.70) Cee-Lo, has been evasive: "You ask me why we're called Gnarls Barkley and I'm asking you 'why not?'. The name Gnarls Barkley isn't anchored down. It's a drifter."

In a 2006 interview, Danger Mouse hedged: "There's no story behind it. The name doesn't have anything to do with anything." Asked about Charles Barkley, he said: "Nope. It's just like everything else, no conscious decision."

The Go-Betweens

This Australian band named from L.P. Hartley's 1953 story *The Go-Between*, later filmed – saying they act as go-betweens between the music and audience.

God

Nickname for ⇨Eric Clapton based on the "miracles" of his virtuoso playing. It was first heard during his membership of John Mayall's ⇨Bluesbreakers from 1965 to 1966. The first example of graffiti saying "CLAPTON IS GOD" was seen near Islington Tube Station and it subsequently appeared on other walls around London. (There were examples round Paddington persisting into the 1970s: some Internet sites wrongly claim there was only the one slogan.)

The Godfather Of . . .

Common nicknames for some of music's elder statesmen: The Godfather of Grunge: ⇨Neil Young. The Godfather of Punk: ⇨Malcolm McLaren, ⇨Lou Reed. The Godfather of R&B: ⇨Johnny Otis. The Godfather of Soul: ⇨James Brown. Cf ⇨The Modfather: ⇨Paul Weller.

The Godfathers

⇨The (New) Sid Presley Experience in 1985 namechecked Francis Ford Coppola's 1972-4 films for their religious and Mafioso associations.

Godspeed You! Black Emperor

These Canadian-based musicians translated *Goddo Supiido Yuu! Burakku Emperaa*, the 1976 film by Japan's Mitsuo Yanagimachi.

Gogol Bordello

This New York multi-lingual gypsy punk band, partly composed of immigrants from Eastern Europe, put on its dancing shoes in 1999. They first named Hütz and the

Béla Bartóks, though leader Eugene Hütz admitted that neither he nor the Eastern European composer was well known. They switched to writer Nikolai Gogol, who also exported Ukrainian culture, and added "Bordello" to emphasise their sexy cabaret.

Go Gos
⇨The Misfits took the same dancing inspiration as the ⇨Au Go-Go Singers when they renamed.

Golden Dawn
The words "cult writer" perfectly fit Aleister Crowley (1875-1947), a British occultist, eccentric, sexual guru and crackpot author of *The Sect Of The Golden Dawn*. Cf ⇨Kula Shaker, ⇨The MacGregors. The best-known Golden Dawn is from Austria.

Golden Earring
This Dutch band formed in 1961 to play soft numbers such as ballads from 1947 film *Golden Earrings*. By the 1970s Golden Earring made driving rock like *Radar Love*.

Goldie
From his home-made gold tooth-caps that also inspired his band Metalheads.

[44] Cheer up, Aleister Crowley: Golden Dawn, Kula Shaker and more love you.

Goodie Mob
This Atlanta hip-hop band, whose members include rapper ⇨Cee-Lo, formed in 1992. The name is spelled out on the 1995 track *Fighting*. It means "The Good Die Mostly Over Bullshit" and "God Is Every Man Of Blackness".

The Good, The Bad and The Queen
Interviews with creator Damon Albarn have him saying both that this band has no name and its 2007 album is "self-titled". Who in the act, if anyone, was good, bad or queenlike wasn't stated, although the album, with its Tower of London artwork, has much to say about modern Britain, which has its good and bad with the monarchy still in place. There was surprisingly little tabloid fury at the apparent impugning of the monarch using Sergio Leone's 1966 *The Good, The Bad And the Ugly*.

Goo Goo Dolls
The New York band formed in 1986 as the Sex Maggots and were offered a gig if they renamed as something less offensive that newspapers could print. They went

back to the papers to try to find something off-the-wall that WAS printable and named after an advert for a toy called a Goo Goo Doll.

Bill Graham

The concert promoter was a refugee called Wolfgang Grajonka who found his name in the Bronx phone book.

Graham Central Station

Former ⇨Sly and The Family Stone musician Larry Graham namechecked himself and New York's Grand Central Station.

Grand Funk Railroad

Named from Canadian route Grand Trunk Railroad.

Grandmaster Flash

Grandmasters, from the chess term, were MCs at music events. Joseph Saddler renamed for his flashy show with rapper Melle Mel (later Grandmaster Mel).

Grant Lee Buffalo

Los Angeles trio led by Grant Lee Phillips, who chose the near-extinct Buffalo in 1993 "as a symbol, of what's gone wrong with this century".

Grapefruit

Tony Rivers And The Castaways were renamed by ⇨John Lennon on signing to Apple in 1968. *Grapefruit* was a book of poems by Yoko Ono. Related: ⇨AC/DC.

The Grapes Of Wrath

Vancouver trio named after a 1939 masterwork about the depression by John Steinbeck. Cf ⇨East of Eden.

The Grateful Dead

What a long, strange trip it has been for this band which started in 1963 as The Hart Valley Drifters. The musicians tried names such as The Sleepy Hollow Hog Stompers and the Thunder Mountain Tub-Thumpers, and then became Mother McCree's Uptown Jug Champs, playing country, before metamorphosing into the rockier Warlocks.

They soon found other bands called The Warlocks. One was the early ⇨Velvet Underground on the other side of America. Another was a precursor to ⇨ZZ Top. ⇨Jerry Garcia was at a party when he decided their psychedelic music warranted a deeper name.

There's agreement he found "Grateful Dead" in a book.

He either found it (1) rapidly and at random, while the band played Valentinian Chance – fortune telling by blindfold-selection of passages; (2) after deliberation.

Some accounts say the others accepted it (1) with varying enthusiasm; other versions say (2) it was backed instantly.

The party's variously said to have been held at (1) bassist Phil Lesh's Palo Alto condo; (2) at the band's manager's house in downtown Los Angeles.

Some say Jerry was on (1) DMT; others that he was on (2) pot; others (3) he was on both and everything else he could get his hands on.

The name itself is said to have come from (1) an entry in an American alphabetical encyclopaedia, Funk and Wagnall's *New Practical Standard Dictionary*; (2) a phrase in *The Tibetan Book Of The Dead*; (3) an Egyptian prayer book; (4) The Oxford Dictionary; (5) The *Oxford Companion To Classical Music* or (6) a volume of Egyptian prayers.

For what it's worth, the best history of the band – as given by their publicist – gives the answers as all (1).

The "quick and grateful dead" legend in folklore tells of people who come back after death to help those still alive who helped them.

Name notes: Often called The Dead. Followers known as Deadheads. Spinoff: ⇨New Riders Of The Purple Sage. Members known as ⇨Captain Trips, ⇨Pigpen. Spinoff: ⇨Dinosaurs. Related: ⇨Jefferson Starship.

Great Society

Grace Slick's band made sardonic reference to U.S. President Johnson's 1964 "Great Society" speech, swept away by the cost of the Vietnam War. Related: ⇨Jefferson Airplane.

The Great Unwashed

⇨The Clean regrouped under this disparaging name for young people, referencing the cleanliness puns which cropped up in New Zealander press whenever the band was reviewed. LP title: *Clean Out Of Our Minds*.

Ric Grech

The ⇨Blind Faith, ⇨Traffic and ⇨Family self-effacing star's birth prenomen was Richard. Before his 1990 death he said he didn't care if he was billed as Ric, Rich and Rick as long as the bank accepted the cheques.

Green Day

The stars who made it big with *American Idiot* started in 1987 as Sweet Children. Larry Livermore, owner of Lookout! Records, recorded their title song *Sweet Children*. Just before its release, they wanted to rename because there was a local act called Sweet Baby.

Livermore says: "I went ballistic. I was like, 'Everybody knows you as Sweet Children. Green Day is dumb. It doesn't mean anything.'"

Their song *Green Day*'s has the singer enveloped in white mist as "my lungs comfort me with joy". It's always seen as about innocence and pot-smoking.

The drummer went from birthname Frank Wright III to Tré Cool. ⇨The Ramones influenced the choice of names of some of their children (there's more in the Ramones entry). Spinoff: ⇨Pinhead Gunpowder.

Green On Red

These rockers from Arizona formed in 1979 and named from one of their early songs.

Green River
This Seattle band named after a North-West region of the U.S., also recalling a 1969 title by ⇨Creedence Clearwater Revival. They'd wisely ditched alternatives The Limp Richards and The Ducky Boys and later became ⇨Pearl Jam.

Grim Reaper
This reference to the skeleton of death was discarded after the band played with Otis Redding on the night he died. They became ⇨Cheap Trick.

Grinderman
This spinoff from Nick Cave's ⇨Bad Seeds, formed in 2006 and had a song called *Grinderman*, in the tradition of ⇨John Lee Hooker's *Grinder Man* and ⇨Memphis Slim's *Grinder Man Blues*. As Slim intoned in 1941, "while everything is quiet and easy/Mr. Grinder can have his way" – a metaphor for society, relations and politics. The band was grinding up these old standards into a rough garage rock.

The Groaner
⇨The Old Groaner, ⇨Bing Crosby.

The Groundhogs
The British R&B band made an LP with John Lee Hooker and named after one of his songs (groundhog = American marmot).

Blind Boy Grunt
⇨Bob Dylan pseudonym, used several times. According to the CD set *The Bootleg Series Volumes 1-3* he used it for a Broadside disc because he was contracted to Columbia. He'd run out of words to sing and had to improvise to test the recording level. He was grunting into the microphone when someone asked for his name.

GTR
Founder Steve Hackett said the name reflected his plan "to re-establish guitar as the foremost rock instrument".

Guadalcanal Diary
Post-punk Atlanta band who liked the title of a 1943 action flick about a group of U.S. Marines.

(The) Guess Who
The Canadian band was floundering after four name changes in less than two years: The Silvertones, The Expressions, Allan And The Velvetones, Chad Allan And The Reflections. When they decided to cover ⇨Johnny Kidd's 1960 hit *Shakin' All Over*, their record company had the idea as marketing it as "Guess Who?" with a press release suggesting it was by a big U.K. group, moonlighting. Cf ⇨? And The Mysterians. Related: ⇨Bachman Turner Overdrive. Unrelated: ⇨The Who.

Guns 'N' Moses

Jewish heavy metal group based in Britain. Referring ⇨Guns N' Roses. Singer Ax'l Rosenberg; guitarists Cohan The Barbarian and Aerial Bombardment; drummer Alastair Arafat.

Guns N' Roses

Part of the band, featuring ⇨W. Axl Rose, had started playing as A.X.L., recalls guitarist Chris Webber: "After A.X.L. we changed the name to Rose, and then Hollywood Rose, because we'd seen a band called Rose from New York in a magazine and wanted to make the distinction."

Axl left to play with L.A. Guns (formed by Tracii Guns) and finally the two bands merged, combining Americans with English-born ⇨Slash. The composite name was chosen in preference to unlikely legends such as Heads of Amazon and AIDS.

Guns N' Roses implied a heavy metal, explosive sound; and recalled protesters putting flowers in the barrels of the guns carried by troops and police. Cf ⇨Guns 'N' Moses. Related: ⇨Velvet Revolver.

Guru

Gang Starr's rapper was born Keith Elam. "Guru" is an acronym for "Gifted Unlimited Rhymes Universal".

Woody Guthrie

Born in 1912 and named Woodrow Wilson Guthrie in honour of President Woodrow Wilson. Inspired ⇨Bob Dylan, ⇨Boomtown Rats; ⇨This Machine Kills; Woody Mellors, one of ⇨Joe Strummer's early names.

Haircut 100

Clean-cut 1980s U.K. popsters, their name suited their image. It was chosen over the ridiculous Captain Pennyworth And The Blatant Beavers.

Bill Haley

Born William John Clifton Haley Jnr. ⇨The Comets.

Half Man Half Biscuit

The Scouse scallies chose this to recall *The Elephant Man* film and Victorian 'freak shows'. Cf ⇨Limp Bizkit.

Hall And Oates

Daryl Hall was born Daryl Hohl. His first record with John Oates was credited to Whole Oates because of a misunderstanding at the printers.

A Dictionary of Rock and Pop Names

Johnny Halliday

Frenchman Jean-Philippe Smet got his stagename while touring with U.S. dancer Lee Halliday.

MC Hammer

Californian Stanley Burrell was a teenage baseball fan and idolised the local Oakland Athletic team, going to see every game. When he became their team mascot, someone remarked on his resemblance to their most famous player "Hammerin' Hank" Aaron. Also known as "McHammer".

Hanoi Rocks

Not from Vietnam, but the U.K. and Finland! From their song *Hanoi Rocks, Bangkok Shocks, Saigon Shakes*. Guitarist called Nasty Suicide.

Happy Mondays

Thought to be a poor joke, or an ironic comment, on fellow Mancunians ⇨New Order's 1983 *Blue Monday*, interpreted by some as a song about Ian Curtis, singer with New Order's predecessor group ⇨Joy Division, who killed himself on Sunday 18 May 1980. Guitarist Mark "Cow" Day simply wanted an antidote to all the doom and gloom which was also being disseminated by another local band ⇨The Smiths. Cf ⇨Oasis.

Hard-Fi

This British rock band formed in 2003. Singer Richard Archer's name inspiration was Jamaican reggae producer and musician ⇨Lee 'Scratch' Perry. In one biography Archer saw, Lee's sound was described as "Hard-Fi". In an interview, Archer added: "Since then I've been desperately trying to find the biography where I read it; but I may have dreamt it."

John Wesley Harding

This British folk-singer was born Wesley Stace. His prenomen was from Methodist founder John Wesley but also in a musical context recalled ⇨Bob Dylan's 1967 *John Wesley Harding*, a tribute to the Texas outlaw John Wesley Hardin, who was shot dead in August 1895. Cf ⇨Tim Hardin, ⇨(p.162) Judas Priest.

Tim Hardin

Discount suggestions that he chose it as a tribute to one Charles Hardin Holley (better known as ⇨Buddy Holly). Hardin is his real name and he's a descendant of outlaw John Wesley Hardin.

Steve Harley And Cockney Rebel

Londoner Steve Nice chose his surname from the street at the heart of the British capital's medical area, and the band name from natives of the city. ⇨Cockney Rejects.

Harlow

Vocalist Teresa Straley was pure platinum Jean Harlow. This American heavy metal band wasn't referencing Harlow in Essex, U.K. Cf ⇨Newtown Neurotics.

Harper Lee

This indie-pop duo formed in Brighton in 1999. They planned to release just one brilliant work and then disappear, like American novelists J.D. Salinger and Harper Lee. Cf ⇨The Boo Radleys.

Harpers Bizarre

Californian vocal harmony combo named from magazine *Harper's Bazaar*. Related to ⇨The Beau Brummels: an attempt to sound English at the height of the British invasion of the American charts.

George Harrison

During the time fellow Silver ⇨Beatles/Beetles were called Johnny Silver and Paul Ramon, he was Carl Harrison – in honour of one of his heroes, Carl Perkins.

Harrison later adopted *alter egos* such as Son of Harry (with Dave Mason); Hari Georgeson (with Splinter and the Ravi Shankar Family); and George Harrysong (with ⇨Harry Nilsson).

Playing with ⇨Cream and Jack Bruce, he became L'Angelo Misterioso ("The Mysterious Angel"). He was dubbed "the quiet one", "the mystery Beatle", "the business Beatle" (because he once asked the accountants how much they were worth) and "dark horse" – later the title of a 1974 LP and record label. He set up Harrisongs for his compositions.

He joined ⇨The Traveling Wilburys in 1988, co-producing their first LP under the name Nelson and then renaming Spike Wilbury to do the same job on their next.

Peppermint Harris

Texas blues record label boss Bob Shad was enthusing to a customer about his new signing: "This boy's gonna be big!" Shad was put in an awkward spot when asked the name of this signing, which he'd temporarily forgotten (it was Nelson Harrison). He was chewing on a mint and, without hesitation, firmly said the first thing that came into his mind.

P.J. Harvey

Polly Jean Harvey shortened to P.J. Harvey for similar reasons as ⇨k.d. lang, though the similarities end there.

Hatfield And The North

This British band formed in 1972. They liked the much-maligned London road signs which give prominence to the middling town of Hatfield. They never found the sign-posted route to Major Fame.

Screamin' Jay Hawkins

Ohio's Jalacy Hawkins named from wild vocals such as on 1956's *I Put A Spell On You*. Cf ⇨Screaming Lord Sutch.

The Hawks

Backers of Ronnie Hawkins. One incarnation of the avian name later flew to success as ⇨The Band.

Hawkwind

The British *Silver Machine* rock purveyors of the 1970s formed from the superbly-named Mobile Freakout and considered The Famous Cure (cf ⇨The Cure later) and Group X.

Their final choice was lauded by a generation of stoned hippies who thought it must mean something heavy: something to do with the slipstream from a predatory hawk perhaps. The connection was enhanced by a hawk logo. The name was originally Hawkwind Zoo, from a story by British author Michael Moorcock (1939-), who also inspired Tygers Of Pan Tang. He appeared with Hawkwind in concert and narrated their 1975 *Warrior On The Edge Of Time*.

Still, the complete truth is so prosaic it's simply hilarious, if you believe one ex-member of the group, ⇨Lemmy (who named ⇨Motörhead from a Hawkwind song and was sacked amid bitterness). He told the author he believed the Moorcock title was picked as an in-joke aimed at flautist/singer Nik Turner, who had aquiline features and a flatulence problem.

"I keep 'earing about some mythical bird, I mean of the feffered kind, called 'awkind," Lemmy said. "It's complete bollocks. ' E [Turner]-'ad a giant 'ook nose like a fucking 'awk's beak. THAT'S why we liked 'awkwind. And 'e was always farting like a bastard. That's it. End of story."

For legal reasons the band briefly was known as Hawklords.

[45] Hawkwind 1972: Lemmy considers revealing the truth behind the name…

H.E.A.L.

This was a loose group including Billy Bragg; rappers ⇨LL Cool J and KRS-One (meant "knowledge rules supreme over nearly everyone"); and members of ⇨Run DMC and ⇨R.E.M. Stood for "human education against lies".

Hear'Say

The British band formed from the winners of the 2001 *Popstars* TV talent show. The apostrophe was not a case of bad grammar, as some have suggested. The quintet was to be called Hearsay, then found there was another band of this name. Tribute band called Near Say. The show's five runners up formed ⇨Liberty X.

Heartbreakers

Among bands called this, an offshoot of ⇨The New York Dolls and ⇨Tom Petty's backers. Name inspirational sources include an ⇨Elvis Presley hit of 1956 and a Clint Eastwood film of 1986.

Heaven 17

The name comes from the novel *A Clockwork Orange*, the 1962 bleak vision of Anthony Burgess (1917-1993), filmed in 1971 by Stanley Kubrick. Burgess may well have been adapting the phrase "seventh heaven".

The anti-hero lists some bands liked by future teenagers. "These young devotchkas had their own like way of govoreeting. 'The Heaven Seventeen? Luke Stern? Goggly Gogol?'" On the opposite page, the hero,

[46] Heaven 17, The Droogs and Moloko were all referenced in *A Clockwork Orange*.

Alex, lists "the new pop-discs – Johnny Burnaway, Stash Kroh, The Mixers, Lay Quiet Awhile With Ed and Id Molotov". Cf ⇨The Mixers. The novel also inspired ⇨The Droogs, maybe ⇨Moloko and ⇨Korova Milkbar. Related: ⇨B.E.F, ⇨Human League.

Heaven West Eleven

This duo had a studio in London's W11 district: Notting Hill and Shepherd's Bush. (Cf ⇨Bush, ⇨East 17).

Heavy D And The Boys

Jamaican-born Dwight Myers wanted to be called McCloud after the U.S. TV cop. Instead, he put on weight and gained a cruel nickname. He tried dieting then changed his name: "It's quicker and easier."

Heavy Metal Kids

British band named after a William Burroughs quote about "heavy metal thunder" in his 1959 *The Naked Lunch*. The phrase soon applied to a whole genre of music, though this band was not typical of the genre. More Burroughs: ⇨Naked Lunch. ⇨Free almost named Heavy Metal Kids too.

Richard Hell

Richard Myers said his stagename fitted his new hell-raising personality. Punk showed it was possible, indeed desirable, to "reinvent yourself". The image was from French 19th-century poet Jean Rimbaud; his stage sparring partner at the time became ⇨Tom Verlaine. ⇨Television, ⇨The Heartbreakers, ⇨The Voidoids.

Helmet

Ex ⇨Band of Susans star Page Hamilton, like many other heavy rockers, was interested in Germany and acquired the nickname Helmut after Chancellor Helmut Kohl. The girlfriend of one of the other band members suggested it for the name for the group and Hamilton thought it would be "cool" with an English spelling to add a sexual connotation.

Jimi Hendrix

Official records list his birthname as Johnny Allen Hendrix, but his father insisted his son should have been James Marshall Hendrix and altered the name four years later. As Jimmy James he played with ⇨The Isley Brothers before forming Rainflowers, later called Jimmy James And the Blue Flames – named after ⇨The Blue Flames.

He reverted to Hendrix and changed the spelling to Jimi on crossing the Atlantic. The name of his best known group, The Jimi Hendrix Experience, was suggested by ex- ⇨Animal-turned-manager Chas Chandler from the slogan "The band you have to experience". This name was in turn the inspiration for the 1967 debut LP title cut *Are You Experienced?* Chandler also managed ⇨Slade and named ⇨Randy California.

Hendrix inspired in whole or part the naming of ⇨Cry Of Love, ⇨Colorblind James Experience, The Jean-Paul Sartre Experience, ⇨The Sid Presley Experience, ⇨Kiss The Sky, ⇨Kinky Machine, ⇨The Red House Painters, ⇨Third Stone and ⇨Voodoo Chile. His roadies included ⇨Lemmy.

Henry Cow

Nobody in the band was called Henry Cow. Their music followed U.S. pianist and composer Henry Cowell (1897-1965), best known for his experimentation after the style of John Cage. They were briefly called ⇨Cabaret Voltaire, a name later made famous by another act. Unrelated: ⇨Blodwyn Pig. Related: ⇨Comus.

The Herd

Late 1960s U.K. bopper band who made a fine pun on the collective for a group of animals and the past tense of hearing – their records were, after all, Heard. Not the greatest band in the world, but they just about win this book's Best Punning Name award (in front of ⇨Felt, ⇨The Jam, ⇨XTC, ⇨U2, The Swankers (⇨Sex Pistols), Riff

Raff, Voxpoppers, N-Trance, The Hit Squad (⇨808 State), ⇨The Hitmen, ⇨The Spin Doctors, Heartbeat, ⇨INXS, The Pop Tarts (⇨Pop Will Eat Itself), Altern8, King L and ⇨Linx.) Related: ⇨Humble Pie.

Herman's Hermits

The U.K. band noticed the similarity between leader Peter Noone and Sherman in the U.S. television programme *The Rocky And Bullwinkle Show*. They got the name wrong, but still thought it "hilariously American". The Hermits was chosen for alliterative effect.

Hetch Hetchy

Athens, Georgia, band who worked with Michael Stipe of ⇨R.E.M. The name from a Yosemite National Park valley.

The Highwaymen

This country band, featuring ⇨Johnny Cash, ⇨Kris Kristofferson, Waylon Jennings and Willie Nelson, named from a J. Webb composition: a folk Highwaymen named after a long poem by Alfred Noyes.

Hinder

This Oklahoma band formed in 2001. Founder and drummer Cody Hanson said the name was a response to the problems that had been hindering them up until that time: "When we first got together, we had our issues. We were all trying to overcome them."

His Latest Flame

After an ⇨Elvis Presley 1961 song. Started as Sophisticated Boom Boom (also title of ⇨Dead Or Alive's 1984 album).

Hitmen

There's been at least two groups called this – one an early 1980s outfit from Australia, an offshoot of Radio Birdman, and the other, a London group who made the LP *Aim For The Feet*. The latter said it combines "business (troubleshooters), firearms (sharp shooters) and pop (records)". Related ⇨Brilliant, ⇨Depeche Mode.

Hole

Another 1990s name short enough to be ambiguous (cf ⇨Blur), chosen by ⇨Courtney Love to "confuse people". Papers called it an "in the face" name recalling ⇨The Slits. Love dismissed their dirty minds, saying it was from Euripides, whose Medea talks of a hole piercing her soul. "It's about the abyss that's inside," she said in an interview.

Billie Holiday

The U.S. jazz singer was born Eleanora Fagan – the second name was her mother's; she later learned her real father was musician Clarence Holiday. Billie was from her favourite movie star, Billie Dove. ⇨(p.171) Lady Day.

Jools Holland
The piano player took the patrician edge off his real first name Julian. ⇨Squeeze.

The Hollies
Manchester, U.K., band formed 1961 as The Fourtones, whose final name was chosen as a tribute to ⇨Buddy Holly, who died in 1959. It seemed obvious, there already having been a band called The Iveys (no relation to the band that became ⇨Badfinger). Bad pun: Album called *Holliedaze*.

[47] Buddy Holly and The Crickets influenced The Beatles, The Hollies – and Hank B. Marvin.

Buddy Holly
Charles Hardin Holley was known as Buddy from an early age in Lubbock, Texas. The "e" in Holley was accidentally dropped when his first record contract was drawn up in 1956, a change he kept (but his grave says "In loving memory of Buddy Holley").

   With ⇨The Crickets, he influenced ⇨The Beatles, ⇨The Hollies and ⇨The Iveys.

The Honeycombs
This 1960s British group punned on their cloying music and featured drummer Ann Lantree who was nicknamed "honey" and a part-time hairdresser.

The Honeydrippers
Honeydripper was a 1945 hit for Joe Liggins And His Honeydrippers; he later set up the Honeydripper label. It was apt for this English R&B club band related to ⇨Chicken Shack, who played 1950s music by Otis Rush and ⇨Gene Vincent. They later teamed with Robert Plant of ⇨Led Zeppelin fame.

The Hoochie-Coochie Men
This band was formed by ⇨Long John Baldry in the 1960s, recalling a ⇨Muddy Waters song which says a hoochie-coochie man has power to seduce any women. Cf ⇨Hoodoo Gurus, ⇨The Mojos, ⇨Wall Of Voodoo, ⇨Voodoo Chile.

The Hoodoo Gurus
This Australian 1980s group named after black magic. They were originally Le Hoodoo Gurus, hoping the French sound was classy, until they got announced as "Three Loose Zulus".

John Lee Hooker
This Mississippi bluesman has used many pseudonyms, sometimes for contractual reasons, including the similar Johnny Lee and John Lee Booker. Inspired: ⇨The Crawling King Snakes, ⇨The Groundhogs.

Hootie And The Blowfish
The misleading moniker refers to two friends, Ervin 'Hootie' Harris and Donald 'Blowfish' Feaster. The nicknames were jokes among the University of South Carolina choir in which band leader Darius Rucker also sung.

Lightnin' Hopkins
Houston singer Sam Hopkins got his name for his fast guitar picking style while playing with piano-bar star Thunder Smith: they became Thunder and Lightnin'.

Hornets Attack Victor Mature
Hollywood leading man Victor Mature's handsome features were not designed to be wrecked by stings. This 1980s band, no great fans of Mature, took it from a Los Angeles paper story about the actor who was playing golf when he had to run for safety after stirring up a swarm. HAVM became famous as ⇨R.E.M. and returned to this name for a small 1985 gig: they guessed only true fans would recognise it.

Horslips
This Irish folk-rock band was at one point (in the 1970s) on the verge of big success despite what is the stupidest of names: "horse lips?" The group was originally "Horslypes," taken from a joke about the Four Horsemen of the Apocalypse, spooner-ised as "The Four Poxmen Of The Horslypse".

The Hothouse Flowers
Taken from a Wynton Marsalis title. A talent nurtured by ⇨U2.

Hot Tuna
This band wanted to be Hot Shit because they thought they had "shit hot tunes". After resistance from RCA, the name was revised. Related: ⇨Dinosaurs, ⇨Jefferson Airplane, ⇨SVT.

The Housemartins
Named after the bird and song. However, the birds are (unlike, say, ⇨Nightingales) not particularly noted for their tunes. Related: ⇨The Beautiful South.

[48] House of Love wore their name origin right on their sleeve for one CD.

The House Of Love

This British band named in 1986 from Anaïs Nin's 1954 poetic and sensual novel *Spy In The House of Love*. It was no connection with the ⇨Was Not Was single of this name, as sometimes reported. That was recorded in 1988. They emphasised their inspiration by picturing the book on an album cover.

Howlin' Wolf

Mississippi-born Chester Arthur Burnett knew that some wolves howl at the moon, and so he did in his evening Memphis KMW Radio slot, adapting Jimmie Rodgers to a tortured blues cry which became *Moanin' At Midnight*. His name was parodied by U.K. 1980s singer *Howlin' Wilf*.

Huang Chung

The exotic name suggests a non-British band, and their music was heavy with Chinese influences. Bassist Nick Feldman said it was the onomatopoeic sound of a guitar chord. Later spelled Wang Chung.

Hues Corporation

This American band named after a conglomerate run by the billionaire Howard Hughes. Los Angeles producer Wally Holmes had wanted to call them Children Of Howard Hues but was informed this was legally dangerous.

Huggy Bear

U.S. detectives *Starsky And Hutch* spent 1975-1979 leaping in and out of fast cars in a TV show that also inspired ⇨Lovebug Starski. Their street-contact is Huggy. The British ⇨Riot Grrrl act named ironically after him.

Human League

The League's antecedents all date from Sheffield, U.K., in the mid-1970s, including the punkish Musical Vomit – not an auspicious beginning. By 1977, Martin Ware and Ian Craig-Marsh were known as The Dead Daughters. They renamed as The Future – a good choice, noting their electronic divergence from punkoid guitar. Phil Oakey saw them and agreed they were "ahead of their time". He joined as the name changed to The Men and The Human League, from the science fiction computer game *Starforce*.

Computer-game fans Ware and Craig-Marsh, the band's founders, later left and formed ⇨B.E.F. and ⇨Heaven 17. Oakey paid them to keep rights to the Human League name. Related: ⇨The Rezillos.

Humble Pie

Press speculation was generated by the group's impressive antecedents including ⇨The Herd and ⇨The Small Faces. Steve Marriott responded with this name to show they weren't suffering from inflated egos. The expression "to eat humble pie" means to act humbly or to eat one's words.

Engelbert Humperdinck

Born Arnold George Dorsey in 1936, he found fame with the ridiculous name performing ballads in 1965. It was suggested by his former flatmate ⇨Gordon Mills, who looked to the past for inspiration. He borrowed it from a 19th century German opera composer, the man behind *Hänsel Und Gretel*. "Enge" later became "Mr Romance".

Hüsker Dü

This critically lauded American mid-1980s band from Minnesota began playing together in 1982. One of their first jam sessions was spent trying cover versions. First they did ⇨Ramones songs and then they tried a rough take on *Psycho Killer* by ⇨Talking Heads. Bob Mould and his fellow group members could not remember the foreign language phrase in the chorus ("Qu'est-ce que c'est?"). Instead they began shouting any other foreign phrases they could think of. One of them said "Hüsker Dü" and the others said, "What?"

[49] The original Engelbert Humperdinck pictured circa 1880.

Hüsker Dü (note the accents) is a Scandinavian game first published in Denmark and then Sweden in the 1950s before being exported under its original name, and in translation, to Britain and the U.S. in the 1970s. The game is meant to encourage memory and means "Do you remember?" in Danish and Norwegian.

Mould said it was mysterious and set them aside from other hardcore punk bands with political names.

HMV

Stands for "His Master's Voice". Name of record label and chain of record stores. Taken from a Francis Barraud painting bought by EMI chairman William Owen, showing Barraud's bull terrier cross, Nipper, looking quizzically at a gramophone. The make of phonograph depicted was changed at Owen's request. Inspired ⇨Bow Wow Wow.

The Hype

This Irish outfit started in autumn 1976 as ⇨Feedback. No relation to The Hype, a band backing Londoner ⇨David Bowie (he reinvented them as The Spiders From Mars); and Hazel O'Connor's group Megahype.

They soon realised that The Hype could alienate record companies and be taken as an admission that they were an empty talent which needed hyping. It could also be seen as self-disparaging as their last name.

[50] The touching His Master's Voice doggie picture that became HMV's logo.

In 1978, fifth member Dick Evans walked offstage during a concert in the Presbyterian Church Hall in Howth. The remaining four completed the concert under the new name they had found, ⇨U2.

I

I Am the World Trade Center

New York couple Dan Geller and Amy Dykes named in 1999 after the twin World Trade Center towers, which dominated their skyline and which they thought symbolized their personal and musical relationship. After the September 11, 2001 attacks, they knew the silly-sounding name could cause offence. They toured as "I Am The World", then added an explanation at the start of each show.

A Dictionary of Rock and Pop Names

Janis Ian
This New York singer, born in 1951 as Janis Fink, adopted her brother's prenomen for her stage surname.

Ibex
A precursor of ⇨Queen; the moniker was suggested by drummer Mike Smith, who thought it sounded Dadaist. ⇨Freddie Mercury renamed the band Wreckage after finding Ibex meant "wild goat".

Icehouse
Australian act Flowers ran into two problems. First was the commercial death of their 1980 debut, entitled *Icehouse*. Second, they faced a challenge from a Scottish act also called The Flowers. They remixed the LP and renamed. An icehouse is slang down under for an asylum, a "cooler" for cooling off lunatics.

Ice T
New Jersey kid Tracey Lauren Marrow needed a cooler name. He abbreviated his prenomen to play on "iced tea". The choice (1) fitted street slang where "ice" means "cool" and (2) honoured black-rights writer Iceberg Slim. This happened before the drug Ice, smokeable methamphetamine, started to appear. The rapper-actor is also called "O.G." or "Original Gangster". Cf ⇨Vanilla Ice.

Vanilla Ice
Rapper Robert Van Winkle recalls his Miami youth: "Ice came from the kids I hung out with. Every one was black, and I had the vanilla skin, so that's what they called me." Cf ⇨Ice T, ⇨Vanilla Fudge.

Idle Race
Jeff Lynne started in this Brummie band who named after an early song. He went on into ⇨ELO, ⇨The Traveling Wilburys and produced ⇨George Harrison and ⇨The Beatles. Not so idle after all.

Billy Idol
William Michael Albert Broad joined ⇨Bromley Contingent, ⇨Chelsea and ⇨Generation X and said of his stagename: "It's a joke, right, but smart and better than ⇨Sid Vicious or Dee Generate [⇨Eater]." In later interviews, he added the story of a teacher in school who wrote "William Is Idle".

Unflattering derivatives: Billy Idle, Bone Idol (because of his leisurely recording schedule). Nickname: Sir William. Son: Willem Wolf Broad.

Immaculate Consumptive
⇨Madonna isn't the only star to take off the religious term "immaculate conception", referring to Jesus being miraculously conceived in the Virgin Mary. (Madge's 1990 CD was called *The Immaculate Collection*.)

This band comprised ⇨Mark Almond, Nick Cave, ⇨Foetus man Jim Thirlwell and Lydia Lunch. They took the name in reference to their thinness – all were skinny, even Lydia Lunch, who looked like she'd had none.

The Immaculate Fools
One of many bands to chose a self-mocking name (cf ⇨Simple Minds etc), this 1980s U.K. outfit accepted they "may not be Einstein" but "wear it well".

The Impediments
The name came because these Minneapolis musicians started with a greater reputation for drinking than performing. They straightened up as ⇨The Replacements.

Incognito
Producer Jean-Paul Maunick, always a backroom boy, chose to keep out of the spotlight with his own band.

Incubus
There have been a few acts of this name. The best known Incubus, signed to Sony, formed in California in 1992. Guitarist Mike Einziger loved the legend of a mythical demon who has sex with sleeping women.

The Ink Spots
The 1930s name came from the days when groups kept things simple: it referred to their individual "spot" in concert as well as their colour.

Inspiral Carpets
Pronounced "In-spiral", as in inspirational, mind expanding, shimmering 1960s songs, spinning records, swirling shirts, even spirals in carpets – possibly as seen after taking acid tabs. All of this was just fantasy to the British schoolboys who launched this band in 1980 as The Furs, a tribute to ⇨The Psychedelic Furs. One of their roadies, Noel Gallagher, said his time with The Inspirals yielded the name ⇨Oasis.

The Intelligent Hoodlum
The real name of this New York teenager, initially a secret, was Percy Chapman. His alias came about because he said he was a reformed criminal. "I was too intelligent for crime!" In 2007, then called Tragedy Khadafi (a reference to dictator Muammar al-Gaddafi), he was jailed for drugs offences. Not so intelligent.

INXS
The pun works if you spell it out. Say "In Excess", not "Inks". They began in 1977 as The Farriss Brothers, three members of the Australian Farriss family. The new name was suggested by ⇨Midnight Oil manager Garry Morris.

In 1997, frontman Michael Hutchence was found dead after living "INXS 2 The Max". He had a daughter with Paula Yates called Heavenly Hiraani Tiger Lily.

IQ

These intellectual U.K. musos lifted the name from a 1960s headline about Oxford-educated Privilege singer Paul Jones: "Can a pop star have too high an I.Q.?" Cf ⇨The Zombies.

Iron Butterfly

Leader Doug Ingle said the name reflected the U.S. band's desire to move between light and heavy sounds. He found it after reflecting on "insect" aliases such as ⇨The Beatles and ⇨The Crickets. He only later heard of the Aztec god Itzapapalotl, meaning "stone butterfly", and wasn't referencing singer Jeanette MacDonald, sometimes referred to as Iron Butterfly. Jimmy Page said the choice had some bearing on ⇨Led Zeppelin's moniker.

Cat Iron

The U.S. blues singer (1896-1958) got his stagename when a reporter misheard his real name William Carradine.

Ironing Board Sam

South Carolina musician Sammy Moore had makeshift-mounted his keyboard on an ironing board for one show. He hated his nickname at first but later gave away ironing boards to concert-goers.

Iron Maiden

This British heavy metal band named after an old-fashioned torture instrument. (This came in two models. The Middle Ages version was a human-shaped cage on a rope to drop unfortunates in water until they drowned or confessed. The later deluxe model enclosed the victim in metal "maidens" – coffin-shaped sections with sharp inward-facing spikes.)

Maiden was formed in 1975 by bassist Steve Harris, who previously played in Smiler, and took the name after seeing a movie adaptation of *The Man In The Iron Mask*. It also became a song of the same title. It's not a reference to East London soccer team West Ham United, sometimes called the Irons, who Maiden support, or to British politician Margaret Thatcher, who became known as "Iron Lady" in 1976 and Prime Minister in 1979.

[51] Iron Maidens: every home should have one. Fun for all the family.

Isley Brothers

They were all brothers, Rudolph, Ronald, O'Kelly, Vernon, Ernie and Marvin. Then they cheated and added cousin Chris Jasper.

It Crawled From The South
⇨R.E.M. put Athens, Georgia, on the rock map. This was a concert billing, recalling films like *It Crawled From The Deep* and *It Came From Outer Space*.

It's A Beautiful Day
Inspired by the weather conditions in San Francisco on the July 1967 day they formed. Their optimism had dimmed by 1978 – or perhaps the weather wasn't so good. They reformed as It Was A Beautiful Day.

The Iveys
"The Iveys" was a tribute to ⇨Buddy Holly. As in *The Holly And The Ivy* Christmas carol. It coincidentally recalled a street in their native Swansea, Wales. Contrary to reports, it wasn't a "holly and ivy" corollary to rivals ⇨The Hollies, who were also just starting out.

   By the time they signed to the infant ⇨Apple label in 1968, a name like The Iveys was looking dated. This hadn't stopped The Hollies from making it big by then, or indeed ⇨The Beatles (both named with Holly in mind). The Iveys also risked confusion with ⇨The Ivy League and they became ⇨Badfinger.

The Ivy League
In the American tradition of "clean-cut" college names (⇨The Crew Cuts, Four Preps, ⇨The Lettermen), they hailed from Birmingham, U.K., but imitated U.S. close-harmonies and referenced the league of "top" American universities. They later became ⇨The Flowerpot Men.

J

The Jackson Five
There were five Jacksons. It took a long time to find a name . . . After Michael left, Randy arrived so the name stayed . . . They became The Jackson Family, then The Jacksons after a label change, because ⇨Motown owned the mark "Jackson Five". Cf ⇨New Edition.

Jackson Heights
Founder Lee Jackson was English and didn't know much about Jackson Heights, New York, but thought it apposite.

Michael Jackson
Michael Joseph Jackson's nicknames, good and bad: Jacko, ⇨The King Of Pop, MJ, ⇨Wacko Jacko, The Gloved One (from his single, white-sequinned glove). Tribute act: Mikki Jay. ⇨Jackson Five.

   His son's Michael Joseph Jackson Jnr, AKA Prince Michael Junior. The name was seen by some as a slight on ⇨Prince. Others said it allowed Michael to invest a future Prince of Pop. In a 1997 interview with *OK!* magazine, he said: "My grandfather and great-grandfather were both Prince, so we have carried on the tradition and now have a third in the family." He also has a daughter, Paris Katherine Jackson.

There are unprintable nicknames, with one Internet band trying to claim the name Michael Jackson Sleepover Club.

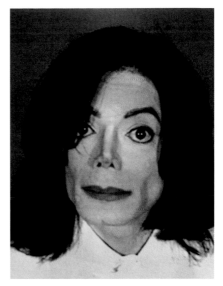

[52] Police booking photo for Michael Jackson, King of Pop.

Mick Jagger
⇨Rolling Stone Sir Michael Philip Jagger, knighted 2003. Nickname Ol' Rubberlips.

Jale
Female quartet from Canada, named ⇨ABBA-style after their initials. Jenny (Pierce), Alyson (MacLeod), Laura (Stein) and Eve (Hartling).

The Jam
This British band named from breakfast conversation among Paul Weller's family. His mother, Ann, recalls: "Nicky [Paul's sister] said: 'We've had the bread and the marmalade, so let's have the jam." (Perhaps referencing bands ⇨Bread, The Marmalade: "jam" is English for breakfast jelly.)

The trio met for "jam sessions" at their school in Woking. Jam was short enough to print up big on posters like that of their idols, ⇨The Who. Spinoff: ⇨The Style Council. Inspired: ⇨Stone Roses.

Jam & Spoon
The surname of one half of this production duo was German for Spoon (Markus Löffel, 1966-2006). He worked with Rolf Ellmer under pseudonyms Tokyo Ghetto Pussy and Storm.

James
This British band took the first name of one of the members. The first choice was "Tim". The singer didn't want his name taken in vain. The line-up had two Jameses. Bassist Jimmie Glennie said it was "simple, unassuming and doesn't give any clues": the same reasons fellow Mancunians ⇨The Smiths named. In their early punk days they were Venereal And The Diseases, then Model Team International. Guitarist Paul Gilbertson's girlfriend worked for an agency of this name, who objected to using it on tee shirts.

The James Gang
Their name came from the outlaws led by Jesse James. Joe Walsh went on into ⇨The Eagles. Unrelated: ⇨James.

Rick James

The singer was James Johnson, briefly Rick Matthews. Some of his name changes were reportedly bids to avoid arrest as a U.S. Navy deserter. ⇨The Mynah Birds, ⇨The Mary Jane Girls, ⇨The Main Line, ⇨Punk Funk Chorus.

Jamie Wednesday

This U.K. band formed on a Wednesday and named after ⇨Jim Morrison of ⇨The Doors. Inspired ⇨Pop Will Eat Itself. Related: ⇨Carter USM.

Jamiroquoi

U.K. star James Kay (1970-) named after an American Indian tribe. He uses Jason as a first name (think "J., son of Kay") and also performs as Jason Kay and Jay Kay. Nickname: ⇨The Cat In The Hat.

Jane's Addiction

This Los Angeles rock-punk band made it big in the 1990s. They claimed Jane was a junkie Hollywood hooker through whom they all met in the 1980s, although this story may be a piece of self-mythologizing. ⇨Perry Farrell, ⇨Lollapalooza, ⇨Porno For Pyros.

Japan

This British synthesiser combo wanted a moniker that showed they weren't another punk guitar act. They hailed from Lewisham and thought Japan more exotic. Their music showed eastern influences (titles: *Life In Tokyo, Visions Of China* etc.) Related: ⇨Dali's Car, ⇨Rain Tree Crow, ⇨David Sylvian.

Jay And The Americans

The 1950s and early 1960s saw some groups striving to project a "decent" short-haired image in the face of McCarthyism and backlash against "unAmerican" values. Hence also ⇨The Crew Cuts. Related: ⇨(p.263) Steely Dan.

Jay-Z

Shawn Corey Carter is one of the richest men in rap and the boss of Def Jam and Roc-A-Fella. Never heard of him? Well, you have of his alter-ego Jay-Z. He was given the nickname Jazzy when growing up and this led to the stagename. It pays tribute to his musical mentor Jaz-O, as well as to the J/Z subway lines in Brooklyn.

Jaz-O

Jonathan Burks is one of many New York rappers to adopt a "jazz" name. The "O" in this case means Originator: his song *The Originators* featured a young ⇨Jay-Z.

Jefferson Airplane

Another origin which is frequently incorrectly reported. It isn't a drug reference. Less credibly, but truthfully, it was the name of a dog they knew – never pictured but reliably reported to have existed.

The pooch's name included "Blind" – the animal wasn't visually impaired; this was a reference to scores of impaired blues players especially Blind Lemon Jefferson, whose work was revered by guitarist Jorma Kaukonen.

Some biographies say the canine's name also contained "Thomas", a reference to the American president. The "Airplane" came from the Jefferson aeronautics company. The name was in place by 1965.

1970s: a Jefferson Airplane was San Francisco slang. It was a clip defined in *Chapman's Dictionary* as any tweezer-like device for holding a smoking joint too small to be gripped without burning. The device was named from the group. However several magazine articles got the truth the wrong way round and suggested the band named from the clip.

1980s: The musicians were trying to correct the flood of incorrect reports, although the Airplane's place in drug culture was by now such that their denials fell on deaf ears. Cf ⇨The Roches and ⇨The Doobie Brothers.

Related: ⇨Great Society, ⇨Hot Tuna, ⇨Jefferson Starship, ⇨Dinosaurs, ⇨SVT. Inspired: ⇨Airhead. Oh, and Grace Slick called her daughter China and her son God.

Jefferson Starship

Part two of the ⇨Jefferson Airplane saga started in 1970 with Jefferson Starship. This higher-flying name originated from co-founder Paul Kantner's sci-fi future vision. He denied naming from *Starship*, the ⇨MC5 track of the year before.

Jellybean

John Benitez (1957-), known for work/relationship with ⇨Madonna, was renamed by his sister because of his fondness for jellybean candy.

The Jesus And Mary Chain

Scots brothers William and Jim Reid have been delivering noise terror since the 1980s. Amid their dark lyrics and heavy menace, it's not surprising they first considered the tag Death Of Joey. Sadly the moniker wasn't inspired by the overdose suicide of a Kilbride mass murderer, as might be supposed, but the demise of the teenage boys' pet budgerigar. Wisely, they decided the choice had to be buried too, before they encountered ridicule.

The author was misled by the band and had to keep going back to find to truth – which is that the choice was an evolution of "Daisy Chain" and intended as meaningless.

When I first approached the Reids' record company, the Chain repeated that the name was inspired by a breakfast cornflakes packet, which had an offer to send for a "Jesus And Mary" linked bracelet. Checks confirmed the obvious: major cereal manufacturers in the U.K. stated that their free gifts would never include such a religious item because of the danger of offence.

When this was pointed out, the Chain switched to another tall story: it came from dialogue in a ⇨Bing Crosby film. I dutifully ploughed through videos of every Crosby film (pity me), with no success.

By now I was aware of various other explanations offers by the duo: that it was a solid gold $200 necklace advertised in a magazine. That it was a chain letter. That it was an order of Catholic nuns (cf ⇨Sisters Of Mercy). That it was a religious shrine in Greece or Mexico. That it was an obscure satanic cult . . . . All false. A more likely theory is that it came from McGee's Club, London, owned by their manager Alan McGee, where they played gigs. The problem with this is that the name came before they moved to the British capital.

William Reid finally said: "These stories are wrong . . . . We knew the word Jesus was sacred to Christians but after all Jesus is the commonest name in some places. Nobody minds the 'Mary." (Cf ⇨Jesus Jones.)

The band's publicists were aware of its shock value, as they later confided in the author (maybe they were impressed or bemused by my persistence). "We know it would upset people." This "likely to offend" aspect rebounded on the Reids when they were banned from U.S. TV shows on account of the name, which they refused to shorten to "J.A.M. Chain" as prudish producers suggested. (Cf ⇨"B.H. Surfers" for ⇨Butt Hole Surfers.)

Related: ⇨Primal Scream.

Jesus Jones

The British band's founders were on vacation, sitting in a Spanish bar and being served by a waiter called Jesus. They commented his religious prenomen was not used for babies back home, where it could be seen as blasphemous. They pictured a few names: Jesus Smith, Jesus Jones . . . started laughing and stopped there.

Jet

There have been almost a dozen professional bands called Jet. The best known formed in 2001 in Melbourne, Australia, named from *Jet*, a track on the ⇨Wings 1973 album *Band on the Run*.

Jethro Tull

The London band was struggling for gigs and forced to give itself a new name almost every time, often chosen by booking agents. After using Navy Blue (not great because their music wasn't blues) they were booked at the Marquee Club as Jethro Tull, after a leading 18th-century British agriculturalist; an agent had by chance seen Tull's book *New Horse Hoeing Husbandry* about a labour-saving seed drill. The club manager John Gee was the first to give them a repeat booking, so the name stayed.

Disregard stories that the name was chosen by Chrysalis in preference to Bag O' Blues – Tull was there before the band signed. A 1968 single, *Aeroplane*, mistakenly credited "Jethro Toe" but flopped, saving them from an unfortunate name. The name's often attached just to leader Ian Anderson, or abbreviated to Tull. Related: ⇨Blodwyn Pig.

[53] Farmer Jethro Tull (1674-1741) contemplates rock music fame.

Jimmy Eat World

This name isn't a reference to this Arizona band's singer Jim Adkins. Guitarist Tom Linton chose it in 1993 to highlight a family joke: the feud between his brothers Ed and Jimmy. The latter would usually win the fights because he was heavier. Eight-year-old Ed responded by drawing a caricature of Jimmy swallowing the globe with the caption, "Jimmy eat world". The drawing was probably inspired by *Tiny Toon Adventures*' sketch *Dizzy Eat World*.

Billy Joel

When fame beckoned Bronx boy William Martin Joel, he rejected a stagey moniker. "Ain't nothing wrong with a downtown name."

Elton John

The British star was born in 1947, in Pinner, as Reginald Kenneth Dwight – a name, he later said, that "sounded like a cement mixer".

At 14 he joined Bluesology. They backed both ⇨The Ink Spots on a British tour and Doris Troy, but the piano man quit, preferring songwriting with his partner Bernie Taupin. Urged to find a showbizzy tag by publisher Dick James (⇨DJM), Dwight cast his mind back to Bluesology – and two latecomers: sax player Elton Dean and front-man ⇨Long John Baldry. He had created Elton John before the end of 1967.

He legally became Elton Hercules John later. Hercules was one of his songs, on the contemporaneous *Honky Chateau* album. He said: "It gave me something to look up to and to remind me always to be strong." It's sometimes said to be after the rag-and-bone man's horse in U.K. TV series *Steptoe And Son*.

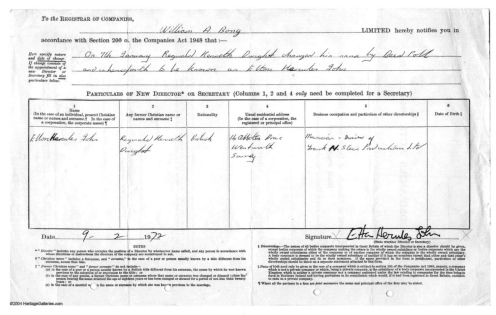

[54] It's official: Company director Reginald Kenneth Dwight becomes Elton Hercules John.

159

John used his original name as the title for the 1988 LP *Reg Strikes Back*. An early budget-priced remake of others' hits was later released on CD as *Reg Dwight's Piano Plays Pop*.

At the end of 1997, he was knighted for services to music. Sir Elton joins other "pop knights" including ⇨Bono (honorary), ⇨Bob Geldof (honorary), ⇨Sir Paul McCartney, ⇨Sir Tom Jones, ⇨Sir Mick Jagger, Sir George Martin and ⇨Sir Cliff Richard.

⇨Captain Fantastic, ⇨The Brown Dirt Cowboy. Spoof act: Elton Jack.

Johnny And The Self-Abusers
The ⇨Simple Minds story starts with this 1977 Glasgow band. The name established their punk credentials before they'd played anything. Inspired: ⇨The Cocteau Twins. Spinoff: ⇨The Cuban Heels.

Johnny The Fox
Nickname for Phil Lynott after 1976 ⇨Thin Lizzy album title track *Johnny The Fox Meets Jimmy The Weed*.

Holly Johnson
The ⇨Frankie Goes To Hollywood singer said he renamed from William Johnson in honour of the transvestite hero of ⇨Lou Reed's 1973 *Walk On The Wild Side* (rather than to ⇨Buddy Holly). Related: ⇨Big In Japan.

Jo Jo Gunne
Early 1970s spinoff from ⇨Spirit, named after a ⇨Chuck Berry song that rhymed with their hit, *Run Run Run*.

Al Jolson
Anglicisation of Asa Yoelson.

John Paul Jones
The English multi-instrumentalist, known for his work for ⇨Led Zeppelin, started life as John Baldwin in 1946. His original name wasn't very appealing, he thought. The stagename was suggested by ⇨Rolling Stone manager Andrew Loog Oldham, who had seen a poster for the film of that name in France. John Paul Jones (1747-1792) was a naval hero.

Oran 'Juice' Jones
This U.S. singer's (1959-) real name Oran produced the 'Juice' nickname joke. No relation to ⇨Orange Juice.

Tom Jones
Thomas Woodward was born in Glamorgan in 1940 and spent eight years singing for small cash, first as Tiger Tom and then as Tommy Scott And The Senators (a bid to sound exotic in Merthyr Tydfil clubs). He chose Scott as a good name for a rocker and for having the right alliterative ring. He was spotted by pop entrepreneur

⇨Gordon Mills, who wasn't impressed with the name: Woodward wasn't Scottish; the Senators weren't American. Mills got inspiration from a film he'd just seen, 1963's *Tom Jones* starring Albert Finney.

Mills thought it would link the singer to the successful movie (based on a 1749 Henry Fielding novel), associate Jones with the raffishly-romantic hero, provide an easy name to remember, emphasise his roots (Jones being a common name in Wales) and provide a visual image. (Jones was soon decked out in tight breeches, backed by The Squires.)

Unflattering derivative: The Prince Of Wails (a nickname also used for ⇨Johnnie Ray). Nicknames: The Voice, Jones The Voice. Jones was later knighted.

[55] Albert Finney in the 1963 movie that gave Tom Jones his stagename.

Journey

This San Francisco AOR combo began as The Golden Gates, after the city's bridge. They held a contest for a new name and rejected all 3,000 entries after thinking of Journey themselves. Related: ⇨Santana.

Joy Division

This celebrated Manchester band started at the height of punk, the summer of 1977. Their singer Ian Curtis sought guidance from ⇨The Buzzcocks manager Richard Boon. Curtis's widow Deborah says Ian was "deeply irritated" when Boon offered The Stiff Kittens as a standard punk name.

Instead they paid homage to ⇨David Bowie by becoming ⇨Warsaw, then reconsidered.

It was vital for bands of the time to have a supposedly shocking name to rival ⇨The Sex Pistols. So the final handle came in 1978, from a 1955 paperback novel about Nazi concentration camps, *The House Of The Dolls*, written by one 'Ka-Tzetnik 135633'. The Joy Division was the area of the prison which housed prostitutes.

Joy Division later evolved into ⇨New Order, a name said to have similar influences. Joy Division was never an apt choice though. While the band delighted the critics, they never sounded joyful, with brilliant

[56] Smile please! Joy Division: never the most appropriate of names. L-R: Peter Hook, Ian Curtis, Bernard Sumner, Stephen Morris.

tracks about isolation, depression and desolation – and Curtis sounding perpetually on the verge of the suicide he later committed.

The Joy Of Cooking

Californian vocalists Toni Brown and Terry Garthwaite wrote feminist lyrics and named from a non-politically correct book which claimed a woman's role is to please her man above all.

Judas Priest

This British band formed in the mid 1960s and used the exclamation "Judas Priest!" – sometimes used in place of "Jesus Christ!"

Many articles have said – wrongly – that the name came from ⇨Bob Dylan's 1968 *The Ballad of Frankie Lee And Judas Priest*. First, the name predates the song – probably anyway, if not certainly. Second, Priest, who started as a pub blues outfit, progressing to rock and heavy metal, never sounded in the slightest like Dylan. Third, they told the author so. They just thought the name gave some idea of what the music sounded like. Influenced: ⇨Exciter.

K

Kaiser Chiefs

This British rock band's members were and are fans of local soccer club Leeds, whose long-serving captain and defender Lucas Radebe once played for South Africa's Kaizer Chiefs. Before retiring from playing he was known as "The Chief."

"We heard the name and thought it was cool," singer Ricky Wilson said. They're commonly called the Kaisers (just occasionally the Chiefs). Not to be confused with Scandinavian act Kaizers Orchestra.

Kajagoogoo

The 1980s British teen idols, who hit number one with their debut single, *Too Shy*, started in 1979 as Art Nouveau. In 1981 they added Christopher Hamill as a singer (⇨Limahl). Nick Beggs (founder, bassist, later lead singer himself) suggested Kajagoogoo.

Beggs told the author in an interview: "I wanted a name that had no meaning. The sound a baby makes sprung to mind. Gagagoogoo. I just changed the first bit. Kajagoogoo." The suitable modification made it nicely memorable. It isn't a reference to Elias Kazanjoglou, birthname of Elia Kazan, the director of *On The Waterfront*.

Limahl later left; the four-piece carried on as Kajagoogoo before reducing to a trio called Kaja (1985-6.) In 2007 Kajagoogoo was back, still as a trio.

A Dictionary of Rock and Pop Names

Kane Gang
Combination of Citizen Kane, and ⇨Sam Cooke's song *The Chain Gang*. They said: "We just took the greatest film ever made and the best song and put them together."

Kasabian
Kasabian's members hail from England, although their name influences are elsewhere. Kasabian's an Armenian name from Turkish "kasab", or butcher. Its meaning is ironic: the Charles Manson cult "family" included Linda Kasabian, who became the star witness in the murder case against him. Former guitarist Chris Karloff found Linda's name while reading up on Manson. Bassist Chris Edwards said the rest of the band thought it was "cool".

Danny Kaye
Anglicisation/ simplification of Daniel Kominsky. Cf ⇨Neil Diamond.

KC And The Sunshine Band
Their leader was Harry Wayne Casey: KC from his surname. "Sunshine": from Sunshine Junkanoo, a style of music.

Keane
The British piano rock band started in 1995 as a covers act called The Lotus Eaters (not the first act to use this). Keyboard player Tim Rice-Oxley has been quoted saying the band was then called ⇨Coldplay, but this name was offered to another student at University College, London, Chris Martin: Rice-Oxley considered joining Coldplay himself.

Either way, he said that in 1997, they renamed Cherry Keane, who was "this really nice old lady who used to look after Tom [Chaplin], the singer". They chose their name while sitting in a Dublin pub shortly before an Irish gig. It was misheard and they were introduced as Cherokee. (Cf the 1960s act ⇨Cherokees.) They dropped her first name because of the confusion.

Kenickie
This U.K. band named after a character played by Jeff Conway in *Grease*, their favourite teen film.

Klark Kent
Inspired by the character Clark Kent, Superman in disguise as a reporter, who is weakened only by Kryptonite. Kent, an *alter-ego* of Stewart Copeland, was on the Kryptonite label. ⇨The Police.

KGB
Almost the last of the boring supergroup dinosaurs in 1976, soon to be killed by punk, featured Ray Kennedy, ⇨Ric Grech and Mike Bloomfield, their surnames echoing the abbreviation for the U.S.S.R.'s feared spy police.

Chaka Khan

The singer was born Yvette Stevens in 1953 in Illinois. Chaka's an African word for "fire" and was used by chief Shaka, founder of the Zulu nation; Khan means "royal".
⇨Rufus.

Johnny Kidd And The Pirates

Singer Fred Heath led a struggling band, improbably called The Five Nutters – until a broken guitar string gave him a defective eye, over which he wore a patch and he was nicknamed Captain Kidd. His band picked up the Pirate image. This simple fancy dress tale contrasts with the complex names of later acts. Time for a new Pirates? Cf ⇨Doctor Hook.

Greg Kihn

This was his real name. The inspiration, however, for some of the worst name-punning album titles of all time: *Next Of Kihn, Rockihnroll, Kihntinued, Kihnspiracy, Kihntageous, Citizen Kihn, Kihnsolidation* and *Unkihntrollable*.

Kilburn And The High Roads

⇨Ian Dury's first London backing band in the 1970s. He knew the north residential area of the capital for its station, Kilburn High Road. ⇨The Blockheads.

The Killer

Jerry Lee Lewis got this nickname in school – he says, from his "ladykilling" looks.

The Killers

When members of British band ⇨New Order were making a video for their 2001 single *Crystal*, they had a fictitious band playing in the background. This act had a bass drum which they decided to emblazon Beatles-style with a name. On impulse, they asked the director to put the word "Killers" on it. The video was seen by Las Vegas musicians Dave Keuning and Brandon Flowers.

Not to be confused with the long-running band Killers, led by former ⇨Iron Maiden singer Paul Di'Anno from 1991 and named after an Iron Maiden album; now usually called Paul Di'Anno's Killers.

Killing Joke

Singer/keyboardist Jaz Coleman recalled a comic book story, pitting Batman against The Joker, entitled *Killing Joke*.

The King

⇨Elvis Presley. Name earned by virtue of his role as the king of rock and given to him by everyone else. Cf ⇨The King Of Pop. Also nickname for ⇨Nat 'King' Cole.

B.B. King

Mississippi boy Riley B. King says of his given names: "The 'B' didn't stand for anything, but the 'Riley' was a combination." His father Albert Lee King had a lost brother called Riley – and worked for a plantation owner called Jim O'Reily, who was present at the birth. The 'O' was dropped because the child "didn't look Irish".

Riley rapidly acquired the tag "The Blues Boy from Beale Street" during his residency on a Memphis, Tennessee, local radio music show. *Beale Street Blues* was one of his numbers. The billing, suggested by deejay Don Kearn, was soon shortened to B.B.

King was one of the inspirations behind ⇨ZZ Top's name.

Ben E. King

Ben Nelson's pseudonym came from his work fronting semi-pro band The Crowns.

Carole King

She was born Carole Klein and, while a struggling songwriter, settled on the more euphonious King. She was becoming established under this name when she married her first husband Gerry Goffin.

King Cole

Old King Cole of the children's rhyme as applied to Cole Porter, the American king of popular songwriting, with dozens of hits to his credit including *I Get A Kick Out Of You* and *I've Got You Under My Skin*. ⇨Nat King Cole.

King Crimson

A 1969 British concert began with the following words: "Ladies and Gentlemen, Giles, Giles and Fripp – who for reasons best known to themselves have changed their name to King Crimson – will have a freakout without the aid of pot, LSD or any other drugs." (Somehow, bands don't get introduced like that any more.)

The "reasons best known to themselves" came from their new composition *In The Court Of The Crimson King*, a narrative track featuring a devil-red character called King Crimson. It was the title cut on their dizzily-pretentious debut LP, subtitled *An Observation By King Crimson*.

[57] King Crimson's first album featured observations by the demonic title character.

The moniker produced some problems in the U.S. because people turned up expecting a soul act like King Curtis. Also known as "Crimso". Other Fripp bands include Discipline (named after 1981's *Discipline* LP), The League Of Gentlemen, The League Of Crafty Guitarists and Sunday All Over The World (this last with his wife, ⇨Toyah). Related: ⇨BLUE, ⇨ELP.

Jonathan King

The U.K. pop entrepreneur/ singer was born Kenneth King – not bad as a showbiz name. Still, he thought it "not very charismatic". So before the release of his first record in 1965: "The boss, the producer and I decided to think of two names each and draw one out of a hat. We all came up with Jonathan, so we forgot the hat."

King named ⇨Genesis, ⇨10CC and others such as Gogmagog, The Piglets and Shag before his career faltered.

King Missile

This New York-based arty group was named by poet-singer John S. Hall. King Missile is a phallic character – half man, half missile – in a Japanese cartoon. It was suggested by an acquaintance, David Sparks: King Missile is all-powerful but lacks confidence, and only achieves anything when his friends rally behind him. Original name: King Missile (Dog Fly Religion). Silly individual member name: guitarist Dogbowl, who was born Stephen Tunney. The (Dog Fly Religion) bit was deleted when he left.

Nosmo King

U.K. singer H. Vernon Watson named from the NO SMOKING sign on open stage doors.

The King Of Pop

⇨Michael Jackson. Name usually said to have been bestowed by his record company. Cf ⇨The King.

The King Of Ragtime

American pianist Scott Joplin (1868-1917), remembered for *The Entertainer* and other ragtime classics.

The King Of Reggae

⇨Bob Marley.

The King Of Skiffle

Skiffle music, often with unusual instruments such as washboards, scored its biggest hit with ⇨Lonnie Donegan's *Rock Island Line*. In a small field, he was the uncontested king.

The King Of Soul

Term applied by fans to ⇨James Brown, ⇨The Godfather of Soul. Also used to describe Otis Redding, partly based on his 1967 album with Carla Thomas, *The King And Queen*, though the epithet was used before its recording.

King Of Swing

⇨Dire Straits claimed to be the sultans of swing years later, yet the true kings of jazz-swing were band leaders Benny Goodman and Ted Heath.

The King Of The 12-String Guitar
⇨Leadbelly to his friends.

The Kings From Queens
From the New York origins of ⇨Run DMC.

Kings of Leon
Three of the group are brothers and the name's an affectionate homage to their preacher father, Leon. The fourth group member's their cousin, and the name also pays tribute to their grandfather, who was also called Leon.

The siblings – Nathan, Caleb, and Jared Followill – spent their youth travelling around the American South with their father as he toured churches. When Matthew Followill joined the Tennessee band as lead guitarist, the brothers were already meshing rock, blues and country in music influenced by religion – Leon-style fire-and-brimstone preaching – and their southern upbringing.

The Kinks
There are divergent accounts about this British group from brothers Ray and Dave Davies. It's agreed they started as the Ray Davies Quartet and renamed The Ramrods after a Duane Eddy instrumental. Other names included The Ravens, after a 1963 Boris Karloff horror movie and meant as a pun on "rave(r)"; and the Bo(ll) Weevils, a track attributed to Eddie Cochran and ⇨Bo Diddley.

Ray recalls: "We were having a drink in a pub with ⇨Larry Page [manager] – and somebody commented on the fake-leather capes Dave and Pete [Quaife, bassist] were wearing. Someone else said we were wearing kinky boots, similar to those worn in Honor Blackman in *The Avengers*." This was 1963; the TV series ran from 1961 to 1969. "Larry concluded . . . we might as well call ourselves The Kinks." Dave maintains the suggestion was from Arthur Howes, their booking agent. Page exploited the choice's curiosity value, with early photos showing The Kinks looking uncomfortable in pink hunting jackets, buckles, frilly shirts and riding whips. Even the drum featured a logo with high-heeled boots.

The brothers thought the tag wouldn't last but agreed the name was short enough to look good on posters (cf ⇨The Who). Dedicated followers of fashion that they were, they knew the epithet was in keeping with swinging sixties London, where "kinky" was in common currency as a fashion-to-sex buzzword.

Related: ⇨Muswell Hillbillies. Influenced: ⇨The Knack.

Kinky Machine
Inspired by ⇨Jimi Hendrix's track *Third Stone From The Sun* on his 1967 debut album *Are You Experienced?* Almost obscured by feedback, a voice declares his spaceship is approaching: "May I land my kinky machine?" Kinky was a very 1960s word, sometimes complimentary (cf ⇨The Kinks). Now, it's usually taken as meaning "perverted", though it has dated retro-chic. Cf ⇨Third Stone.

The Kinsey Report

Named after their lead singer, 'Big Daddy' Kinsey, who shared his name with psychologist Alfred Kinsey (1894-1956), whose *Kinsey Report* was a survey of American sexuality.

Rahsaan Roland Kirk

Most people rename for pragmatic reasons. Ronald Kirk said he did so because a spirit told him to do so. Unfortunately the spirit was not available for comment to the author on the reasons. Inspired: ⇨Rip Rig + Panic.

Kiss

This U.S. band formed in 1972 and toyed with the name Wicked Lester. Kiss was from ⇨The New York Dolls (singers of 1973's *Looking For A Kiss*), the idea of singer-guitarist Paul Stanley (born Stanley Harvey Eisen). It was the most intimate activity they thought they could get away with as a moniker. It also fitted in with surname of original drummer Peter Criss (born Peter Crisscoula). Bassist Gene Simmons, born Chaim Klein in Israel, was called Gene from an early age and so lifted his Americanised stage prenomen from actress Jean Simmons.

Their first record was released with marathon kissing contests. KISS is often reproduced in capitalised form to fit in with their logo , which makes the 'SS' look like lightning bolts. This was the idea of lead guitarist Paul 'Ace' Frehley. This seemed cool until (1) someone noticed the 'SS' happened to look like Nazi SS insignia, now illegal in Germany, and forced them to change the KISS logo there to KIZZ; (2) the capitals promoted speculation that it's an acronym. The group's members deny it stands for anything, be it "Knights/Kids In Satan's Service" or "Keep It Simple Stupid". More kissing: ⇨The Pogues.

Kiss The Sky

From ⇨Jimi Hendrix's 1967 *Purple Haze*, where he tells us he's actin' funny, but doesn't know why. He then adds "'scuze me while I kiss the sky."

Klaatu

This Canadian band's members were science fiction fans and named in 1975 from the 1951 Edmund North-Robert Wise film *The Day The Earth Stood Still*, which tells of a flying saucer landing. One of its occupants, Gort the robot, is controlled by the key word "Klaatu". ⇨Ringo Starr's admiration for the movie – he had just featured a still on a 1974 LP cover – sparked rumours that Klaatu were ⇨The Beatles in disguise. The record company played on this with a teasing campaign similar that for ⇨The Guess Who.

Klaxons

This British rock band formed in 2004 called "Klaxons (Not Centaurs)" taken from a line in the art text *The Futurist Manifesto*. (The essay, written by the Italian poet Filippo Tommaso Marinetti, makes a passing reference to a centaur, no klaxons). The modern word klaxon, from the Greek verb klazō, meaning "to shriek," is used for many forms of alarm call (cf ⇨The Alarm) or warning instrument such as car horns.

The KLF

Or "Kopywright Liberation Front". Leader Bill Drummond had a number of copyright problems after sampling other artists' records to create something new. Related: The JAMS (or Justified Ancients Of Mu Mu), taken from the Shea and Wilson *Illuminatus* novels.

KMFDM

This industrial rock band said in an interview it tore German words from a newspaper in 1984 and reshuffled them into the ungrammatical phrase "Kein Mehrheit Für Die Mitleid", sometimes written as "No majority for the pity". In one of their songs, *Megalomaniac*, they use the phrase "Kein Mitleid Für Die Mehrheit" or "no pity for the majority". The non-user-friendly name was shortened to KMFDM in 1985. The band suggested as alternatives "Kill Mother Fucking ⇨Depeche Mode" and "Keep ⇨Madonna From Doing Music".

The Knack

This 1970s Los Angeles band chose a name like ⇨The Kinks. It was also a ⇨Beatles tribute: the 1965 film *The Knack* was directed by Dick Lester, fresh from his success with *A Hard Day's Night* – the cover of which was mimicked by The Knack's debut LP.

Kokomo

This name, used by both a U.K. bluesy band and an American jazz-tinged rock outfit, came from a southern U.S. town.

Kooks

⇨David Bowie's song *Kooks* on the album *Hunky Dory* is about his family: it was written in 1971 after the May 30 birth of his son Zowie. It's a playful song, even though Bowie's marriage to Angie was not as idyllic as it seemed and both were already going their separate ways. The British band formed in Brighton in 2004 and took the name, with its ⇨Kink-like sound. A separate Swedish band in the 1990s had also used the name Kooks.

[58] Kooks look to the future, with naming debts from Bowie and The Kinks in the past.

Kool And The Gang

Founder Bob Bell was always "Cool". They renamed from Kool And The Flames to end confusion with ⇨James Brown's Famous Flames.

KoRn

Offensiveness alert. An inoffensive-sounding name which *Q* magazine said was "taken from a homosexual practice too 'alternative' to detail". A full explanation appeared on the *KoRn On The Kob* Web site. Leader Jonathan Davies overheard two gays talking at a party. Let's just say, the sweetcorn in question was found during intimate contact. Davies said everyone told this story started retching in disgust. It's not from the U.S. police slang for "Kiddy pORN".

Korova Milkbar

Another name from Anthony Burgess' 1962 novel *A Clockwork Orange*, later made into a motion picture. The thuggish anti-heroes hung out in a café of this name, indulging in all the things kids did in milkbars in the 1950s (taking amphetamines, taking liberties, playing music on the jukebox, playing the fool, trying to smoke and look cool) with updated ultraviolence to boot (i.e. "flip horrorshow boots for kicking"). Korova is Russian for cow, apt for a milkbar.

Cf ⇨The Droogs.

Kraftwerk

The German electronic band rehearsed in an old factory and recorded in a refinery, producing music that reflected their industrial environment. They continued the theme by naming themselves (in translation) "Power Station". Inspired ⇨VCL XI. Spinoff: ⇨Neu!

Billy J. Kramer

Briton William Ashton wanted to sound like he came from the other side of the Atlantic. He added a J. to his name to further Americanise it, in a move suggested by ⇨John Lennon. Cf ⇨Hank B. Marvin. ⇨The Dakotas.

[59] Kraftwerk, 1970. About to switch on their power station studio.

Kris Kristofferson

At a time when long foreign names were considered bad for rock stars, U.S. singer Kristoffer Kristofferson performed as Kris/Chris Carson for impresario ⇨Larry Parnes. With the advent of acts like ⇨Simon and Garfunkel, such monikers became more acceptable and he successfully reverted.

Kula Shaker

The writings of 1960s guru Aleister Crowley convinced leader Crispian Mills that K was a special letter, shared by political and spiritual leaders from Kennedy to Krishna.

His first band name, The Kays, was the same as a U.K. mail order catalogue and didn't inspire many. Then Mills met Krishna devotee Kula Sekara, named after a well-known religious figure. Mills said in an interview: "The original was a ninth century mystic and emperor. We felt we needed a bit of regal patronage and that if we took his name he would look after us." Their 1996 first album was called *K*. More Crowley: ⇨Golden Dawn.

The Kursaal Flyers

Canvey Island's finest, they formed in the Essex, U.K., seaside resort in 1974. They took their name from the most daring of the big dipper rides in Southend's funfair.

L

Sleepy LaBeef

Thomas La Beff changed his surname to avoid confusion. His somnolent appearance was caused by a droopy eyelid. Cf ⇨Sleepy John Estes.

Patti LaBelle

Patricia Holt renamed Patti LaBelle in the 1960s to front a group called The Blue Belles. The act became LaBelle as she eclipsed the superbly-named Cindy Birdsong. ⇨Laura Nyro.

Lady Day

Saxophonist Lester Young was a friend of ⇨Billie Holiday, who said in 1959: "We called my mother 'Duchess', so he [Young] named me 'Lady Day' and I called him 'Prez'. We were the royal family."

Ladysmith Black Mambazo

This South African group named from their township and a fondly-remembered act, 'Mambazo', which means an axe.

Lambchop

These Nashville country twangers enjoyed their first success in 1995. Leader Kurt Wagner said the name was chosen because "I like the way a beautiful woman's lips make the words sound, like with a smile at the end."

A Dictionary of Rock and Pop Names

Lambrettas
These British musical revivalists came from Brighton, scene of clashes between motorbiking rockers and Lambretta-scooter-riding mods. Cf ⇨The Merton Parkas.

Lois Lane
Lois Wilkinson of British 1960s female duo ⇨The Caravelles was called Lois Lane from her shared first name with Superman's girlfriend. Cf ⇨Klark Kent (sic).

k.d. lang
Canadian Kathryn (not Karen, as sometimes reported) Dawn Lang is of the feminine persuasion but chose to disguise this. The lower-case letters were part of the process: "Kathy's mundane, K.D.'s generic and it's a name not a sexuality." ⇨The Reclines. Cf ⇨P.J. Harvey.

The Larry Mullen Adventure
Irish schoolboy Larry Mullen Jnr., 14, put up a notice asking for musicians in 1976. They were to be called The Larry Mullen Adventure – until Paul Hewson arrived and took charge. They became ⇨Feedback, ⇨The Hype and ⇨U2.

The La's
John Power recalled: "(Guitarist) Mike Badger had this name The La's and we were like: 'What, The La's? As in all right, la?' And he was like: 'No (sings) La, la la."

To explain: that's "la la" as in music such as *There She Goes*; not L.A. as in Los Angeles; this lot come from Merseyside, U.K. where "la" is slang for "lad". Related: ⇨Cast.

The Last Poets
This collective named from a poem by the South Africa's Keorapetse Kgositsile, who said he was in the last era of artists before guns took over.

Lawnmower Deth
Like Death By Milkfloat, a simple ⇨Killing Joke. Individual member names: Concorde Face Ripper, Qualcast Mutilator, Mr Flymo, Mighty Mo Destructimo.

Leadbelly
Louisiana-born Huddie Leadbetter (1888-1949) learned the blues during the years he spent in prison for violent crimes. His fellow convicts christened him Leadbelly, a joke on his surname and testament to his toughness.

There are many incorrect theories such as that it related to his sexual prowess, a buckshot wound or ability to consume the worst prison chow. Nickname: The King Of The 12-String Guitar.

Led Zeppelin
1: **Yardbirds**. Session guitarists Jimmy Page and ⇨John Paul Jones recorded with ⇨Yardbird Jeff Beck in 1966. As they cut *Beck's Bolero*, Page and Beck thought of forming a band, possibly adding ⇨The Who's rhythm section of John Entwistle (bass)

and Keith Moon (drums), who weren't happy at the time. For vocalists, they liked ⇨The Small Faces' Steve Marriott or The Spencer Davis Group's Stevie Winwood. Nothing came of the group at once. Page instead joined the Yardbirds. When later Beck quit, Page was left in charge, though he didn't have rights to the name.

2: **New Yardbirds**. Manager Peter Grant and Page started a tour with The New Yardbirds. The Scandinavian gigs of 1968 made it clear they weren't the Yardbirds any more and a new moniker was needed.

[60] Led Zeppelin didn't crash as predicted, though Hindenburg images are never far away.

3: **Very Heavy Lead**. When Page's band visited New York in 1968, road manager Richard Cole was hanging out at the Salvation disco with Moon and Entwistle, by now openly saying they too wanted to form a band with Page and Winwood, who had moved to ⇨Traffic.

Author Steve Davis quotes Cole: "Entwistle said, according to Cole: 'Yeah, we'll call it Led Zeppelin. Because it will fucking go over like a lead balloon.' Moon roared out his maniacal bray and Cole told Jimmy [Page] the minute he got back to the hotel."

Entwistle, up to his death, maintained the phrase was his. Many sources, also quoting Cole, attribute the remark to Moon. Cole is sticking to the Entwistle version – while saying the alternative is not implausible because Moon used a similar phrase to describe disastrous concerts. Page and Jones also thought it was Moon – although, if Cole is to be believed, they weren't there at the time. They later asked Moon if they had his permission to use it for a band different in composition to the one he first proposed. Moon, pleased to be approached, said it was fine. He also maintained, throughout his life, that the phrase was his.

Everyone thought a ⇨Cream-like supergroup would be heavy not just with talent but with egos, personality clashes and differing styles. It could have flown, crashed or been too heavy to ever get off the ground. Page compromised and had recruited Jones, along with two promising, unknown Birmingham men: singer Robert Plant and drummer John Bonham.

4: **Led Zep**. Page was again thinking of names and came up with Mad Dogs – the moniker was later used by ⇨Joe Cocker – then Whoopee Cushion. If he'd chosen this ludicrous name, history might have been different.

It was only then that he remembered the zeppelin comment. He told Davis in the book *Hammer Of The Gods*: "It had something to do with the expression about a bad joke going over like a lead balloon. There's a little of the ⇨Iron Butterfly light-and-heavy connotation."

It also fitted imagery such as the ⇨Blind Faith album cover of a rocket. Led Zep soon had its own album imagery featuring Graf von Zeppelin's airship.

The "Lead" was respelled by Grant because (1) it would not be pronounced as

"Leed Zeppelin" and (2) "nobody can spell in America, so they won't notice." (Cf ⇨Def Leppard.) They were soon simply "Led Zep" or "the Zeps".

5: **Four Symbols**. By the time of their fourth LP, Zep became known by various runic symbols, thereby pre-dating the one adopted by ⇨Prince.

Page chose the symbol usually rendered as "Zoso". The glyph is similar to the alchemical symbol for amber. Unflattering derivative: Led Wallet – their first rehearsal ended with the rich Page asking the hard-up Brummies to chip in for beer.

Jones': symbol: Three ovals cutting through a circle representing confidence and competence.

Bonham's symbol: Three interlocking circles. He was dismissive of runes idea but his logo, also from a book of runes, represents man, woman and child. It also resembles three drums and looked like the Ballantine drinks company logo. Bonham's son Jason has drummed with Zep for reunions after his father's death. ⇨Bonzo, ⇨Bonham.

Plant's symbol: A feather in a circle, designed by Plant and representing his lyrical-writing, derived from a sign of the Mu civilisation. ⇨'Percy' had been singing with the ridiculously-named Hobstweedle (a Tolkien reference), ⇨Black Snake Moan and ⇨The Crawling King Snakes. At one stage he might have joined ⇨Slade, which again would have made history different.

6: **Other names**. On tour in Copenhagen in 1970, the band was confronted by Eva von Zeppelin, a relative of the airship designer. She said: "They may be world famous but these shrieking monkeys aren't going to use a privileged name without permission." Zep appeared for the night as The Nobs. Fears of court action proved groundless.

Unflattering derivatives: 'Dead Zeppelin' – referring either to Bonzo's death or their flagging "dinosaur" appeal in the aftermath of punk. 'The Stairlifts To Heaven' – referring to their reunion at more advanced age playing *Stairway To Heaven*.

Tribute bands include: ⇨Dread Zeppelin, ⇨Fred Zeppelin and the all-female Lez Zeppelin.

7: **Aftermath. Spinoffs**: ⇨The Firm, ⇨The Honeydrippers, ⇨The MacGregors, ⇨Unleded.

8: **Afterword**. Zeppelin took off quickly and flew high to success, so proving the name ironic. Page said the name didn't matter as long as the music was accepted: "We could have called ourselves the Vegetables or the Potatoes . . . . What does a Led Zeppelin mean? It doesn't mean a thing."

Brenda Lee

Brenda Lee Tarpley dropped her surname as not stagey enough. Always MISS Brenda Lee. Cf ⇨Crystal Gayle.

Lemmy

Ian Kilmister confirmed "Lemmy," rather than being meaningless, came from his frequent remark "lemme a fiver"! ⇨Hawkwind, ⇨Motörhead. Inspired: ⇨Dare.

The Lemonheads

Evan Dando's band, from Massachusetts, said it named from a U.S. candy brand "because Lemonheads are sweet on the outside and sour on the inside". However, "lemon" is narcotics-speak for a Quaalude: Lemmon the name of a business which once made it. A "lemonhead" is someone who used this product.

John Lennon

John Winston Lennon was born in 1940, his middle name tribute to U.K. Prime Minister Winston Churchill. The former ⇨Beatle who was shot dead 40 years later was John Ono Lennon, a tribute to second wife Yoko Ono.

[61] Button badge warning of the drugs danger for Lemonheads.

The early Beatles were Johnny (Lennon) and The Moondogs, then Long John And The Silver Beetles (sic). The Long John tag, recalling Long John Silver, was more legitimately used by the tall ⇨Long John Baldry. Lennon rejected being Johnny Silver on their first tour to fit The Silver Beetles. While others in ⇨the Fab Four used pseudonyms more readily, he disliked such "pretence".

Lennon excluded from this dislike, jokes like Dr Winston O'Boogie (with ⇨Elton John); The Walrus and The Dreamweaver (sundry song references). His wordplay, evident in his books as well as the naming of the Beatles, showed in naming of ⇨Cyrkle and ⇨Grapefruit. Related: ⇨Billy J. Kramer, ⇨The Dakotas, ⇨Poco.

Les Negresses Vertes

A misleading name, on a par with ⇨The Fat Lady Sings and ⇨Five Guys Named Moe. This French group got their name from abuse thrown at them by drunken bikers at an early gig.

Lettermen

Like ⇨The Ivy League and many others, a clean-cut U.S. name to assure the public they were respectable guys of the sort you'd find at Yale. Lettermen are student sporting stars; this harmony trio wore preppy lettered sweaters.

Level 42

Bassist Mark King named his 1980s British jazz-funk band after Douglas Adams's *The Hitch Hiker's Guide To The Galaxy* where "42" is the mysteriously succinct reply to the question "What is the meaning of life, the universe and everything?" He added "Level" because the number looked bare on its own. In 1996 newspapers reported that astronomers indeed found the number 42 significant in explaining the distances between stars.

[62] Sam Rockwell and Garth Jennings make *The Hitchhiker's Guide to the Galaxy* in 2005. The book inspired Level 42 in 1980.

Levellers

This politically-aware group's philosophy is similar to the Levellers, a puritanical party of the English Civil Wars (1642 on), who advocated "levelling" people to same wealth and status.

Huey Lewis And The News

American singer Hugh Anthony Clegg III, known as Huey, renamed after poet Lewis Welch. The Beat writer was a friend of his mother, Magda Cregg, and the future star saw him as his stepfather. Huey's record company urged Huey's band Clover to find a more newsworthy name. They obliged.

The Libertines

This English rock band named in 1997 after Marquis de Sade's *Lust of the Libertines*. They liked the sexual knowingness and that a libertine is free from restraints. Related: ⇨Babyshambles, ⇨Dirty Pretty Things.

Liberty X

This U.K. band formed from the five runner-ups on the 2001 *Popstars* TV talent show. The winners formed ⇨Hear'Say. The others chose Liberty to show they were free from the TV and record demands on the winners. While this band was dubbed "Flopstars" by some, they went on to success. After being challenged by an existing band called Liberty, they became Liberty X.

Lieutenant Lush

⇨Malcolm McLaren chose the name for ⇨Boy George to fit *The Mile High Club*, a song about airliner sex.

The Lightning Seeds

From *Raspberry Beret*, a song by ⇨Prince on 1985 album *Around The World In A Day*. The line used is: "The thunder drowns out what the lightning sees." They misheard it as "lightning seeds". Related: ⇨Big In Japan.

The Lilac Time

"Lilac time" is a phrase similar to "purple passage" used by Walt Whitman and others. It turns up in 1969's *River Man* by British singer-songwriter Nick Drake. It was from here that it was taken by leader ⇨Stephen Duffy.

Limahl

Former singer with British band ⇨Kajagoogoo, Chris Hamill made an anagram of his surname.

Limp Bizkit

There are so many explanations for this Florida rap-metal band's name that the author was honour bound to try to find out which was correct. The record company was keener for me to review the latest CD or interview leader Fred Dirst for a serious newspaper and couldn't understand interest in a name in place since 1994. The answer from Dirst was: "It's just a stupid name, the stupidest we could think of at the time".

Other theories: (1) "Limp biscuit" is a well documented – I mean in slang diction-aries – male masturbation game played in teenage male groups, with the loser having to eat a somewhat worse-for-wear cookie. (Cf ⇨Circle Jerks.) (2) Former band member Rob Waters claimed a friend of Dirst's said his brain was "like a limp biscuit" after trying marijuana. (3) A number of fan sites, based on a lot of limp-biscuit-brained speculation, have said it was the name of Fred's dog, which had a limp.

The band, discovered by the similarly-charmingly-named ⇨Korn, has sometimes written its name as limpbizkit. Cf ⇨Half Man Half Biscuit.

Lindisfarne

Founded in Newcastle, U.K., in 1967. Named from a nearby island which houses a monastery founded in 635 A.D.

Linkin Park

The Grammy winning Californian band formed in 1996 as Xero. In 1999 they added singer Chester Bennington, who wasn't crazy about their planned new name Hybrid Theory.

He liked Lincoln Park, a public space he passed in Santa Monica. He found the domain name www.lincolnpark.com was taken, so adjusted the spelling to "Linkin Park".

Linx

David Grant chose this for its double-meaning; a big cat and "connections". His bassist was called Sketch, born Sketch Martin, who joked: "My real name is Preliminary Drawing . . . most people found that a bit of a mouthful!"

Lipps, Inc.

This Minneapolis band punned on "lip sync". Infamous lip-synchers ⇨(p.193) Milli Vanilli should have taken notes.

Little Caesar And The Romans

Roman Emperor Julius Caesar has inspired small-time imitators down the years. One was 1920s gangster Al Capone, source of the name ⇨Dennis Alcapone, inspiration behind this band and 1931 film *Little Caesar*.

Little Eva

Eva Boyd was a babysitter for Gerry Goffin and ⇨Carole King before she started singing their songs. They named her from a character in Harriet Beecher Stowe's *Uncle Tom's Cabin*.

Little Feat

Founder Lowell George (1945-1979) recycled his nickname "Little Feet".

Guitarist Paul Barrere said: "Lowell had unusually little, fat feet and Jimmy Carl Black of ⇨The Mothers happened to make mention of them. The name was born with Feat instead of Feet just like ⇨The Beatles, neat huh?"

Inspired: ⇨Dixie Chicks.

Little Richard

Georgia kid Ricardo Penniman became Richard Johnson when he was adopted. He was 'Little' when he started singing at 14. Nickname: The Georgia Peach. Cf ⇨Cliff Richard, ⇨Scritti Politti.

Living Colour

Taken from a phrase beloved of photographers and moviemakers. This American band called their first album *Vivid*. "There were too many monochrome names and people wearing black . . . we wanted to put some colour back into music, make it real." (They chose the English spelling, as opposed to color, to "make it better".)

The Lizard King

⇨Jim Morrison's alter-ego The Lizard King grew out of his *Celebration Of The Lizard*, a piece of self-mythology on grand scale. He said lizards and snakes are identified with "unconscious forces of evil".

L.L. Cool J.

This New York rapper was born James Todd Smith. "Ladies Love Cool James" was a piece of graffiti in Queens. Related: ⇨H.E.A.L.

Lollapalooza

American music festival founded by ⇨Perry Farrell. From the American idiom for a remarkable thing or person, usually spelled "lollapalootza", Farrell heard it in a Three Stooges film.

London SS

This band namechecked German Schutz Staffeln storm-troopers, following the punk trend for Nazi shock tactics. Related: ⇨The Clash, ⇨The Damned.

The Long Ryders
This 1980s California band named from *The Long Riders* western, released a few months before they formed. The Ryders denied the respelling was a tribute to ⇨The Byrds. It was merely "to be different from the movie".

Loop
Named after the first ⇨Velvet Underground single, released in December 1966 as a seven-minute flexidisc.

Loop Guru
The techno-dance experts became the self-styled "gurus of loops" because of their samples. It's a coincidental echo of French *loup garou*, "werewolf".

Lord Kitchener
Jamaican Aldwyn Roberts took the name of one of Britain's greatest war figures, known for his recruitment poster: "Your country needs YOU". Reggae artists have appropriated names both famous and infamous (⇨Sir Coxsone Dodd, ⇨Dennis Alcapone).

Lords Of The New Church
British band The Wanderers and were taken on by manager Miles Copeland, who also looked after the business for his brother Stewart's ⇨The Police. Miles suggested Lords of Discipline and the band came up with the portentous name. Related: ⇨The Damned, ⇨The Dead Boys, ⇨Sham 69. Copeland also helped name ⇨Wishbone Ash.

Los Lobos
Spanish Chicanos in California, they identified with their Tex-Mex audience by calling themselves "The Wolves". Hence titles such as *How Will The Wolf Survive?*

Lostprophets
The Welsh alt-metal band incongruously named after a ⇨Duran Duran bootleg of a 1988 concert in Italy. They thought it an interesting collective and removed the space between the two words.

Lothar And The Hand People
This 1965-1970 band was led by Richard Willis, who said he had dreamed of an enslaved race called the Hand People being saved by a hero called Lothar.

Love
Group mainstay and mainspring Arthur Lee, speaking in 1967's summer of love, insisted Love means not just romance but "universal love and cosmic peace". Related: ⇨Band Aid (no, not THE Band Aid). Inspired: ⇨Alone Again Or.

Love And Rockets

From an American cartoon strip, flagship of the Fantagraphics comics empire. Related: ⇨Bauhaus.

Courtney Love

She was born Love Michelle Harrison in San Francisco, on 9 July 1965, to Hank Harrison and Linda Carroll. Her parents split when she was a toddler. She became Courtney Michelle Harrison ("love" seemed wrong after the break), then Carroll (after her mother's divorce) then Rodriguez (after her mother's second marriage; she became Ari Rodriguez, after an obscure ⇨John Denver song) and Manley (following her mother's third marriage).

She star-to-be tried the "decent, normal" prenomen Michelle then decided that of the names foisted upon her Courtney and Love were the ones she liked most.

She formed Sugar Babylon with future ⇨L7 members and was kicked out of ⇨Faith No More and ⇨Babes In Toyland before founding ⇨Hole and playing a leading part in ⇨Riot Grrrl. She's the widow of ⇨Kurt Cobain.

The Lovin' Spoonful

John Sebastian started with ⇨The Mugwumps and graduated to this group, whose name refers to the *double entendres* in Mississippi John Hurt's *Coffee Blues*: "I love my baby by the lovin' spoonful". Cf ⇨10CC, ⇨Cream.

Nick Lowe

⇨Basher. Terrible punning LP title: *All Time Lowes*.

The Low Numbers

A tribute to the early ⇨The Who, who were briefly The High Numbers. This 1970s outfit specialised in obscure numbers by Pete Townshend and others.

L7

This Los Angeles female band named after a postwar slang term for "square", a conventional person. This is attributed to the rectangular visual pattern made by joining the capital L and the number 7.

Ludacris

Rapper Christopher Bridges' stagename punned on "ludicrous" and his prenomen.

Lulu

The little Glaswegian started with a big name – Marie McDonald McLaughlin Lawrie. Her manager, Marian Massey, introduced her at one club as a "lulu of a kid," meaning she was amazing for her age. Inspired ⇨Flesh For Lulu.

Larry Lurex

This aspiring glam-rocker named after the shiny lurex thread used in stage clothes of the time. Lurex's parodying attempt to jump on the ⇨Gary Glitter bandwagon failed. It cleared the way for him to become ⇨Freddie Mercury.

Loretta Lynn

She was born Loretta Webb, sister of Brenda Webb, whom she renamed ⇨Crystal Gayle. Loretta was in tribute to movie star Loretta Young; Lynn came later when she married. Nickname (shared with others): The Queen Of Country Music.

Lynyrd Skynyrd

All of the original group but one came from Jacksonville, Florida, where most attended the same high school.

They started in 1964 as My Backyard, referencing Willie Dixon's *Back Door Man*. Over the next five years the quintet tried The Noble Five ("Nobel Prize" pun), The Wild Cats, Sons Of Satan, The Pretty Ones, Conqueror Worm, and finally the One Percent, used for several years until 1970.

The inspiration for the final moniker was Leonard Skinner, a gym teacher at Robert E. Lee High School in Jacksonville. Skinner hated long-haired students and would strictly enforce the boys' dress code of no hair touching the collar or sideburns below the ears.

At some point in the 1960s he disciplined (budding guitarist) Gary Rossington and (drummer) Bob Burns for letting their hair grow. Skinner said in a 1978 interview that he couldn't remember who he suspended. Either way, the young musicians dropped out of school, partly because of his actions – and remembered the hassle.

Rossington tells the story on Judy Van Zant Jenness' web history. He and others slicked back their hair with Vaseline, but showers were compulsory after gym. "Skinner would come through the showers while you were doing it, and if he caught you with your hair down touching your ears or something he'd kick you out. After about 20 or 30 times of doing that to me, and kicking me out for two weeks of suspension, I just quit school."

According to the band's site: "In 1970, the band – playing as the One Percent – had a gig at a local club called the Forest Inn and Ronnie [Van Zant, singer] called

[63] Lynyrd Skynyrd, Atlanta, Georgia, July 1976.

out to the crowd, 'Hey, we're Leonard Skinner and we're gonna play for y'all tonight.' Since most of the crowd had run into Coach Skinner at one point or another the name was an instant hit. Eventually, the vowels were changed 'to protect the guilty' — as Gary put it."

They were Lynard Skynard until 1973 when they adopted the more skewed spelling Lynyrd Skynyrd. The band's debut album was called *pronounced 'lĕh-'nérd 'skin-'nérd*, commonly referred to as *Pronounced*.

The tribute worried Rossington, with friends telling him for months: "Gary, got a call for you – someone called Leonard". The unfortunate teacher wasn't pleased with his resulting fame/infamy!

Within years of leaving school, the by-now very-long-haired band were worth millions: far more than their short-haired contemporaries who had obeyed Skinner's commands. Skinner still looked like a marine and moved into real estate and personal training.

[64] "Still haven't got ya hair cut, boy?" Band name inspiration Leonard Skinner (right) greets Lynyrd Skynyrd's Artimus Pyle.

Skynyrd was torn apart in 1977, with a plane crash which claimed the life of singer Ronnie Van Zant. They re-emerged, initially as "Lynyrd Skynyrd 1991".

Later Skinner introduced them at a 2006 concert and saw them enter the Rock and Roll Hall of Fame that same year.

Skynyrd has had 22 members over its life. The current version has two members of the original line up – keyboardist Billy Powell and Rossington, one of those who was disciplined by Skinner 40 years ago.

Related groups: ⇨Rossington Collins Band, ⇨.38 Special.

M

Paul McCartney

The ⇨Beatles bassist, ⇨Fab Four mop-top, lovable long-haired Liverpudlian lad, known as 'Macca', was born James Paul McCartney.

He had two flirtations with the stagename Paul Ramon (chosen "because it sounded really glamorous . . . Valentino-ish"). He first toyed with it in 1960, when the Silver Beetles adopted stagenames during their tour supporting ⇨Johnny Gentle. It was revived when he dropped in on a London recording session for The Steve Miller band in February 1969. (Hence ⇨The Ramones).

Some of his 1960s material was credited to writers A. Smith or Bernard Webb, said to be anonymous French students, because Macca feared people would say the songs were only hits because of his name. (His brother recorded as ⇨Mike McGear in a bid to avoid comparisons.)

Other one-off stagenames include: Apollo C. Vermouth (producing ⇨The Bonzo Dog Doo-Dah Band) The Country Hams (playing a song written by his father Jim) and Percy "Thrills" Thrillington (a Muzak version of ⇨Wings's 1971 *Ram* LP).

He was knighted in 1997. ⇨The Smoking Mojo Filters.

The McCoys
American teenage brothers Rick and Randy Zehringer started playing with their neighbour Dennis Kelly, who taught them an instrumental from The Ventures LP *The McCoys* – and realised he had hit on a name. Related: ⇨Derringer.

Country Joe McDonald And The Fish
"Country": from their acoustic-folk sound. "Joe": because the Californian singer was named Joseph Stalin McDonald, after the Soviet dictator, by his politically-motivated parents. "The Fish": Joe's early songs were protests. Chinese communists said that revolutionaries should move through the people like fish.

The Fish name was variously used by journalists to either refer to Joe's backing band or main member Barry Melton. Melton insisted it related solely to him. (⇨The Fish.) Spinoff: ⇨The Dinosaurs.

Mike McGear
Peter Michael McCartney, younger brother of the more famous ⇨Paul McCartney, wanted to make it on his own terms. He considered Mike Blank then used the 1960s phrase "fab gear" (⇨The Beatles were always "fab"). It was a little to close to his real name to successfully show he was trading without any link to 'Macca'.

The MacGregors
AKA Roy Harper and ex- ⇨Led Zeppelin guitarist Jimmy Page. They named after an old alias of Aleister Crowley, the sex guru who also inspired ⇨Golden Dawn and ⇨Kula Shaker.

Roger McGuinn
James Joseph McGuinn III was known as Jim as ⇨The Byrds flew to stardom. In 1965 he joined the Subud faith which maintains that everyone has a spiritual identity, "the verbal sound of the soul", behind the earthly one. He was told his real name was "Roger" and in 1968 officially assumed the name. Cf ⇨Carlos Santana.

Machine Head
These rockers loved ⇨Deep Purple's 1972 album of the same name. Cf ⇨Stormbringer – who almost named Machine Head.

Malcolm McLaren

Stars named/managed by the U.K. entrepreneur and sometime star-in-his-own-right: ⇨Bow Wow Wow; ⇨Sex Gang Children; ⇨The Sex Pistols. AKA ⇨The Godfather Of Punk, a title also applied to ⇨Lou Reed.

Madder Rose

This New York indie rockers poetically reversed the pigment name "rose madder", said guitarist Billy Cote. Singer Mary Lorsen said it was a surreal choice ("How can a rose be mad?") and not a riposte to the antics of ⇨W. Axl Rose.

Madness

The nutty boys from London had a three-year apprenticeship as The (North London) Invaders. They considered Morris and The Minors or Morris Major And the Minors but, in the end, decided to leave this to the unrelated ⇨Morris Minor And The Majors.

They went for Madness because they liked the old ska song of this name by ⇨Prince Buster. They recorded *The Prince* in his honour . . . it was their first hit in 1979. It also matched their "Nutty Sound". Above all, they were mad (in the English sense of being insane, rather than the American sense of enraged). Spinoff: ⇨The Nutty Boys.

Madonna

Born in 1958 in Rochester, Michigan, Madonna Louise Veronica Ciccone was named after her mother. Like many other stars she has always preferred the single name, but initially ran into misunderstandings. For one early session she had to fill in a form asking for Christian and Surnames and consequently was billed as "Madonna Madonna".

Madonna, like Jesus, is used freely in some Latin American lands but is seen as sacrilegious in most other Christian countries. She said: "I didn't have a hard time

growing up as Madonna because I went to a Catholic school."

Dictionary definitions hint at the controversy: "Madonna – a lady, especially a brothel madam; a designation of the virgin birth and Mary Magdalene – from Italian *ma donna*, or 'my lady'." This connection of raunchy and religious icons, prostitution and piety made for plenty of

[65] Madonna, Madge, The Material Girl, The Queen Of The Pops. Live Earth, Wembley, 2007.

184

publicity. This sparked titles such as *Like A Virgin* and *The Immaculate Collection*.

Name notes: Inspired ⇨Ciccone Youth, ⇨Take That. Anagrams: Madonna Louise Ciccone = "Occasional Nude Income"; Madonna, The Material Girl = "Real Dim Man-Eating Harlot". Husbands Sean Penn and Guy Richie have both been dubbed "Mr Madonna". Nicknames: ⇨The Material Girl, ⇨The Queen Of The Pops, ⇨The Queen of Disco/Disco Pop, Maddie. Madonna's first band was called ⇨Emmenon.

Her children include Lourdes Maria Ciccone Leon, Rocco John Ritchie and David Banda Mwale (adopted with last names Ciccone Ritchie).

Magazine
⇨Howard Devoto liked the juxtaposition between pop covering issues like a periodical – and a case full of bullets.

Taj Mahal
Henry St Clair Fredericks, a multi-instrumentalist, took the name of one of the wonders of the world in a bid to be mysterious and memorable. (The name was also used by a U.S. rapper.)

Mahavishu Orchestra
From leader John McLaughlin, who renamed Mahavishu after converting to the Sri Chinmoy faith.

The Main Line
⇨Rick James liked innocent names which hinted at naughtiness. While he said this was to do with trains, mainlining is also drugs-speak for injection. Cf ⇨The Mary Jane Girls.

The Mamas And The Papas
Taken from San Francisco Hell's Angel-speak for men and women; at one point there were two couples in the band. Ellen Naomi Cohen, AKA Cass Elliot, became known as Mama Cass (Elliot).

Related: ⇨The Mugwumps; ⇨Spanky And Our Gang; ⇨Wilson Phillips.

Manassas
Promo pictures for Stephen Stills' new band were shot in this Virginia town. A location sign was prominently featured in the best picture, hence the name.

The Manhattan Transfer
This New York band's early act was based on visual style taken from 1920s and 1930s swing. The name recalls one of the best books which summed up the N.Y. of that time, John Dos Passos' *The Manhattan Transfer*.

Manic Street Preachers
This Welsh rock band's members can be manic and preach didactic messages. Richey Edwards was quoted saying the group was walking along the street and listening to

a "hallelujah come-to-Jesus man" berating the passers-by when they overheard someone remarking: "Oh look, there's a manic street preacher".

A slightly different account has guitarist James Dean Bradfield busking in the street when the remark was made about him. Unfortunately Richey isn't around any more to cross-check events after vanishing in 1995.

Unflattering derivative: Janet Street Porters (reference to a British journalist of similar name).

Barry Manilow

The world's famous nose was born Barry Pinkus in Brooklyn, New York. At 13 he became Manilow, his mother's maiden name, after his father left the family. Manilow he has been ever since, apart from cutting an early single as Pinkus. It flopped – he took this as an omen.

The Man In Black

⇨Johnny Cash and ⇨Roy Orbison. Cf ⇨The Men In Black.

The Mannish Boys

Early ⇨David Bowie band inspired by ⇨ (p.291) Muddy Waters' 1955 blues standard single *Mannish Boy*.

Manfred Mann

Manfred Mann was born Michael Lubowitz. The Mann name was from a German legend and this band named after him. Related: ⇨Emanon. Album title: *Mannerisms*.

Mano Negra

⇨Clash-style politico posing by these Parisian neo-punks, who were named after an Andalucian anarchist group they admired.

Marilyn Manson

Brian Warner mixed convicted killer Charles Manson with screen star Marilyn Monroe as an attention-grabbing comment on the duality of American culture. The name chiefly applies to Warner, a younger ⇨Alice Cooper, although it's also a credit for his band. At first they also renamed to follow the diva-icon/criminal idea: Madonna Wayne Gacy, Zsa Zsa Speck etc. Shocking name rip-off in best ⇨Dead Kennedys mode. Unrelated: ⇨Mansun, ⇨Marilyn, ⇨The Misfits, Norma Jean.

[66] Marilyn Monroe with Tom Ewell in *The Seven Year Itch*, about to blow away rock stars for years to come.

Mansun

This 1995-2003 British combo was for some time A Man Called Sun, after a ⇨Verve B-side. Their record label thought this too similar to ⇨A Man Called Adam, so it was crunched to Mansun. This wasn't a reference to Charles Manson.

Mantronix

Leader Curtis Khalee said it was a combination of "human and machine, man, mantra and electronics".

The Marcels

American harmony band named after a popular layered hairstyle worn by lead singer Cornelius Harp.

Marillion

This British band formed in the late 1970s with influences such as ⇨Genesis and the literature recalled in their original name Silmarillion: the title of a J.R.R. Tolkien tome, published posthumously in 1977. Tolkien inspired ⇨Cirith Ungol, ⇨The Pink Fairies, ⇨Shadowfax and ⇨Steve Peregrin Took. Related: ⇨Fish.

Marilyn

Born Peter Robinson, U.K., he became friendly with ⇨Boy George in London and developed the nickname Boy Marilyn for his transvestism and his attempts to recreate the appearance of U.S. film star Marilyn Monroe (Norma Jean Baker, 1926-1962; Peter was born in the year she died).

[67] Tolkien's Middle Earth has echoed through music, with Marillion and more getting hot about hobbits.

The Marine Girls

This U.K. band recorded sea-themed songs. They also recorded more nautical songs under the silly tag Grab Grab The Haddock. Related: ⇨Everything But The Girl.

Mark-Almond

Formed by former ⇨Bluesbreakers guitarist Jon Mark and sax man Johnny Almond. Unrelated: ⇨Marc Almond.

Bob Marley And The Wailers

⇨The Wailers. ⇨The King Of Reggae.

Marquee Moon

Berlin band named after the title track of the 1977 ⇨Television album. Cf ⇨Friction, ⇨Elevation.

M/A/R/R/S

The first name initials of the musicians behind the 1978-88 hit *Pump Up The Volume.* (Martyn, Alex, Russell, Rudi and Steve.) Cf ⇨M.A.R.S.

M.A.R.S.

The last name initials of the musicians: Macalpine, Aldridge, Rock and Sarzo. Cf ⇨M/A/R/R/S.

The Mars Volta

Leader Cedric Bixler-Zavala explains "Volta" is taken from a term used by film director Federico Fellini to denote a sudden change of scene: the "Mars" denotes an interest in science fiction. Related: ⇨At The Drive-In, ⇨Sparta.

Marshall Tucker Band

None of the members of this South Carolina country rock band had the name Marshall or Tucker. Marshall Tucker was the owner of a hall they used for early jam sessions. They adopted his name in thanks.

Martha And The Muffins

These Toronto funsters insisted they were just joking with vocalist Martha Johnson by including the Muffin cartoon character – they weren't poking pun at ⇨Martha And The Vandellas.

Martha And The Vandellas

Martha Reeves named her band in homage to Van Dyke Street near her Michigan home and the vocalist ⇨Della Reese.

Hank B. Marvin

⇨The Shadows star Brian Rankin needed a U.S.-sounding handle as he modelled himself on ⇨The Crickets, right down to the ⇨Buddy Holly glasses and Fender. Rankin became Hank; Brian abbreviated to an American-sounding initial: the Marvin, from a friend called Martin, just sounded right. Cf ⇨Billy J. Kramer.

The Mary Jane Girls

Another "not-so-innocent" ⇨Rick James name. Mary Jane is slang for marijuana.

Massive Attack

This British band named from a newspaper splash. "Massive" and "attack" are common headline words, along with ⇨ Clash. The choice was neither meant as phallic nor a statement of intent. They briefly abbreviated to Massive during the 1991 Mid-East conflict. Related: ⇨Tricky.

Masters Of Reality

They formed in 1980 in New York, naming after ⇨Black Sabbath's LP *Master Of Reality* to turn off the "punk snobs".

Matchbox
Britons dedicated to the revival of 1950s rock 'n' roll – 20 or more years later. They named after one of their favourite tunes: ⇨Carl Perkins's *Matchbox*.

Matching Mole
At first glance meaningless or surreal, it's a pun on the French for "soft machine", *machine molle*. Founded by ⇨The Soft Machine's Robert Wyatt.

The Material Girl
Nickname for ⇨Madonna. Based on her 1985 hit *Material Girl* and her massive commercial success.

Matt Bianco
This U.K. jazzy band started in 1983 after the demise of ⇨Blue Rondo A La Turk. The name sounds like a drink or a personal name. The group said it was "a made up spy; we love TV themes and film scores". Related: ⇨Basia.

Matthews Southern Comfort
Ian Matthews McDonald, late of ⇨Fairport Convention, wrote an LP of this name referencing the well known U.S. whisky blend – and recycled it when he formed a band.

Max Webster
Nobody in this early 1980s Canadian rock band was called Max Webster. They thought it would give too much prominence to an individual member to name the group after him, so they chose a name at random.

MC5
"MC" usually means "master of ceremonies" for rappers and deejays: ⇨MC Hammer etc. Here it means "Motor City": the five came together in "motor town" or ⇨Motown, Detroit in 1967. Spinoff: ⇨Destroy All Monsters. Inspired ⇨Shakin' Street, although not ⇨Jefferson Starship, as is sometimes suggested.

M.C. 900 Ft Jesus
American rapper Mark Griffin, from Dallas, took the name from a sermon by Oral Roberts.

MDC
Originally this group from Texas was Millions Of Dead Cops: Singer Davey got fed up of explaining this. Hence they became MDC, which could and did mean a wealth of other things, such as "Multi-Death Corporation".

Meatloaf
Texan schoolkid, meaty Marvin Lee Aday, weighed 240lbs in seventh grade. He was 13 when, loafing around as usual, he stumbled onto his football teacher's foot (and

his nickname) during a game. The Dallas teacher yelled in pain: "Gerroff me ya great hunka meatloaf!"

The Meat Puppets

This American band said that sometimes they felt like someone else was pulling the strings; they were slaves to computer-programmed instruments, promotional duties and concert tours.

Mega City IV

From a cartoon strip featuring Judge Joe Dredd, the anti-hero who keeps law and order in Mega City. The band liked Dredd even though he's a cross between Dirty Harry and Mussolini.

Megadeth

One of many "death rock" monikers, this was taken from the American army term for the impact of a large-scale conflagration resulting in the deaths of a million people or more. Related: ⇨Metallica. The band which became ⇨Pink Floyd had considered the similar Meggadeath.

The Mekons

There is only one mekon, although he cropped up several times in science fiction, always as an awesome and awful threat to the human race. The Manchester Mekon and The Mekons, from Leeds, both thought it unusual and a symbol of possible world domination.

John Cougar Mellencamp

A story of an artist renamed by management without being consulted. (Cf ⇨Gary 'U.S.' Bonds, ⇨The Beach Boys).

John Mellencamp from Indiana was signed by ⇨David Bowie's management company, where Tony De Fries thought John's surname too long. People have coped with names far worse (⇨Humperdinck, Garfunkel) yet he chose Johnny (after ⇨Chuck Berry's *Johnny B. Goode*) and Cougar (another cat name – after an American puma).

It was only when a bewildered Mellencamp was handed his first record in 1976 he discovered the change. Seven years later he added his real name and in 1989 reverted back to this. His commercial standing increased as Mellencamp, suggesting the U.S. public had more intelligence than De Fries realised.

Members

This U.K. punk group intended it as an anatomical reference rather than to themselves. Cf ⇨Penetration.

Memphis Slim

The Memphis bluesman (1915-1988) was born John Len Chatman, not Peter Chapman as sometimes reported, though he used this a writing credit in honour of his father.

The Men In Black

Tribute band named after ⇨The Stranglers' monochrome garb. The Stranglers album of 1981 was called *The Men In Black*. Cf ⇨Johnny Cash and ⇨Roy Orbison.

Menswear

The short-lived British 1990s hopefuls named because of their sartorial eloquence, expressed in a range of snappy suits. The name, sometimes written Menswe@r, was dubbed "really 80s" by ⇨Paul Weller.

Mental As Anything

The Australian ⇨Madness, as nutty as the Nutty Boys, named after Oz slang and titled one album *Fundamental*.

Me Phi Me

This 1990s rapper renamed after black college campus fraternities such as Alpha Phi Alpha.

Freddie Mercury

This cosmopolitan ⇨Queen singer's given name and origins have been incorrectly given in many encyclopaedias and even biographies, which say his parents were Persian. In fact they were from Gujarat in western India and were Zoroastrian Parsees. The future star was born on 5 September 1946 in Zanzibar with the surname Bulsara, which refers to a town north of Bombay and south of Ahmedabad.

His prenomen, according to his brother-in-law Roger, was Farok, not Farookah or Farookh as many books have it. He became Freddie at boarding school, and so he stayed, through to his Parsee-style funeral wreath in 1991.

There are also mistakes in many biographies about his rebirth as a star in the 1970s under the name Freddie Mercury. Many fans assumed it was a quicksilver reference to glam rock and sparkling stars (cf ⇨Quicksilver Messenger Service). After all, the

[68] Freddie Mercury: The Queen who wanted to be King. Or vice versa.

late Freddie also worked as ⇨Larry Lurex. The official Queen biography states he christened himself in 1970 after the messenger for the Gods. His brother-in-law said that Mercury was Freddie's rising planet. "I said it was a bloody good job it wasn't Uranus. Freddie never forgave me for that."

Related: ⇨Sour Milk Sea.

Ethel Merman
The most celebrated lady of the Broadway musical was born Ethel Agnes Zimmermann. She started a tradition of anglicising, simplifying and abbreviating real names. Another famous Zimmerman to rename was ⇨Bob Dylan.

Merseybeats
Named after the River Mersey which dominates this 1960s act's native city of Liverpool. It was a lucky pick just before ⇨The Beatles popularised "The Mersey Sound" round the world.

Merton Parkas
Neo-mod act named after their London neighbourhood, Merton Park, and parkas – the long coats which were essential mod garb. Related: ⇨The Style Council. Cf ⇨The Lambrettas.

The Metal Gurus
⇨The Mission light-heartedly remaking glam rock in the 1990s and named after ⇨T Rex's 1972 *Metal Guru*.

Metallica
L.A. band whose name was chosen to reflect their music. Several articles had already called heavy metal "metallica". Spinoff: ⇨Megadeth.

Miami Sound Machine
At first all-male and called Miami Latin Boys, from their Florida base. Then their lead singer became Gloria Estefan (née Fajardo; she married band member Emilio Estefan), "sound machine" was taken from a local disco.

George Michael
The British star was born Georgios Kyriacos Panayiotou (spelling confirmed to author directly). The first name is often pronounced "Gorgeous". His original name Yog survived as a family nickname. The ⇨Wham! man was nicknamed 'The Bubble With The Stubble' (cockney rhyming slang: bubble and squeak = Greek).

Bette Midler
"The Divine Miss M" used her real name, the Bette after Bette Davis.

Midnight Oil
Named from their habit of holding late-night rehearsals. Inspired ⇨Candlebox.

A Dictionary of Rock and Pop Names

Mighty Lemon Drops
This Wolverhampton, U.K., band decided they preferred lemon drops to their original sweet soubriquet, The Sherbet Monsters. Not a drugs reference (cf ⇨The Lemonheads).

Steve Miller
Aliases include The Space Cowboy and The Gangster Of Love, both inspired by 1973 hit *The Joker*.

The Million Dollar Quartet
Sun Studio's name for the 1956 Memphis jam between ⇨Elvis Presley, ⇨Jerry 'The Killer' Lee Lewis, ⇨Carl Perkins and ⇨Johnny Cash. "What else would you call them?" asked Sun's owner Sam Phillips, who taped the session.

Milli Vanilli
They weren't called Milli or Vanilli: this German act named after a New York discotheque.

Gordon Mills
U.K. pop businessman who named ⇨Engelbert Humperdinck, ⇨Tom Jones and ⇨Gilbert O'Sullivan *inter alios*.

The Mindbenders
Originally The Jets, they were renamed by ⇨Wayne Fontana after a U.K. science fiction/spy movie. By 1968, "mindbending" was a term applied to drugs, not something he'd intended. Related: ⇨10CC.

Zodiac Mindwarp And The Love Reaction
The 1980s British psychedelic revival band said they chose an "appropriately psychedelic" name. Fashion students making all the right moves; less of the right music. Leader Mark Manning led by example as Mindwarp. The rest managed some of the best monikers around: Trash D. Garbage; Flash Bastard; Cobalt Stargazer and Slam Thunderhide. Names worthy of ⇨Captain Beefheart's Magic Band. Proof positive that a name isn't everything.

Morris Minor And The Majors
U.K. comedy star and group who named after the much-loved Morris Minor car. Cf ⇨Madness.

M.I.A.
This usually means "Missing in Action". In the case of M.I.A., it also means "Missing in ACTON" – a London suburb where Mathangi 'Maya' Arulpragasam was living when she started out as a visual artist and album cover designer. She grew up in Sri Lanka; learned English at 11 and sometimes felt she missed out as a result. She's another in the long tradition of single-name artists: ⇨Shakira. ⇨Mika ⇨Pink.

Mika

Michael Holbrook Penniman was always known to his Lebanese family as Mica and changed the spelling.

The Minutemen

That's "minute" spoken as in 60-to-an-hour time, not "minute" as in tiny. All of their early tracks clocked in at around a minute or less – making for 45-song albums. Related: ⇨fIREHOSE.

The Miracles

⇨Smokey Robinson's band decided to rename from the Matadors and, wanting to keep an initial M, chose democratically with each member putting a name in a hat. More ⇨Motown random choice: ⇨The Commodores.

Miranda Sex Garden

The British trio had no name just minutes before a 1990 charity concert. The moniker was suggested by American Tim Sheperd, singer with British grunge band Heisenberg. Sometimes abbreviated to MSG (no relation to ⇨MSG).

The Misfits

Founder Glenn Danzig "misfit" joke is a tribute to Marilyn Monroe, taken from the title of her final movie, from 1961. Related: ⇨Danzig.

The Mission

The British 1985-on Goth-rock band, a break-away from ⇨The Sisters of Mercy, named after the Mission brand of speakers. They liked its extra devotional associations. The original Sisters, led by ⇨Andrew Eldritch, claimed a Sisters LP had been pencilled in under the working title *Left On A Mission Of Revenge*. What glorious revenge to filch it!

It's sometimes wrongly suggested the name's a film reference. The musicians were referring to neither the Ennio Morricone-soundtracked 1968 movie nor the De Niro Oscar-winner that emerged about the time they were forming. They were called "The Mish" by fans, who were called Missionaries. Related: ⇨The Metal Gurus.

Mr Mojo Risin'

Anagram for ⇨Jim Morrison (as J. Morrison) of ⇨The Doors; used most notably on the title track of the group's 1971 album *L.A. Woman*. Also near-anagram Mr. Mojo Riser.

Mr Pitiful

Otis Redding nickname, from his singing style.

Mr Wonderful

Actor-singer Sammy Davis Junior acquired this nickname after his role in the Jerry Bock-George Weiss show and film.

Joni Mitchell

Canadian Roberta Joan Anderson, always known as Joni, was first married to folk singer Chuck Mitchell. The two became known for their joint concerts and she kept the surname when they separated in 1966. Inspired: ⇨Clouds.

The Mixers

Like ⇨Heaven 17, a moniker of the future mentioned in 1962 novel *A Clockwork Orange*.

MN8

Perhaps the best thing about these 1990s teen idols was their punning name, which they chose over ORIGIN8. The street cred was wrecked when it was revealed Kule-T's mum called him Terry and KG wasn't really a Kool Guy or a Krazy Geezer but a Kevin.

Moby

The American who released the multi-million-selling CD *Play* in 1999, after some two decades making music, was born Richard Melville Hall in 1965. He recalled that this big, adult-sounding name didn't suit his especially tiny being: "My parents nicknamed me Moby . . . kinda like naming a Chihuahua 'Killer.'"

It was also a reference to his great-great-great-great uncle, novelist Herman Melville, who wrote *Moby-Dick, Or, The Whale* (1851) a mixed-narrative tour de force about life at sea and a killer whale.

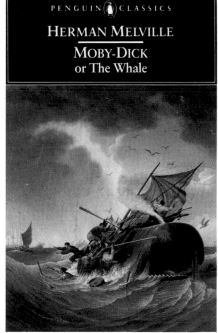

PENGUIN CLASSICS

HERMAN MELVILLE

MOBY-DICK
or The Whale

[69 + 70] Moby. And his *Moby-Dick* roots.

A Dictionary of Rock and Pop Names

Moby Grape
This 1960s San Francisco troupe named after the punchline of a joke about Moby Dick: "What's blue, large, round and lives in the sea?" After a 1974 reformation they were known as Maby Grope. More jokes: ⇨Camper Van Beethoven, ⇨The Cranberries. Unrelated: ⇨Moby.

Modest Mouse
This American indie rock band formed in 1993 and only started enjoying chart hits a decade later, working with former ⇨Smiths guitarist Johnny Marr. The name was chosen by guitarist Isaac Brock from Virginia Woolf's story: *The Mark On The Wall*. The piece refers to "the minds of modest mouse-coloured people".

The Modfather
The name probably should apply to members of ⇨The Small Faces and ⇨The Who, but it's most often linked to ⇨Paul Weller. The ⇨Godfathers-style appellation pays tribute to his mod image and music.

moe.
Five Guys Named Moe, the Louis Jordan song and musical, was the inspiration for this band, which started in 1990 in New York. They thought it was funny, said guitarist Al Schnier, even though Jordan's music didn't sound much like theirs. Because there weren't five of them (though there were later), they became Moe. When they discovered a Brooklyn act called this, they decided to lower-case the "m" and added a full stop to the name to make the faintly-ridiculous "moe." More odd capitalisation or punctuation: ⇨Wham! ⇨fIREHOSE.

moe. fans, have tagged themselves "moe.rons". Cf ⇨Five Guys Named Moe.

Mojos
Mr. Mojo; Mojos; Mojo Men. Those bands have in common an African word meaning a good luck token. These voodoo charms include dried and pickled animal heads. Cf ⇨Muddy Waters; ⇨The Hoochie-Coochie Men.

Molly Hatchet
These Florida rockers named after a lady who ranks in the annals of criminal legend alongside Sweeny Todd and Jack The Ripper. The notorious Hatchet Molly was a whore in Massachusetts.

Moloko
Another reference to *A Clockwork Orange*. Moloko plays a central part in the book and film. It's Nadsat slang from Russian for milk, which in the book is laced with drugs. The band developed the name into that of "a dark child". Cf ⇨Heaven 17.

Monaco
Peter Hook, of ⇨New Order fame, said: "Well, it's a lot more interesting than Scunthorpe, innit?" Related ⇨Revenge.

Zoot Money And His Big Roll Band

The British combo's name fitted its zoot-suited leader who was born in the money (real name, George Money).

The Monkees

A manufactured group launched in 1965 as America's answer to ⇨The Beatles, with their own television show modelled on *A Hard Day's Night* and *Help!* Brain-storming in committees resulted in a name short-list of The Boyz and The Monkeys, soon re-spelled in a Beatlesque way. The name of member Davy Jones later turned another British singer of the same name into ⇨David Bowie.

Thelonious Monk

This jazz genius is a fine example of real names being stranger than their fictional equivalent. Nicknames: The High Priest Of Be-Bop (appropriately religious) and The Mad Monk (making fun of his surname and referring to Russian "mad monk" Rasputin).

Monochrome Set

This British band named in reaction to "colourless music" and all-black-clothes bands. (Cf ⇨Living Colour.) It gave rise to a 1983 compilation named after buttons seen on black and white TV sets: *Volume, Brilliance, Contrast*.

Matt Monro

Singer Terry Parsons renamed, in part, after pianist Winifred Atwell's father. The prenomen came from reporter Matt White, the first journalist to write about him.

Marilyn Monroe

The screen star made a few records and inspired ⇨Marilyn, ⇨Marilyn Manson, ⇨The Misfits and Norma Jean. ⇨Elton John's single *Candle In The Wind* makes reference to her real name, Norma Jeane (Mortenson). Norma was renamed by talent scout Ben Lyon, who thought she resembled actress Marilyn Miller. Marilyn was keen to use her grandmother's name Monroe. Lyon agreed it had a good alliterative effect.

Chris Montez

Part-Anglicisation and simplification of Christopher Montanez.

Monty Python

The U.K. comedy act made records, had a musical spinoff in ⇨The Rutles and influenced ⇨Toad The Wet Sprocket. Their show was nearly called *Owl Stretching Time* or *Gwen Dibley's Flying Circus*. "Monty" was suggested by Eric Idle, after a drinking companion, and John Cleese (born John Cheese) offered "Python".

The Moody Blues

"The Moodies", British synth kings of the 1960s-70s came together from Birmingham acts El Riot And The Rebels. To get club work, they agreed sponsorship with brewer Mitchell & Butler, and named The M&B Five after studying M&B logo beermats. On stage, they were the Moody Blues Five to fit their R&B music, which included a track *Moody Blues*. Spinoff: ⇨The Blue Jays.

Mookie Blaylock
Seattle band named from their favourite basketball player. Related: ⇨Pearl Jam, ⇨Temple Of The Dog.

Moondog
Kansas blind street musician Louis Hardin named in 1947 after a mutt "who used to howl at the moon more than any dog I ever heard of". Hardin kept it despite a challenge by disc jockey Alan Freed, who started *Moondog's Rock 'n' Roll Party Show*. The moniker was used by the early ⇨Beatles (Johnny And The Moondogs) and by Moondog Jnr.

Keith Moon
⇨The Who. His penchant for rock excess of the highest order led to his nickname: The Loon.

Martin Moon
Nickname for John Martin, from his lyrical obsession with the night sky.

Moors Murderers
A textbook example of how to produce maximum U.K. tabloid outrage by "cashing in on misery". ⇨Steve Strange and Chrissie Hynde (later of ⇨The Pretenders) named after the notorious U.K. killers of children on the moors above Manchester. Cf ⇨The Smiths.

Jim Morrison
In typically rebellious form, ⇨The Doors singer claimed both his parents were dead and further distanced himself from them by dropping one "S" from his last name. ⇨The Lizard King. Inspired ⇨Jamie Wednesday.

Van Morrison
George Ivan Morrison (the middle name came from the Russian in his family). No relation to: Sterling Morrison of ⇨The Velvet Underground or Jim Morrison of ⇨The Doors. Nicknames: The Belfast Cowboy, Van The Man. Related: ⇨Them.

Morrissey
The British vocalist/lyricist with ⇨The Smiths, for many years now a solo artist, was born Steven Patrick Morrissey in May 1959. He became known by the surname during his Mancunian schooldays, used in an apparent bid to stop excessive familiarity. Known to some fans as Moz/Mozzer. Unflattering nicknames: Moaner, Dorrissey (coined by former songwriting partner Johnny Marr). Related: ⇨The Nosebleeds, ⇨Slaughter And The Dogs.

Jelly Roll Morton

Ferdinand LaMenthe Morton wrote *Jelly Roll Blues* at the start of his career, playing Los Angeles pool halls and brothels. It's a *double entendre* about the perils of having a large jelly (jam) roll. Also known as Mr Jelly Roll.

Tex Morton

New Zealander Robert Lane was always getting in trouble with the police when busking. He came up with the name "Tex Morton" when stopped by an officer one day. It was taken from a nearby garage sign.

Mother Of The Blues

As opposed to ⇨Empress Of The Blues or ⇨Queen Of The Blues. An apt title for "big mama" Ma Rainey.

The Mothers (Of Invention)

⇨Frank Zappa's band was at first The Soul Giants, then The Muthers and The Mothers. Nervous record company executives feared the all-male group could be adopting "the oedipal compound word": Zappa added to the name because "necessity is the mother of invention".

Spinoff: ⇨Little Feat. Related: ⇨Captain Beefheart, Ruben And The Jets (1968 project, named for "a nice 1950s feel" and mixing doo-wop with zany lyrics).

Individual members included The Winged Eel Fingerling (Elliott Ingber – also with Beefheart), Jim 'Motorhead' Sherwood (a drugs reference – cf the unrelated ⇨Motörhead) and Arthur Dyre Trip III (more drugs).

Mötley Crüe

This heavy metal group formed in Los Angeles, California, in 1980. Guitarist Mick Mars (born, Bob Deal) remembered that one of the members of predecessor act White Horse had called his fellow musicians "a motley looking crew." (Mars confirms this story to the author. This is another tale often mistold: it was NOT a passer-by commenting on the new band.) They added umlauts, inspired by the labels on German beer cans. More heavy metal umlauts are sported by ⇨Motörhead and others.

Motorhead/Motörhead

This British metal band was formed by ⇨Lemmy after he was sacked from ⇨Hawkwind. He wanted to have a dig at his former band by calling his group ⇨ Bastard but was talked out of it by manager Doug Smith, who accepted "Motorhead", perhaps thinking it to do with bikers. Lemmy said in an interview: "Like petrolhead, someone driving fast."

Lemmy's song *Motorhead*, on the B-side of Hawkwind 1974 single *Kings Of Speed*, references slang for a speed freak, or amphetamine-addict. (⇨The Mothers' Jim Sherwood was called 'Motorhead'.)

The band is usually credited as Motörhead, following the heavy metal trend for excessive umlauts.

Motörhead's personnel includes excessive louts: Wurzel (Michael Burston – the name came from his physical similarity to Worzel Gummidge, a scarecrow who comes to life in books by Barbara Euphan Todd, later televised); Animal (Phil Taylor's stagename came from his habits and nickname Philthy Animal; he has had two stints with the band); and 'Fast' Eddie Clarke (⇨Fastway). Motörhead briefly teamed up with Girlschool as Headgirl. Fan club: Motorheadbangers.

Motown
Detroit, the centre of the U.S. motor industry, was known as "Motor City" or "Motown". Hence Motown Records, ⇨Tamla Motown, ⇨MC5.

Mott The Hoople
The Doc Thomas Band was renamed by A&R man/producer Guy Stevens (who also named ⇨Procol Harum) from the title of a 1967 book by Willard Manus. Related: ⇨Bad Company.

M People
It originally stood for Mancunian leader Mike (Pickering), though after award-winning success *Q* reported: "Now it could stand for Money or Manchester or Marketing or Mercury Prize." Tribute band: TheM People.

MSG
Michael Schenker Group, often abbreviated to MSG. Related: ⇨UFO.

The Mugwumps
These New York folkies name from the mugwumps in *The Naked Lunch*, who are compulsive killers and ruthless rulers. Related: ⇨The Lovin' Spoonful, ⇨The Mamas And The Papas. More William S. Burroughs: ⇨Naked Lunch.

The Mullanes
New Zealander Neil Finn formed this band in 1984 as a stop-gap between his time in ⇨Split Enz and ⇨Crowded House. Mullane was the middle name of both Neil and mother Mary.

Mungo Jerry
This happy-go-lucky British skiffle/rock band took their name from a serious source: Nobel laureate T.S. Eliot. One of the characters in his 1939 *Old Possum's Book of Practical Cats* is called Mungojerrie. Singer Ray Dorset just liked the name.

MUSE
The muse that led to the creation of the album *No Nukes*. It stands for Musicians United For Safe Energy.

Muse
This British rock band formed in Teignmouth, Devon, in 1997 and took part in a local talent contest. The number of entries made them remark there must be a muse

hanging over the town to produce so many. They unexpectedly won (under the temporary moniker Rocket Baby Dolls).

They reasoned Muse would look good on posters (see ⇨U2 and many other acts who have partly named for similar reasons). Unrelated: ⇨Throwing Muses, the Muses and ⇨MUSE.

Muswell Hillbillies
Alter ego for ⇨The Kinks after signing to RCA in 1971. It led to an album recalling characters from Ray and Dave Davies' youth in Muswell Hill, London. The name is partially derived from U.S. TV show *The Beverly Hillbillies*. The show also inspired ⇨The Bodines, ⇨The Notting Hillbillies and ⇨The Stamford Hillbillies.

Mwandishi
Herbie Hancock projects, named from Swahili for "composer".

My Bloody Valentine
This Irish combo had buzzsaw bass, cutting lyrics and a name that combines a story of genocide with *My Funny Valentine*, covered by ⇨Frank Sinatra, ⇨Elvis Costello and more.

My Chemical Romance
The U.S. band formed in 2001. The bassist Michael 'Mikey' Way was working in a New Jersey bookstore when he came across *Ecstasy: Three Tales of Chemical Romance*, a 1996 novella collection by Irvine Welsh.

The Mynah Birds
⇨Rick James and ⇨Neil Young. The name reflected their relatively unknown status compared to ⇨The Byrds. Mynah birds are excellent mimics.

The Mystery Girls
This 1970s Liverpool band consisted only of guys. It was the gender-bender activities of singer Pete Burns which inspired the namecheck of ⇨New York Dolls track *Who Are The Mystery Girls?* Related: ⇨Dead Or Alive ⇨Wah! ⇨The Teardrop Explodes.

Mystery Trend
This Californian band named after mishearing the ⇨Bob Dylan song *Like A Rolling Stone* which refers to "a mystery tramp".

N

The Naked Lunch

This act named after U.S. writer William S. Burroughs' most famous novel, 1959's *The Naked Lunch*. A highly-regarded piece of cut-up prose by an author famous for his guns, sex, drugs and rock books. It documents the life of a drug addict in surreal detail.

Named from Burroughs: ⇨Clem Snide*; ⇨Dead Fingers Talk; ⇨Heavy Metal Kids*; ⇨The Mugwumps; The Naked Lunch*; ⇨The Nova Mob; ⇨Sex Gang Children; ⇨The Soft Boys; ⇨Soft Machine; ⇨Steely Dan* and ⇨Thin White Rope. (*= directly from this novel).

[71] *The Naked Lunch*: A scary, surreal book. And a band.

Nas

American rapper Nasir Jones abbreviated his first name. His first recordings were credited to Nasty Nas.

Nazareth

This Scottish combo named from a line in ⇨The Band's 1968 *The Weight*, about Joseph and Mary.

The Nazz

The word "naz" was part of the street-talk of the New York black community. It meant "Jesus-of-Nazarath-like" or "very good". It was adopted by jazz musicians and comedians such as ⇨Lord Buckley, whose *Sermon On The Mount* was delivered by a character called The Naz. There were two bands of this moniker; first, a nascent version of ⇨Alice Cooper named after Buckley. Second, a Philadelphia group named by Todd Rundgren after ⇨The Yardbirds' track *The Nazz Are Blue*.

Ned's Atomic Dustbin

The 1950s BBC radio comedy show *The Goons* was a hit in the 1950s and revived in the 1980s. *Ned's Atomic Dustbin* was the title of a 1959 show involving some irradiated jolly japes: nuclear power was a hot issue at the time.

This British rock outfit's singer Jonn Penney said his mother read him *Goons* scripts as a kid. In a 1995 interview he said: "If we'd ever thought we were going to have a career out of it, we'd have called ourselves Tinkle or something succinct like that."

Ricky Nelson

He slightly changed his birthname Eric Hilliard Nelson when he became a teenage TV star. He later (1960) became Rick Nelson in a bid to indicate maturity.

Nena

Gabriele Kerner, from Germany, was on holiday in Spain aged three when she was addressed as "Niña" by a local (Spanish for little girl). Her parents nicknamed her "Nena" and it stuck.

Neu!

German for "New!"

This ⇨Kraftwerk spinoff's first LP sported a *NEU!* sticker, like improved soap powder.

Neutral Blue

This was how Scottish singer Roddy Frame remembered how to wire a plug. This band evolved into ⇨Aztec Camera.

Neutral Milk Hotel

The best known of dozens of bands on the Elephant 6 record label from Athens, Georgia. This band was named after a schoolboy story written by leader Jeff Mangum.

New Edition

Manager Maurice Starr named this band because he was trying to mould them into a new edition of ⇨The Jackson Five. Cf ⇨New Kids On The Block. Inspired ⇨Boyz II Men.

New FADS

This 1988-1995 British dance rock band's name was nothing to do with fads and fashion. They were also called New Fast Automatic Daffodils after an Adrian Henri poem, which is a cut-up of Wordsworth's *Daffodils* and a Dutch advertising leaflet promoting the DAF (Daffodil) motor car. Unrelated: ⇨DAF.

New Kids On The Block

Manager Maurice Starr had named and guided ⇨New Edition to stardom. When they fell out, he decided to try the same with a bunch of white kids. He said the moniker was "pretty obvious when you know the story". Often abbreviated to New Kids and NKOTB.

Randy Newman

Singer Randall Newman's stage prenomen has been the target of amusement in the U.K. where to be "randy" translates as to be "horny" in American English. Cf Randy Jackson of ⇨The Jackson Five.

New Model Army

This British troupe liked the name of the 1645 model Roundhead army which was victorious against Royalists. Vocalist: Slade The Leveller (who later reverted to plain Justin Sullivan). Cf ⇨The Levellers.

New Order

⇨Joy Division was doomed after the singer Ian Curtis' 1980 suicide. The new moniker revived allegations of fascist sympathies. Journalist Biba Kopf wrote in NME: "It's a stupid choice of name for a group previously steeped in gloomy, magnificent gothic romanticism."

Joy Division was a Nazi term. Hitler wrote of "a New Order", his world plan, in *Mein Kampf.* ⇨Factory Records sleeves were said to have celebrated "Nazi chic". The use of two Nazi-derived names seemed more than coincidental. The boss of Factory, Tony Wilson, confirmed in an interview with the author that the band's manager Rob Gretton took pleasure in stirring up the rock press with false leads, thus generating more publicity. The source wasn't Germanic: Gretton saw a television report that the Khmer Rouge had renamed as The New Order of Kampuchean Liberation.

The musicians have denied allegations of right-wing bias, and say the handle was accepted because they were making a fresh start. The new vocalist, born Bernard Dicken, sometimes called Bernard Albrecht in Joy Division, became Barney Sumner and claimed to be so politically naïve he didn't understand "left-wing" and "right wing".

Wilson added: "It never dawned on the band until they started reading about it in the papers."

Name notes: No relation to The New Order, a U.S. band related to ⇨MC5 and ⇨The Stooges. Spinoffs: ⇨Electronic, ⇨Revenge, ⇨The Other Two, ⇨Monaco. Inspired: ⇨Happy Mondays.

New Riders Of The Purple Sage

⇨Grateful Dead spinoff, named after Zane Grey's adventure novel.

Newtown Neurotics

U.K. group named after their native postwar "new town" of Harlow, Essex, the influence of which apparently "makes people neurotic". Unrelated: ⇨Harlow.

New York Dolls

The New Yorkers' name was lifted from the 1970 Russ Meyer film *Beyond The Valley Of The Dolls* – his first for a major studio and spoof of the earlier 1967 film *The Valley Of The Dolls*. In both cases "doll" is narcotics slang for an amphetamine or barbiturate drug in capsule form. It carried an extra meaning for the doll-like all-male band whose transvestite tendencies were celebrated by their first name Actress: "It got us noticed."

Name notes: Sylvain Sylvain was previously called Ronald 'Syl' Mizrahi and inspired the naming of ⇨David Sylvian of ⇨Japan (note spellings). The Dolls also included Johnny Volume (later Johnny Thunders, né John Genzale). Inspired: ⇨The Mystery Girls and ⇨Kiss.

Nickelback

The Canadian band was formed by singer/guitarist Chad Kroeger. He moved to Vancouver in 1995 to use a friend's studio, supporting himself with part-time jobs.

"Even after we recorded a few songs, I was a cashier at Starbucks and coffee was

$1.95," he said in an interview. He often had to give customers change, since few gave the right amount. The words "Here's your nickel back" became a tired mantra, repeated dozens of times a day. Nickelback saw the name as a tribute to all those with jobs in places like Starbucks, having to repeat things many times, and as a comment on commercialism.

Nico

Christa Päffgen (1938-1988) was still a model when she got her professional name – not yet a singer, still less a collaborator with the ⇨Velvet Underground. She was rechristened by German photographer Herbert Tobais in 1956 after the man he loved, filmmaker Nico Papatakis. Tobais said models should have single names and Christa didn't suit her.

Nico later invented false stories that her real name was Nico Pavlovsky: she was named by artist Salvador Dali as an anagram of "icon" and she was given the name by Coco Chanel, who based it on her own name.

Nigel And The Crosses

⇨R.E.M.'s 1989 Green world tour included a part-time band called Worst Case Scenario featuring Peter Buck. They renamed at one point in honour of Nigel Cross, the original editor of the magazine (sic) *Bucketfull Of Brains*.

The Nightingales

This post-punk band took its avian inspiration from *Luscinia Megarhynchos*, a small bird of the thrush family mainly noted for the rich love-song of the male, heard at night.

Nilsson

Harry Edward Nelson III changed the spelling to avoid links with England's famous admiral and ⇨Rick(y) Nelson.

Nine Inch Nails

This American industrial rock band's leader Trent Reznor chose "Nine Inch Nails" in 1988 because it "abbreviated easily" and not for any literal meaning. The logo features NIN in a box, with the second N reversed.

This statement has not prevented the usual internet idiots whose 'friend of a friend' told them that maybe it's a reference to the spikes used to crucify Jesus. Or perhaps they read "somewhere" it applies to Reznor's fingernails. (His nails aren't of Freddy Krueger or even Flo Jo length.)

999

This U.K. band named from their theme *Emergency*: 999 is the British number for urgent calls, equivalent to ⇨911 in the States.

911

From the U.S. emergency number, coincidentally echoing ⇨Public Enemy's *911 Is A Joke*.

The Nipple Erectors

This punk band name's orgasmic reference led to the abbreviation: The Nips. ⇨The Pogues.

Nirvana

There've been at least three professional bands called this. One, from Seattle, is credited with changing music history, popularising grunge and featuring Kurt Cobain (1967–1994) who shot from nothing to superstardom – then shot himself.

They played a local Community World Theater show billed as "Nirvana: also known as ⇨Skid Row, Ted Ed Fred, Pen Cap Chew and Bliss." They also considered Throat Oyster and Windowpane. Cobain said: "I wanted a name that's beautiful and nice and pretty instead of a mean, raunchy punk name like ⇨The Angry Samoans."

Nirvana originally meant Buddhist beatitude or blessedness. Its origin is Sanskrit for extinction: here, the breaking down of individuality and absorption into a supreme spirit. It suggests reflective folk, trance-like ambient music or soothing mantras rather than Cobain's pain. Grunge contemporaries ⇨Sanctuary and ⇨Soundgarden had similarly misleading names.

A different band called Nirvana was a 1960s-onwards British group led by Patrick Campbell-Lyons, who took legal action. This ended with a payment to him and his partner: Cobain agreed not to perform psychedelic rock.

Cobain's widow is ⇨Courtney Love of ⇨Hole. Related: ⇨Foo Fighters. It's Kurt CO-bane, not C'bane.

Nitty Gritty Dirt Band

U.S. outfit named because of their down-to-earth aim of wanting to get back to the basics of country music.

Nomad

Leader Damon Rochefort didn't like his prenomen and reversed its letters to become a wanderer.

The Nosebleeds

Never a true heavy metal band, they jokingly named after the fans' nosebleeds produced from standing too close to speakers. Among those to work with the group after the departure of ⇨Ed Banger: ⇨Morrissey.

The Notorious B.I.G.

Rapper Christopher Wallace, who was murdered in 1997, at first used the stagename Biggie Smalls (because he reminded a friend of a gangster in the 1975 movie *Let's Do It Again*). He later changed this to The Notorious B.I.G.

The Notting Hillbillies

Notting Hill is the London area where ⇨Dire Straits's Mark Knopfler and Steve Phillips had met and also formed ⇨The Duolian String Pickers. The name's a reference to their country sound via the U.S. TV series *The Beverly Hillbillies*.

Nova Mob

This mob named from U.S. writer William S. Burroughs' story *Nova Express*. Cf
⇨Naked Lunch.

*NSYNC

This American "boy band" lasted from 1995 to 2002. Like many other manufactured
bands (⇨B*Witched etc) its name came with a newspaper-friendly story which
reflected well on the group. In this case, it was claimed that Justin Timberlake's
mother was impressed when she heard the five's voices totally "in sync".

   Coincidentally, the last letters of each member's first names spelled: JustiN, ChriS,
JoeY, JasoN, JC. Also written as 'N Sync.

NTM

Offensiveness alert. French rap group whose name means *nique ta mere* or "fuck
your mother". Related: LHOOQ, *elle a chaud au cul* or "she has a hot ass", inspired
by Duchamp.

Ted Nugent

⇨The Amboy Dukes, ⇨Damned Yankees.

Nugerte

Anagram of Atlantic Records boss Ahmet ERTEGUN (1923-2006) – used as a credit
name when composing music.

Gary Numan

The British synth star was born (1958) Gary Anthony James Webb, but like ⇨Cliff
Richard (born Harry Webb) thought the name had little stage appeal. Webb chose
Newman to reflect his futuristic-sounding synthesiser music, picked from the *Yellow
Pages* directory then given a "nu-style" spelling. Fans called Numanoids, unbeliev-
ably. Apart from a short spell with The Lasers, Numan was solo, though he disguised
this under Tubeway Army for a time.

The Nurk Twins

Nickname for Lennon and McCartney, sometimes spelled Nerk Twins. (Cf Jagger-
Richards, ⇨The Glimmer Twins; Perry-Tyler, ⇨The Toxic Twins.)

The Nutty Boys

⇨Madness spinoff by Chris Foreman and Lee Thompson. Album title: *Crunch!*

NWA

Like ⇨The Beatnigs, this Californian rap band wanted a name which expressed their
positive response to being black and their fight against prejudice. They wanted to be
called Niggers With Attitude. The U.S. slang is now worldwide: "attitude" = to have
a strong manner. They abbreviated to NWA after misunderstandings by ignorant radio
disc jockeys who couldn't comprehend how "nigger" could be used in any way but
pejoratively.

The Nymphs

Singer Inger Lorre said: "A nymph is a bug lava and I joke that one day we'll grow into ⇨The Beatles."

NYoil

The name means "New York's Original International Lover" said *Time Out New York*. It's pronounced as "N-Y Oil".

Laura Nyro

The white New York singer-songwriter was born Laura Nigro and renamed to avoid possible racist "negro" confusion. She worked with ⇨LaBelle.

◐

Oasis

As the crown of the best British group is passed to ⇨The Arctic Monkeys and ⇨Radiohead, Oasis sails on with a career that began in Manchester, in 1991. Noel Gallagher, now the band's lead guitarist/songwriter, had been a roadie for ⇨The Inspiral Carpets since 1988. His singer brother Liam formed his first band called The Rain. (There was an obscure ⇨Beatles track called *Rain*.)

On the *Definitely Maybe* singles box set interview CD, Liam says: "It's on a poster on me bedroom wall just sitting there, and I saw the word 'Oasis' and I just thought: 'That's very nice.' I thought: 'I'd have a bit of that." The poster showed Inspiral dates including one at the Swindon Oasis.

In 1996 Noel dismissed some other name theories: "There was a clothes shop in Manchester called Oasis where you could buy these decent trainers and is where all the football hooligans used to go. And a lot of people say it's the name of the local taxi firm in Burnage, or it's the name of the local curry house."

Two unlikely sources that Noel didn't mention: (1) the track *Oasis* by fellow Mancunians ⇨The Happy Mondays; and (2) the Oasis Club in Manchester, where The Beatles played in 1963. Oasis as a word has been applied to everything from clubs to financial products and flower-holders. The band has avoided challenges over the use, apart from the clothing chain over "Oasis" tee-shirts.

Oasis has also been used in a musical context before: ⇨Oasis of the 1980s. There was also a pub duo in Leeds, Yorkshire, called Oasis; the first time the Gallaghers played at The Duchess of York in the city, there were only about 12 people there, perhaps because everyone thought it was the other Oasis.

Tribute bands: Blurasis, The Gallaghers, No Way Sis and Oasisn't. Related: ⇨The Smoking Mojo Filters. Liam has a son called Lennon after ⇨John Lennon.

A Dictionary of Rock and Pop Names

Oasis (1980s)
Everyone's heard of the Gallaghers' ⇨Oasis. Not so many know Oasis was also used by a short-lived "supergroup" – Mary Hopkin, Peter Skellern and Julian Lloyd Webber – aiming to be "an oasis in a desert of modern music".

Ocean Colour Scene
This Birmingham, U.K., band said Ocean, Colour and Scene were "three words we liked which sounded good together". Cf ⇨Living Colour.

Sinéad O'Connor
Sinéad Marie Bernadette O'Connor. Unflattering derivative: Skinhead O'Connor. Pronunciation guide: "Shin-aid" not "Sigh-need".

Odetta
The folk singer and ⇨Bob Dylan interpreter's birthname was Odetta Holmes Felonius Gorden.

O' Jays
This band from Canton received advice from Cleveland deejay Eddie O' Jay. "Eddie helped us loads. Even in gettin' the record contract," Eddie Levert said. "We thought of the best way of thanking Eddie, by naming after him."

Ol' Dirty Bastard
American rapper Russell Tyrone Jones (1968-2004) has one of the funniest names in rock. He named ⇨Wu-Tang Clan from his love of martial arts movies, and used the same source for his stagename. Group members told him his unique vocal style had "no father" and he remembered a similar plotline in 1980 kung fu film *Ol' Dirty & The Bastard*. Often shortened to ODB.

Omar
Omar Hammer used just his first name because he hated being compared to ⇨MC Hammer.

On A Friday
This group of friends at Abingdon School, Oxfordshire, named "On A Friday" in 1986 because this was the weekday they rehearsed at the music room. The band was put on hold while they attended university and, after only eight gigs, they signed to EMI in 1991. The matter of the name came to a head after a February 1992 concert review in *Melody Maker* by John Harris, who started: "Terrible name. Apt for beer-gutted pub rockers, but ill-suited to the astonishing intensity of this bunch."

Interestingly, they went on to become ⇨Radiohead.

One Dove
This 1990s band started as The Doves. They ran into trouble with the already-existing Thrashing Doves. The group became One Dove, a reference to an ecstasy tablet, not the ⇨Bob Marley reggae song *One Love*.

One Little Indian

This British record label was set up as a bedroom concern by Derek Birkett, the former bass player of ⇨Flux of Pink Indians. One of his early signings: ⇨The Sugarcubes.

101'ers

An R&B-style outfit starring ⇨Joe Strummer, later of ⇨The Clash, and Don Kelleher, later of ⇨Public Image Ltd.

They didn't name after the rat torture room in George Orwell's 1949 novel *Nineteen Eighty Four*. The truth is more prosaic: it was the address of a London squat, 101 Walterton Road, home of Strummer and friends.

13111

Spinoff project from ⇨R.E.M. : Bill Berry took the name from the record's matrix number.

The Only Ones

Formed 1976. The *NME* quoted vocalist Peter Perrett saying it came from a fantasy about the end of the world and the band being the only ones left alive.

The Opium Eaters

Liverpool band of 1978, whose members went on into ⇨Frankie Goes To Hollywood, ⇨The Slits and ⇨Wah! They were encouraged by Mick Jones of ⇨The Clash, who suggested the name from *Confessions Of An English Opium-Eater*, the 1822 book by Thomas De Quincey.

Orange Juice

No relation to ⇨Oran 'Juice' Jones! They adopted their off-beat name as a refreshing change amid rancid punk. Inspired ⇨Strawberry Switchblade.

The Orb

This English electric/ambient group formed in 1988 and likes psychedelic, spacey and sci-fi themes. They named after a disco-ball type object in the 1973 Woody Allen film *Sleeper*. This orb produces trance or drug-like effects when touched. The same movie also inspired the naming of ⇨Sleeper. Founder Dr Alex Paterson got his "doctorate" from the initials of his first two prenomens Duncan Robert.

Woody Allen masquerades as a robot to avoid detection in "Sleeper".

[72] Woody Allen looked into the future – and maybe saw groups called The Orb and Sleeper.

Roy Orbison

Roy Kelton Orbison, or 'The Big O', joined the 1988 aggregation ⇨The Traveling Wilburys as Lefty Orbison, a studio joke based on a political discussion. Their next album was dedicated to the late Lefty. Punning LP title: *Orbisongs*.

Orbital

Orbital play spacey music – but named after London's main orbital road, the M25 motorway, the quickest way of getting to the warehouse parties at which they performed.

Orchestral Manoeuvres In The Dark

Liverpudlian keyboard players Andy McCluskey and Paul Humphreys went through many early groups. They included Hitlerz Underpantz (a jejune name guaranteeing commercial failure and reflecting the punk fascination with shocking Nazi references). There was also ⇨VCL XI, The Id and ⇨Dalek I.

One of their first tracks featured tank sounds and explosions off a sound effects record, *Orchestral Manoeuvres In The Dark*. The name was gradually shortened: O.M.I.T.D., O.M.D., OMD. They said similarities with ⇨ELP and ⇨ELO were coincidental. It wasn't intended as an anagram, though some come close including "Uncontroversial Remarketed Hash".

The Orioles

One of the first of many "bird" bands, they came from Baltimore, Maryland, and named after the mascot associated with sports teams from the city.

Orson

These pop musicians formed in 1999/2000 in their native Hollywood. Singer Jason Pebworth said in an interview that they loved director Orson Welles' work: "He was a maverick, yet his art stood the test of time." The name came to him from a list of snacks in a coffee shop: the Greta Garbo, the Clark Gable, the Orson Welles. The last was a sandwich filled with Gouda cheese and pickles. None of the band ate one. Cf ⇨Kane Gang.

Ozzy Osbourne

Born 1948, known as Ozzy from his surname. Some journalists interviewing him have been told to call him by his proper name. "I'm bleedin' John Michael Osbourne here, y'know." He may then regale reporters with the similarity between his name, the magazine *Oz* and musical *The Wizard Of Oz*. (I know. I've been there). Related: ⇨Black Sabbath, Blizzard Of Oz. No relation to the rock bands Oz or Ozz.

Osibisa

African-tinged rock band formed by Teddy Osei which played bisaba, the West African native music, in a rock style.

Gilbert O'Sullivan

The Irish singer-songwriter was born Raymond O'Sullivan. Gordon Mills, manager (and namer) of both ⇨Tom Jones and ⇨Engelbert Humperdinck, thought his songwriting matched some of the greats of the past. The fledgling star became Gilbert, while retaining his surname, in reference to British composers Sir William Gilbert and Sir Arthur Sullivan.

The Other Two

In 1990 two ⇨New Order members were going their own ways with solo records: Barney Sumner's ⇨Electronic and Peter Hook's ⇨Revenge. This left the "quiet ones", married couple Stephen Morris and Gillian Gilbert. They said the moniker had "plenty of ironies" and "it was getting late and we're crap at names".

Johnny Otis

This U.S. pop talent scout and recording artist anglicised his real (Greek) surname, Veliotes. ⇨The Godfather of R&B.

OutKast

This hip hop duo based in Georgia found their name in a dictionary in 1991. They thought it was appropriate because rap was dominated by East Coast and West Coast rappers who saw those from the south as outcasts.

Ox

⇨The Who bassist John Entwistle formed this band after ⇨Rigor Mortis. The nickname was for his taciturn nature and still stature on stage. A remark by Entwistle (and/or Keith Moon) inspired the naming of ⇨Led Zeppelin.

The Ozark Mountain Daredevils

Mountain range in Oklahoma and Arkansas. The Daredevils' 1975 *The Car Over The Lake Album* illustrated the name with a daredevil automobile in mid-flight.

P

Larry Page

British singer Leonard Davies renamed in honour of the *Jolson Story* star and became "Larry Page, the teenage rage." He renamed ⇨The Kinks, ⇨The Troggs and ⇨Reg Presley.

Patti Page

Oklahoma-born Clara Ann Fowler took her new prenomen from opera singer Adelina Patti. It fitted the surname Page which she had to adopt in a radio show sponsored by the Page Milk Company, a Tulsa dairy, when she was 18.

Palladium

The band formed in 2006 as the Peppernotes, after singer Peter Pepper. They renamed to Palladium because it rhymed with "stadium", Pepper said: "We've big aspirations, that's what we're aiming for."

Papa Roach

This Californian rock band formed in 1993 and named as a joke from singer Jacoby Shaddix's step-grandfather, Howard William Roach, nicknamed Papa Roach. The cockroach covers did not prevent huge CD sales.

The Paramounts

Members of this British band, formed in 1959, were cherry-picked from various groups from Southend-on-Sea. In combination they were "Paramount". The name, therefore, was not a movie reference, as might be assumed.

Paramount Gary Brooker became famous soon after with ⇨Procol Harum. Other former Paramounts later joined Procol. It wasn't until 1970 that everyone in Procol had at some time played with the Paramounts.

Colonel Tom Parker

Eminence grise behind ⇨Elvis Presley. The manager was born Andreas Cornelius van Kuijk in the Dutch town of Breda. The "respectable" all-American name was assumed when he arrived as an immigrant. The military "rank" was an honorary title bestowed by the Tennessee Militia.

Parliament(s)

Young ⇨George Clinton was looking for a name for the vocal group he was forming in the 1950s . . . and found it in his pocket. Where he had a packet of Parliament cigarettes. ⇨Funkadelic.

Larry Parnes

This U.K. businessman named or managed among others: ⇨Vince Eager, ⇨Georgie Fame, ⇨Lance Fortune, ⇨Billy Fury, ⇨Johnny Gentle, ⇨Duffy Power, ⇨Dickie Pride, ⇨Tommy Steele and ⇨Marty Wilde.

He was known as Larry "Mr Parnes, Shillings And Pence" Parnes because of his financial savvy. He gave all his stars similar names – usually a two-syllable "soft" first name followed by a simple, short, "hard" surname. The names were sometimes suggested to fit in with some character of the auditioning singer.

Parnes failed to rename one artist in his stable, Joe Brown, who had decades of solo success despite the non-stagey name. He might not have enjoyed the same success under the proposed moniker Almer Twitch.

The Alan Parsons Project

Code name used by London's Abbey Road Studios for bookings made by Alan Parsons (⇨The Beatles' engineer) as he recorded with musical partner Eric Woolfson. He kept it as a group name.

Bill Parsons

Singer Bobby Bare got a shock when his record came out. It was mistakenly credited to Bill Parsons, another artist on the same label. The song, 1958's *All-American Boy*, was a hit and he was renamed for life.

Gram Parsons

Cecil Ingram Connor became known as Gram, an abbreviation of his middle name. ⇨The Byrds, ⇨The Flying Burrito Brothers. Inspired ⇨Angelband.

Billy Paul

Paul Williams reversed his birthnames so as not to clash with the Paul Williams in ⇨The Temptations or an actor of the same moniker.

Pavlov's Dog

This U.S. band, formed 1973, paid tribute to ⇨The Rolling Stones, whose 1971 song *Bitch* includes the line "when you call my name I come running like a Pavlov Dog." Pavlov's Dog's second album was 1976's *At The Sound Of The Bell*. Both bands referenced experiments by psychologist Ivan Pavlov.

Peaches And Herb

Herbert Feemster, better known as Herb Fame, formed this duo with Francine Barker, whose Peaches childhood nickname came from her friendly disposition. When Francine left, four other female singers in turn were drafted in as the new "Peaches".

Pearl Jam

Seattle's Pearl Jam formed in 1990, mainly from bands called ⇨Green River and Mother Love Bone. They first played under their new line up as ⇨Mookie Blaylock.

Bassist Jeff Ament really wanted "Pearl" in the name and they added "Jam", after musical jamming, and seeing ⇨Neil Young play. It's a less colourful account than that originally offered by singer Eddie Vedder, who said Pearl Jam came from American Indian great-grandmother, Pearl, and her finest recipe: a fearsome jam that supposedly had hallucinogenic properties. He said the jam was made from Mexican cactus yielding mescaline, boiled and distilled with the spines removed.

Pearls Before Swine

This U.S. band recycled the proverb, adapted from The Bible – Matthew 7:6: "Do not throw your pearls before swine, lest they trample them under foot and turn to attack you." This U.S. band regarded its art as 'pearls', though it said its audience were not 'swine'.

Pencey Prep

This New Jersey punk band 2000-2002 named after the school attended by Holden Caulfield, anti-hero of the 1951 J.D. Salinger novel *The Catcher In The Rye*. Related: ⇨My Chemical Romance.

Penetration
Late 1970s British punksters, whom the *NME* later reported as playing "penetrating music". Any resemblance to a term beloved of advertising agencies was accidental . . . any coincidence with sex: deliberate.

Percy
Robert Plant's nickname "Percy" was born during ⇨Led Zeppelin's tour to promote their first album. It was an in-joke because he was a plant and the most famous English gardener at the time was Percy Thrower. Disregard reports that the tight-trousered one's appellation came from the film *Percy* about a man who has a penis transplant. The film was made in 1971; the nickname dates from 1969.

Pere Ubu
The Cleveland band named from the anti-hero of Alfred Jarry play *Ubu Roi*, made into a film by animator Jan Lenica in 1976. They liked the name Peru Ubu even though he's self-centred, stupid and sadistic. Spinoff: ⇨Friction.

A Perfect Circle
Maynard James Keenan, founder of this Californian band, said the name was picked in 1999 because relationships between group members formed "a perfect circle" of friendship. APC had a song at the same time called *Orestes*, with the opening lines: "Metaphor for a missing moment/Pull me into your perfect circle."

Carl Perkins
The rock 'n' roll singer made a slight modification to Lee Perkings, the name misspelled on his birth certificate.

Peter, Paul And Mary
Wisely chosen in preference to their surnames Yarrow, Stookey and Travers, which sounded like "a firm of morticians". Stookey's first name was Noel but renamed because it went better with Peter and Mary.

Pet Shop Boys
London-based Neil Tennant and Chris Lowe struck up a conversation in a King's Road hi-fi shop and formed a duo tentatively called West End in 1981.

They worked with record producer Bobby O (Robert Orlando) who knew three local lads who worked in an Ealing pet store: Tennant thought Pet Shop Boys sounded like an American rap act, "twee and camp".

Tennant was "absolutely horrified" in 1986 when journalist Betty Page told him the name was being linked to a sado-masochistic ritual – decadents were said to be anally inserting small animals to induce a masturbatory high. Tennant now believes this to be apocryphal, having spoken to "some people in New York who might know".

Answering questions at the Oxford Union later, Tennant was asked about the origin, and paused before answering: "You know, it's funny to think that people are looking at you and thinking: 'There goes a man who puts hamsters up his bottom." He brought the house down.

A Dictionary of Rock and Pop Names

Probably the legend about the name has been helped along by three traits. First, Tennant says it has been "endlessly referred to". Second, the PSB affect an air of knowing satire at all times, which suggests that things are not what they seem. Third, is their sexuality. There's some confusion of issues here. It's obvious that someone can be gay without knowing of, or condoning, animal torture. Unfortunately, this isn't so obvious to some tabloid journalists.

Tom Petty
Petty might have never made it if he had stayed as a member of the unpleasantly-named Mudcrutch, homage to Florida's muddy alligator swamps. Related: ⇨The Heartbreakers, ⇨The Traveling Wilburys.

Nanker Phelge
⇨Rolling Stones songwriting credit for some 1960s all-group compositions. Bill Wyman said: "Phelge came from Edith Grove's flatmate Jimmy Phelge, while a Nanker was a revolting face that band members, Brian [Jones] in particular, would pull."

!Phfft
The British record label's onomatopoeic name is meant to represent a lager can being opened, although less savoury theories are rife. Not a reference to 1954 U.S. movie *Phfft*.

Little Ester Phillips
Texas blues singer Ester Jones took her name from a poster for Phillips Gasoline.

Phish
This U.S. rock band formed at the University of Vermont in 1983 and named after the drummer, Jon Fishman.

The Photos
These British new-wavers wanted to be obscure and dual-meaning-sounding. The photogenic members' debut was *I'm So Attractive*. Related: ⇨Strange Cruise.

Edith Piaf
France's greatest cabaret star (1915-1963) was born Edith Giovanna Gassion. She was given her stagename in 1935 by night-club owner Louis Leplée: *la môme piaf*.

Piano Red
Pianist Willie Perryman's albino condition and pink eyes gave rise to the nickname. Inspired ⇨Doctor Feelgood.

Pigpen
⇨Grateful Dead member Ronald McKernan (1945-1973) was given his nickname in school because of his "funky' approach to life and sanitation," according to the Dead's website. It's probably a reference to the always-filthy Pig-Pen character in *Peanuts*.

Pinhead Gunpowder

San Francisco drummer Aaron Cometbus discovered Pinhead Gunpowder, described as a "high octane" green tea, in a local shop in 1991. ⇨Green Day's Billie Joe Armstrong, who joined him, liked it because his heroes ⇨The Ramones were known for their "pinhead" jokes.

Pink

Alecia Beth Moore said she has been known as Pink since the age of 15 when she had her trousers pulled off at summer camp. She blushed bright pink. Some profiles suggest a resemblance to Steve Buscemi's character Mr. Pink in the 1992 Quentin Tarantino movie *Reservoir Dogs*, although the author can't see it himself. Her pink hair came only after the stagename, which is often written P!nk.

The Pink Fairies

A tongue-in-cheek name that some people did not know whether to take seriously or not. It was meant to be a joke. As you can tell with albums which have titles like *Oh, What A Bunch of Sweeties*. It may have been a reference to J.R.R. Tolkien. Cf ⇨The Pretty Things.

Pink Floyd

The U.K. band came together from the wreckage of Sigma 6, also called Meggadeath (cf ⇨Megadeth), the Architectural Abdabs, The Screaming Abdabs and finally The Tea Set.

Drummer Nick Mason recalls they needed another moniker when they were offered a gig at which another band called Tea Set was playing. New recruit Syd Barrett (ex-Hollering Blues) "without further ado" namechecked two music heroes: Pink Anderson (1900-74) and Floyd Council (1911-76) to suggest The Pink Floyd Sound. While there is no suggestion in this case he owned records by Anderson or Council, "the name stuck", albeit in slightly abbreviated form.

Still, there are many false reports out there. The London *Evening Standard* had said: "Roger Waters shared a flat in 1967 in Earls Court with artist Duggie Fields and someone called Mick Steadman. They had two cats called Pink and Floyd. Although the name is widely believed to derive from a synthesis of two Georgia blueser's monikers . . . we think it came from the cats."

It's true that Waters was friendly with a Mike Leonard, who lived in Highgate with two cats – called Tunji and McGhee, one a Burmese and one a Siamese. Waters was fond of the cats. Tunji McGhee doesn't have the same ring to it as Pink Floyd.

Barrett later left the band; he inspired ⇨Gigolo Aunts. He didn't give any interviews so it is difficult to clear up the mystery before his death in 2006. The Floyd went on to become one of the best-selling bands of all time. And to think they could have been known as Anderson Council . . .

Members have recounted versions of a story about meeting a music industry executive – who apparently showed his ignorance by asking, "Which one's Pink?"

For another band-naming story involving a cat and some mystery: ⇨Procol Harum.

A Dictionary of Rock and Pop Names

Pink Kross
All-female trio, described by *NME* as: "Glasgow's foremost purveyors of Day-Glo escapist fuzzy garage punk." They named after their favourite act ⇨Redd Kross.

The Pips
They were named after a cousin of leader Gladys Knight, Pip Woods. It became an acronym for "Perfection In Performance".

Pitchshifter
The English band named from the audio device that changes the pitch of a signal. The group played industrial music as Pitch Shifter until 1996, then rock as Pitchshifter from 1998.

Pixies
This hard-rocking American band made it big on the back of a name found in a dictionary by guitarist Joey Santiago. Arguably, the moniker is more misleading than meaningless, sounding like the name for a fey folk-rock band. Like their fellow Bostonians ⇨Throwing Muses, they eschew the definite article. Related: ⇨The Breeders.

Placebo
Brian Molko and Stefan Olsdal formed the band in London in 1994. They noticed that many other acts at the time had a name influenced by drugs. They decided to go for one with no effect.

PM Dawn
From the duo's stagenames, Prince Be and Minutemix – respectively brothers Attrell and Jarrett Cordes.

Poco
The band formed after the 1968 breakup of ⇨Buffalo Springfield as Pogo, who named after the U.S. newspaper comic strip by Walt Kelly, because their manager looked like the Pogo character himself. They encountered legal difficulties with the owners of the cartoons but decided to change it as little as possible. *Poco* is a musical term – from Italian – meaning "slightly". Contrary to several books on ⇨John Lennon, he didn't name Poco. They were named before they met him.

The Pogues
Shane MacGowan – he with the teeth like sharks', skin like shrapnel, voice like tearing sandpaper and drunk-set eyes – was a member of lost punk stars ⇨The Nipple Erectors, later abbreviated, before forming this riotous Irish band in the early 1980s. Again, he chose a saucy name and was forced to abbreviate.

This one, suggested by band member Peter Stacy, came from Irish "póg mo thón", or "kiss my arse". The pronunciation of the Gaelic is Pogue Mahone. The band played in the 1987 film *Straight To Hell* as The McMahon Gang. ⇨Joe Strummer.

The Police

⇨Sting's men chose Police because the word is "internationally known". It fitted similarly-named enterprises by manager Miles Copeland, brother of drummer Stewart Copeland. These included CIA, FBI, the Illegal record label and the Outlandos (i.e. outlaws) Charity Trust. The names were inspired by their father, a former executive with the Central Intelligence Agency.

Miles played a part in naming ⇨Lords Of The New Church and ⇨Wishbone Ash. Tribute band: The Secret Police. Related: ⇨Curved Air, ⇨Klark Kent, ⇨Soft Machine ⇨Zoot Money.

The Pop Group

It can be argued The (Strictly Non-Radio-Friendly) Punk Group would have been a better name for this lot. The name can be seen as refreshingly modest or one with the arrogance of ⇨The Band (THE Pop Group, as if no other matters). Related: ⇨Rip Rig + Panic.

Iggy Pop

Michigan-born James Newell 'Jewel' Osterberg took the Iggy from his time as a member of failed punk band, The Iguanas (1964). With ⇨The Stooges (to the 1970s), he became Iggy Stooge.

The "Pop" related to local personality and well known drop-out Jim Popp. The star told *Rolling Stone* in 2007: "Jim Popp was a friend of the Ashetons and Dave Alexander [The Stooges]. They were part of a gang that cut school and sniffed glue together. I always thought Pop was a cool name. And it goes good with Iggy." The "Pop" was added when he worked with ⇨David Bowie. Iggy in turn helped inspire ⇨Ziggy Stardust.

Pop Will Eat Itself

The U.K. band said the phrase "Pop Will Eat Itself" came from *NME* reporter David Quantick, who coined the phrase while interviewing ⇨Jamie Wednesday. Often abbreviated to PWEI.

Porcupine Tree

The author is inclined to give this English progressive band minimal publicity. The response to questions on "why the name" was "don't ask!" It would be helpful if you confirmed many curious fans' speculation that it's about a cactus that provides a psychedelic drug (Cf ⇨Pearl Jam). That would perfectly fit the creation of the band, along with an imagined backstory stretching back to the 1970s. Fans say Steve Wilson hasn't even told other members of the band and wants it to remain a mystery.

Porno For Pyros

More shock-rock from ⇨Lollapalooza founder ⇨Perry Farrell. He named the band in 1992 after the L.A. riots.

Portishead

This British band from Bristol unassumingly named from the nearby coastal town.

Cat Power

American singer/songwriter Charlyn "Chan" Marie Marshall (1972-) has attracted some predictably stupid Internet comments by fans. There is speculation she sees herself as a cat or intends it as a vegan statement.

Marshall recalls it happened like this: when she was a cashier at a pizza restaurant, she received a call from a friend who had formed a band. She was the lead singer, and they needed a name as they had their first concert that night. "Just as she [her friend] was on the phone telling me all this shit, which I was furious about, this real old man in a CAT diesel power cap was asking for a beer. So that was where the name came from."

[74] Chan Marshall noticed a guy with a CAT POWER hat... and had an idea...

Duffy Power

Singer Ray Howard's name was misheard by ⇨Larry Parnes.

The Power Station

This ⇨Duran Duran spinoff named from The Power Station, the New York studio where they recorded in 1985. If had translated the name into German, they would have got ⇨Kraftwerk. Related: ⇨Arcadia.

Prefab Sprout

Leader Paddy MacAloon found the name in 1973 after mishearing the words "pepper sprout" in Nancy Sinatra (⇨Boots) and Lee Hazlewood's 1967 song *Jackson*. They sing about their love for each other being hotter than the aforesaid sprout. MacAloon formed a band under the name in Newcastle in 1982. Bored with the true story, he then told reporters it was an attempt to link unrelated words: "The second choice was Chrysalis Cognos".

The handle was as surreal as ⇨The Chocolate Watch Band, ⇨The Electric Prunes or ⇨The Soft Machine from the 1960s, and ⇨Aztec Camera in the 1980s. MacAloon admits being inspired by deliberately strange progressive rock names of the 1970s. He told the author: "You hear it and think, 'what does that mean?'"

"Prefabs" were quickly-built pre-fabricated houses built in large numbers in the U.K. to replace blitz-damaged property after the Second World War. How a naturally-growing sprout can be "prefabricated" has never been explained.

The Prefects

U.K. punk band, counterparts to ⇨The Cortinas. In this case, named not after the Ford Prefect, but school pupils.

The Presidents Of The United States of America

The Seattle group named in 1993 following guitarist Chris Ballew's suggestion of "the most significant name we could chose in America."

Elvis Presley

Elvis was born in Tupelo, Mississippi in 1935: named after his father, Vernon Elvis Presley, and Mr. Presley's friend in Tupelo, Aaron Kennedy. He had no need of stagenames – at first, as a modest kid, later, as perhaps the greatest of all stars. Elvis was his father's middle name and was fortunately unique in showbusiness. It was uncommon except in poor white communities in the U.S., who imported it from the English Helwiss.

[74] Forget Costello, Jackson and Mercury: here's the true King leaving his stamp on music.

Of his middle name, Aron was the spelling the Presleys chose, apparently to make it similar to the middle name of Elvis' stillborn identical twin, Jesse Garon Presley. Elvis later sought to change the spelling of his middle name to the biblical Aaron but learned that official state records, inexplicably, had already listed him as Aaron. It has been suggested some officials just thought it a spelling error and changed it without checking with Elvis' parents. Aaron is the spelling on his grave and the one his estate regards as his official middle name.

To many he was Elvis, El, (Elvis) The Pelvis (from his provocative hip thrusts, judged too racy to be shown on U.S. television) or ⇨The King. He was also known as the Mississippi/Memphis Flash and The Hillbilly Cat. ⇨Million Dollar Quartet. His name and music inspired ⇨Elvis Costello, ⇨Vince Everett, ⇨The Sid Presley Experience, ⇨Death In Vegas, ⇨Reg Presley, ⇨The Heartbreakers, ⇨Wayne Fontana, and ⇨Kid Creole.

Reg Presley

Keith Altham, *New Musical Express* journalist and PR man extraordinaire, recalls a 1966 phone call from music entrepreneur ⇨Larry Page about his signing ⇨The Troggs. "He said, 'I'm a bit worried about the lead singer. His name is Reginald Maurice Balls.' [Sic: actually the name was Ball, singular.] He said, 'Now what can I call him?' I said: 'Presley!' for a joke on the phone. He said, 'That's great!' I said, 'No, I was only kidding."

Ball, an apprentice bricklayer with a strong rural accent, said in an interview: "I thought, 'Oh my God.. couldn't they have thought of a less well known name, like Crosby or Sinatra?"

The Pretenders

Taken from ⇨Sam Cooke's version of The Platters' 1956 hit single *The Great Pretender*. Leader Chrissie Hynde admired the song. Tribute band: Pretend Pretenders.

A Dictionary of Rock and Pop Names

Pretty Boy Floyd

First, there was Kansas gangster Charles Floyd. Second, there was an admiring prostitute who gave him his nickname. Third, there were two groups – from L.A. and Canada – who named after Floyd. Last, there was Ugly Kid Joe, who named after the Californians.

Pretty Girls Make Graves

This Seattle band (2001-2007) named after a song of the same name by ⇨The Smiths. ⇨Morrissey took the title from Jack Kerouac's *The Dharma Bums*.

The Pretty Things

Dick Taylor, founder-bassist of the ⇨Rolling Stones, left them on the brink of their turning professional in 1962. His new band played dirty R&B – showing their liking for ⇨Bo Diddley and naming from his just-released 1963 composition *Pretty Thing*. Related: ⇨The Pink Fairies.

Dory Previn

Née Langdon, the singer-songwriter kept her name from her brief marriage to composer André Previn.

Dickie Pride

⇨Larry Parnes expanded his stable of stars with commendable speed. One young hopeful named Knellar was picked for his voice and promptly told that from then on his surname was Pride. First name? Richard? Make that Dickie.

   This was 1958, when naïvety was normal, but even cursory consideration should have told Parnes that the attention-grabbing name would produce plenty of phallic-size sniggers.

Primal Scream

Formed in 1982 by ex – ⇨The Jesus And Mary Chain drummer Bobby Gillespie and named after psychologist Arthur Janov's essay *The Primal Scream*. It advocates the vocal release of tension and anxieties, returning to the emotional freedom of babyhood. Janov inspired ⇨Tears For Fears and some ⇨John Lennon songs. Spinoff: Spirea X, named after a B-side by the parent group.

The Primitives

This U.K. indie group was inspired by ⇨Lou Reed twenty years before. In his 1963 pre- ⇨Velvet Underground days, he played in a garage band called The Primitives.

Prince / ♀

The star's story starts in Minneapolis, where his father, pianist John Nelson, using the stagename Prince Rogers or Roger Prince, led a jazz band called the Prince Roger Trio. John's wife, singer Mattie Nelson, was also in the band. They named their son Prince Rogers Nelson after the family concern, although they called him "Skipper".

   The Symbol: The situation later became more confused. Prince renamed with a hieroglyphic sign:

A Dictionary of Rock and Pop Names

The symbol was explained by fanzines as covering the masculine and feminine sides of his personality. The circle represented the brain and unity, while the crossover meant music. ⇨Led Zeppelin had used runes years before.

Nobody knew how to pronounce the symbol. Some papers couldn't print it. Prince became "Symbol", "The Artist Formerly Known As Prince", TAFKAP or "The Artist".

The formal renaming came on 7 June 1993, Prince's 35th birthday. Prince also became known as "Retired" on his 35th birthday, when he threatened to release only vaulted material. The threat proved false.

In a late 1996 American interview, TAFKAP said that, contrary to near-universal reports, he'd decided to change his name long before a row with Warner Bros.

In an interview with Liz Jones, TAFKAP said: "Changing my name made perfect sense to me. I'm not Nel's son, Nelson, that's a slave name. [Prince shares the same surname as ⇨Rick Nelson and ⇨Nilsson.] My wife just says: 'Hey.' If she said: 'Prince, get me a cup of tea', I'd probably drop the cup."

He has now been back as Prince for some time, and still uses the symbol for some things: for example his 2007 O2 gigs had a vast stage in the shape of the symbol, and he has custom-made guitars in the shape.

Pseudonyms include: ⇨Camille; Christopher (writing for ⇨The Bangles); Joey Coco; Mr. Goodnight (for the track of this name on 2007 *Planet Earth*); The Kid (the main character in *Purple Rain*, revisited in *Graffiti Bridge*); Alexander Nevermind;

[75] A symbol of guitar rock to come? Prince wows the 2007 Superbowl.

Paisley Park (also the name of his studio); Jamie Starr (producing The Time, Vanity 6 and other bands); Tora Tora (on the NPG's *Exodus* CD) and Victor (which at one stage he even considered as his new "official" name).

Nicknames and unflattering derivatives: His Royal Badness, His Royal Purpleness, Prance, Ponce, and Princess (the latter used by his school contemporaries – he recalls: "They used to call me names . . . anything small"); Squiggle (after his renaming); the Imp of Perverse; The Artist Formally Known As Sane, The Artist Formally Known As Talented and The Artist People Formally Cared About (the last by American shock jock Howard Stern).

His groups include: Grand Central; Champagne; The Royal Family; Time, Madhouse and The Revolution. A number of these can be seen as the names of Prince himself since he was the sole "band" member. Sheila Escovedo became known as Sheila E.

Trivia: He inspired the name ⇨The Lightning Seeds. ⇨Michael Jackson was annoyed when Prince rejected an invitation to duet on the song *Bad*. Jackson's son Prince wasn't named after Prince.

Prince Buster

Colin Bustamente Campbell's middle name (after politician Alexander Bustamente) made him "Buster". He added Prince when he started in music. He inspired ⇨Judge Dread and ⇨Madness.

Procol Harum

No. 128858

The Governing Council of the Cat Fancy

14ᵗ OCTOBER 1964

This is to Certify that the undermentioned Cat has been registered as follows :—

No. of Breed 27A	Colour BLUE
Name of Breed S.H	Sex M

Name of Cat PROCUL HARUN

Sire Ch BALLARD BILIN
Reg. No. 93184 Breed No. 24A Colour BLUE

- Grandsire Ch LAMONT BLUE BURMABOY
  Reg. No. 86140 Breed No. 24A Colour BLUE
- Grandam ANGELA VANESSA
  Reg. No. 86924 Breed No. 24A Colour BLUE

Dam LA-SUN HARMONY
Reg. No. 114435 Breed No. 24 Colour BROWN

- Grandsire Ch CHINDWIN CHEE-KEE
  Reg. No. 101195 Breed No. 24 Colour BROWN
- Grandam AILANTHUS TIDDLY WINKS
  Reg. No. 99488 Breed No. 24 Colour BROWN

Date of Birth 19-6-64   Breeder OWNER
Owner MRS E V CHAPMAN
Address 253 SOUTH AVENUE, ABINGDON BERKS

.... 64/S.H. Registrar

"Notify any errors within seven days. Any subsequent corrections will necessitate the issue of a new certificate for which a fee of two shillings must be paid."

[76] A cat breeder's certificate that wrote its way into rock history, respelled as Procol Harum.

In 1966, British lyricist Keith Reid and pianist Gary Brooker got together, on request of A&R man Guy Stevens, to work on original songs, distinct from the covers Brooker had played with ⇨The Paramounts.

The two formed a band. Within six months, they had a worldwide hit with *A Whiter Shade of Pale*. Reid, in a 2008 interview with the author, confirmed they got Procol Harum from a cat name suggested by Stevens. Brooker told writer Chris Welch on a 1997 CD sleevenote that it was from a pedigree certificate.

It's intriguing to note the confusion about the cat's ownership, breed, name spelling and over how Stevens told the band. Detective work by author Marcus Gray shows the cat was a Burmese Blue male, breed name Procul Harun, called Claude, owned by Elisabeth Coombs and Bob Rowberry, who once shared a London flat.

The Burmese Cat Club was bequeathed the certificate from breeder Eleonore Vogt Chapman, the club's Rosemary Hale said in a 2008 interview.

Coombs, now Mrs. Liz Rice, told Gray that Stevens saw the papers, on his own, when he visited. Rowberry agrees – although they differ at which property this happened. Brooker is pretty sure the band heard it over the phone from Stevens.

Reid remembers a London party: "We were all there. It was a 'happening'. Bob showed its [pedigree] certificate."

For a long time, the Procol Harum site at www.procolharum.com concluded it was "one of the mysteries of rock".

The band accepted the name because it seemed to have no meaning. "Harem", however spelled, sounded right. Only later they heard it was Latin for "beyond these things". (Though name expert Adrian Room notes procul should be followed by the ablative 'his' not the genitive 'harum'.)

If the band can't agree on recollections, perhaps we're past caring. The members of ⇨Barclay James Harvest can't recall how they named either.

The confusion resembles mix-ups over ⇨Jefferson Airplane – possibly named after a dog – and ⇨Pink Floyd – named from two bluesmen – or, according to incorrect reports, two cats.

Professor Longhair
Neither a professor of title nor long of hair, Henry Roeland Byrd (1918-1980) was not however, the fraud he seemed. He was one of the New Orleans' best blues pianists and singers. And he once had long hair: his first band was called Professor Longhair and The Four Hairs. In later years he lost the locks (and was billed as Roy 'Bald Head' Byrd).

Psychedelic Furs
Leader Richard Butler took the name from ⇨The Velvet Underground's 1967 cut *Venus In Furs*. (This song also inspired ⇨Steve Severin.) Psychedelic Furs were at the forefront of 1981's psychedelic revival attempt in Britain. The celebration of unfashionable hippies and fur coats proved distracting. Influenced ⇨Inspiral Carpets.

Psychic TV
The reasons for this name are so complex, convoluted, philosophical and pretentious it hardly seems worth starting. Their first album is dedicated to an obscure faith

called "The Temple of Psychic Youth". They also wanted to use the most powerful medium of today – television – to advance their case. It was all explained by their leader, the vocalist who began life as Neil Megson and who is now known as Genesis P. Orridge.

Psychotic Pineapple

These 1980s comedians were poking fun at fruity hippy names such as Colossal Pomegranate, Ballpoint Banana and ⇨The Strawberry Alarm Clock.

Public Enemy

The phrase "public enemy number one" emerged in America in the early part of this century. F.B.I. director J. Edgar Hoover used it to refer to bank robbers like ⇨Pretty Boy Floyd and George 'Babyface' Nelson.

These criminals had inspired the naming of Jamaican reggae artists such as ⇨Dennis Alcapone and ⇨Dillinger. By 1982 it was the turn of the New York rappers: Chuck D (Carlton Douglas Ridenhour; he says "D" means "Dangerous") used it for a record which challenged the perception of young black men, and then formed a band of this name.

Inspired: ⇨Buster Rhymes, ⇨Follow 4 Now.

Public Image Ltd.

Ex ⇨Sex Pistol Johnny Rotten reverted to his real name John Lydon in 1978 and chose this band moniker as a reaction to mainstream rock, which he felt was based on media-led hype and public image. After the LP *Public Image Ltd*, the band became known as PiL. In the early days, it was conceived as one of a group of companies with similarly-faceless names. Chief among these were P.E.P. – Public Enterprise Productions, which handled production – and M.I.C. – Multi Image Corporation, for video projects.

Gary Puckett And The Union Gap

Gary Puckett was born in Hibbing, Minnesota in 1942, but was brought up in the historic town of ⇨Union Gap. He chose it as the name for his band and extended its famous association by wearing Civil war togs. Still, groups in uniforms were being swept away by the British invasion, as ⇨Paul Revere And The Raiders discovered too.

Pulp

Pulp's typical of the 1990s vogue for short names: ⇨Bush, ⇨Blur etc. The moniker gained its own fashionability with Quentin Tarantino's 1994 *Pulp Fiction* which both parodied and celebrated kitsch, camp and violence. Meanwhile the band were on their way to the top with *Different Class*.

Leader Jarvis Cocker (who isn't related to singer ⇨Joe Cocker, also from Sheffield) said the name was originally Arabicus Pulp, taken from a coffee bean commodity. He uncovered the term in 1978 in school: "We were in economics and someone had the *Financial Times*. It was unwieldy so soon became Pulp. I like the idea that it means ephemeral material that gets thrown away, like the cheap novels printed on crap paper."

Punk Funk Chorus

Critics called ⇨Rick James' music "punk funk". So he replied by giving this name to his backing singers.

Pussy Galore

The U.K. author Ian Fleming, and later scriptwriters, chose the names of the molls in James Bond thrillers for their laugh value. The Washington DC attempt-to-shock quintet (1985-1990) stole this particular name from 1964's *Goldfinger* in which Honor Blackman was Galore.

Pylon

Named from the 1935 novel *Pylon* by U.S. writer William Faulkner, which paints a depressing picture of the American south. "And we should know," said the close neighbours of ⇨R.E.M.

[77] "One day there will be a band called Pussy Galore." "I must be dreaming." Honor Blackman and Sean Connery, 1964.

Quarterflash

This U.S. AOR band named after an antipodean colloquialism, "a quarter flash and three parts foolish". They said: "It sums us up very well."

Suzi Quatro

The 1970s star shortened her birthname Susan Kay Quatrocchio. Her Italian father often abbreviated his surname to Quatro.

Queen

The British band's name was suggested by ⇨Freddie Mercury in 1970, sitting in the Truro kitchen of Win, mother of drummer Roger Meddows-Taylor (who dropped the 'Meddows' for added brevity and street-cred). She recalled: "He kept saying how regal it sounded." Queen was simple, short, had royal references and endless visual possibilities.

Mercury had to fight for his choice. "Queen" was then the usual British euphemism for homosexual, as opposed to "gay" – which was still used in its original meaning, as in "happily carefree". Freddie wasn't referring to the House of Windsor either. It was an appropriate parody of his outrageous flamboyancy – before anyone else made fun of it. The man always had a sense of humour.

Queen won over The Grand Dance (from C.S. Lewis' *Out Of The Silent Planet* books) and ⇨Rich Kids, a Cocteau reference later used elsewhere. Band members had also worked with Smile (a name considered by ⇨Iron Maiden), ⇨Ibex and ⇨Sour Milk Sea. Tribute bands include: Kween; Magic; The Royal Family.

Queen Latifah

New Yorker Dana Elaine Owens was 8 when she was nicknamed Latifah by her cousin. It means "nice" or "delicate" in Arabic.

Queen Of The Blues

Title applied to Dinah Washington and, especially, Bessie Smith. The latter is also ⇨Empress Of The Blues. Ma Rainey's ⇨Mother Of The Blues.

The Queen Of Country (and Western)

There are those who think ⇨Patsy Cline should be atop this list. Country's Leading Cowgirl carved a special place in C&W hearts with *I Love You So Much It Hurts* and others, but her career was short and the nickname only came later.

There are those who dubbed themselves "The Queen Of Country Music": Muriel Deason, ⇨Loretta Lynn, Dolly Parton and Kitty Wells. That leaves Tammy *Stand By Your Man* Wynette as The Queen Of Country And Western; and Minnie Pearl, The Queen Of Country Comedy.

The Queen Of Disco

⇨Donna Summer: from her run of disco hits in the 1970s including *Love To Love You Baby* and *I Feel Love*. The title, or Queen Of Disco Pop, was later applied to ⇨ Madonna.

Queen Of Flash

⇨Cher has been referred to as this. Flash, as in flash trash: showy. And flash, especially, as in to teasingly display. Décolletage with an exposed tattooed buttock here, a naked breast there, or a bellybutton diamond.

The Queen Of Soul

Usually applied to Aretha Franklin – a 1968 LP was called *Lady Soul*. A highly-contested tag claimed by others too.

The Queen Of The Pops

⇨Madonna by any other name. Cf ⇨The King of Pop.

Queensrÿche

This U.S. heavy rock band, known for their ⇨Queen-like sound and name, added Germanic influences. The name means "Queen's country", decorated with a heavy metal umlaut.

? And The Mysterians

Like ⇨The Guess Who, a naïve attempt to create interest through mystery. The name was taken in 1963 from a Japanese film about a race planning world domination. The singer legally changed his name to "Question Mark" and still wears sunglasses constantly. Some interest evaporated when it was discovered he wasn't a Martian, as claimed, but Rudy Martinez from Michigan.

Tommy Quickly

A protégé of ⇨The Beatles, his stagename produced behind-cupped-hands jokes about Quickly being fast with the ladies or lacking sexual control. It was a simplification of his birthname Thomas Quigley. He stands alongside ⇨Dickie Pride in the pantheon of badly-named stars.

Quicksilver Messenger Service

All four founders shared the same birth sign, Virgo: two were born on August 24, the others September 4. Astrology buff and bassist David Freiberg said they also had Mercury as their joint ruling-planet.

It wasn't taken from the name of a U.S. wild west telegraph and delivery service, as sometimes reported, egged on by records with western themes. ⇨Spinoff ⇨Dinosaurs.

Quiet Riot

The bunch of guys initially wanted the misleading Little Women. Still, you couldn't get much louder than this lot, said ⇨Status Quo's Rick Parfitt: "I had been saving up 'Quite Right' for some time but hadn't found any suitable chance to use it. I met the guys and gave it to them for free. They loved it."

The Quireboys

The musicians formed in 1984 as The Choirboys, from the title of a 1977 movie. They worked on a building site – arriving for work in eyeliner after clubbing the night away – and their foreman's reaction to the moniker was: "Queer Boys, more like!" So they went on the college circuit as the Queerboys, figuring this would have an impact. It did: "gay soc" protests. Hence the Quireboys compromise. Unflattering derivative: Not The Hoople. Cf ⇨Mott The Hoople.

Raconteurs

Spinoff from ⇨The White Stripes by Jack White. He said in an interview that lyrics were "a form of storytelling" and the tradition of stories passed on orally by travelling musicians or families was being lost. He noted: "It would be stupid to call ourselves the Storytellers in America. So I guess we'll suffer in France." They also suffered in Australia: where an existing Raconteurs forced them to be known as the Saboteurs.

Radiohead

The British alternative rock band started in 1986 and signed to EMI in 1991 as ⇨On A Friday. The record company wasn't impressed by the name, but didn't immediately force the band's hand, as is sometimes reported.

[78] Radiohead, Seattle, 1993: a long way from their "On A Friday" origins.

Dave Newton, who knew the band, said he was told "Keith Wozencroft [who had just started as an A&R man] drew up a list of five names – all taken from other bands' song titles – and presented it to them, saying: 'Pick one of these and do it soon.'" As with the list presented to ⇨Blur, it would be fascinating to see the alternative offerings.

The source was *Radio Head* on the 1986 ⇨Talking Heads album *True Stories*. Radiohead members have said the name was chosen with minimal discussion, though guitarist Ed O'Brien commented they all liked Talking Heads, a band breaking up at the time. *Radio Head* is a slight pseudo-reggae tune and some members of the band have suggested it was picked as the least annoying on the album – not the best Heads outing.

Yorke said in 1993 on the *Radiohead: The Interview* (Talking Music) disc that the name had "loads of great connotations . . . It's about the way you take information in, the way you respond to the environment you're put in."

The choice was far from unique, though Oxford's finest went on to be more influential, commercially-successful and critically-lauded than most of its original "-head" name rivals (cf ⇨Portishead etc).

Rage Against The Machine

From the 1960s anarcho-slogan of the San Francisco "tune in, turn on, drop out" rallies. "Rage against the machine" had become a bumper sticker by the 1990s. The same soundbite culture permeated tracks such as *Settle For Nothing* and *Know Your Enemy*. Related: ⇨Audioslave.

Rainbow

The Los Angeles Rainbow Bar was visited by ⇨Deep Purple guitarist Ritchie Blackmore and inspired a song and album title, cut with New York band, Elf. He renamed the group (who included ⇨Dio), saying the handle was more colourful. Related: ⇨Wild Horses.

The Raincoats

The group formed in London in 1977, influenced by ⇨The Slits, which founder-member Palmolive went on to join. Band member Gina Birch said: "Ana's (da Silva, co-founder) from Madeira and was fascinated by London, rain and dreary old days."

Rain Tree Crow

A one-off-album reunion of ⇨Japan in 1991 under ⇨David Sylvian – who refused to revive the earlier name. He said this name was a symbol of his work over four years – "a dark period" – with music a healing process.

The Ramones

⇨Paul McCartney briefly assumed the stagename Paul Ramon as a leather-clad rocker. As ⇨The Beatles swept all before them, one of their American fans was New York bassist Douglas Colvin. He was excited to read of McCartney's renaming. "I was lost in fantasy, and changed from Douglas Colvin to Dee Dee Ramone."

In 1974, Colvin formed his first serious group and became Dee Dee. When the issue of a

[79] Leather-jacketed Beatle Paul Ramon pointed the way for The Ramones.

collective name came up with fellow musician Tommy, Dee Dee suggested "How about the Ramones?" In an interview he said he "wasn't that serious" but everyone else took Ramone as a surname.

Recruits adopted both the image – ripped jeans, rancid sneakers, pinhead stares – and pretended to be brothers: Joey, Johnny, Dee Dee, Tommy, Marky, Richie, CJ and Elvis.

Inspired: ⇨Bad Brains, ⇨Exploding White Mice. Influenced ⇨The Runaways, though not their naming, as is sometimes reported. ⇨Green Day members named children after the band: Billie Joe Armstrong named his son Joey as tribute to Joey Ramone, and Tré Cool called his daughter Ramona.

Shabba Ranks

Jamaican Rexton Gordon's first three letters already made him a king: "Shabba" means "African king" (he didn't take it from the Queen of Sheba.) "Ranks" was Kingston slang for top stars, as in *Up Town Top Rankin'* (it wasn't from local bandit Trevor Ranks, though many stars of the "slacking" scene named after gangsters: ⇨Dillinger etc).

Rapeman

Another misunderstood choice by Chicago musician Steve Albini, ex- ⇨Big Black. This 1980s name was intended as an anti-rape comment. Albini was fascinated by Japanese comics which favoured "gokan" rapes.

Rare Earth

There are cases of a record label named after a group: for example Harvest from ⇨Barclay James Harvest. This is the reverse and taken from a ⇨Motown subsidiary.

Sun Ra

Alabama-born jazz bandleader (1914-1993) Herman Blount's fascination with mythology led to him claiming to come from outer space (Saturn) as one of the Angel Race and son of Ra, the ancient Egyptian sun god. The "Sun" came from his nickname "Sonny," even if he might claim higher origins. Hence his band Solar Arkestra.

Ratt

This American metal band liked the sound of cartoon character Mickey Rat's name. When the cartoon artist objected, they became Ratt.

Rattlesnake Annie

Named because she wore a rattlesnake's tail in her right ear. Example of a simple "character" we don't get these days, like ⇨Barbecue Bob, ⇨Daddy Stovepipe and Grass Skirt Girt.

Raw Power

Rock combo named after the 1973 album by their proto-punk heroes ⇨The Stooges.

Johnnie Ray

Because of his tendency to cry during emotionally-fraught numbers, he acquired the nicknames The Cry Guy, The Howling Success, The Nabob Of Sob and the Prince of Wails (the last shared with Welsh ballad king ⇨Tom Jones).

The Real Roxanne

NYC radio was flooded in 1984-5 with rap raves about a girl called Roxanne. ⇨UTFO's *Roxanne, Roxanne*, then *Roxanne's Mother, Roxanne's Doctor* etc. Singers claiming to be Roxanne followed – and this one did better than most, hitting at rival Roxanne Shante.

Real Westway

The Westway is the road west from London's Paddington towards Oxford, over-looked at one point by towerblocks. It was from one of these apartments that early ⇨The Clash songs were written. Hence this band name. Related: ⇨Big Audio Dynamite.

The Rebel Rousers

Formed 1959 by ⇨Cliff Bennett in Drayton, U.K., in tribute to Duane Eddy single hit *Rebel Rouser*.

The Reclines

⇨k.d. lang's first band, playing country music and with a name paying tribute to country star ⇨Patsy Cline.

The Red And The Black

Mike Scott of ⇨The Waterboys lifted the title of Stendhal's 1830 *Le Rouge Et Le Noir*.

Redbeards From Texas

Tribute to ⇨ZZ Top, two have reddish beards, the other is called Beard.

Redbone

Los Angeles band formed by American Indians; "rehbon" is slang for half-breed. Cf ⇨Cher. Unrelated: Leon Redbone.

Redd Kross

This Californian band named after a scene in *The Exorcist* film of 1973, in which a cross gets covered in blood. The name "worked on many levels". The International Committee Of The Red Cross was red-faced and cross. The band was forced into idiosyncratic re-spelling (similar to that by Red Krayola after Crayola concern). Inspired ⇨Pink Kross.

The Red Hot Chili Peppers

This American 1980s-on rap-funk-punk-rock band formed from bands such as Anthym and were originally called, in mock-hippy style, Tony Flow and the Miraculously Majestic Masters of Mayhem (or Masters Of The Universe). The Red Hot Chili Peppers was considered "a perfect hatstand name". The Chilis developed a chilling penchant for wearing not much apart from strategically-placed socks.

Individual names include: Antwan The Swan – who was born Anthony Kiedis – and ⇨Flea – originally Mike Balzary. Unrelated: ⇨Chilli Willi And The Red Hot Peppers.

The Red House Painters

This Californian band of the 1990s loved the casual greatness of ⇨Jimi Hendrix's one-take blues workout, *Red House*.

The Redskins

Punk and *Oi!* bands were awash with Nazism: ⇨4 Skins combined sexist, racist and political slurs. By contrast, this British act (which started as No Swastikas) named to show skinheads could also be socialists.

Lou Reed

Most accounts give his birthname as Lewis Allan Reed. Still, some reports claim he was Louis Allan Firbank/Firbanks. It seems this was a joke started by Lester Bangs for *Creem* magazine. ⇨Velvet Underground drummer Mo Tucker also denied that Reed changed his name.

Reed was once a member of The Shades (wore sunglasses – which he has done a lot in his later career too); The Jades (wore sequins); LA and the Eldorados (stood for "Louis Allan"); surf band The Beach Nuts and ⇨The Primitives, a name borrowed two decades later by another ensemble.

⇨Drella. ⇨The Godfather Of Punk. Inspired: ⇨Berlin, ⇨The Waterboys, ⇨Sid Vicious, ⇨Holly Johnson.

Reef

Singer Gary Stringer denied this 1993-2003 British band used an anagram for "Free". "But I think ⇨Free are rad." Stringer also denied it was from "reefer" (which would make sense, given titles such as *Mellow, Good Feeling* and *Comfort*) and says the name "just emerged . . . we wanted to be living rock animals."

Della Reese

Based on her real name, Dellareese Taliaferro. Inspired ⇨Martha And The Vandellas.

R.E.M.

Perhaps the most critically-acclaimed band of the last 30 years. Their ambiguous, sometimes mumbled, lyrics are pondered over by students worldwide. Their name, and its offshoots, produced as many myths as the oblique songs.

The singer-lyric writer, born John Michael Stipe, said the early amateur group needed to find a name after being offered a gig in 1980. At the time they were rehearsing in a near-derelict church. Stipe's account is given in *It Crawled From The South: An R.E.M. Companion* by Marcus Gray: "We sat up one night and just got completely drunk and rolled around the floor. We had this chalk, and we took every name someone could think of and wrote it on the wall."

By morning, the top names were R.E.M., Negro Eyes – which they knew would provoke racist allegations – and the punky Slut Bank: Cans Of Piss and Twisted Kites.

Elsewhere it's reported that they were still unnamed when they had a local radio spot to promote the first gig. Stipe, Peter Buck, Mike Mills and Bill Berry asked WUOG listeners to vote on such names as Third Wave, Negro Wives (a slightly different name to that above) and Twisted Kites. Mills recalls they had no name for the gig, although Buck liked Twisted Kites and has said in interviews they used this (one poster with a handwritten addition "with Twisted Kites" confirms this).

Biographies often say R.E.M. itself came at random, either from sequences of letters or the dictionary. Mills said they wanted an almost-meaningless combination which did not fix them to a particular era in the way the Revolting Cocks or the ⇨Circle Jerks both did. How Cans Of Piss was even considered, then, is a mystery. Buck loved the surreal ⇨Strawberry Alarm Clock but wanted something "concise".

[80] Michael Stipe's band opted for R.E.M. over Negro Eyes, Slut Bank and Twisted Kites.

Stipe said: "We just like the dots.' 'R.E.M.' means nothing." The fact that it fitted several abbreviations is said to be coincidental, particularly the scientific term "Rapid Eye Movement", a phenomenon in sleep when eyeballs move rapidly as an indication of the dreamer 'looking around' at the visual events in his dream world.

Despite this, R.E.M.'s early posters featured eyes prominently and they named a record "Rapid Ear Movement". They found there'd been at least four other groups called REM/Rapid Eye Movement, while REM Inc. is a company supplying people with disabilities.

Related: ⇨Adolf And The Casuals, ⇨The Back Door Band, ⇨The Frustrations, ⇨H.E.A.L, ⇨Hetchy Hetchy, Hindu Love Gods (with Warren Zevon; naming after an earlier, abortive R.E.M. offshoot), ⇨Hornets Attack Victor Mature, ⇨It Crawled From The South, ⇨13111, ⇨Nigel And The Crosses, ⇨Shadowfax, ⇨1066 Gaggle Of Sound, ⇨The Troggs. Inspired: ⇨Concrete Blonde.

Renaissance
Formed ⇨The Yardbirds in 1969, they fused classical, folk, jazz, blues and rock "to create a renaissance".

REO Speedwagon
⇨Buffalo Springfield chose an old steamroller for name inspiration, and this Illinois outfit named after a type of antique fire truck. It was the suggestion of keyboardist Neil Doughty. He came across a truck made in about 1920 by Ransom E. Olds, the father of the Oldsmobile, and thought the name "kinda sexy". So it didn't look like a reference to Rio De Janeiro, "we made it capitals – R-E-O Speedwagon. It was at the start of Olds' career, so that connotation was right for us too."

The Replacements
⇨The Impediments' impediment was booze. The group turned up to play their first concert, in their home town of Minneapolis, so drunk they could hardly stand. They sobered up when owners of local clubs threatened to ban the accurately-named act and switched to something similarly apt.

The Residents
The minimalist band achieved what ⇨? And the Mysterians failed to do by maintaining total anonymity, wearing masks at all times and at first rejecting any name. In 1971 the fledgling Californian combo sent off four album-length demo tapes to radio stations and record labels. The packages included their San Mateo address and no names. One company returned the tape as a rejection addressed to "The Residents".

Return To Forever
Massachusetts keyboard whiz Chick Corea chose this as the far-out title of his 1972 album. It was liked so much by the jazz musicians he worked with that they named after it the following year.

Revenge

Bassist Peter Hook, "Hooky" to his friends, formed this band in 1989 as his main group ⇨New Order took a break. The obvious conclusion to reach would be that this name indicated Hooky's revenge on Barney Sumner for setting up ⇨Electronic. Though Hook said: "It's not a rivalry."

Other members of the band noted that Revenge was a word on a leather jacket worn by ⇨George Michael in the video for *Faith*. Some scepticism at this explanation of its source is in order. After all by then Hook had his Revenge and by 1995 moved into another spinoff, called ⇨Monaco.

Paul Revere And The Raiders

Paul Revere (1735-1818) was an American patriot who is said to have ridden from Charlestown to Lexington in 1775 to warn American colonists of the approach of British troops.

His modern namesake from Idaho, birthname Paul Revere Dick, was named in tribute. His backing musicians, The Night Riders, adopted Eighteenth Century stage outfits, similar to ⇨Gary Puckett And The Union Gap. Revere was not the only star to cut off his "Dick": cf ⇨Fish and ⇨Byrds drummer Michael Clarke.

The Rezillos

Scottish punky band, named after a club in Edinburgh. Later became The Revillos. Related: ⇨The Human League.

Rhinoceros

West coast band formed by ⇨Doors producer Paul A. Rothchild. The name was suggested by his assistant Barry Friedman, to fit Rothchild's view it was a heavy "supergroup". Inspired: ⇨Atomic Rooster.

RIB

Leader of Euro band Quadrophenia, rapper RIB Master, says his handle means "Rootless Intelligent Being", taken from science fiction jargon for UFOs.

Cliff Richard

He was born Harry Rodger Webb, 1940, in India. No relation to poet Harry Web or another famous Webb, ⇨Gary Numan, who thought the name fine for "a solicitor, scrap metal dealer, shop assistant or a soldier but not a star".

Harry Webb and The Drifters were offered gigs by London promoter Bob Greatorex – if the singer renamed. The names Russ Clifford, Cliff Russord and Cliff Russard were suggested. This in turn became Cliff Richards. Some reports said Greatorex had a cousin called Richard Cliff, although this version is now disputed.

Guitarist Ian Samwell suggested dropping the final S of the surname, so Richard could correct radio interviewers when they got it wrong, ensuring the name was mentioned twice.

Cliff said in an interview: "It paid tribute to ⇨Little Richard. It was two Christian names which was good and unusual." (Richard is a committed Christian.)

Down the years the surname has become redundant, in Britain at least: like Elvis,

Bruce and Jesus, Cliff is enough. Or perhaps "Sir Cliff" after the sword of knighthood fell on his shoulders.

Unflattering derivative: Riff Pilchard. Related: ⇨The Shadows, ⇨The Drifters, ⇨The Young Ones. ⇨Keith Richard(s).

Keith Richard(s)

Born Keith Richards, in Dartford, Kent, he dropped the last letter from his surname on leaving home – a change inspired by ⇨Cliff Richard, whose rocker credibility was still intact. Still, journalists persisted in spelling Keith's name as "Richards". He gave in to the inevitable in 1977 and, after a reconciliation with his father, reverted to Richards.

This ⇨Rolling Stone's nicknames include ⇨Keef, The Walking Laboratory, The Living Skull, The Human Riff and The World's Most Elegantly Wasted Human Being. ⇨The Glimmer Twins, ⇨The Ex-Pensive Winos.

Rich Kids

A name considered by early ⇨Queen and used by a ⇨Sex Pistols spinoff joined by ⇨Midge Ure. From Jean Cocteau's book *Les Enfants Terribles*.

Ricky And The Red Streaks

⇨The Beatles dallied with the *alter ego* Long John And the Silver Beetles in their early days, in tune with the "and the" trend of rock 'n' roll monikers. This didn't last long.

By 1969 they were thinking of going full circle. Paul wanted to rehearse the band, revive old songs and go out on the road incognito. The tour never happened and the tag's only reference comes on *Anthology 3*. Cf ⇨Sgt. Pepper.

The Righteous Brothers

These Californians weren't brothers. Nor were they religious. Nor were they black, as many listeners initially assumed. Billy Hatfield and Bill Medley started in 1962 as The Paramours and made an impact with their gospel voices, dubbed "Blued-Eyed Soul Brothers" and "Righteous Brothers".

Right Said Fred

The perpetrators of the 1991 British hit *I'm Too Sexy* named after a 1962 novelty by Bernard Cribbins. The phrase is an in-joke because one of the band was called Fred.

Rigor Mortis

⇨Who bassist John Entwistle formed the band for his 1973 concept album, *Rigor Mortis Sets In* which said rock had died and music was stiff and contrived.

Riot Grrrl

A movement including ⇨Babes In Toyland, ⇨Hole, ⇨Huggy Bear and ⇨L7 with a name of "snarrrling" anger.

Rip Rig + Panic

These Britons named after a ⇨Rahsaan Roland Kirk 1965 bop album, *Rip, Rig and Panic*. One of the band's members was Neneh Cherry, daughter of trumpeter Don Cherry, who owned the Kirk record. Related: ⇨The Pop Group.

Smokey Robinson

Detroit boy William Robinson in Detroit was known as Smokey from an early age. His band The Matadors became ⇨The Miracles, which forced a name change for ⇨The Temptations. His name forced U.K. band Smokey to become Smokie.

The Roches

Members of this all-girl family kept their surname Roche despite people thinking it was about cockroaches or roach clips for smoking cannabis.

Kid Rock

Speaking at age 36 he said in an interview: "My real name is Robert James Ritchie. But when I was young they used to call me the little white kid that could rock the turntables. When I was 14 it seemed cool. Most people call me Bobby." As with other rock kids, it will be interesting as to how long he sticks a kid and if he ever grows up namewise.

Rock Lobsters

Like Rock Salmon, a pun that keeps recurring. The best known Rock Lobsters mimic ⇨The B-52s and their *Rock Lobster* hit.

Rockpile

Dave Edmunds named a 1972 album and this band, with ⇨Basher, after his Welsh studio.

The Rolling Stones

Rolling stones may gather no moss, but rock has been littered with them: The Temptations' *Papa Was A Rolling Stone*, ⇨Bob Dylan's 1965 *Like A Rolling Stone* (written with the band in mind) and ⇨Muddy Waters' *Rollin' Stone*, his Chess debut. The last – which also inspired U.S. magazine *Rolling Stone* – was taken as the name by early leader Brian Jones, who wanted to reflect his love for rhythm and blues.

Their first credit was to "Brian Jones And Mick Jagger And The Rollin' Stones": the band also included one ⇨Michael Philip Jagger, who had met ⇨Keith Richards on a train in 1960. (⇨The Glimmer Twins). This title lasted a year before manager Andrew Loog Oldham changed it to The Rolling Stones, though they soon were The Stones to many.

The name has allowed many word associations, with records including *Heart Of Stone*, *Stone Age* and *Hot Rocks*. The Rock And Rock Hall of Fame citation for the "Greatest Rock Band In The World," says the name hints at elements of the Stones' style: rock 'n' roll, getting stoned and rolling on down the road.

Jones gave himself the suitably authentic name Elmo Lewis when he played blues. This happened to be the name of ⇨Jerry 'Killer' Lee Lewis' father; Jones' full name

[81 + 82] Muddy Waters cut a song called *Rollin' Stone*; Mick Jagger's band has been rolling ever since.

was Lewis Brian Hopkin-Jones but like ⇨Queen's Roger Taylor and others after him, decided a double-barrelled name was not good for proletarian rock credibility. On the other hand, new bassist Bill Perks decided his surname was too proletarian, and became Wyman.

Related: ⇨The Ex-Pensive Winos, ⇨Nanker Phelge, ⇨Willie And The Poorboys. Inspired: ⇨Pavlov's Dog, ⇨The Stone Roses, ⇨Wild Horses. Tribute bands: The Rolling Clones and The Counterfeit Stones (front man: Nick Dagger).

Plenty of bands have named partly because of the ease of abbreviating their names Stones-style, ⇨The Boomtown Rats and ⇨The Black Crowes are among them. Unflattering derivative: The Strolling Bones.

Ronettes
Their leader was Veronica Bennett, known by her family as Ronnie. The name fitted the popularity of similar sounding groups such as the Marvelettes.

Rosebud
"Rosebud" was the dying word of the anti-hero of *Citizen Kane*. This band loved the ending of the epic film with the meaning becoming clear only in the closing seconds. Cf ⇨The Kane Gang, Eden Kane.

W. Axl Rose
The ⇨Guns N' Roses star was born in Indiana in 1962. He was – so he thought – William Bailey, eldest son of L. Stephen and Sharon E. Bailey. He was 17 when he

discovered his real father was William Rose, a local hellraiser whom his mother had married while still at school. He had left Sharon when little William was two and she remarried. William reverted to Rose, soon abbreviating his prenomen to W. to distance himself from his real father who "was an asshole." W. naughtily made an anagram of "Oral Sex" by adding A.X.L. – the name of his first band.

Rossington Collins Band

From Gary Rossington and Allen Collins, survivors of the plane crash which ended the first version of ⇨Lynyrd Skynyrd.

Johnny Rotten

John Joseph Lydon was so mistrustful he still hadn't told ⇨The Sex Pistols his surname three months after their conception. "Johnny" was always spitting, blowing his nose and inspecting his rotting teeth. Band member Steve Jones (guitar) found this repulsive and his catchphrase became: "You look rotten/you sound rotten/you're rotten".

⇨Malcolm McLaren liked stagenames. He liked "Rotten" because it was the opposite of the pop entrepreneur names such as those by ⇨Larry Parnes. As ⇨Neil Young told the world in 1979, Elvis was dead but not forgotten: it was now the story of Johnny Rotten. Lyndon reverted to his birthname in ⇨Public Image Ltd.

Roxette

The Swedish pop band named from a song they liked by ⇨(p.99) Doctor Feelgood.

Roxy Music

Bryan Ferry chose "Roxy" in honour of a favourite cinema; rock music and old-style Ritzy glamour. The "Music" distinguished them from an act just called Roxy. The name was originally put in ironic inverted commas.

⇨Eno radically abbreviated his name while Phil Manzanera, also keen to avoid "toff" jokes, trimmed his real name Phillip Targett-Adams. ⇨Bananarama.

Rufus

The soul-funk group gave the origin away with 1977 album *Ask Rufus*. This was the title of a "write-in" question column in the magazine *Mechanics Illustrated*. ⇨Chaka Khan.

Rumblefish

⇨Police spinoff named from Francis Ford Coppola's 1983 *Rumble Fish*, about a boy who draws parallels between aquarium fish and urban unrest.

The Runaways

It was neither from ⇨Del Shannon's 1961 *Runaway* nor ⇨*The Ramones Leave Home* from 1977 – the Runaways started in 1975. The name was "a rebellious dare to romance and adventure." Related: ⇨The Blackhearts.

Run DMC
From New York vocalists: Joe 'Run' Simmons and 'DMC' Darryl McDaniels. ⇨H.E.A.L.
⇨The Kings From Queens.

Runrig
They started in bucolic mode as The Run-Rig Dance Band, playing Scottish Highland ceilidh music with Gaelic lyrics. Singer Donnie Munro said the name referred to ploughing furrows.

Runt
It was applied by Patti Smith to Todd Rundgren, from his surname (pronounced "Rundt-grun") and a term of abuse ("runt"). In return his 1973 album *A Wizzard, A True Star* was dedicated to her.

Rush
Canadian band formed in 1968, in Toronto, Ontario. Drummer John Rutsey's brother suggested the name because of the 'rushed' need to find one before a gig.

The Rutles
From ⇨*Monty Python's Flying Circus* spinoff, *Rutland Weekend Television*. The name combines Rutland (England's smallest county) with ⇨The Beatles, whom they parodied.

The Ruts
This reggae-punk act named after their first song, *In A Rut*. After singer Malcolm Owen's death in 1980 they became Ruts DC – DC from the Italian musical abbreviation, *Da Capo* meaning back to the start. Cf ⇨Klaatu.

Bobby Rydell
This 1960s U.S. star simplified his name Robert Ridarelli (thus providing the name of the college in musical *Grease*).

Mitch Ryder
Singer William Levise Jnr., AKA Billy Lee, was urged by his record company to find a more inspiring name before his first major release. They told him: "Almost any name's better than yours." The story that follows sounds like an urban myth but is confirmed by the star. He took them at their word, walked to the nearest phone booth and opened a directory at random. His finger stabbed on "Mitch Ryder". Related: ⇨The Detroit Wheels.

Sad Café

Members of this British band formed in 1977 and loved *The Ballad Of The Sad Café*, a 1951 novella by U.S. writer Carson McCullers (1917-1967) about unrequited love. The group's 1979 album *Façades* was an anagram.

Sade

The singer was born in Nigeria as Helen Folasade Adu. Her debut CD made the pronunciation clear: "Sade (SHAR-DAY)".

St. Etienne

This British band named in tribute to a French town. Challenged by *Melody Maker* on why name after "a crap soccer team", they said that they thought it "sounded good".

Salt 'N' Pepa

Cheryl 'Salt' James and Sandra 'Pepa' Denton, from Brooklyn and Jamaica respectively, named, because of their appearance, by producer Hurby Aznor after a Sammy Davis Junior film.

[83] Sad Café liked this Carson McCullers book so much they named after it.

Sanctuary

Seattle thrash-metal: A beautiful name chosen not from any literary reference (such as William Faulkner) but as an ironic reference to their music, from the same school as ⇨Soundgarden.

The Sandpipers

There have been several bands of this name. One was a Florida vocal group, backed by the early ⇨Allman Brothers as the Allman Joys. The trend for bird names was then at its height. Another act, an easy listening trio, named after the 1965 Elizabeth Taylor film *The Sandpiper* after finding their first choice ⇨The Four Seasons already taken.

Santana

Originally Santana Bluesband, from Mexican-born founder Carlos Santana. Santana later became enamoured with the teachings of Bengal mystic Sri Chinmoy at the instigation of friend John McLaughlin, AKA ⇨Mahavishu and was for a time called

Devadip (it means "enlightenment of the lamp of the Lord"). Cf ⇨Roger McGuinn. Related: ⇨Abraxas Pool, ⇨Journey. Unflattering derivative: Sultana.

Satchmo

Jazzman Louis Armstrong used his "satchel mouth" to play passages with no pause for breath. ⇨Dippermouth.

Savage Garden

This Australian duo formed in 1994 as *Interview With The Vampire* came out. Singer Darren Hayes was an admirer of *The Vampire Chronicles* by Anne Rice, which inspired the movie, with its words: "The mind of each man is a savage garden."

Leo Sayer

Jackie, wife of manager ⇨Adam Faith, named Gerard Sayer "little Leon lion" from his mane of hair and 5ft 4ins height.

The Scaffold

Liverpudlian band including ⇨Mike McGear and Roger McGough, referencing Miles Davis' LP *Lift To The Scaffold*.

Boz Scaggs

The singer-songwriter was born in Texas in 1944 as William Royce Scaggs. He was given the nickname Bosley by school acquaintance Don Lively aged 14. Another schoolfriend Lewis MacAdams recalled: "This guy [Lively] was able to spot somebody who was from the country, though Boz never seemed a country boy."

Scissor Sisters

This band, formed in 2001, mixes New York disco, glam rock and camp attitude. The name is from a lesbian sexual position, tribadism. The act's logo, featuring two pairs of interlocking scissors with leg-shaped blades, says it all.

On the interview sections of the 2004 DVD *We Are Scissors Sisters . . . And So Are You*, they seem amazed that anyone should find the name anything other than a subject suitable for polite chatter.

Bon Scott

⇨The late AC/DC singer was born in Scotland as Ronald Belford Scott and called "Bonny Scotland" when he moved to Australia in 1952. "My schoolmates threatened to kick the shit out of me when they heard my Scottish accent. I didn't take any notice!"

Scratch

Nickname for Lee Perry based on his first hit, *Chicken Scratch*, in 1961. While it was just one of many pieces produced under the aegis of ⇨Clement 'Coxsone' Dodd, it gave him a lasting nickname. ⇨The Upsetter.

Scritti Politti

It was taken from Italian for political writing, *scritti politichi*, used by Communist theoretician Antonio Gramsci (1891-1937). The respelling recalled ⇨Little Richard's *Tutti Frutti*. It tied in with the early left-wing leanings of Welshman, Cardiff-born Green Strohmeyer-Gartside, later Green. Influenced: ⇨Wet Wet Wet.

Scroobius Pip

British maker of the 2007 song *Thou Shalt Always Kill*. A misspelling of the Edward Lear poem, *The Scroobious Pip*.

Seal

Disregard reports that he was born Bernard Young and the moniker came from a collection of porcelain seals. Seal told the author that his name is Sealhenry Samuel. He does have a small collection of seals, mainly sent in by fans – long after he became famous as Seal.

The Searchers

The Liverpool combo, seeking a new sound and name, saw the 1956 John Wayne western *The Searchers*.

Seasick Steve

The U.S.-born blues singer was born Steve Wold but became Seasick Steve after an unfortunate fishing accident he wants to forget. Also sometimes called C16.

See For Miles

From ⇨The Who's 1967 hit *I Can See For Miles*.

See You Next Tuesday

Michigan death metal band formed 2005. The apparently innocent phrase is an acronym starting with "C-U-".

The Selecter

The Special AKA lacked the money to record a B-side for 1979 single *Gangsters*. Instead they let some friends use the flip side for a ska track, *The Selecter* (sic). It was hastily credited to The Selecter but they couldn't spell "selector". As they recorded more, they said it had political, mechanical, sexual and racial connotations. ⇨The Specials.

Captain Sensible

⇨The Damned bassist Raymond Burns got his name in 1976 when the band played a punk festival in south-west France. The bands travelled there in coaches, Sensible said: "I got this shirt with epaulettes. I was pretending to be the pilot, and shouting: 'It's all right! Everything's under control! It's on autopilot!' Someone said: 'Oh, it's Captain Fucking Sensible.' I thought it would last five minutes. I didn't know I would still be Captain Sensible at 35." He would have preferred a more macho name, "like Duane Zenith or Bert Powerhouse".

Sepultura

This Latin American heavy metal act formed in 1984 and named after "grave" in Portuguese. Founder Max Cavalera discovered it when translating ⇨Motörhead's *Dancing On Your Grave*.

Sgt. Pepper's Lonely Hearts Club Band

⇨The Beatles first came up with this in 1967 as they contemplated touring again, according to artist Peter Blake – the man responsible for the packaging of their landmark album with this title. He said a "smokescreen" name would allow them to play smaller venues. In the event, the Fabs never went back on the road properly.

The original *Dr. Pepper's . . .* was dropped because of fears of action by the soft-drinks maker.

Cf ⇨Ricky And The Red Streaks.

Set The Tone

U.K. popsters, named from Andy Warhol's *Popism*, seen by design expert Kenny Hyslop (ex ⇨Simple Minds).

702

This Motown revival female trio from Las Vegas named from their telephone area code. Cf ⇨Area Code 615.

7 Year Bitch

This Seattle grunge band inevitably got unfavourably compared to ⇨Nirvana, with a silly name not helping. Singer Selene Vigil liked the twist on 1955 movie *Seven Year Itch*. Monroe also inspired ⇨Marilyn Manson, ⇨The Misfits.

Steve Severin

In the beginning there was a naughty 1870s novel by Leopold von Sacher-Masoch called *Venus In Furs*, narrated by the pervy Séverin. Masoch was a name borrowed by psychologist Krafft-Ebbing to describe the condition of enjoying pain.

In 1967 the title was recycled as a song by ⇨The Velvet Underground. A decade later, punk was exploding in England. Steve Bailey was going under the name Steve Havoc as ⇨Siouxsie And The Banshees came into being. He heard *The Velvet Underground And Nico* and named from the sado-masochism paean. Cf ⇨The Psychedelic Furs. Related: ⇨The Glove.

Sex Gang Children

An early version of ⇨Culture Club. Some accounts tie this to writer William Burroughs and say it was the choice of ⇨Malcolm McLaren, trying to boost his shop 'Sex' (cf ⇨The Sex Pistols). However ⇨Boy George says he created it: "I came up with pretentious names: In Praise Of Lemmings, The Sex Gang Children, a line stolen from a ⇨Bow Wow Wow song". ⇨Lieutenant Lush.

The Sex Pistols

The musical equivalent of one of those adverts which starts: "SEX!!!" And then continues: "Now we have your attention." The Pistols would have probably grabbed attention anyway through their music, headline-grabbing publicity stunts and much else. But the name kick-started their career which has extended to reunions in 1996 and 2007.

They began in 1974 as The Swankers. This swanky choice might not have been understood in the U.S. ("wank" is a term of British abuse) and ⇨Malcolm McLaren reconsidered. He was keen on stagenames. John Lydon became ⇨Johnny Rotten; Paul became "Slave" Cook; bassist Glen Matlock added an extra "N" to his name but was replaced with ⇨Sid Vicious.

[84] The Sex Pistols' name helped boost trade at Malcolm McLaren and Vivienne Westwood's London shop.

"Sex" was McLaren's clothes shop at 430 King's Road, Chelsea. Under Vivienne Westwood it has gone through many names, including Let It Rock and Too Fast To Live, Too Young To Die. On its own, McLaren said Sex was too short and provocative for airplay. He said he liked ⇨Sex Gang Children for the same reason.

So "Pistols" was a misspelling of Sex Pistils, a botanical term meaning the male sexual parts of flowers. It was about as close as McLaren dared go to "The Penises". Lydon said: "I liked that name very much. I thought it was hilarious. The word 'Sex' had never been used in that blatant way before. I thought it was perfect to offend old ladies."

McLaren recalled: "Rotten just wanted to be called 'Sex'. I wasn't having it: I was in control and I wasn't going to waste my time with a bunch of herberts going out with a name like Sex. I was out to sell lots of trousers."

Because of venue bans, they completed a 1977 tour under the names Acne Rabble – cf ⇨Cockney Rebel – and – continuing the skin problem theme – SPOTS, which meant "Sex Pistols On Tour Secretly".

Related: ⇨Public Image Ltd, ⇨Rich Kids. Inspired, in whole or part: ⇨The Buzzcocks, ⇨The Celibate Rifles, The Tex Pistols (Spoof "Texan" version), ⇨The Sid Presley Experience. McLaren played a part in forming ⇨The Damned, who might conceivably have been called The Sex Pistols – but only if they had met McLaren before Rotten and his crew. Anagram: Sex Pistols = Sexist Slop.

Seymour

This indie group named from a character whose name meant "see more" and seems closely related to the one in U.S. writer J.D. Salinger's story *Seymour: An Introduction*. Bassist Alex James said it was suggested by friend Paul Hodgson: "We all liked [Salinger's] *The Catcher In The Rye*", while others credit singer Damon Albarn: either way, the band became better known as ⇨Blur.

Shadowfax
Another reference to author J.R.R. Tolkien, from Gandalf's horse in *The Lord Of The Rings*. The name's been used by two U.S. outfits: a 1970s band from Chicago; and a short-lived 1975 group, one of the antecedents of ⇨R.E.M.

The Shadows
⇨Cliff Richard's U.K. backers The Drifters (a suitably romantic name when drifting was okay) faced legal action from the U.S. black group of the same name when they planned to release a single in the States in 1959. They became The Four Jets – the single was called *Jet Black* and the band included Jet Harris. He and ⇨Hank B. Marvin later switched to the Shadows because of their role shadowing Richard.

Shakespears Sister
Virginia Woolf (1882-1941) wrote an essay asking what would have happened if England's greatest writer, William Shakespeare, had been a woman. ⇨Morrissey of ⇨The Smiths lifted this for 1985's *Shakespeare's Sister*. In 1989 this band, with links to ⇨Bananarama, named after the song: "It says something poetic about women." They claimed mistakes on their first record cover, omitting an "E" and an apostrophe, were the fault of a graphic designer.

Shakin' Street
Taken from a song by ⇨MC5 on the 1970 album *Back In The U.S.A.*

Shakira
Shakira Isabel Mebarak Ripoll has Colombian, Spanish, Italian and Lebanese ties; Shakira means "grateful" in Arabic. ⇨Pink and ⇨M.I.A. are among other female stars to strip to a single name.

The Shamen
The word often turns up in music, applied to ⇨Jim Morrison and just about every other voodoo-inspired act. Shamen perform wild or emotional rites – like early concerts by this British group. Related: ⇨Alone Again Or.

Sham 69
Founder Jimmy Pursey took the name in 1975 from faded soccer graffiti seen on a wall that originally said "Walton and Hersham '69". In 1969, the hippy apotheosis had been marked with "love and peace." By 1979, punks replaced this with "hate and war". It was a rejection of the hippy "sham" ⇨Ten Years After. Fans called: Sham Army.

[85] Shakira Isabel Mebarak Ripoll has shed unwanted names on the road to fame.

Del Shannon

Charles Westover renamed after (1) his favourite car, the Coup De Ville L or "Coup Del" and (2) his helper, Mark Shannon. The name is quite coincidentally similar to the U.S. mystery writer Dell Shannon. ⇨The Runaways.

Sandie Shaw

Sandra Goodrich, born Dagenham, U.K., blagged her way into a meeting with future manager Eve Taylor, then kicked off her shoes and sang. She often appeared barefoot on stage, as if walking on a sandy shore.

Shed Seven

The rock band from York, North England, named after a railway shed, marked SHED 7, outside York station. Shed Seven confirmed this in several broadcast interviews. The name's attracted loads of inaccurate speculation by people who obviously hadn't seen these interviews. Ideas include: (1) there were six sheds and they imagined a seventh; (2) there were seven schoolfriends who used to play in a shed; (3) there were originally 11 of them and they were urged to "shed seven" in order to be a success. If you don't know, SHUT UP.

Pete Shelley

Peter McNeish renamed within hours of christening ⇨The Buzzcocks. His new stage-name was no direct homage to poet Shelley. It was simply what his parents would have called their child had it been a girl.

Shinehead

Edmund Aiken had a very full head of hair: the appellation was a joke after he considered shaving it off one hot day.

The Shins

The Oregon-based indie rock band began in 1997. The name was that of a fictional family featured in *The Music Man*. The Broadway show was also a favourite of guitarist James Mercer's father.

Michelle Shocked

She won't reveal her real name: "I've always been shocking!" Although the "me shell-shocked" pun was clearly too contrived to have been missed if it really was selected as a baptismal name. She was born Karen Michelle Johnson: her middle name gave rise to the pun. A few reference books give her birthname as Michelle Schacht, which is plausible but wrong. She has become softer since her early CDs, though Michelle Mellowed doesn't have quite the same ring.

Showaddywaddy

Many barber-shop groups, rockabilly and doo-wop bands used the "showaddy-waddy" backing line. This band specifically referenced Maurice Williams's *Little Darlin'*. Sha Na Na did much the same.

A Dictionary of Rock and Pop Names

The Sid Presley Experience

The South London band aimed to combine the energy of ⇨Sid Vicious of ⇨The Sex Pistols with the excitement of ⇨Elvis Presley and the exhilaration of ⇨The Jimi Hendrix Experience. Related: ⇨The Godfathers.

Sigue Sigue Sputnik

This 1980s British band were lauded as "the fifth generation of rock 'n' roll" and "the biggest hype of all time".

S.S.S. mastermind Tony James told the author it was inspired by a gang of Moscow street ruffians whom he had read about in *The International Herald Tribune*. "Russia's the place." Subsequent lengthy perusals of the *Herald Trib* archive have not yielded the name. The band rapidly became known as "The Sputniks" (artificial unmanned satellite, especially that launched by the U.S.S.R.) Related: ⇨The Sisters of Mercy.

The Silencers

The source was a 1966 film. The ⇨Magazine-like ammunition reference was "intended to leave fans speechless".

Simon And Garfunkel

Paul Frederic Simon and Art (short for Arthur) Garfunkel. Their earliest recordings (1957) were as ⇨Tom and Jerry.

Simon released material as Jerry Landis, Paul Kane, True Taylor and Tico And The Triumphs while Garfunkel tried Artie Garr before they reunited in 1964. At this stage Simon had some folk success of his own and they decided to override fears about Garfunkel being too long to pronounce, figuring it was unusual enough to remember.

The decision was initially rejected by the record company, which preferred Simon And Garfield – the credit name for the 1964 LP *Wednesday Morning, 3AM*. This would now provide associations with another cartoon cat, Garfield. Simon recalled: "I was frightened people might think that we were comedians or something, but at least we were honest. I always thought it was a big shock when ⇨Bob Dylan turned out to be Bob Zimmerman."

Nina Simone

North Carolina singer Eunice Waymon simplified her name after one too many mishearings.

Simple Minds

Their success would be inconceivable under their original punk name ⇨Johnny and The Self-Abusers.

Simple Minds was chosen as a similarly self-depreciating laddish moniker. The source was ⇨David Bowie's *The Jean Genie*, an astronaut "so simple-minded" that he cannot drive his module.

The choice is worthy of many other bands who apparently do not take themselves too seriously: ⇨The Animals, ⇨Bad Brains, ⇨The Blockheads, ⇨The Electric Prunes, ⇨The Immaculate Fools, ⇨Madness, ⇨Mental As Anything, ⇨The Zombies and more.

Simple Minds rapidly became known as The Minds, while the rest of The Self-Abusers became ⇨The Cuban Heels. Related: ⇨Set The Tone.

Simply Red

Mancunian vocalist Mick Hucknall, whose early bands included ⇨The Frantic Elevators, insisted on being called Red. His most striking feature was unruly hair, the target of "ginger nut" school jests. He noted it was also a reference to the soccer team Manchester United and the U.K. Labour Party, whom he supported.

Backed by some of ⇨Durutti Column, Hucknall suggested Red And The Dancing Dead, All Red and Simply Red, punning on "simply read".

Frank Sinatra

The future singer, born 1915, was meant to be christened Martin Albert Sinatra. The priest got confused and named the baby Francis after his godfather Frank Garrick.

At the age of 22 he was a singing waiter in New Jersey calling himself Frank Trent. Bandleader Harry James wanted to change his stagename to Frankie Satin. Sinatra's mother Dolly typically put her foot down: "Your name is Sinatra and it's going to stay Sinatra. So tell him to fuck off with this Frankie Satin crap." Sinatra agreed his own name was more musical, evoking sonata, among other words.

Inspired ⇨(p.89) Danny Wilson, ⇨The Trash Can Sinatras. Daughter: Nancy "Boots" Sinatra (⇨Boots). A headline said to be about Sinatra led to ⇨Frankie Goes To Hollywood. Nicknames: The Guv'nor, The Hoboken Canary, Ol' Blue Eyes and The Voice. Tribute act: Come Fly With Me (after a 1957 album).

Siouxsie And The Banshees

⇨Bromley Contingent punkette Susan Janet Dallion, born 1957, was always known as Susy, although this came to be spelled the American Indian way. She took the banshees from a 1970 Vincent Price horror film. Related: The Creatures (Siouxsie and group member Budgie, born Peter Clarke). ⇨Steve Severin.

Sir Douglas Quintet

Texan Doug Sahm decided that U.S. groups looked outdated at the height of the British Invasion. He played the part of an English gentleman, becoming Sir Douglas. After his accent gave him away, he fronted Doug And The Texas Tornadoes.

Sister Ray

⇨Velvet Underground 1968 song covered by many bands including ⇨Joy Division and the inspiration behind naming of fellow Mancunians Sister Ray, a precursor to ⇨The Smiths, and several groups in the U.S.

Sister Sledge

Real siblings made up this Pennsylvania act, unlike many others such as The Coyote Sisters, The Davis Sisters, The Kaye Sisters, ⇨The Sisters of Mercy, Sisters Unlimited, and The Vernon Girls.

More genuine sisters: The Beverly Sisters, Fontane Sisters, Jones Girls, The King

Sisters, The Lennon Sisters, The Lucas Sisters, McGuire Sisters, Paris Sisters, The Peters Sisters, The Pointer Sisters, Shepherd Sisters, and The Sinclair Sisters.

The Sisters of Mercy

This band's founder, ⇨Andrew Eldritch, includes a rant on his Web site under "Boring FAQ" about how the name question "plagues" every band on the planet. The question is irritating and insulting, he suggests.

Eldritch then condescends to answer it just one more time: "Leonard Cohen wrote a song in which – like us – 'The Sisters Of Mercy, they are not departed or gone'. He should know. Is that why we picked the name? Almost. We did feel that the song would help the dimmest of the dim to interpret the name."

The 1968 song sounds doom-laden and depressing on first listen, though Eldritch rightly notes that critically-acclaimed songwriter Cohen's "droll and erudite" tunes are often misunderstood. The name's a popular reference to prostitutes and there's also a Catholic order of nuns of the same name. Eldritch liked the contrast between sisters of sin and sanctity. "A nice 50/50 balance between nuns and prostitution, which seemed like a very suitable metaphor for a rock band," he told *Melody Maker*'s Adam Sweeting in 1983.

Like ⇨Echo And The Bunnymen, their first drummer was a machine, which was retained for far longer than Echo and called Doktor Avalanche.

Eldritch said the Sisters started as "a very, very, very dry joke". When the joke went sour with a break-up in 1985, both halves of the band toyed with the name The Sisterhood. The row was finally won by Eldritch. He released one record as The Sisterhood and the row was sorted out.

The rest became ⇨The Mission. Later Sisters included Tony James, ex ⇨Sigue Sigue Sputnik. Their record company was called Merciful Release.

[86 + 87] Spot the difference: The Sisters Of Mercy (here, Andrew Eldritch and Tony James) and the Sisters of Mercy (nuns, putting on a charity show). Could they be related?

A Dictionary of Rock and Pop Names

The author, who was educated at a Catholic Sisters of Mercy school at one point, and thinks *Floodland* one of the best 1980s rock CDs, has respectfully written this entry without resorting to stereotypical references to "princes of darkness" or "black clad Goths". Almost.

Sixpence None the Richer

The Texan band named in 1992, to play Christian music, and took the name from ideas in C. S. Lewis' anthology *Mere Christianity* which suggests that monetary value is only part of the value of any gift.

Skid Row

The word skidroad was used in lumberjacking to refer to slippery, steep or muddy tracks for rolling logs to saw-mills. It's come to mean any street of cheap shops or slums. Like ⇨Dire Straits, it's a name which can describe the penniless state of many fledging bands.

It's been used at least three times by professional musicians. The first outfit started in Eire in 1968 and has released occasional albums since, some with Gary Moore; the second formed in New Jersey in 1986 and with help from ⇨Jon Bon Jovi made undistinguished heavy metal fare, and the third was a short-lived group from Seattle in 1987. The last seemed unaware of the others and renamed – so avoiding the possible name-clash legal action which would have undoubtedly ensued sooner or later – finding acclaim as ⇨Nirvana.

The Skids

The uninitiated may imagine this vague moniker refers to skid row, car accidents or moving fast. In fact it's a post-punk name like ⇨The Photos that works on several levels and is mainly a shock reference to underpant stains. Richard Jobson's fault. Spinoffs: ⇨The Armoury Show, ⇨Big Country.

Skinny Puppy

This industrial band from Vancouver, Canada, said the name was chosen "in solidarity with animals treated cruelly and the oppressed everywhere. One day even a skinny puppy will grow up to be well fed and happy."

Skunk Anansie

The 1994-2001 British rockers liked the African folk tales of Anansie the spider-man. They added Skunk "to make the name nastier."

Slade

At a time when many other bands were long-haired sandal-wearers, this British Midlands act adopted the braces, bovver boots and razored heads of skinheads as a publicity stunt. They were originally called Ambrose Slade. "Slade" was the name of a heath near their Wolverhampton base. Manager Chas Chandler abbreviated the name. Titles included *Slayed?*, *Sladest*, *Slayed Alive*.

Slash

The guitarist was born Saul Hudson in England, and moved to America where he often visited the Los Angeles house of character actor Seymour Cassel, father of his friend Matt. Cassel Senior would often address him as "Slash" – as in "Slash, where you dashing to now?" It was only years later that Slash, touring with ⇨Guns N' Roses for *Use Your Illusions*, actually asked why the name. "I never stood still for more than five minutes; he [Cassel] saw me as someone who was always working on his next scheme. He was right." ⇨Velvet Revolver.

Slaughter And The Dogs

This Manchester, U.K., punk band, who formed 1976, and showed a strong glam rock influence, named after their favourite albums: ⇨David Bowie's *Diamond Dogs* and Mick Ronson's *Slaughter On Tenth Avenue*. Related: ⇨Morrissey.

Sleeper

This Britpop band (1993-1998) started out as ⇨Surrender Dorothy, then found other acts had this name. Singer Louise Wener took the new moniker from a 1973 Woody Allen film (which also inspired ⇨The Orb). "It could mean a secret agent (like in the song *Spies*), someone sleeping or a railroad car." It could also mean an unexpected hit, and that "ultimately described the band". Guitarist Jon Stewart added: "It had lots of Es in it. Es are good . . . in a band name, at least."

Slim Chance

⇨Led Zeppelin named because of a comment that such a band would go down like a lead balloon. Ronnie Lane latched onto similar remarks. "I'd high hopes. Nobody thought we had a chance," he told the *NME*. ⇨The Faces.

Slim Shady

An alter-ego for ⇨Eminem. He said the name "just popped into my head. Then I started thinkin' of twenty million things that rhymed with it". Slim Shady is his "dark, evil, creatively sick part".

The Slits

Billed as "the female equivalent of ⇨The Sex Pistols", this British all-girl bunch of minimalist punk rockers chose a feminist equivalent of the phallus.

Sloan

Members of this Nova Scotia pop act named in 1991 from an in-joke about a friend, Jason Larsen, whose picture is on the cover of their 1992 *Peppermint* EP. Founder Jay Ferguson recalled: "Jason worked in a warehouse. His boss always called him 'slow one', but with the French accent it turned into 'Sloan'."

Slowhand

Fans' 1960s nickname for guitar hero ⇨Eric Clapton who would painstakingly restring guitars when strings broke. It was not from his measured playing style on ballads such as those on his 1977 album *Slowhand*.

Sly And The Family Stone

Sylvester Stewart, known as Sly, was in The Stoners and therefore was Sly Stone. He then formed a new band with other members of his Hollywood commune "family". Cf ⇨Family. Related: ⇨Graham Central Station.

The Small Faces

The fashion leaders of the 1960s London mod scene were called "faces". Hence *I'm The Face* by ⇨The Who, a band of musicians trying to be mods and undisputed "faces" revered by West Londoners. Their rivals were Steve Marriott and Ronnie Lane, mods who tried to be musicians from East London. They named Small Faces in reference to their stature. Related: ⇨The Faces, ⇨Foreigner, ⇨Humble Pie, ⇨The Rolling Stones, ⇨Slim Chance.

Smashing Pumpkins

There have been many reports that this band named after the fate of pumpkins (hollowed out into faces for jack-o-lantern candles) after Halloween has passed. Songwriter Billy Corgan played down the surrealism: "It just came to me. It means absolutely nothing. It's the most ambiguous name I could think of."

Smiley Culture

British reggae star Smiley, AKA David Emmanuel, used to "chat up" girls by asking them for a smile.

The Smithereens

This American band formed in 1980, pre-dating similarly-named ⇨The Smiths. They heard "smithereens" on television and thought it wondrous.

Hurricane Smith

Musician Norman Smith, ⇨Beatles' engineer, ⇨Pink Floyd producer, borrowed it from the 1952 Nat Holt movie.

The Smiths

⇨Morrissey, lyricist and vocalist extraordinaire, met potential band members Gary Farrell and Johnny Marr – guitarist born John Maher – in 1982 and produced a postcard on which he had scrawled three suggested names: "Smiths", "Smithdom" and "Smiths' Family".

They all liked the first. Morrissey wanted a name as short and normal as possible. He selected the most common English surname to put the spotlight on the words and music, not the individual group members. The Smiths implied a back-to-basics approach and an unexotic Englishness that promised songs about real people. The humdrum name also had its bad points. It was prosaically boring, in contrast to Morrissey's poetic and Marr's musical brilliance.

It has other associations which have been denied as inspirations: (1) fellow Mancunian Mark E. Smith of ⇨The Fall; (2) "punk poetess" Patti Smith; (3) Manchester club Mr Smiths in Brazil Street and (4) the Moors Murders near Manchester. Sadistic killers Myra Hindley and Ian Brady were turned in to the police in the 1960s by David Smith, Hindley's brother-in-law. Morrissey wrote the song *Suffer Little Children* about the killings. It closes the group's debut album of 1984. Cf ⇨The Moors Murderers.

Related entries: ⇨The Nosebleeds, ⇨Slaughter And The Dogs, ⇨Sister Ray, ⇨Electronic, ⇨The Adult Net, ⇨Rough Trade. Inspired ⇨Pretty Girls Make Graves.

Smokie

. . . started as Kindness, became Smokey then changed the spelling to avoid links with ⇨Smokey Robinson. The band's reluctance to say much on the name reinforces suggestions that it's to do with illicit substances.

The Smoking Mojo Filters

Taken from the lyric of ⇨Beatles song *Come Together*. This one-off 1995 trio was ⇨Paul McCartney, Noel Gallagher and ⇨Paul Weller, who performed the track for the *Help!* charity album.

[88] The Smiths: ordinary name, extraordinary music. L-R: Johnny Marr, Morrissey, Andy Rourke, Mike Joyce.

The Sneaker Pimps

This British act named in 1995 after hearing ⇨The Beastie Boys hired a man to track down classic sports shoes.

Snoop Dogg/Snoop Doggy Dogg

A crazy pseudonym – yet better than Cordozar Calvin Broadus, Jnr., his real name. When still a kid, he was called Snoopy by his mom because he liked the cartoon *Peanuts*. This could have led to legal problems from the Charles M. Schulz company. He became Snoopy Doggy Dogg, after his cousin Tate Doggy Dogg. More recently, the West Coast rapper has been Snoop Dogg.

[89] Watch out y'all: Snoop Doggy Dogg and 2Pac leader Tupac Shakur hit the town in 1996.

Snow Patrol

The Scotland-based alternative rock band formed in 1995. They were known as Polar Bear until they discovered that the ⇨Jane's Addiction bassist had a side project of this name. This had already led to a friend calling them Snow Patrol. Discount the suggestion of Internet bloggers that it's a reference to an antarctic bird, the Snow Petrel.

Soft Boys

This band was simultaneously referencing William Burroughs's *Soft Machine* – from 1961 – and *Wild Boys* – from 1962. It was intended as a comment on modern wimps but spawned "Mr Flopsy" sexual jokes. Cf ⇨Naked Lunch.

Soft Cell

⇨Marc Almond combined 'soft sell' and 'padded cell'. Fan club: ⇨Cell Mates.

The Soft Machine

The title of a novel by William Burroughs, sequel to *The Naked Lunch*. It's about the effect of drugs on the "soft machine" of the body and brain. Daevid Allen had worked with Burroughs and decided to ask permission to use it for a band. "I arranged to meet him on a street corner in Paddington. He (Burroughs) appeared, hat over his eyes, and said: 'Can't see whaa not.'" Cf ⇨Naked Lunch. Related: ⇨Matching Mole, Whole World.

BY WILLIAM BURROUGHS
AUTHOR OF "THE NAKED LUNCH"

[90] "Can I use this title?" said Daevid Allen. "Can't see whaa not," said Burroughs.

Sonic Youth

This New York group named by leader Thurston Moore from reggae act Big Youth and Sonic's Rendezvous Band, the post-⇨MC5 outfit that Fred 'Sonic' Smith led. He wanted to marry reggae "toasting" with discordant rock. Related: ⇨Ciccone Youth. Anagram: Touch Noisy.

David Soul

David Solberg simplified his name. He became a singer following his role in the 1970s TV series *Starsky And Hutch* which also inspired ⇨Lovebug Starski and ⇨Huggy Bear.

Soul II Soul

Selected by founder/disc jockey Jazzie B (born Beresford Romeo) based on his rap: "I gonna put my soul into your soul." Cf ⇨Boyz II Men, Reel 2 Real.

Soundgarden

Named in 1984 after a sculpture in Magnuson Park, Seattle. Douglas Hollis' *A Sound Garden*, dedicated in 1983, features Aeolian pipes to make a constantly-changing

[91 + 92] Soundgarden and *A Sound Garden*... the band and the sculpture they named after.

sound. It's both "bleak" and "sublime" and makes for a not-obvious name, said guitarist Kim Thayil: "It sounds like Pure Joy or Rain Parade. It fools people."

Soundgarden broke up in 1997. The sublime Hollis sculpture was still in place and cranking out its spooky sound. Related: ⇨Audioslave.

Sour Milk Sea

This Oxford band named from a Jackie Lomax song *Sour Milk Sea* (written by ⇨George Harrison) and got a footnote in rock history for rejecting ⇨Freddie Mercury.

Southside Johnny And The Asbury Jukes

Singer Johnny Lyon was a New Jersey kid like ⇨Bruce Springsteen and ⇨The E Street Band, who he worked with. He named from his favourite blues which began in clubs on Chicago's South Side. Origins include Springsteen's Dr Zoom & The Sonic Boom, and the delightfully-named Blackberry Booze Band.

Bob B. Soxx

A bobby-soxer was an adolescent girl following the 1930s–40s trend of wearing bobby socks (white cotton, worn below the knee). Producer ⇨Phil Spector chose it for singer Bobby Sheen, usually joined by The Blue Jeans.

Spandau Ballet

The *NME* joked in April 1991: "Apparently Gary Kemp visited Spandau jail in Berlin and decided that for entertainment they might have ballet. Honest." Funny, but wrong.

Members of Gentry and The Makers became part of a London club scene documented by writer Robert Elms. He saw "Spandau Ballet" written on a wall in the still-divided city of Berlin and offered it to the musicians. Spandau is an area famous for its now-demolished prison which housed former Nazi leader Rudolf Hess until his 1987 death. The graffiti was probably a dig at the Nuremberg executions of Nazi leaders.

Gary Kemp's group were criticised for abandoning their homeland to peddle fascist chic. But they said the new romantic image was a refreshing break from drab British recession – and Islington Ballet didn't sound right.

Spanky And Our Gang
Movie producer Hal Roach gathered child actors for slapstick routines called *Our Gang* in the 1920s. These continued into the 1940s with new stars, including chubby George 'Spanky' McFarland.

Cut to the 1960s. Scene: Chicago. Elaine McFarlane was called Spanky because her name was like George's and she too was plump: she later joined ⇨The Mamas And The Papas as a replacement for the late Mama Cass. The films also inspired ⇨The Young Rascals.

Sparklehorse
This American alternative band's only member is Mark Linkous. Asked about the name he links it to some of his songs (which came after the name). "Might be from like carousels . . . like in *Cow* . . . 'metal teeth of . . . carousels . . .' like the sparkly horses on 'em and rocking horses too, as on the *Chords I've Known* cover . . . or it might be how motorbikes are sometimes called Iron Horses . . . *Gasoline Horseys* is all about that." So that clears that one up, then. Not.

Sparks
Idiosyncratic brothers Ron and Russell Mael were Halfnelson – until their zany records were likened to The Marx Brothers film.

Sparta
Like ⇨The Mars Volta, a spinoff from ⇨At The Drive-In and named from their minimalist style, which started with a razored-down 2002 EP, *Austere*.

Spearhead
Michael Franti, from San Francisco, was inspired by his hero King Shaka's redesign of Zulu weaponry. Related: ⇨The Disposable Heroes Of Hiphoprisy.

Spear Of Destiny
The Spear of Destiny is a warhead with Biblical associations, later owned by European dictators, tyrants and despots. Leader Kirk Brandon told the author: "We use it as a symbol of the conscious movement of young people's minds." Unflattering derivative: SOD, Spear of Broccoli.

The Specials
This English Midlands ska band named from 'special' one-off records manufactured for toasters and deejays. Individual names: Roddy Radiation (guitarist Rod Byers); Sir Horace Gentleman (bassist Horace Panter). Related: ⇨The Selecter.

Phil Spector

The U.S. record producer was born in the Bronx in 1939 as Harvey Philip Spector. Author Tom Wolfe dubbed him "the first tycoon of teen". ⇨Bob B. Soxx, ⇨The Ronettes.

Spice Girls

The revival of this British band in 2007/2008 came a decade after the five girls stormed the pop world.

They were first recruited and given the name Touch by Heart Management, run by the father and son team Chris and Bob Herbert with financier Chic Murphy. Spice Girl Geri Halliwell recalled Touch was "OK, but perhaps a little wet." Murphy then suggested High Five, Five Alive and Take Five. Mel B said the last sounded too much like ⇨Take That.

That night, at an aerobics class, Halliwell got an idea to call the band Spice because "we're all so different." Victoria Beckham says Geri pitched it to others: "It's got five letters and it's us. One word for five different tastes." They later changed management and added "Girls" because there was a hit record by U.S. rapper called Spice 1, and besides they were always called "the girls".

At a press conference, the author asked the girls (well, Victoria and the two Mels) about the name. Mel C. said: "We didn't like Touch – The Spice Girls is better." Victoria agreed: "Yeah, it's more direct." They confirmed the accounts, later given in their autobiographies.

They differ from that of Ian Lee, who ran Trinity Studios in Woking, Surrey, and

[93] The Spice Girls return: Vancouver, 2007. Sporty, Posh, Ginger, Baby and Scary.

was quoted in one newspaper: "They got their name from Tim Hawes, who co-wrote a song with them and titled it *Sugar and Spice*. They were sitting around afterwards and he said: 'There's your name. It's perfect because you're a bunch of spicy bints.' They loved it." It's interesting though, that in line with that title they could have been The Sugar Girls. (Cf ⇨Sugababes.)

They inspired many tribute bands, including All Spice and Nice N' Spicey. *If you wannabe my soundalike . . .*

SPICE GIRL NAMES

In 1996, Peter Lorraine of the BBC's *Top of the Pops Magazine* interviewed the Spice Girls and wrote a piece under the headline *Spice Rack*. It was, Geri Halliwell said, "a marketing man's dream", assigning nicknames based on the *Wannabe* video.

Ginger Spice: Geraldine Estelle Halliwell. She's also known as Geri and Ginger, after her red hair. She was the only girl named after an actual Spice. Some newspapers preferred Sexy Spice though she stuck to Ginger. Because she's two years older than the others, she's also been called Old Spice.

Posh Spice: While Victoria Caroline Adams has tried to play down "posh" in recent years, her love of designer dresses instead of jeans made it obvious. She's also been called Suga, Shopgirl and Chav Spice. She might have the last laugh if her husband is knighted, which would make her Lady Victoria Beckham.

Scary Spice: Melanie Janine Brown was named from her fright of curly hair, Leeds accent, and animal-print dresses. Also known as Mel B, or (later) as Melanie G/ Mel G.

Baby Spice: Emma Lee Bunton is the youngest Spice Girl (Spice Women now? Spice Mums?) with babydoll dresses and an "innocent" appearance.

Sporty Spice: Melanie Jayne Chisholm, or Melanie C/Mel C, was often to be found in a tracksuit and was a gym fanatic.

At first the Spices played up to their names. Their characters became more cartoon-like, said Geri: she made her hair redder, Baby looked "about fifteen", Sporty did backflips on demand, Scary's hair got wilder and Posh "bought 25 pairs of Gucci shoes".

The Spin Doctors

The idea came from a tutor of guitarist Eric Schenkman, who said a political spin doctor distorts a newsworthy story: a cricket spin doctor tampers with the ball. The American pop act said it linked with records "spinning," "doctors" as in scores of other musical "medics" and the 1988 U.S. presidential election, during the course of which they formed.

Spirit

They started as Spirits Rebellious, after a book by Kahlil Gibran, they later abbreviated as they turned from alcoholic to holy spirits. Related: ⇨Jo Jo Gunne.

Spitfire

British rock bands recalling the famous wartime fighter plane. One Spitfire has links with ⇨Elastica and ⇨Suede.

A Dictionary of Rock and Pop Names

Spizz
Vocalist Kenneth Spiers, named Spizz in school, recorded as Athletic Spizz 80, Spizzles, Spizzoil, Spizzenergi etc.

SPK
Australian band whose name stood for System Planning Korporation. Later they added Sozialistisches Patienten Kollektiv and even Surgical Penis Klinik.

Split Enz
They named Split Ends in about 1970 after one of their friends who was always complaining about her hair condition. When they moved to Australia they included a reference to their New Zealand homeland by becoming "Enz". Related: ⇨The Mullanes, ⇨Crowded House. Terrible title: *The Beginning of the Enz*.

Dusty Springfield
The singer (1939-1999) was born Mary Isobel Catherine Bernadette O'Brien in Hampstead, London. Dusty was a childhood nickname because she was a tomboy, according to a Philips record-company biography. Springfield was from her mother's maiden name and first used as the name of family band 'the Springfields' with her brother Tom.

Bruce Springsteen
Yup, the U.S. superstar's name, hair and teeth are his own. He was born Bruce Frederick Joseph Springsteen. Nicknames: ⇨The Boss and ⇨Brooce. Groups: ⇨The E Street Band, ⇨MUSE, The Castiles, Earth, Child, Steel Mill and Dr Zoom & The Sonic Boom. ⇨Southside Johnny also sent greetings from Asbury Park.

[94] Bruce and the band come home to E Street where they named, 2002. L-R: Roy Bittan, Clarence Clemons, Bruce Springsteen, Patti Sciafla, Steven Van Zandt, Garry Tallent, Danny Federici, Max Weinberg and Soozie Tyrell.

A Dictionary of Rock and Pop Names

Spyro Gyra

This New York jazz fusion band formed, about 1970, by saxophonist Jay Beckenstein at a weekly jam session at Buffalo club named Jack Daniel's. As its popularity grew, the owner wanted to put a name of the group on a sign and Jay said, "Call it spirogira" (algae commonly known as 'pond scum'). The next week, that name was on the sign – spelled as 'Spyro Gyra'.

Squeeze

These Britons picked their name in 1974. Several were ⇨Velvet Underground fans and this was a joke about the below-par 1972 LP cut by an ersatz Underground, kept going by Doug and Billy Yule after ⇨Lou Reed left.

Stamford Hillbillies

A hilly part of London, seizing on the *Beverly Hillbillies* joke. Cf ⇨Notting Hillbillies.

Alvin Stardust

The British singer was born Bernard Jewry but failed to make it big as the leader of the American-sounding Shane Fenton And The Fentones. A ⇨Gary Glitter-like change to leather trousers, silly shades and Elvis sideburns was inspired by ⇨Ziggy Stardust.

Ziggy Stardust

Ziggy was the hero of ⇨David Bowie's 1972 album *The Rise And Fall Of Ziggy Stardust And The Spiders From Mars*.

"Ziggy" came from a clothes shop Bowie passed on the train. It reminded him of his friend ⇨Iggy Pop: like "ciggie" but with an unusual Z. "Stardust" was from The Legendary Stardust Cowboy who was on Mercury Records at the same time. The character and creator inevitably became confused. When Bowie announced the character had played his "last show", many thought he was announcing his own retirement. Inspired: ⇨Alvin Stardust.

Ringo Starr

The ⇨Beatle's grandfather had the patronym Parkin but renamed on impulse. Richard 'Ritchie' Starkey found the new surname useful because it abbreviated to give him a stagename in Rory Storm And The Hurricanes. His Butlin's Holiday Camp drum solos were introduced as "Starr Time". He was called Rings because of his fondness for ostentatious finger jewellery. He has a drummer son Zak, who has played with ⇨Oasis among others.

Starry Eyed And Laughing

This British act, with stars in their eyes, named from a phrase in ⇨Bob Dylan's *Chimes Of Freedom*.

Lovebug Starski

New Yorker Kevin Smith renamed after the *Starsky And Hutch* TV show. Cf ⇨David Soul.

A Dictionary of Rock and Pop Names

Status Quo

This British act started life in 1967 as The Spectres (record flopped, risked confusion with ⇨Phil Spector), switched to Traffic (eclipsed by ⇨Traffic almost at once) and Traffic Jam (single banned because of its lyric). The band desperately considered seeking publicity as The Queers (cf ⇨The Kinks) or The Muhammad Alis (writing to the boxing star to ask permission). Then manager Pat Barlow suggested "Quo Vadis" or "Status Quo".

Neither Francis Rossi nor Rick Parfitt knew that it was Latin for "the present position" and even when they were aware, they insisted it had no special significance and could have been worse: "Caveat Emptor" or "Quod Erat Demonstrandum" maybe "and who knew what ⇨Procol Harum meant, anyway?"

Widely known as The Quo. Inspired: ⇨Quiet Riot. Tribute band: Fake Us Quo.

Tommy Steele

Another of the stable of 1950s/1960s U.K. pop stars groomed by ⇨Larry Parnes. Steele was born Thomas Hicks. It's often said the Steele name was suggested by PR man John Kennedy first.

Steeleye Span

Ashley Hutchings used his friend Martin Carthy's suggestion of a wagoner's name in the traditional song *Horkston Grange*. Related: ⇨The Albion Band, ⇨Fairport Convention.

Steely Dan

New Yorker singer-songwriters Donald Fagen and Walter Becker chose the name from William Burroughs' 1959 *The Naked Lunch*: the nickname for a special, steam-powered, milk-squirting, extra-large dildo, of course. The choice is surprising given that "The Dan" produced highly-tasteful, sophisticated jazzy music. Related: ⇨Jay and The Americans. Inspired: ⇨Deacon Blue. Cf ⇨Naked Lunch.

Steppenwolf

Der Steppenwolf was a novel by Hermann Hesse (1877-1962). It fitted the background of vocalist John Kay, who was born Joachim Krauledat and escaped from Communist East Germany as a child. Fanclub called: Wolfpack.

[95] Author William Burroughs on the set of *The Naked Lunch*, surrounded by creatures from the film, 1991. Steely Dan was just one band to name from the book.

[96] Steppenwolf found literary insight before *Born To Be Wild*.

Cat Stevens

Of Greek extraction, London-born Steven Georgiou combined his first name with "Cat", a fashionable 1960s term. His conversion to the Moslem faith resulted in a change to Yusef Islam. In 2006, Islam returned with his first album of western pop in decades.

Rod Stewart

Roderick David Stewart (1945-) became known as Rod The Mod at 20, after appearing in a TV documentary of the same name about "a typical mod". Anagram: Rated Worst. Related: ⇨The Faces.

Stiff Little Fingers

Band from Belfast, Ireland (who started the Rigid Digit label) were inspired by a B-side by The Vibrators, which included the lyrics: "If it wasn't for your stiff little fingers nobody would know you are dead." (Not a reference to aliens in 1960s TV science fiction series called *The Invaders*.)

Sting

Meeting this star, the author found he can happily give a full answer to questions about his name. I'm told that more recently he simply suggests reporters haven't done their homework before daring to interview him and could we now get back onto discussing the brilliant new album please?

Turn to the dictionary and what do you get? "STING, noun, verb. 1. Sharp-pointed section of insect etc used for defence or attack . . . " Relevance to 1970s-2000s rock?

The answer we gain from the man himself is this. 21 year old primary school teacher Gordon Sumner, born in Newcastle, U.K., found his stagename during his time as a part-time jazz bassist/singer for various local bands.

"It was just a joke," he says. "An accident." The young Gordon habitually used to wear a horizontally striped yellow and black jumper: it was all he could afford. This made him look like a bee or a wasp, and the nickname Sting(er) was suggested by local jazz player Gordon Soloman.

[97] Stripey jumper = Sting. L-R: Andy Summers, Sting, Stewart Copeland. The Police *Walking on the Moon* cover session 1979.

This might come as a surprise to those journalists who have speculated that the name must be profound and deep-meaning given Sting's serious tone for the last decade. Among the incorrect but amusing theories peddled in explanation are the following:

It's a reference to Scott Joplin's *The Sting*;

It was picked as an insect name like ⇨The Crickets and ⇨The Beatles;

It's a comment on being stung by cupid's arrows as in Elvis Presley's *I Got Stung*;

It's a "police and criminal" type name, with a "sting" meaning a bank robbery.

⇨The Police, ⇨The Blue Turtles. Unflattering derivative: Stink.

The Stone Poneys

Linda Ronstadt-led trio named after U.S. blues singer Charley Patton's *(Stone) Pony Blues*.

The Stone Roses

This Manchester band's evolution took half a decade, starting in 1979, evolving into English Rose – an acoustic track on ⇨The Jam's 1978 album *All Mod Cons* – and finally The Stone Roses, inspired by ⇨The Rolling Stones.

The name had a light-heavy/surreal/ ⇨Led Zeppelin/ ⇨Iron Butterfly quality. No relation to ⇨Guns N' Roses or Stoned Rose, a predecessor of ⇨Ultravox.

Stone Temple Pilots

Or how the record label signed a Californian band with a logo which resembled the STP oil company logo. "Hey guys, we're a bit worried about the logo: STP might not like it. Say, what does it stand for? Maybe we could use that instead."

"Yeah. Forgot to tell ya: 'Shirley Temple's Pussy.'" Cue mass corporate heart attacks.

Much to their publicists' relief, STP chose Stone Temple Pilots. Unflattering derivative: (because of a similarity with ⇨Pearl Jam): Clone Temple Pirates.

The Stooges

The name was suggested while the band, in suitably-stoned disarray, watched a programme by the Three Stooges American comedy troupe. Their singer became Iggy Stooge, and, later, ⇨Iggy Pop. Related: ⇨Tin Machine, ⇨Destroy All Monsters. Inspired: ⇨Raw Power.

Stormbringer

Swiss rock band with a name filched from their heroes ⇨Deep Purple. The Purps recorded a 1974 album of this name. "It was a hard choice between this and other titles," they told the author. "We also like ⇨Machine Head."

Strange Cruise

After ⇨Steve Strange's time in ⇨Visage he attempted a comeback in Strange Cruise. He was working with Wendy Wu, ex- ⇨The Photos, by then renamed Wendy Cruise.

The Strangeloves
The protest name came from the 1963 film *Dr Strangelove (Or How I Learned To Stop Worrying And Love The Bomb)*.

Steve Strange
Welshman Steve Harrington got his name after moving to London, where he became a leader of the New Romantic club movement. He recalled: "I was living in West Hampstead and my hair was white and cut spiky on top. I was sharing with a girl named Suzy so the postman used to call us Mr and Mrs Strange." He told the author: "My dear, it's because I am on stage 24 hours a day . . . "
⇨Moors Murderers, ⇨Strange Cruise, ⇨Visage. Unflattering derivative: Nobby Normal (because he was a down-to-earth and matter-of-fact Welsh boyo at heart).

The Stranglers
This U.K. punk-new wave band originally called themselves The Guildford Stranglers. The serial killer struck many times in the Surrey area: the group was formed near the town in 1974. Spoof band: ⇨The Men In Black.

Strawbs
It was short for the Strawberry Hill Boys, after the London area where they first worked. Sandy Denny often sung with them, so the "boys" tag was dropped. (Note no definite article, Strawbs NOT The Strawbs.)

Strawberry Alarm Clock
This U.S. West Coast band knew strawberries were big in the summers of love in the 1960s. Some accounts say an alarm clock went off when they were debating the name. It wasn't a tribute to ⇨The Beatles single *Strawberry Fields Forever* because the band was "christened" before the record came out.

Strawberry Studios
Manchester, Northern England, studios co-owned by >10CC members. Named after the 1967 ⇨Beatles single *Strawberry Fields Forever*.

Strawberry Switchblade
Glaswegian glamour dolls with colourful image recalling psychedelia of ⇨The Strawberry Alarm Clock for their 1980s successes. ⇨Orange Juice leader James Kirk gave it to them – he'd written a song called *Strawberry Switchblade*.

The Stray Cats
At least two bands have used this variant on the popular "cat" name. One, a 1970s outfit, featured Keith Moon of ⇨The Who and David Essex for the films *That'll Be The Day* and *Stardust*. The other was a U.S. rockabilly act who named after the earlier group. Both Stray Cats were produced by ⇨Dave Edmunds, who did the same for The Polecats.

A Dictionary of Rock and Pop Names

The Streets
This English rapper from Birmingham said his birthname Mike Skinner wouldn't make for an exciting stagename and he was happy to hide behind a group moniker. His first record started off in about 2000 as a band project. He said in an interview the name was "a suburban rather than an inner-city thing" which has "a different street sound".

Streetwalkers
Former ⇨Family men Roger Chapman and Charlie Whitney named Chapman Whitney to record a 1974 LP called *Streetwalkers*. They soon reconsidered.

Joe Strummer
John Mellors (1952-2002) got his name from a combination of 'Joe Cool', his ukulele playing as a London busker: and his nickname Strumboli from his temper, which could produce explosions to rival Italy's Mount Stromboli. He was also known as Woody Mellors after ⇨Woody Guthrie. ⇨The Clash, ⇨The Pogues.

Stryper
The Christian rockers named from the Bible, the King James Version of Isaiah 53:5: "The chastisement of our peace was upon him; and with his stripes we are healed."

The Style Council
Paul Weller had moved to the left and early gigs were called Council Meetings. It all sounded like a British official body such as The Design Council. The political 1984 single *Soul Deep* was credited to The Council Collective.

Poly Styrene
⇨X-Ray Spex vocalist Marion Elliot said the name was a protest against "plastic artificial living".

Styx
This band liked the legend of the River Styx, one of the waterways of the underworld in *The Inferno* by Dante, part of *Divina Commedia*. Cf ⇨The Divine Comedy. Spinoff: ⇨Damned Yankees.

The Subterraneans
These beat-literature fans namechecked a book by Jack Kerouac, who inspired ⇨The Dharma Bums and more.

Suede
This British band's name followed the 1990s fashion for short monikers and the tradition of "fabric" names seen by dozens of groups: cf ⇨Felt etc. It also puns on "swayed", fitting singer Brett Anderson's androgynous appearance.

    The cooler-than-thou band uncoolly took it from a dry-cleaning shop called THE PERSUEDERS, on Stoke Newington High Street. They laughed at the dreadful shop sign, which had the SUEDE highlighted in red.

They had to be known as (the) London Suede in the U.S. because of a name clash with an American female pop, cabaret and jazz singer/ instrumentalist called Suede. Related: ⇨Elastica. Unflattering derivative: Pseud.

Sugababes

This British pop trio formed in 1998, just after the peak of "Spice Mania". It's ironic to note that since ⇨The Spice Girls might have had a Sugar name, according to one account, this act might have been the Spicebabes – on their way to smashing sales records set by their predecessors. Keisha Buchanan's nickname in school was "Sugar baby".

The Sugarcubes

The first album by ⇨The Jesus And Mary Chain was described by one reviewer as "an innocent little sugarcube just waiting for the tongue." This (unrelated) band's name sounds innocent, suggesting sweet music, but as many drug users know, LSD is often taken soaked up into sugarcubes. They included ⇨Björk.

The Sugarhill Gang

Rappers assembled by Sylvia Robinson for her label Sugarhill, named after Sugar Hill, New York.

Donna Summer

Née LaDonna Gaines, she became LaDonna Sommer after her marriage to Austrian actor Helmut Sommer. She anglicised it, shot to fame and divorced in 1976. ⇨The Queen Of Disco.

Super Furry Animals

This Welsh rock band's frontman Gruff (pronounced Griff) Rhys initially deflected questions from the author in 1996, for *The A-Z Of Names In Rock*, by saying enigmatically: "The name came out of something in a comic." Nice, but wrong.

The band formed in 1993, and the name came from T-shirts being made by Gruff's sister. Her Super Furry Animals T-shirts were printed for the fashion group Acid Casuals. The band's since given plenty of clues: their record label became Placid Casual and a 1997 song was *The Placid Casual*. Often called SFA or the Furries/Super Furries.

Supergrass

The British indie rockers were briefly known as Theodore Supergrass before abbreviating. They've claimed it came from a newspaper headline about a big-time criminal informer who got a lighter sentence in return for information on his buddies. However, this is probably just a 'smokescreen': many fans assume it to be a coded reference to cannabis.

Supertramp

They came together under patronage of Dutch millionaire sugar daddy Stan Miesegaes and began to rehearse as Daddy.

The new name was suggested by sax-playing recruit Dave Winthrop to suit their initially super-scruffy image. In 1969, "Tramp" was a fashionable word for everything from clothes shops to clubs. It was also a reference to the 1910 memoir by Briton W.H. Davies, *The Autobiography Of A Supertramp*, relating his experiences of roaming the U.S. incognito as a down-and-out.

A 1986 compilation album was called *The Autobiography Of Supertramp*.

The Supremes

This female group called themselves The Primettes, after The Primes, whom they backed. After The Primes went solo in 1960, record company Motown ordered a name change (which the vocal trio did not want) and offered a list of suggestions. Founder Florence Ballard reluctantly picked Supremes. (The Primes soon became ⇨The Temptations, so the name could have stayed.) After Diana Ross became the new boss they became Diana Ross and the Supremes.

Surrender Dorothy

There have been many bands of this name, the best known of which later became ⇨Sleeper. Group member Jon Stewart said: "It comes from that bit in *The Wizard Of Oz* when the witch paints it on the sky with her broomstick and suddenly, this amazing phrase appears before you." ⇨Toto named in part from the film.

Screaming Lord Sutch

David Sutch (1940-1999), a British commoner but never a common man, said "screaming" came from his singing style, which reminded many of American singer ⇨Screamin' Jay Hawkins. He changed his name by deed poll to Screaming Lord Sutch, 3rd Earl of Harrow, becoming a toff to fit his trademark top hat. He told the author in an interview: "I later tried to change my name to Margaret Thatcher, but I was told it would be too confusing." Sutch's band featured future stars of ⇨Deep Purple and ⇨Led Zeppelin.

SVT

Former ⇨Hot Tuna and ⇨Jefferson Airplane member Jack Casady is usually said to have named after the Ampeg SVT amplifier. After reports suggested he wanted to play music to "get hearts racing and blood pressure raised," someone told him this was called supra ventricular tachycardia. Only later did he discover SVT was an undesirable condition.

Sweethearts Of The Rodeo

From the influential countryish album by ⇨The Byrds called *Sweetheart Of The Rodeo*. ⇨Flying Burrito Brothers.

Switchfoot

This Californian band formed in 1996 and named after a surfing technique, said singer Jon Foreman. Switchfoot surfers change stance to keep going as long as possible. He said that the term could just as much apply to life and music.

David Sylvian
Chosen during his early ⇨Japan days as more exotic than his own name, David Batt (hardly a suitable name for someone dubbed "the world's most beautiful man"). It was a tribute to Sylvain Sylvain of ⇨The New York Dolls.

System of A Down
This Los Angeles rock band said *Victims Of A Down* was a poem that singer-guitarist Daron Malakian composed in high school. Shavo Odadjian, their manager at the time, thought the word "victim" was passive and depressing: lead singer Serj Tankian backed "system" as an alternative. The band's often called System or SOAD.

T

Take That
⇨Boyz II Men, ⇨Boyzone, ⇨Bros., ⇨New Kids On The Block, ⇨East 17. Just some of the teen idols of our time who said "take that" to the critics and enjoyed massive commercial success. Take That's 2005 plus revival proves the men don't know, but the little girls still understand.

Discount erroneous reports that they came together from TWO bands called "Take That" and "Party". Gary Barlow met Mark Owen in 1987 while in The Cutest Rush; Jason Orange and Howard Donald were in Street Beat; chunky body popper Robbie Williams later enjoyed solo success.

The official version says "someone caught sight" of a tabloid headline: "Take That And Party". Owen said: "We all really liked it, so we called ourselves Take That And Party, but we dropped the Party bit when we heard about the American group, The Party."

An often reported alternative is that it comes from a ⇨Madonna video, where she grabs at her crotch and shouts at the audience: "Take That".

Either way, Barlow noted on the band's Web site that it was "the best of a bad bunch of ideas, but it could have been worse – the first idea was Kick It." Take That sounded as if it was lifted from a *Tom And Jerry* show, or like ⇨Wham! a decade before. *Take That And Party* became the title of their first album, released in August 1992.

Talking Heads
This 1975-1991 American band – makers of some exceptional music in the 1980s – said a fellow graduate of the Rhode Island School of Design, Wayne Zieve, saw the term "talking heads" in New York's *TV Guide*. It's television speak for an onscreen speaker. David Byrne liked it for many reasons, including his hope that the group would communicate: he rejected other collectives such as The Portable Crushers, The Vague Dots and The Artistic Blocks.

Fans called the band "The Heads". Reformed in 1996 by the ⇨Tom Tom Club faction, this name was formally used briefly. Also related: ⇨Bonzo Goes To Washington, ⇨Tom Tom Club, ⇨Brian Eno (whose record *King's Lead Hat* is an anagram of "Talking Heads"). Inspired: ⇨Radiohead.

Talk Talk

Mark Hollis recorded a track *Talk Talk* which became his band's "theme tune". He came to regret the double name which reinforced comparisons with ⇨Duran Duran, who shared the same label and producer.

Tamla Motown

The American hit-making record label began as two companies, ⇨Motown and Tamla, which was originally to be Tammy, after the Ray Evans song from 1957 movie *Tammy And The Bachelor*. Oscar Brodney was writing more Tammy films, so the company became Tamla.

The Teardrop Explodes

'Saint' Julian 'Pope' Cope was looking for a name for his psychedelic group A Shallow Madness when he chanced upon an old D.C. Marvel comic, *Prince Namor*, number 77, dating from June 1971.

The cartoon says: "Filling the wintered glades of Central Park with an unearthly whine . . . painting the leaf-bare branches with golden fire . . . THE TEARDROP EXPLODES!! . . . for echoing seconds the sky is filled with silver webs of lightning – and, with the glow's fading, a new menace is revealed!"

In an interview, Cope said he liked it because he thought most hip bands of the time had 'cold' names and it was "warmer, more colourful, emotional." Related: ⇨Dalek I, ⇨Echo And The Bunnymen, ⇨The Mystery Girls, ⇨Wah! Possibly inspired: ⇨Aztec Camera.

[98] The Teardrop Explodes – and a new band is revealed in Liverpool. ©2008 *Marvel Characters, Inc.*

Tears For Fears

U.S. psychologist Arthur Janov was the pioneer of Primal Therapy, a technique set out in *Prisoners Of Pain*. It suggests using "tears for fears" – releasing emotion to relieve depression.

The emotions of this British new wave band were therefore supposed to help the anxieties of the performers – and listeners. Their 1983 debut LP was called *The Hurting* while their second, 1985's *Songs From The Big Chair*, was a reference to a psychiatrist's couch. Janov influenced ⇨John Lennon, ⇨Primal Scream and ⇨Sting.

Television

This New York group started in 1971 as The Neon Boys, revamping in 1973 as guitarist Thomas Miller became ⇨Tom Verlaine. Television was ⇨Richard Hell's suggestion; Verlaine backed it enthusiastically. He was inspired by literature but decided "hardly anyone reads" and wanted to communicate via the mass media. And it fitted his new initials.

Second guitarist Richard Lloyd said: "'Television' just seemed to fit that bill 'cause it's something that's in every home in America."

Inspired: ⇨Marquee Moon, ⇨Friction, ⇨Elevation and, in part, ⇨The Frantic Elevators. Related: ⇨The Heartbreakers, ⇨The Voidoids, ⇨The Waitresses. Cf TV names such as ⇨Terrorvision.

Temple Of The Dog

Members of ⇨Mookie Blaylock and ⇨Soundgarden paying tribute to the late Andrew Wood, vocalist with Mookie predecessors Mother Love Bone. The name's a line in his song *Man Of Golden Words*.

The Temptations

This Michigan band considered ⇨The Miracles but ⇨Motown had already signed an act of this name. Otis Williams came up with the alternative with record label employee Billy Mitchell. Related: ⇨The Supremes.

10CC

Many people have bought 10CC records without knowing what this refers to: a small car engine? The combined size of their brains? It was dreamt up – literally – by ⇨Jonathan King.

The businessman told a paper that he had gone to bed, perchance to dream, slept on the subject, and woke up with a firm idea. The words, repeated with a wink, led to suggestions that it's a reference to ejaculation achieved during orgasm. In a 1988 interview, guitarist Lol Creme (born Lawrence Creme) backed this account.

However, King later said his dream was simply that he would have a band with a number one single in both America and Britain, and it would be called 10CC. Songwriter Eric Stewart said King's dream was "a hoarding over Wembley Stadium or Hammersmith Odeon or something and it said, '10CC, The Best Group In The World." Kevin Godley agreed, though noting "the ejaculate theory makes better after dinner conversation."

It was said the immodest King chose to make the figure up to a round ten, more than the usual nine cubic centimetres. However, the average ejaculate volume is more like three cc of semen, much less than the 0.35195 fluid ounces the name implies.

Cf ⇨Cream, ⇨The Lovin' Spoonful. Related: ⇨The Mindbenders; ⇨Frabjoy and Runcible, ⇨Strawberry Studios.

1066 Gaggle O'Sound

Michael Stipe solo project in the early days of ⇨R.E.M.: 1066 is his "favourite year in history".

10,000 Maniacs

The alt rock band, which included Natalie Merchant, formed in 1981 in New York. The source was a low-budget splatter flick, *2,000 Maniacs!* (not another B-movie called *Ten Thousand Clowns*).

Ten Years After

This rock band formed in 1966. Leader Alvin Lee was referencing 1956. He gives this as the date when "rock became the dominant form of popular music" thanks to ⇨Elvis Presley. They reformed in the 1970s as Ten Years Later.

Terrorvision

Taken from the title of a 1960s TV horror film, in protest against violence on the small screen. Cf ⇨Television.

Texas

. . . were nearly called Paris . . . and they were from neither Dallas nor France . . . but Glasgow. They thought that the name was still a good description of their music and "means having room to grow". It was homage to *Paris, Texas*: they loved Ry Cooder's soundtrack. Cf ⇨Travis.

The The

The moniker for projects by British studio master Matt Johnson, who said in an interview: "The purpose of a band's name is to be remembered, which is why I chose this one, and everybody remembers it." It was a swipe at bands obsessed with "the": ⇨THE Sex Pistols, ⇨THE Damned and ⇨THE Clash.

Them

⇨Van Morrison's band named from a 1950s film, where the "them" of the title, a race of invaders, were so awesomely terrible that nobody dared speak the name.

Thin Lizzy

The Irish group came together in 1969, naming from British comic strip in *The Beano* about a robot called Tin Lizzie (from a Model T Ford motor car). They respelled the words, pointing out that the Irish won't pronounce the "H". ⇨Dare, ⇨Wild Horses, ⇨Johnny The Fox.

The Thin White Duke

The opening words of ⇨David Bowie's 1976 track *Station To Station* refer to "the return of the Thin White Duke". He planned a book of the same name at this time. Thin White Duke well described Bowie's pale, emaciated mid-1970s phase.

Thin White Rope

A reference to male ejaculate, I'm afraid – blame William Burroughs. More Burroughs: ⇨Naked Lunch.

Third Stone

⇨Jimi Hendrix's *Third Stone From The Sun* which described the earth, inspired ⇨Kinky Machine and this group.

The 13th Floor Elevators

Going Up: This 1960s Texas band is remembered as being in the apogee of hippiedom. Elevators: because they were making psychedelic music which they hoped would be uplifting (cf ⇨Otis "Elevator" Gilmore). 13th Floor: a drug rather than a superstitious reference: 13th letter = M = marijuana; getting high. **Going Down**: Guitarist Stacy Sutherland was imprisoned and then shot dead by his wife. Inspired: ⇨The Fire Engines.

.38 Special

This U.S. band said one rehearsal generated a noise complaint and a visit from police wielding .38 calibre handguns. The name recalled the blast of late Ronnie Van Zant's ⇨Lynyrd Skynyrd – .38 special singer Donnie is his brother.

30 Seconds To Mars

This Los Angles emo band formed in 1998. Singer Jared Leto said the moniker came from a manuscript called *Argus Apacase* about the speed of technology. Fans have been looking for the source with bafflement.

36 Crazyfists

There has to be some way of warming up the cold nights in Alaska. For Anchorage guitarist Steve Holt, in 1994, it was Jackie Chan films, especially 1977's *The 36 Crazy Fists*. Singer Brock Lindlow said: "Now we're all fans."

This Machine Kills

This band named from U.S. folk singer ⇨Woody Guthrie's guitar inscription "this machine kills fascists". ⇨Donovan had a similar guitar.

This Mortal Coil

From words Shakespeare gives Hamlet: "when we have shuffled off this mortal coil". Related: ⇨The Cocteau Twins. Cf ⇨The Darling Buds.

Thompson Twins

There are three of them. Not twins and not called Thompson. They named from Hergé's Belgian comic strip *The Adventures Of Tintin*, which featured bungling Thompson twins sleuths. Hergé uses other names for the characters outside English-speaking countries and the band escaped the legal problems ⇨Stephen 'Tin Tin' Duffy faced.

[99] The Thompson Twins namechecked sibling sleuths from Herge's Tintin cartoons.

The Three Chuckles

New York promoter Charlie Bush heard the yet-unnamed trio and sent them away to look for a moniker. His next interview was with a mother-and-son act. The child wasn't interested in performing, just chomping on a Chuckles candy bar. Bush told the woman: "You haven't got the job . . . but your boy's just given me a great idea."

Three Dog Night

Californian Danny Hutton founded a group with three lead singers and wanted a name to reflect this. He found an expression from Australia; aborigines used to keep warm at night by sleeping alongside their dogs: one dog night, chilly: two dog night, colder: three dog night, freezing.

311

The Nebraska band was named by bassist Aaron Wills (AKA P-Nut) after he, founder Jim Watson and friends were caught skinny dipping by police. Watson was charged for violating Omaha code 311 (indecent exposure). They agreed 311 would not limit the band because it said nothing about its music.

For a while 311 kept quiet about the origin, even after Watson had left in 1991; they suggested that 3:11 was the perfect length of song and had astrological significance. They were more forthcoming in 1996 after suggestions it referred to the Klu Klux Klan (as in three times 11, K being the eleventh letter of the alphabet).

Throwing Muses

The alt-rock band formed in 1981 in Rhode Island. Leaders Kristin Hersh and Tanya Donelly liked The Muses and added "Throwing" to make it less gender-specific as they moved from an all-female act. Related: ⇨Belly, ⇨Breeders and ⇨50 Foot Wave. Cf ⇨Muse.

Thunderclap Newman

Named as a joke on jazz pianist Andy Newman. The producer who thought of the name was Bijou Drains – better known as Pete Townshend of ⇨the Who.

Tiffany

She was born Tiffany Renee Darwish in California.

Timbaland

Rapper and producer Timothy Z. Mosley, known as "Timbo," was renamed by mentor DeVante Swing, punning on Timberland clothes popular in hip-hop.

The Ting Tings

This much-lauded 2008 duo from Manchester, U.K. mysteriously say the name came from an old work colleague of singer Katie White ("we think it means an old bandstand in Mandarin.")

Tin Machine

⇨David Bowie's 1988-1992 band named after the noise they made on *Tin Machine*. Using some of ⇨The Stooges, Bowie wanted to recreate their *Raw Power* album which he'd thinly mixed to give a tinny transistor sound.

Tiny Tim

New Yorker Herbert Boutros Khaury hated his real name. He was being ejected from one club after an audition when a member of the audience called out "Hey, Tiny, do us a set!" He told the author in a phone interview: "It's because I'm about a foot less than the Empire State building". The singer was actually 1,466ft shorter than the landmark, but never mind. Tiny Tim was a minor character in Charles Dickens.

TLC

The familiar abbreviation meaning "tender loving care" fitted their first names to produce an ⇨Abba-style acronym: T = Tionne 'T-Boz' Watkins; L = Lisa 'Left-Eye' Lopez and C = Rozonda 'Chilli' Thomas.

Toad The Wet Sprocket

Californians who named from a comedy skit by the U.K. ⇨Monty Python troupe making fun of silly group monikers.

Tom And Jerry

Early ⇨Simon And Garfunkel. Their guise for a single *Hey Schoolgirl* was taken from the MGM cartoon cat and mouse characters produced by Fred Quimby. When they first met in a school play, Garfunkel was playing a Cheshire Cat so he became Tom (Graph) and more diminutive Simon became Jerry (Landis).

[100] Comedy travels a long way. Britain's Monty Python had musical fruit in The Rutles and Toad The Wet Sprocket in California.

Tom Tom Club

⇨Talking Heads bassist Tina Weymouth and drummer Chris Frantz had the honour of naming a studio in the Bahamas, where they were the first to work. It became Tom Tom, after Chris' native drums on the LP, credited to their "club".

Steve Peregrin Took

Stephen Porter (1949-1980) renamed from hobbit J.R.R. Tolkien's Peregrin Took and came to fame in ⇨Tyrannosaurus Rex. Aptly the band's Tolkienesque lyrics went down a storm at the Middle Earth Club.

Toploader

The English rock band (1997-2002) said the name had multiple meanings – a toploader is, after all, a type of washing machine. But why would anyone name after a washing machine? Most people assumed it meant a rolled cigarette of cannabis and tobacco, with most of the cannabis put at the front end by whoever prepares it.

Peter Tosh

⇨Wailer Peter McIntosh's surname has led to credits as "Tosh" and "Touch" (how it's pronounced in Jamaica).

Toto

This is another of those names which book after book, Web site after Web site gets wrong. The myth is that singer Robert Kimball was born Robert Toteaux, pronounced "Toto". The band's former bassist David Hungate started this as a joke.

[101] Toto's name recalls Dorothy's cute dog in *The Wizard Of Oz*. Aaaah.

The truth is that the new Los Angeles MOR band members were looking for a short, simple name while recording their 1977 debut. Founder Jeff Porcaro jotted down the word Toto, which Hungate noted was Latin for "in total", apt since the members had many styles. It was also, crucially, the name of Dorothy's dog in *The Wizard Of Oz*, so "cute and memorable".

Cf ⇨Jefferson Airplane – also named after a dog but widely believed otherwise.

The Tourists

This British band named from their itinerant lifestyle – though they were nearly The Spheres Of Celestial Influence. These backdated hippies straightened up as ⇨Eurythmics.

A Dictionary of Rock and Pop Names

The Toxic Twins
Joe Perry and Steven Tyler of ⇨Aerosmith: a riposte ⇨The Nurk Twins and ⇨The Glimmer Twins.

Toyah
Toyah Ann Willcox was born in 1958 in Birmingham. Her mum Barbara found the first name in a ballerina book. As a single-name artist Toyah was The Princess of Punk. Now, married to Robert Fripp of ⇨King Crimson, she's Toyah Willcox again for acting.

T'Pau
British couple Carol Decker and Ronnie Rogers took it from the *Star Trek* TV series. T'Pau was a stateswoman from the planet Vulcan. The duo thought it sounded like a comic book ⇨Wham!

Traffic
One of the most pivotal U.K. groups of the late 1960s and early 1970s was named after they had a hard time crossing the road because of the volume of the traffic. Not a reference to ⇨Jimi Hendrix's *Crosstown Traffic*. The moniker was also used by early ⇨Status Quo.

The Tragically Hip
The band formed in 1986 and named from former ⇨Monkee Michael Nesmith's film *Elephant Parts* – not ⇨Elvis Costello's song *Town Cryer*, which featured the words "so tragically hip".

The Transformers
Punks inspired by ⇨Lou Reed, whose 1972 LP *Transformer* featured *Walk On The Wild Side*.

The Transmitters
Like ⇨The Transformers, a punky name working on two levels. The Transmitters were post-punk, like ⇨Pere Ubu.

The Transporters
"Transport" as in to move physically and emotionally. Cf the above two entries.

Trash
The band started off as White Trash and ran into a race row. They pointed out they were white: what was wrong with calling themselves trash? (Cf: ⇨Average White Band.)

The Trash Can Sinatras
Named for the 1990s, after ⇨Frank Sinatra – and possibly his singing daughter Nancy (⇨Boots). They wanted to reflect "the two sides of music . . . the tinsel and the trash".

Traveling Wilburys

The band, billed as 'the ultimate superstar aggregation', began as a fantasy by former ⇨Beatle ⇨George Harrison and Jeff Lynne, of ⇨ELO fame, who wanted a "dream band" featuring all the people they most admired.

When Lynne was helping produce Harrison's 1987 *Cloud Nine*, a joke was started about small errors, common in studio production, often called "gremlins". The duo called them "wilburys", as in "we'll bury them in the mix".

They used the same term, to the amusement of the others, when this supergroup came together, at first for a planned Harrison B side. They wanted a jokey, "homely" name which understated their fame and suggested a non-pro, part-time family hill-billy outfit who toured, despite incurable stage fright. Hence their original choice: The Trembling Wilburys. They were joined by ⇨Bob Dylan, ⇨Tom Petty and ⇨Roy Orbison.

Travis

Like ⇨Texas, another British band to take inspiration from *Paris, Texas*. They named after the main character Travis played by Harry Dean Stanton in the Wim Wenders-directed 1984 film.

This is one name origin that's often reported incorrectly, based on the information that Travis named after a desperate movie character. This has led many people to choose a different char-acter. Their guess, usually stated as fact, is that Travis

[102] Travis was desperate. Would he be consoled to know a band named after him?

named after Travis Bickle in the 1976 film *Taxi Driver*, played by Robert De Niro. In an interview for this book, the band confirmed the Wenders origin. A 2007 song, *New Amsterdam,* even namechecks the right movie.

The Tremeloes

From the musical term tremolo, a succession of up and down pitches. The band accepted by ⇨DECCA Records instead of ⇨The Beatles.

T Rex

⇨Tyrannosaurus Rex was impracticably long for posters, said producer Tony Visconti. So were titles like *My People Were Fair And Had Sky In Their Hair But Now They're Content To Wear Stars On Their Brows*. The fey folk songs about fairies were also an acquired taste. In reply, Marc Bolan slashed the name to T Rex in October 1970. There was no full stop: T Rex not T. Rex, despite fears of legal action by food company Trex.

Bolan sacked ⇨Steve Peregrin Took, brought in Micky Finn, trimmed titles to efforts like *Tanx*; and launched glam rock. The T-Recstasy (T-Rextasy?) later inspired: ⇨Eater and ⇨The Metal Gurus.

A Tribe Called Quest

Many 1990s rappers were in posses or tribes: cf ⇨Boo-Yaa T.R.I.B.E. This bunch named after their leader, Q-Tip.

[103] Marc Bolan went for the simple approach with T Rex after wordy efforts like this.

Tricky

Adrian Thaws was raised in Bristol, U.K., and nicknamed Tricky Kid because of his delinquent behaviour. Related: ⇨Massive Attack.

The Triffids

Australian band named from English writer John Wyndham's (1903-1969) most famous novel, 1951's *The Day of The Triffids*, about nasty walking plants with lethal stings. The Midwich Cuckoos also named from Wyndham.

Troggs

These British rockers took "trogg", 1960s slang for a troglodyte or cave-dweller, to describe their primitive sound. ⇨Reg Presley.

The Tubes

They wanted a name with an oral reference and found it with The Tubes – in this case a key part of the human ear, although it has many other possible meanings with TV tubes just a starting point.

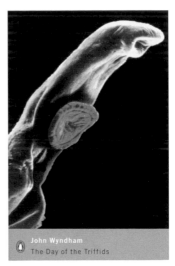

John Wyndham
The Day of the Triffids

[104] The Triffids threatened civilisation as we know it – and invaded rock too.

Tina Turner

She had a star voice, looks and charisma, but Tennessee girl Annie Mae Bullock knew she hadn't the right name. That came with her marriage to Ike Turner, who chose Tina because it fitted alliteratively. Nickname: Duchess.

12Rods

This Ohio rock band looked on the verge of success at various points during its 1992-2004 career. Bassist Matt Flynn came across a school Bible and found "The 12 Rods of the Apostles" as a heading (*Numbers* 17:1-13).

24-7 Spyz

This New York band said music was a fulltime job: "24-7" (something done all the time, as in "twenty-four hours a day, seven days a week") "spies" because they were secretly seeking out new ideas for songs.

23 Skidoo

This 1979-84 British post-punk band's name is a "mysterious Illuminati phrase" in the work of Aleister Crowley, William Burroughs (cf ⇨Naked Lunch) and filmmaker Julian Biggs says the All Music Guide. Some profiles explicitly link it to Crowley's *Book Of Lies*. (Cf ⇨Golden Dawn etc.)

However "23 skidoo/skiddoo" is also a long-standing U.S. phrase for "get out now". The band said it just reflected a desire to "stay out of a rut". They got fed up of being asked about the origin and claimed it was from a stone in London's Highgate Cemetery. (The author found several graves there defaced with "23 skidoo", effectively saying "time to split").

Twiggy

Lesley Lawson was named "Sticks" at school for her thin appearance. The English model/singer later changed to Twiggy.

Conway Twitty

It seems natural to assume that this was chosen for a joke – like ⇨Engelbert Humperdinck.

In fact Harold Lloyd Jenkins was serious when he chose the names from towns in Texas and Arkansas, after a day leafing through the atlas and considering various combinations. He told the author that the "Conway" was found quite quickly. He was stuck on Arkansas for hours, rejecting names such as "Baldknob and Smackover." Shame! Jenkins was born in Mississippi. His real name was a tribute to actor Harold Lloyd.

Two Five

Michael Francis is a cousin of ⇨50 Cent and got the nickname "25 Cent" as a teenager.

2 Men, A Drum Machine And A Trumpet

Andy Cox and David Steele of ⇨Fine Young Cannibals made an amusing, unpretentious choice that beats many carefully-crafted, elaborate appellations.

2Pac

From leader, Tupac Amuru Shakur (1971-1996), who was killed in a gun attack. His real name was Lesane Crooks.

2.13.61
Harry Rollins-led projects named after his birthdate.

Tyrannosaurus Rex
British band started in 1968 as Tyrannosaurus Rex, named after the large prehistoric dinosaur. Leader ⇨Marc Bolan said: "Tyrannosaurus Rex was the largest animal that ever lived. That's rather nice isn't it?" Manager Simon Napier-Bell added that Bolan chose it "because he was going to be that big too". At first that looked unlikely as the acoustic duo of bongo player ⇨(p.277) Steve Peregrin Took and Bolan won only a small audience. ⇨T Rex.

The Tyrell Corporation
   This U.K. dance act named from the company that makes robots in the film *Blade Runner*.

U

UB40
These Birmingham reggae musicians were unemployed in 1979, as were about one in 10 of British workers.

[105] The hated British "signing on" card, shown on the front of UB40's first album.

A Dictionary of Rock and Pop Names

Legend has it that they met in a dole queue. In fact, they told the author that several of them knew each other before. It's true that they took the number from the British unemployment benefit attendance card, UB40, issued by the Department of Health and Social Security. (Many Internet sites get this one wrong: the UB40 was NOT an initial-fill form so the band couldn't have met while "filling it in".)

Their first album, in 1980, was called *Signing Off* and featured a reproduction of the hated card. Singer Ali Campbell said: "The name summed up where we were and where we'd been. We didn't want to go back. A lot of people understood."

UFO
The best-known UFO loved hard rock and science fiction (related: ⇨Fastway, ⇨MSG, ⇨Waysted). Another, from Tokyo, meant United Future Organisation.

Ultravox
British band named from Latin "ultra", meaning "beyond", "better than" or "best". And "vox", meaning "voice". Translated as "the ultimate voice" or more accurately "the voice from beyond".

Founder member Warren Cann recalls they also might have gone for punk name The Zips or ⇨The Damned before settling on Ultravox! The exclamation mark, homage to ⇨Neu!, was later dropped.

Christopher St. John became Chris Cross (no relation to ⇨Christopher Cross) and original singer Dennis Leigh became John Foxx. (Cann recalls Leigh had considered becoming Johnny Vox, giving him nominal leadership; Cann stopped this by threatening to trump him as Warren Ultra.) Cf ⇨Bono Vox. Later vocalist: ⇨Midge Ure.

The Undertones
The Belfast band found the word "undertones" in a history book. Inspired: ⇨Wednesday Week.

Unleded
Jimmy Page and Robert Plant vowed never to reform ⇨Led Zeppelin after the death of John Bonham. When they got back together, though without John Paul Jones, they chose this punning name. Led Zep has reformed with Jones for Live Aid and other charity concerts. One, in December 2007, had more than a million online applicants for 20,000 tickets. ⇨Percy, ⇨Bonzo, ⇨Dread Zeppelin etc.

Upsetter, Upsetters
Lee Perry is known as ⇨Scratch and The Upsetter for 1960s hits including *The Upsetter*, the latter was also attached to his bands.

Midge Ure
Born James Ure in Glasgow, Scotland, the nickname was a phonetic reversal of his Christian name (MIJ), not a dig at his stature as sometimes suggested. Related: ⇨Visage, ⇨The Rich Kids, ⇨Ultravox.

Urge Overkill

This Chicago band named after a song by ⇨Funkadelic, an early influence.

Uriah Heep

Heep, full of false "'umbleness", is a villain in Charles Dickens' 1850 master-work *David Copperfield*. The British band's name was suggested by manager Gerry Bron: Dickens was everywhere in Britain around 1969-1970 since it was the 100th anniversary of his death and a TV version starred Robin Phillips. Their 1970 debut: *Very 'Eavy, Very 'Umble.*

[106] Ron Moody as Uriah Heep in the film which led to the band Uriah Heep. (Also L-R: Susan Hampshire, Edith Evans and Robin Phillips).

UTFO

Brooklyn rappers whose name means "Un-Touchable Force Organisation". Inspired: ⇨The Real Roxanne.

U2

This Irish act started in 1976-1977 as ⇨(p.172) The Larry Mullen Adventure/Band, ⇨Feedback and ⇨The Hype – then rose to world domination.

Bassist and then amateur manager Adam Clayton approached Dublin musician Steve Averill, AKA Steve Rapid of The Radiators, for advice in 1978.

In the 2006 biography *U2 By U2*, ⇨Edge says: "Steve gave us a list of about six possible names, none of which we really liked." Singer ⇨Bono wasn't impressed with Flying Tigers or The Blazers. Clayton said U2 was the one "everyone disagreed with the least."

Eventually they all came round to it. U2 prints up big, avoids the definite article (1978 punk names often had a "the") and didn't pin them down. Bono told *NME* in 1980 it was ambiguous, so avoided wrong assumptions.

As a pun, means "you too" or "you two". U2 was quite coincidentally also a type of submarine (the reference that Bono first thought of); an American plane used for intelligence gathering (the first association Adam Clayton made); a size of battery and a railway line in Berlin.

Two incorrect stories that often show up are (1) the list was supplied by manager Paul McGuinness and (2) the name was V2, a reference to The Virgin Prunes. McGuiness hadn't taken them on at the time and U2 got billed at one early concert as V2, but only after a misunderstanding.

[107] Rare picture of U2, shortly after naming in 1978. The Dublin band had rejected Feedback and Hype.

A Dictionary of Rock and Pop Names

Notes: U2 patronage/participation helped ⇨Clannad and ⇨The Hothouse Flowers. Tributes: Doppelganger, The Joshua Trio, We Will Follow. The name is said "u-two", though is "u-dos", "u-deux" to some fans.

Ritchie Valens
Born Richard Valenzuela of Indian-Mexican parents in Los Angeles, his name was only shortened/Anglicised just before his first single in 1958.

Valley Of The Dolls
This British band named after a 1967 film about a naïve actress who's lured into a life of lust, drink and "dolls" – or drugs. It was based on a Jacqueline Susann novel. Cf ⇨The New York Dolls.

Frankie Valli
Anglicisation of his real name Francis Castelluccio.

Vampire Weekend
This New York band formed in 2006, named after a mock horror movie they made when studying at Columbia University. The video featured a character called Walcott, who pops up in one of their songs. The song, film and group name are more about vacations than vampires. (The band's initial press said they were more geeks than Goths.)

Van Der Graaf Generator
This British band recalled U.S. scientist Robert Van de Graff, who built a generator at M.I.T. in the 1930s. They read about his death in the newspapers and thought his name "really original".

Vangelis
He was born Evangelos Odyssey Papathanassiou in Greece. His record company christened him simply Vangelis – they knew the problems people had with Greek names like Nana Mouskouri.

Van Halen
They started under the punk handle Rat Salade, then named after Dutch-born Eddie Van Halen, and his drummer brother Alex Van Halen. Yet David Lee Roth was the primary attraction for many fans: *Kerrang!* said the choice was "amazing . . . given the size of his ego".

Vanilla Fudge

This U.S. band started as The Vagrants and described themselves as "white guys doing black music". Cf ⇨Average White Band. This prompted one fan to say their sound was like "tasty fudge in a white colour".

VCL XI

Early ⇨Orchestral Manoeuvres In The Dark, named from a valve number on ⇨Kraftwerk's 1975 *Radio Aktivitat*.

Bobby Vee

Simplification of his real name Robert Velline. He reverted for an attempted 1970s comeback.

Velvet Revolver

Guitarist ⇨Slash had already been in a band where two sides compromised to get the name. That was when Hollywood Rose and L.A. Guns became Guns N' Roses. He wasn't directly involved in that naming, but was with the next; his own act, formed in 2002, initially called The Project.

The night before the name was picked, Slash went to the movies. While he cannot remember what he saw, one name in the credits hit him: Revolution Studios. This led to "Revolver". In the 2007 *Slash* autobiography, he says: "Not only did it evoke a gun, but there was also the subtext of a revolving door, which, considering how many members of other bands this band was composed of, seemed entirely right." Plus it was one of the best ⇨Beatles albums.

Singer Scott Weiland had come up with "Black Velvet". They compromised on Velvet Revolver.

The Velvet Underground

The name conveyed the 1960s New York group's interest in dark, fetishist, and underground interests. ⇨Lou Reed took it from *The Velvet Underground*, a book by Michael Leigh. A friend, Tony Conrad, had found a battered copy of the sexual exposé and brought it to Ludlow Street, where he had been living.

The name was liked both for its sound and the sado-masochistic theme. The front

[108] Velvet Underground record design based on the Michael Leigh book cover that gave them their name.

cover showed a whip, mask and kinky boots. The same themes were explored in the song *Venus In Furs* about Séverin.

In one interview, Lou Reed recalls meeting author Leigh's daughter soon after the name was adopted; Leigh had just died. Band member Sterling Morrison said it was proved right because CBS News was doing a feature on an "underground" film being made; moviemaker Piero Heliczer the involved the group.

They directly/indirectly inspired names of ⇨Dream Academy, ⇨Loop, ⇨The Primitives, ⇨The Psychedelic Furs, ⇨Sister Ray, ⇨Squeeze, ⇨Steve Severin and ⇨Verve. Related: ⇨Drella, ⇨Nico, ⇨The Dream Syndicate.

One of their early names was The Warlocks, a name shared with the early ⇨Grateful Dead, the west coast band who renamed after they heard of their east coast namesakes. The Velvet Underground also considered The Falling Spikes – entertainingly in view of their song *Heroin*. Sometimes abbreviated to V.U. – also an album title. Often called The Velvets: no relation to a Texas R&B group of the name.

Tom Verlaine

New Jersey vocalist/guitarist Thomas Miller renamed after French poet Paul Verlaine, friend of Arthur Rimbaud. It's fitting that a man with initials T.V. should found ⇨Television.

Veruca Salt

This Chicago band formed in 1993, naming after the spoilt, rich, precocious brat who appears in British writer Roald Dahl's 1964 cautionary tale *Charlie And The Chocolate Factory*, filmed 1971 and 2005.

Because a verruca is an unpleasant boil-type lump on the foot, they called their music "wart-core" as opposed to "hard-core". Anagram: Veruca Salt = A Vast Ulcer.

[109] Veruca Salt named in 1993 after a poor little rich girl, here played by Julia Winter in 2005.

The Verve

This British group (formed 1989, reformed 2007) named after the U.S. Verve record label, known as the home of ⇨The Velvet Underground, whom they admired. Originally Verve, the name was a typical 1990s short choice (cf ⇨Blur). Unrelated: The Verve Pipe, a U.S. grunge band. Influenced: ⇨Mansun.

Vice Squad

Named for their scatological lyrics, the sort of stuff Scotland Yard's Vice Squad was set up to hunt out. Civil liberty groups – and this punk band – said it was no business of the police to investigate personal morality. Included ⇨Beki Bondage.

A Dictionary of Rock and Pop Names

Sid Vicious

London schoolboy John Simon Ritchie (1957-79) was also known as John Beverley, because his mother had married again. John Lydon (later ⇨Johnny Rotten) met him in the early 1970s and recalls: "I called him Sid, after my pet hamster. One day, the hamster took a bite out of my father's hand. We named Sid the hamster Vicious after that."

Vicious, used from 1973, self-consciously echoed ⇨Lou Reed's *Vicious*. The name was in the background as Ritchie formed ⇨The Flowers of Romance.

As a Pistol, Sid wasted no time in attacking a journalist who came to interview him. This is sometimes cited as the origin of the name, though it was in place long before. Like ⇨Johnny Rotten's, it was the antithesis of "nice" names given to stars by McLaren's starmaker predecessors such as ⇨Larry Parnes.

Vicious lived his name to the last. He was charged with the murder of his girlfriend, Nancy Spungen, and while on bail suffered a fatal heroin overdose. He's one inspiration for ⇨the Sid Presley Experience.

The View

This quartet formed in 2005 and used to meet at The Bayview pub in Menzieshill, Dundee, near their homes.

Butch Vig

The U.S. producer and ⇨Garbage man was born Bryan Vigorson in Viroqua, Wisconsin. He abbreviated his surname. Vig said: "My father used to shave my head to a 'butch' haircut every two weeks. Since then, everyone called me that."

Gene Vincent

Virginian Vincent Eugene Craddock shortened his names. Unrelated: ⇨Gene.

The Violent Femmes

The Milwaukee band hasn't been forthcoming on why the name was picked: it was apparently "written in the sky" and they just had to form "a band worthy of the name". The "violent" bit led some promoters to fear possible riots (cf ⇨Quiet Riot) while the all-male band's choice of "femmes" prompted allegations of sexism and homophobia. (denied).

Virgin

Richard Branson chose it for his company, at that time distributing records, because he was a business virgin and it had a subversive sound. His runner-up choice: Slipped Disc Records. Later V2.

Visage

The British 1980s studio band chose French for "face", "because it sounded classy". The Face had been a mod buzz-word (cf ⇨Small Faces) and was the title of the magazine that chronicled the rise of its leader ⇨Steve Strange.

The Voice Of The Beehive

Two American sisters who moved to England. They'd first called themselves The Beehive Girls. In interviews at one stage, they claimed it was from a Bette Davis movie. When people couldn't find it, they switched and said it was an Italian film. Then they admitted it was another hairstyle name like ⇨The B-52s. Cheeky album titles: *Let It Bee*, *Honey Lingers*.

The Voidoids

⇨Richard Hell – born Richard Myers – said their name was supposed to represent "emptiness, future". Hence a novel he started in 1973, *The Voidoid*. (He's since published other books.)

Voodoo Chile

Band of the nineties inspired by a child of the sixties. ⇨Jimi Hendrix was known as Voodoo Chile after his songs. *Voodoo Chile (Slight Return)* was a hit, spawned by the much longer jam on 1968's double LP *Electric Ladyland*.

Wacko Jacko

Unflattering derivative for ⇨Michael Jackson. Long known as Jacko from his patronym, he became "wacko" after reports about plastic surgery; skin colour changes; 'funky monkey' Bubbles, and so on. The humour drained away after accusations and court cases.

Wah!

Liverpool bands led by Pete Wylie, who found the name when cycling one hot day and said "Wah! Heat". This developed into monikers such as The Mighty Wah! and Shambeko Say Wah!, after a group of Nazi-fighters (cf the many names of ⇨Foetus). It isn't a reference to New York's Café Wah, the starting point for folk acts including ⇨Bob Dylan. Related: ⇨The Mystery Girls, ⇨The Opium Eaters, Oedipus Wrecks.

The Wailers

Like ⇨Siouxsie And The Banshees, their sound gave them the name; "Wailing Wailers" first coined by Jamaican manager ⇨Clement 'Sir Coxsone' Dodd.

Waitresses

Ohio lyricist Chris Butler wanted to write songs from a woman's viewpoint. (Most astute effort: *I Know What Boys Like*.) He said: "The waitress character is always an ordinary woman put upon by difficult circumstances."

Walker Brothers

Actors Noel Scott Engel and John Maus were cast as the Walker brothers in a 1964 TV play and kept the illusion for records. More bogus brothers: ⇨The Chemical Brothers, ⇨The Doobie Brothers, ⇨Flying Burrito Brothers, ⇨The Righteous Brothers.

Junior Walker And The All-Stars

Walker, called Junior by his family, said an ecstatic punter at a gig cried out: "These guys are all stars".

Wall Of Voodoo

Los Angeles musician Stanard 'Stan' Ridgway was trying to produce horror and sci-fi film music and effects with his partner Marc Moreland under the name ACME Soundtracks. One stormy night they were trying to create a "wall of sound" effect for a movie but the power kept mysteriously failing in their rented office.

Marc whispered: "Stan, this is no longer like a 'Wall Of Sound'." He got the reply: "Yeah, it's creepy.. more like a 'Wall Of Voodoo.'"

Variants of this story, told to the author and many other journalists, suggest it's grown in the telling. Stan has gleefully grafted on voodoo details and says his mother was a faith healer, which made it spookier.

War

The Creators, a funk black band from Long Beach, renamed as former ⇨Animal, Briton Eric Burdon, joined them in 1969. They suggested War to contrast with the peace preoccupations of many groups. Vietnam was a major issue. Burdon was less sure, having just done his *Love Is* album. Their 1970 LP was called *Eric Burdon Declares War*. The next had a worse title: *Black Man's Burdon*.

The Warm Jets

The Warm Jets (⇨Roxy Music minus ⇨Bryan Ferry) backed ⇨Eno on his 1974 *Here Come The Warm Jets*. Eno said the guitar on the title track "sounded like a tuned jet". He denied any sexual reference. Another Warm Jets formed in London in 1996, naming after Eno's LP because "it sounded good".

Warsaw

Early ⇨Joy Division, from ⇨David Bowie's experimental track *Warszawa* on his 1977 *Low* LP. The choice was dropped because of London group Warsaw Pakt. Reference: *Warsaw* on the *Substance 1977-1980* CD.

Dionne Warwick

Marie Dionne Warrick changed her surname in a bid to end confusion (though her name's pronounced "War- wick", not "Worrick" as the English town is said.)

Was (Not Was)

The enigmatic studio wizards and 'brothers' Don and David Was left their name clouded in mystery for years. Was or not Was, that was the question? David was born

Weiss, sometimes incorrectly spoken as "Was" or "Wass" although it should be said "Vice". Don was never Was, was never David's brother, instead born Don Fagenson. So the one was Vice Not Was and the other was always Not Was. Fagenson's young son gave him the idea by contradicting words he was given. "Blue." "Not blue."

WASP

This Los Angles heavy metal band's choice wasn't an insect name. For a long time it was thought to refer to "White Anglo-Saxon Protestants". They said in a 1980s interview it meant "We Are Sexual Perverts", although this may have been to avoid ⇨KISS style accusations of Satanism: "We Are Satan's People/ Preachers" was being mooted.

The Waterboys

Rock critic Robert Christgau, reviewing the 1973 album *Berlin*, castigated ⇨Lou Reed for the song *The Kids* with its repeated "I am the waterboy". Christgau asked: "what is a waterboy anyway?" Mike Scott, of this British band, said he didn't know either but loved the word. He chose the name to provide an answer, having rejected Funhouse, from a ⇨Stooges LP. Related: ⇨The Red And The Black, ⇨World Party.

Muddy Waters

The U.S. blues singer had an inauspicious start. McKinley Morganfield was born in poor surroundings on the Mississippi delta in 1915. The river itself is called "Old Muddy". One of his favourite play areas as a child was a dirty creek and his long-suffering grandmother, who had to clean him, called him "Muddy". Inspired ⇨The Mannish Boys, ⇨Mojos, ⇨The Rolling Stones.

Johnny 'Guitar' Watson

Texan musician John Watson Jnr. (1935-1996) named in 1954 from the Sterling Hayden film *Johnny Guitar*.

Watts 103rd Street Rhythm Band

Named after the Watts area of L.A., California.

Waysted

British heavy metal band with punning name on their leader (cf ⇨Fastway). In this case, Pete Way, ex-⇨UFO. He laboriously explained this in an interview with the author in case it wasn't clear (you know, Pete WAY so, like, WAYsted, good eh?). Not as elegantly wasted as ⇨Ex-Pensive Wino Keith Richards.

The Weathermen

Tribute to ⇨Bob Dylan, whose 1965 *Subterranean Homesick Blues* includes the lines "You don't need a weather man/To know which way the wind blows". The song inspired ⇨fIREHOSE.

The Weavers

Political-folk band named after Gerhart Hauptmann's German play. *Die Weber* gained a new audience in the U.S. after it was translated.

The Wedding Present

Guitarist-singer David Gedge explains this Northern English band chose it because it sounded "deep and classy, like a play or a film". Fans called them The Weddoes.

Wednesday Week

Los Angeles band named after a 1980 song by The Undertones, not the ⇨Elvis Costello B-side.

Weezer

This nickname was given to singer Rivers Cuomo because he had childhood breathing problems. He decided to apply it to his band, formed in 1992.

Paul Weller

Weller was born in Woking, in May 1958. His mother was unwell when his birth was registered. Amid confusion her son was named John William Weller, his father's name. Later he was renamed Paul. Nicknames: The Cappuccino Kid, ⇨The Modfather, The New Eric Clapton, The Uncle of Britpop. Bands: ⇨The Jam, ⇨The Style Council, ⇨The Smoking Mojo Filters.

Kitty Wells

The Tennessee-born country singer Ellen Deason was named for her version of *My Sweet Kitty Wells*.

Westlife

The Irish band named in 1998 because most of its members were from the west coast. They had to pass on their first choice Westside because there already was one.

Wet Wet Wet

This Scottish pop band named from a ⇨Scritti Politti song they adored, *Gettin' Havin' and Holdin'*, which says "his face is wet, wet with tears". It's on the 1982 album by Scritti Politti, *Songs To Remember*. The third wet was an attempt not to be associated with double names as ⇨Duran Duran, ⇨Talk Talk etc. They were known as The Wets – an abbreviation seen as inevitable though not uncomplimentary.

Wham!

⇨George Michael and Andy Ridgeley started in 1979 with an unsuccessful ska act, The Executive. Their starting point as a duo was a Michael song with a "Wham bam thank you ma'am" line. It evolved into 1982's *Wham! Rap (Enjoy What You Do)*.

The punchy name quite coincidentally recalled comics such as Batman and especially the American artist Roy Lichtenstein's 1963 two-canvas image *Whaam*.

Note the exclamation mark at the end of the name, cf ⇨Wah! Their backing singers included ⇨Dee C. Lee. Tribute band: Club Tropicana.

Whippersnapper

Folk fiddler Dave Swarbrick formed Whippersnapper in 1984 during a break from ⇨Fairport Convention reunions.

A Dictionary of Rock and Pop Names

'Swarb' told me in an interview that he just liked the cheeky-sounding name. The band was nearly called "Morgan" after the car, because it had "an old-English feel to it". "One of our songs is about *Hard Times In Old England*, so it would have been right. There were a few names about. Whippersnapper won in the end, it's a good fun word."

Whitesnake
Ex- ⇨Deep Purple star David Coverdale named his band after the title of his 1977 first "solo" LP. ⇨'Percy', Robert Plant, used to call him "David Coverversion".

The White Stripes
The name used by this duo from Detroit, Michigan, explains much of their philosophy. Jack Gillis married Meg White in 1996, taking her last name. He kept the surname when they divorced, though they continued their musical partnership, describing themselves as "brother and sister". They celebrated their first decade together as The White Stripes in 2007, still clad in the red, white and black clothes they referenced at the outset – all inspired by Meg's surname.

Spinoff band: ⇨Raconteurs. No relation to German band The Stripes which included singer ⇨Nena.

White Zombie
American movie buff Robert Straker named himself Rob Zombie and took the name of this 1990s band from the title of a 1931 Bela Lugosi film. Unrelated: ⇨The Zombies. Cf Bodysnatchers.

The Who
They started at school in Acton, London, backing one Roger Harold Daltrey as The Detours. This lasted for some time until U.K. television show *Thank Your Lucky Stars* featured a nine-piece Irish combo also called The Detours.

Guitarist Peter Dennis Blandford Townshend – those really are Pete "Beaky" Townshend's middle names – and friend Richard Barnes suggested No One, The Group or The Who. The aim was to curtail the Detour jokes from the smarmy MC at the Oldfield Tavern, their regular concert venue.

Townshend also suggested the Hair because it was becoming a major moral issue. Older people accused youth of decadency, dirtiness and sexual confusion. The younger generation was pointing out it wasn't the coiffure on top but the mind underneath that mattered. However, the band didn't have especially long hair and knew the name could date. Townshend suggested The Hair and The Who? as a compromise. The Who was favoured by Daltrey as short enough to print big on posters. (The Who later were heroes of ⇨The Jam, who favoured the same "keep it short" thinking.)

The musicians were taken on by publicist Peter Meaden, who thought their handle "airy-fairy". He decided to mould them into the archetypal mod outfit, put them in mod clothes and renamed them The High Numbers (mod lingo for "very good"; cf ⇨The Low Numbers).

When a Meaden single flopped, they gained a new manager, Kit Lambert. He thought a change might shake off their unwelcome reputation for wrecking venues;

and make them sound less like a housey-housey session. So they reverted to The Who. Bingo!

Lambert thought the name a gimmick but agreed it was interestingly confusing. "The Who made good conversation fuel, provided ready-made gags for disc jockeys. It was so corny it had to be good."

Name notes: Cf ⇨The Guess Who – similar name but not related. Townshend (nickname Towser) also worked with ⇨Thunderclap Newman. Drummer ⇨Keith Moon (1947-1978) often called The Loon. Bassist John Entwistle (1944-2002) formed ⇨Ox and ⇨Rigor Mortis. A remark by Entwistle – probably, although it may have been Moon – led to another band becoming ⇨Led Zeppelin. Inspired: ⇨See For Miles. The name led to titles such as *Who's Next* and *Who Are You*.

Wilco
This Chicago-based band came together in 1994 from the remnants of alternative country act Uncle Tupelo. They renamed after the word used by CB radio fans for "I will do that" or "will comply". Inspired: ⇨Cherry Ghost.

Wild Cherry
Accident victim Rob Parissi woke up in hospital and looked at his bedside table . . . and saw a box of cherry-flavoured cough drops called Wild Cherry. As the Ohio singer recovered, the image stuck in his mind.

Kim Wilde
Born Kim Smith, the daughter of ⇨Marty Wilde and sister of Ricky Wilde. She continued the family name tradition first given to her father by ⇨Larry Parnes.

Marty Wilde
British singer Reginald Smith was performing as Reg Patterson when he met manager ⇨Larry Parnes, who chose the name from a list on the toss of a coin. The new star liked Marty, but wasn't wild about Wilde. "I think I wanted to be called Marty Patterson after the Word Heavyweight Champion." Though he agreed it was a lot better than Reg Smith, which wasn't a "star-quality name". (Cf ⇨Elton John's Reg Dwight.) His band was called The Wilde Cats. Daughter: ⇨Kim Wilde.

Wild Horses
Spin-off from ⇨Rainbow and ⇨Thin Lizzy, named after the ⇨Rolling Stones 1971 track *Wild Horses*.

Hank Williams
The Alabama country singer was born Hiram Williams – although it was incorrectly spelled Hiriam on the certificate. He preferred the more authentic American Hank.

Willy And The Poorboys
Short-lived mid-1980s group formed by ⇨Rolling Stone Bill Wyman, who named them with conscious irony; he isn't one of this world's paupers and the project was

designed to raise cash for charity. Equally a tribute to ⇨Creedence Clearwater Revival's 1969 LP *Willy And The Poorboys*.

Wilson Phillips

Some progeny of famous parents try to play down their parent's links. An increasing number – Arlo Guthrie, Julian Lennon and Zak Starkey – are open about it. Some are shameless . . . .

⇨Beach Boy Brian Wilson's daughters Wendy and Carnie were two-thirds of the trio. Chynna Phillips was the daughter of Michelle and John 'Wolfking Of L.A.' Phillips.

Wind In The Willows

This folky New York outfit purloined the poetic title of *The Wind In The Willows*, the 1908 children's novel by British writer Kenneth Grahame (1859-1932). Included Debby Harry, soon to form ⇨Blondie.

Amy Winehouse

Amy Jade Winehouse, a Grammy-winning British R&B/jazz singer, made it into newspapers for the wrong reasons: drugs, drink, bulimia and stormy marriage among them. She also makes it into this book for unflattering derivatives such as Amy Wino, Amy Wineglass (slip by Jon Snow in *Channel 4 News*) and Declinehouse plus nickname ⇨The Camden Caner. Amid the irony of tracks such as *Rehab*, she released a DVD called *I Told You I Was Trouble*. She might be better helped by sympathy not laughter.

[110] Call her Wino, Declinehouse, Wineglass or Winehouse, she's a great singer. Amy out and about in London, 2008.

Wings

If it's hard thinking of a name for a band, consider the problems facing ⇨Paul McCartney as he pondered what to call the outfit he was forming after what is widely regarded as the greatest-ever pop group. How do you top ⇨the Beatles?

The Fabs' name was not as brilliant as their music – but 'Macca's' choices are hardly among the greatest to be found in this book. The Turpentines was his first choice – unusual but long. Paul McCartney and The Dazzlers next idea. It sounded a bit retro and was not dazzling. Wings came last.

Reports at the time said it was chosen to indicate the star's desire to travel again. While he did not wish to be so tied to the studio as in his later Beatle days – Wings soon went on a low-key tour – this was not really the reason.

McCartney told British newspapers at the time that the name was "futuristic", "optimistic" and "hopeful". His wife Linda was pregnant at the time. Actually the name's creation is a little more dramatic than he first revealed.

The birth of his second child, Stella McCartney (now a fashion designer), was difficult, "a bit of a drama," he recalled in the 2001 film *Wingspan*. McCartney said that both Linda and the baby almost died. He was praying for them when the image of wings came into his head. The wings could be those of a stork's, as well as a jet-setting star with a band, which was soon on the run.

Even this explanation left another origin lying off the page, although many fans speculated – many correctly. Their surmises were confirmed at a press conference when McCartney was asked, by the author and others, if it was anything to do with The Beatles' song *Blackbird*. Of course it was: *Blackbird*, seen by some as one of 'Macca's' greatest achievements, was recorded in the studio in the wee small hours after the others had left, and is essentially just McCartney solo. In retrospect it can be seen, like *Hey Jude*, as a coded message – in this case, not on the break-up of Lennon's first marriage but on the break-up of The Beatles: "take these broken wings," it goes, "and learn to fly".

Another Macca name: ⇨Percy "Thrills" Thrillington. Inspired: ⇨Jet.

Wire

This British arty quartet survived and outgrew their punky origins as The Geezers. They wanted a minimalist name to reflect their minimalist songs, which they described as "not short, just not long". Guitarist Bruce Gilbert suggested The Wires. Singer Colin Newman said there were a lot of other plural names around: Wire could refer to guitar strings, electric flex or much else.

Wishbone Ash

This British prog-rock band started in 1966 and were playing as Tanglewood when new manager Miles Copeland urged a more attention-grabbing name, suggesting Third World War or Jesus Duck.

Desperate to avoid these, founder Andy Powell suggested all the band members wrote down ideas. They ended up with two lists, one of which had the word Wishbone on it and the other of which had Ash. Powell said: "The combination sounded intriguing. Actually, it sounded like more than it was."

Wizzard

Leader Roy Wood (born Ulysses Adrian Wood) moved on from The Move to adopt the visual image of a crazed wizard, shown most clearly on the album cover of 1973's *Wizzard Brew*. The "zz" spelling was deliberate, coming from English schoolboy slang. Related: ⇨ELO.

A Dictionary of Rock and Pop Names

WOMAD
Stands for World Of Music, Arts And Dance. Created in large part by British musician Peter Gabriel, ex- ⇨Genesis.

Stevie Wonder
His prenomen's Steveland. ⇨Motown billed the blind star as Little Stevie Wonder on the release of his first LP at the age of 12. His father's name was Judkins; and Little Stevie's early songwriting credits at Motown were to S. Judkins, though his mother said he signed to the label under the surname Morris, "an old family name". He added Hardaway as his mother remarried.

The "little" went in 1964 as he grew to six feet but the wonder remained; he formed the Wonderlove vocal group and played one record as Eivets Rednow, Stevie Wonder backwards.

Wonder Who
⇨The Four Seasons in disguise for a 1966 single designed to prove that they could have hits without the prop of their famous name. The group's members were proved right as the song reached the top five. The point would have been better proved with a totally anonymous name. "Wonder Who", like ⇨The Guess Who, suggested somebody famous was involved.

The Wonder Stuff
The band formed in the 1980s; informally known as The Stuffies. Strangely, not The Wonders . . . .

Vocalist Miles Hunt had, for a long time, claimed the name "doesn't mean anything." In the 1990s a tall story was put about suggesting his uncle Bill Hunt, keyboard player with ⇨Wizzard, knew ⇨John Lennon. The former ⇨Beatle, it was claimed, supposedly met the energetic young Miles and remarked that the boy had "the wonder stuff".

In a previous book this author disputed this as "incredible"; while Lennon visited The Big Apple several times before settling there, he left Britain on 3 September, 1971, and never returned.

Brenton Wood
Alfred Jesse Smith wanted to make enough money to live in the Hollywood suburb of Brentwood.

World Party
This British pop/rock band started in 1985 when Karl Wallinger left ⇨the Waterboys. Its name reflects his world and environmental concerns. The first album had a track called *World Party* on it; the second, 1990's *Goodbye Jumbo*, has him wandering an elephant graveyard on opening track, *Is It Too Late?*

Johnny Worth
Songwriter Les Van Dyke named after his local London telephone exchange.

Wu-Tang Clan

The Kung fu movie *Shaolin and Wu Tang* is about warriors, trained Wu-Tang style. The name came from the central Chinese mountain Wu Dang, associated with Ming dynasty emperors and martial arts. The group's earliest releases pit Shaolin fighters against the Wu-Tang. The movie was admired by members ⇨Ol' Dirty Bastard and RZA.

X

There were some interesting pseudonyms in this single-letter-name band, including Billy Zoom (Tyson Kindale) and D.J. Bonebrake. However they paid tribute to the so-strange-it-didn't need-changing real name of singer Exene Cervenka and became X.

X-Clan

New York band "fighting for the black cause", named after activist Malcolm X. One of his civil rights campaigner colleagues was Sonny Carson, whose son Lamumba founded the band. Lamumba met Malcolm X as a child.

X-Ray Spex

Brilliant name recalling the punk enthusiasm for toy spectacles which can "see through" things. An even more brilliant name for their singer, ⇨Poly Styrene (born Marion Elliot). The name was taken from the adverts in the back of *True Detective* magazines.

XTC

The British band's "ecstasy" referred to happiness, not the drug ecstasy, which wasn't known when they started and only became "fashionable" at raves about ten years later. Bands with similar punning names include ⇨INXS and ⇨U2.

Yanni

Yanni Chryssomallis to his bank manager. A ⇨Vangelis-style abbreviation for a fellow Greek keyboard star.

A Dictionary of Rock and Pop Names

Yardbirds

These British 1960s little red roosters, who liked doing purist versions of old songs, were paying a tribute to ⇨"Bird" Charlie Parker, whose name came from his fondness for chickens – or, more accurately, eating them; he called them "yardbirds". They later became New Yardbirds and then ⇨Led Zeppelin. Related: ⇨Eric Clapton, ⇨Renaissance. Inspired: ⇨The Nazz.

Yazoo

Vince Clarke's first band after ⇨Depeche Mode, with vocalist ⇨Alf. Alf had suggested the name based on labels she had seen of old blues albums. Clarke later said she had confused the words yazoo and kazoo.

Contrary to other sources it is nothing to do with ⇨Bob Dylan's Basement Tapes track, *Yazoo Street Scandal*. The name was later abbreviated to Yaz in the U.S.A., because a small record company had registered Yazoo.

Yazz

The British singer, who made her name working with The Plastic Population and Coldcut in the 1980s, shortened her full name, Yasmin Evans.

Yeah Yeah Yeah

From ⇨The Beatles. Specifically *She Loves You (Yeah Yeah Yeah)*. This 1990s rock band is no relation to the below 2000s New York band.

Yeah Yeah Yeahs

That's not "yeah Yeah YEAH!" in a naïve, positive *Harry Met Sally* way. It's a shrugged "yeah yeah yeah" as in New York open-eyed dismissive patois. Say it along with "Yeah right" or "whatever" in response to some ridiculous statement which you can't be bothered to argue about.

Singer Karen O (Karen Lee Orzolek) has made this clear in a few interviews after being asked if she was paying tribute to ⇨The Beatles. Cf ⇨Clap Your Hands Say Yeah.

Yello

Reportedly means "a yelled hello" rather than being a Germanic misspelling of "yellow". Singer/lyricist and former artist Dieter Meier, from Switzerland, is much too sophisticated to do a thing like that.

Yes

The zenith – or nadir, depending on where you stand – of British art-rock in the 1970s, Yes evolved from Mabel Greer's Toyshop. Singer Jon Anderson wanted a change while guitarist Peter Banks admitted the toy moniker was "silly". The name was chosen – like the final word of Irish writer James Joyce's magnum opus *Ulysses* – because "it's the most positive word that can be conceived, and one of the shortest". Later the band splintered, with one faction considering The Affirmative and becoming ⇨AWBH. Related: ⇨Asia, ⇨BLUE.

Yesterday's News

New York 1980s *a capella* act, formed in 1979. They were looking for details of a forthcoming gig in the *Daily News*. After going through the news section they found the answer in . . . yesterday's news.

Yo La Tengo

Spanish for "I've got it". It is roughly the same as "Eureka!" in Greek and represents this band's joy at finding a name.

It is used as a cry by Spanish-speaking outfielders in baseball. Ira Kaplan took it in honour of a Latin ballplayer for the New York Mets, shortstop Elio Chacon.

The Youngbloods

These 1960s American hit-makers were named to fit in with star member ⇨Jesse Colin Young, who had already released two albums, the second of which in 1965 was entitled *Youngblood*.

Jesse Colin Young

Perry Miller said that he renamed in tribute to: JESSE James, the legendary American Robin-Hood style criminal; COLIN Chapman, the racing driver; Cole YOUNGER, a cowboy hero. ⇨The Youngbloods.

Neil Young

⇨Buffalo Springfield, ⇨Crazy Horse, ⇨The Mynah Birds, ⇨The Godfather Of Grunge.

The Young Ones

U.K. alternative comedians, professing to be fans of ⇨Cliff Richard, named their TV series about young students after Cliff's 1962 film and song. They later joined with Richard on a charity remake of his 1959 hit *Living Doll*.

The (Young) Rascals

Producer Hal Roach made a 1920s series of single-reel movies called *Our Gang*. The comedy was revived on TV in the 1950s as *The Little Rascals*. This inspired ⇨Spanky And Our Gang and New York band The Young Rascals, who later became The Rascals.

Z

Frank Zappa

Francis Vincent Zappa Jnr. was born to Greek parents. Father of the band ⇨The Mothers of Invention and valley girl Moon Unit Zappa. She later went on to form ⇨Fred Zeppelin with brothers Dweezil and Ahmet Rodin.

A Dictionary of Rock and Pop Names

Zombies

This intellectual British pop band members were photographed reading university books and playing chess together. Their original bassist, Paul Arnold, qualified as a doctor. The name was therefore ironic. For more "we're stupid" names, see the entry on ⇨Simple Minds. Unrelated: ⇨White Zombie.

ZOX

From the drummer, John Zox, whose U.S. band mixes violin and reggae.

ZTT

British record company and production force, best known for work with ⇨Frankie Goes To Hollywood, formed by Trevor Horn. ZTT should be said as "Zang Tumb Tuum", which is the onomatopoeic version of the sound of a machine gun, as written by Italian futurist Luigi Russolo. Cf ⇨Art of Noise, a band on the label.

Zucchero

The Italian pop star was born Adelmo Fornaciari but got the nickname Zucchero ("sugar") in early childhood.

The Zutons

The British rock band from Liverpool took their name in 2001 from ⇨Captain Beefheart's sidekick Bill Harkleroad, better known as Zoot Horn Rollo.

During a conversation about names, group member David McCabe misheard this as "Zuton Rollo". The others liked the error and went on to develop "Zuton" as a sci-fi concept on their debut album, with comic-book cover asking *Who Killed . . . The Zutons?*

ZZ Top

The Texas-raised trio's name has been the subject of debate. Lets start with the "ZZ". The *Q Encyclopedia Of Rock Stars* says it came from an open pair of hay-loft doors with "Z" beams seen by guitarist Billy Gibbons. He's given this account to *Goldmine* magazine as long ago as 1991.

The musicians now tell me it was an attempted parody of venerable blues players like ⇨B.B. King and Z.Z. Hill. "We wanted to be like a crusty bluesman". "Z.Z." was always going to make their records easy to find in record shops – and their entry easy to find in books like this. The barn doors just knocked home the idea.

Many accounts give the origin of "Top" from cigarette rolling papers: Top, Zig Zag or Rizla brands, which share some similarities with the band's ZZ logo. Gibbons says it actually just came to him one day to fit the "ZZ". "It was a top name."

Name notes: (1) They formed after the break-up of The Warlocks – a name also considered by ⇨The Grateful Dead and ⇨The Velvet Underground – and the psychedelia-influenced Moving Sidewalks. (2) The "Z"s are said U.S.-style: "Zee Zee Top", not "Zed Zed Top". (3) Tribute band: Redbeards From Texas. (4) ZZ Top achieved their greatest success after Gibbons and bassist Dusty Hill grew long beards. Note that the clean-shaven one is called Frank Beard. As we have seen throughout this book, names can be misleading things.

Photo Permissions

[1]   Rex Features;
[2]   Hulton Archive/ Getty Images;
[3]   Reproduced by permission of Penguin Books Ltd;
[4]   Fernando Manos/ Corbis;
[5]   Courtesy Randall-Reilly Publishing Co.;
[6]   Badly Drawn Man used with kind permission of Viz, first published in Viz in 1983;
[7]   Hellestad Rune/ Corbis Sygma;
[8]   Alinari Archives/ Corbis;
[9]   Michael Ochs Archives/Getty Images;
[10] Offshoot Sports Photography Ltd;
[11] Kim Hee-Chul/epa/ Corbis;
[12] Lynn Goldsmith/ Corbis;
[13] Robbie Jack/ Corbis;
[15] Bettman/Corbis;
[16] Alta Vista Productions/Kobal Collection ZZB419AA.jpg;
[17] Universal Music Group;
[18] Graham Keogh/ Hot Press;
[19] Eric Schaal/Time & Life Pictures/Getty Images;
[20] Ronald Grant Archive;
[21] Retna Pictures;
[22] Frank Trapper/ CORBIS SYGMA;
[23] Michael Ochs Archives/Getty Images;
[24] Universal Music Group;
[25] Ian Dickson/ Redferns ID1030;
[26] Groupe Femmes d'Aujourd'hui;
[27] Lynn Goldsmith/ Corbis BE078740 (RM);
[28] UrbanImage.tv/ Adrian Boot;
[29] Penguin Books Ltd;
[39] Shelley Gazin/ Corbis;
[31] Joel Brodsky/ Corbis;
[32] Ronald Grant Archive;
[33] Ronald Grant Archive;
[34] Henry Diltz/Corbis;
[35] Nick Cooper;
[36] MARK BEECH;
[37] MARK BEECH;
[38] Harry Goodwin/ Redferns;
[39] Hulton-Deutsch Collection/Corbis;
[40] Eve Production Inc/Kobal Collection;
[41] Peter Foley/epa/ Corbis;
[42] Leacock Pennebaker/Kobal Collection;
[43] Neal Preston/ Corbis;
[44] Bettmann/Corbis;
[45] Jorgen Angel/ Redferns;
[46] Ronald Grant Archive;
[47] John Rodgers/ Redferns;
[48] Universal Music Group;
[49] Hulton Archive/ Getty;
[50] Archives Charmet/ The Bridgeman Art Library;
[51] Mary Evans Picture Library;
[52] Santa Barbara California Sheriff Dept/epa/Corbis;
[53] The Bridgeman Art Library;
[55] Woodfall/Kobal Collection;

[56] Harry Goodwin/ Rex Features;

[57] Robert Fripp;

[58] Virgin Records;

[59] GAB Archives/ Redferns;

[60] Bettman/Corbis;

[62] Touchstone Pictures/ZUMA/ Corbis;

[63] Neal Preston/ CORBIS;

[64] The Florida Times- Union;

[65] Daniel Deme/epa/ CORBIS;

[66] Ronald Grant Archive;

[67] Ronald Grant Archive;

[68] Neal Preston/ CORBIS;

[69] Wyatt Counts/ Corbis;

[70] Penguin Books USA Ltd;

[71] Flamingo Books;

[72] Ronald Grant Archive;

[73] Tim Mosenfelder/ Corbis;

[74] Maiman Rick/ CORBIS SYGMA;

[75] Keystone USA/Rex Features;

[76] Rosemary Hale and the Burmese Cat Club;

[77] Ronald Grant Archive;

[78] Karen Mason Blair/ Corbis;

[79] Hulton/Getty Images;

[80] GAB Archives/ Redferns;

[81] Rex Features;

[82] Terry Cryer/Corbis;

[83] Penguin Books Ltd;

[84] Sheila Rock/Rex Features;

[85] John A. Angelillo/ Corbis;

[86] CORBIS SYGMA;

[87] Bettmann/Corbis;

[88] Stephen Wright/ Redferns;

[89] Mitchell Gerber/Corbis;

[90] The Random House Group Ltd.;

[91] Corbis;

[92] Ebet Roberts/ Redferns;

[93] Kim Stallknecht/ epa/Corbis;

[94] William Mckim/ Getty Images;

[95] Jean Louis Atlan/ Sygma/Corbis;

[96] Penguin Books Ltd;

[97] Fin Costello/ Redferns;

[98] 2008 Marvel Characters, Inc.;

[99] 'HERGE-MOULIN- SART 2007' AFP/ Getty Images;

[100] Ronald Grant Archive;

[101] CinemaPhoto/ Corbis;

[102] Ronald Grant Archive;

[103] Universal Music Group;

[104] Penguin Books Ltd;

[105] EMI Group;

[106] Ronald Grant Archive;

[107] Sheila Rock/ Rex Features;

[108] Rex Features;

[109] Ronald Grant Archive;

[110] Beretta/Sims/Rex Features;

Index

304

A Dictionary of Rock and Pop Names

A Dictionary of Rock and Pop Names

A Dictionary of Rock and Pop Names

A Dictionary of Rock and Pop Names

A Dictionary of Rock and Pop Names

311

A Dictionary of Rock and Pop Names

A Dictionary of Rock and Pop Names

A Dictionary of Rock and Pop Names

A Dictionary of Rock and Pop Names

A Dictionary of Rock and Pop Names

A Dictionary of Rock and Pop Names

A Dictionary of Rock and Pop Names